GOLDWIN SMITH: VICTORIAN LIBERAL

GOLDWIN SMITH, AGED 24
From a portrait at Eton College, painted by George Richmond in 1847. Reproduced by kind permission of Eton College.

GOLDWIN SMITH

VICTORIAN LIBERAL

Elisabeth Wallace

UNIVERSITY OF TORONTO PRESS

Copyright ©, Canada, 1957
University of Toronto Press
Printed in Canada
London: Oxford University Press
Reprinted in 2018
ISBN 978-1-4875-8536-5 (paper)

PREFACE

GOLDWIN SMITH was not a markedly original thinker or political philosopher. What, then, was his significance? An intelligent liberal and on many subjects a representative Victorian, he speculated with unflagging interest on the problems of his day. Unpopular as his ideas often were, they reflected characteristic strains in nineteenth-century liberal thought, and in particular the Victorian concern about questions raised by the two great forces of democracy and imperialism. In lucid prose he analysed the major problems of the Anglo-American community and the beginnings of Canadian national life. A master journalist in the great age of modern journalism, he was seldom a constructive critic, but as a publicist of remarkable fertility he brought into sharp focus the issues of the time. On one matter his perception was unrivalled. He fully appreciated the profound significance of the common traditions and interests which linked the English-speaking peoples.

The first half of his life was spent in Britain, the second in North America. To the end of his days he remained first and foremost an Englishman, but preferred to describe himself as an Anglo-Saxon, since he was as much interested in the political ideas and institutions of Canada and the United States as in those of England. In all three countries he not only followed public affairs closely, but as the champion of a liberal creed tried to shape opinion and thus the course of events. It was perhaps inevitable that Canadians and Americans often considered him an alien who misinterpreted their point of view.

Goldwin Smith was the first person to stress the close relationship between these countries, and the importance of the links which united them. An intelligent concern for the common problems confronting the peoples of the English-speaking world was his most original contribution to the questions of his day. From his writing insularity and provincialism were conspicuously absent. He was interested in what Englishmen, Canadians, and Americans (and to a lesser extent South Africans and Australians) thought about the major issues of the Victorian age, about intellectual and ethical as well as political and social problems. To all these peoples he tried to explain what the others believed, how they had dealt with similar situations, and why they thought and behaved as they did.

A journalist by profession, he had a scholar's interest in comparative government and a student's curiosity about the way in which transplanted British ideas and institutions were modified by the history and environment of new lands. The only contemporaries who attempted a similar comparative analysis were his friends Sir Charles Dilke and James Bryce. An observer rather than a participant in public affairs, Goldwin Smith was at least their peer in felicity of style. In an age of great writers the effectiveness of his prose was unsurpassed. Through the pages of some two hundred English, American, and Canadian journals he sought to mould contemporary thought by timely editorials and articles, rather than by longer studies on less evanescent themes. His hobby was writing letters to editors, to which he attached almost as much importance as to essays and editorials. At the same time he kept up a voluminous correspondence with friends in Great Britain and the United States. His papers in the Cornell University Library contain letters from leading statesmen, journalists, and literary men, with some of whom he corresponded for almost half a century. Many of these played a more responsible and important part in public affairs than he did, and their reflections on the contemporary scene are full of interest. Their letters and his present a revealing picture of Victorian liberalism.

Ostrogorski suggests that during the third quarter of the nineteenth century Goldwin Smith's influence on the rising generation in England almost equalled that of John Stuart Mill.[1] In Canada his impact on the course of events was less, because he failed to understand the nascent nationalism which ran counter to his vision of continental unity. But the encouragement he gave Canadian letters and the standard he set Canadian journalism can scarcely be overestimated.

A volume of *Reminiscences*, prepared during the last years of his life, was edited and published after his death in 1910 by his secretary, Arnold Haultain. Goldwin Smith did not intend this as an autobiography, since he considered his life too unimportant to record. The book is what the title suggests: an old man's recollections of people and places. Full of anecdotes about men and events, it contains much repetition, and for most part deals with his early life in England. The later years in Canada fill only three brief chapters. In 1913 Mr. Haultain published two further volumes: *Goldwin Smith, His Life and Opinions*

[1]*Democracy and the Organization of Political Parties* (London, 1902), I, 91.

and *A Selection from Goldwin Smith's Correspondence*. An unpublished thesis on Goldwin Smith by R. A. McEachern is in the University of Toronto Library. Half a century after his death, the time seems ripe for a reassessment.

The somewhat unusual plan of the present study requires explanation. It is divided into two parts: the first on his life, the second and longer section on his ideas. As he himself recognized, what he did was less interesting than what he thought. He was unduly modest, however, in considering his life not worth recording at all. As he once observed when reviewing a biography, the career of a man in public life affords matter for narrative, "but the actions of literary and scientific men are their works. Interest, in their case, properly attaches to events or circumstances which influence thought or are sources of inspiration."[2] Goldwin Smith sought primarily to influence thought. The second section on his ideas is divided topically, not chronologically. The reason for this arrangement is that as a prolific journalist for more than fifty years he discussed ideas which interested him. A strictly chronological analysis would involve wearisome repetition.

No bibliography has been included, as Goldwin Smith's books are listed chronologically in the index under his name, and there are full footnote references throughout the text. A complete bibliography of all his fugitive writings, pamphlets, articles, editorials, and letters would be extremely long and would largely duplicate information already given in footnotes.

Before Goldwin Smith left England in 1868 he destroyed his private correspondence; hence the major sources for the first forty-five years of his life are his published writings and letters to newspapers. The Cobden and Gladstone Papers in the British Museum contain his letters to these statesmen; those to James Bryce are among the Bryce Papers at the Bodleian Library. A number of his letters to the 3rd and 4th Earls Grey are in the Grey Papers at the University of Durham. The Lang Papers at the Public Library of New South Wales in Sydney, Australia, include one letter from Goldwin Smith to the Reverend J. D. Lang. I am indebted to the South African Library at Cape Town for microfilm copies of letters between John Xavier Merriman and Goldwin Smith from the Merriman Papers, and to the Merriman trustees for permission to quote passages from his letters. The Seward Papers at the Rochester University Library contain the letters cited to and from W. H. Seward. The W. Bourke Cockran Papers in the New York Public Library include his

[2]Review of "Thomas Wright's Life of William Cowper," *Nation* (New York), LVI (March 2, 1893), 163–5.

letters to Cockran. The Walter Dymond Gregory Papers in the Douglas Library, Queen's University, Kingston, have a number of Goldwin Smith's letters to Henri Bourassa. His letters to George W. Curtis are in the University of Toronto Library. To all these libraries I am most grateful for permission to use their collections.

Goldwin Smith's Autograph Album at the Art Gallery of Toronto contains some four hundred letters to him from various British, American, and Canadian friends. These the director, Mr. Martin Baldwin, and the librarian of the Gallery were good enough to let me use. The letters to A. J. Beresford Hope, referred to in the text, were very kindly presented to me by the Reverend Charles Feilding of Trinity College, Toronto.

With these exceptions all the letters cited both to and from Goldwin Smith (unless otherwise specifically noted) are at Cornell University in Ithaca, New York, which owns the great bulk of his private papers. These were presented to Cornell by his secretary and literary executor, Mr. Haultain, in fulfilment of Goldwin Smith's wishes. I am much indebted to Mr. Stephen A. McCarthy and Mr. G. F. Shepherd Jr., of Cornell University Library, for kindly allowing me to use these papers and to reproduce the charcoal drawing of Goldwin Smith by A. F. Sandys which is in the Cornell Library. Their very helpful staff put all facilities at my disposal on numerous occasions. Mr. Shepherd, Dean R. M. Ogden, and Mrs. Edith Fox, the Cornell University archivist, were all good enough to read the section on Cornell, and to give me advice on various pertinent details.

I am also grateful to the librarians of the Public Archives of Canada, the Ontario Provincial Archives, the Ontario Legislative Library, and the University of Toronto Library, for many kindnesses.

In each case where excerpts from letters have been quoted I have tried to get in touch with the heirs of the writer, in order to ask their permission. In several instances I have been unable to locate them, but hope they will take the will for the deed. I acknowledge gratefully the courtesy of the following heirs of Goldwin Smith's correspondents, in allowing me to quote from unpublished letters to him: Miss Anne Bourassa, Miss Margaret V. Bryce, Mr. R. Cobden-Sanderson, Mr. C. A. Gladstone, the Marquess of Lansdowne, Mr. Goldwin Longley, Mrs. C. S. MacInness, Mrs. R. S. Messenger, Mrs. M. E. Miller, the Earl of Minto, Mr. D. S. Perigoe, Mrs. Guy Morley, the Earl of Rosebery, Mr. L. P. Scott, the Earl of Selborne, Mr. Arnold Whitridge, and Messrs. Thorold, Brodie, Bonham-Carter and Mason. To Mr. and Mrs. John Strachey I am grateful for permission to examine the private papers of

Mr. J. St. Loe Strachey. Premier Leslie Frost and Professor D. C. MacGregor kindly allowed me to use a copy of a letter from Goldwin Smith to Mr. Alexander MacGregor, which is in the possession of Premier Frost.

I am greatly indebted to Mr. Herbert Staples for much help in locating pictures of the Grange, for allowing me to use the etching of its portico by Mr. Owen Staples, and for obtaining permission from *The Telegram* to reproduce the drawing of the Grange first published in the Toronto *Evening Telegram* in 1896.

Miss S. Pantazzi, librarian of the Art Gallery of Toronto, has most generously assisted me in a great many ways, particularly with regard to the portraits of Goldwin Smith in this volume. Mr. C. K. Adams, the director of the National Portrait Gallery, Mr. Peter Murray of the Courtauld Institute, and Mr. Tom Lyon, the librarian of Eton College, have also given me much helpful advice and information about portraits of Goldwin Smith.

The Eton leaving portrait by Margaret Sarah Carpenter (Mrs. William Hookham Carpenter), was painted in 1841 for the Provost of Eton, who at his death left it to Mrs. Goldwin Smith. The director of the Art Gallery of Toronto has kindly allowed me to reproduce this picture from their collection. To Eton College I am indebted for permission to reproduce the George Richmond portrait, painted in 1847, which is now at Eton. A watercolour copy of it by Catherine Lyons was given to the Very Reverend Dean Llwyd of Nova Scotia in 1911 by Francis Pigou, Dean of Bristol, who was Goldwin Smith's first cousin. In 1933 Dr. Llwyd gave this to the Art Gallery of Toronto. The charcoal by A. F. Sandys in the Cornell University Library is probably the one which Sandys exhibited at the Royal Academy in 1882, but may well have been drawn some years earlier. Among the portraits of Goldwin Smith not reproduced in this volume is one by E. Wyly Grier, painted in England in 1894, and given to the Bodleian Library by some of Goldwin Smith's Oxford friends. A replica hangs in his old library at the Grange, which is now occupied by the Art Gallery of Toronto. Another replica of a portrait of him by Mr. Grier was given to the University of Toronto Library by John Ross Robertson in 1899. A portrait by John Russell was presented by J. B. Hurry to the Corporation of Reading in 1912. The picture reproduced at page 208 of Arnold Haultain's edition of *Goldwin Smith's Correspondence* used to hang in the Senior Common Room of University College, Oxford. It is no longer there, and its present whereabouts seem uncertain. This was an oval miniature, in watercolour on ivory, which is mentioned in Mrs. R.

L. Poole's *Catalogue of Oxford Portraits*. The Toronto artist, J. W. L. Forster, painted three different portraits of Goldwin Smith as an octogenarian. One of these was commissioned for the Goldwin Smith Hall at Cornell, a second for the National Club in Toronto, where it still hangs, and the third remained at the Grange, where it is now in the collection of the Art Gallery of Toronto. A death mask of Goldwin Smith by the Canadian sculptor, Walter Allward, is in the collection of the Art Gallery of Toronto.

I am grateful to the University of Toronto Press for a very pleasant collaboration in preparing this volume for publication, and also for permission to reprint here some sentences from articles of mine in the *University of Toronto Quarterly* and the *Canadian Historical Review*. I am also indebted to the University of Chicago Press for permission to use portions of an article of mine published in the *Journal of Modern History*, and to the American Historical Association for allowing me to use passages from an article which appeared in the *American Historical Review*.

I wish also to express my gratitude to the University of Toronto and to the Rockefeller Corporation for grants which helped me to complete this work.

The manuscript has been read by Professor Vincent Bladen, Dr. Eugene Forsey, and Professor F. H. Underhill. I am most grateful to them for their generous expenditure of time and their helpful suggestions. Above all, I am indebted to Professor Alexander Brady, who first suggested the subject, who read many rough drafts, and whose advice and criticism at every stage has been invaluable.

ELISABETH WALLACE

February, 1957

CONTENTS

Preface		v
Illustrations		xii

PART I—LIFE

I.	England	3
II.	United States	27
III.	Canada: Early Years and Marriage	53
IV.	Canada: Journalism and Public Affairs	82
V.	Canada: Later Life	109

PART II—IDEAS

VI.	Liberal Creed	133
VII.	State and Individual	162
VIII.	Critique of Imperialism	183
IX.	Religion and Ethics	211
X.	Democracy in Canada	226
XI.	The Destiny of Canada	253
XII.	Epilogue	281
	Index	289

ILLUSTRATIONS

Goldwin Smith, aged 24 — *Frontispiece*

Goldwin Smith at Eton, aged 18 — *facing page* 18

Columned Porch and Gable of "The Grange" — *facing page* 84

Goldwin Smith — *facing page* 116

The Grange in 1896 — *page* 127

: PART I—LIFE

I. ENGLAND

BORN IN 1823, in the third year of George IV's reign, Goldwin Smith lived to see the accession of George V in 1910. As a boy of nine he remembered the excitement over the passage of the First Reform Act, and as a ten-year-old the abolition of slavery. His memory went back to the days when gentlemen wore knee-breeches and powdered hair, the stocks and the curfew were both common, the night-watchman still called the hours through the streets, and the morning fires were lit in the bedrooms with the flint and steel of the era before matches. "I opened my political eyes," he wrote Lady Dilke during the Boer War, "on the great promises of moral progress, peace and all the political and social beatitudes after the Reform Bill of 1832. I shall close them on a great relapse."[1] In after days he liked to recall that he had heard Addington, Prime Minister of England in 1802, talk of Pitt, and remembered Lord John Russell who had seen Napoleon at Elba. The Duke of Wellington, who lived in the next parish, was long familiar to him as a neighbour, riding about the countryside with a little cape over his shoulders, and leaving immense calling cards for his friends. Goldwin Smith lived to deplore the hazards created by the influx of horseless carriages in the once peaceful streets of Toronto.

A born controversialist, he devoted most of his energy, throughout his eighty-six years, to supporting causes in which he believed and attacking abuses which he detested. He never lacked convictions, nor suffered from doubts as to their rightness. Controversy, when conducted temperately, he thought no evil. In John Morley's opinion no one—not even Disraeli himself—was Goldwin Smith's equal in pungent controversy. Complete freedom of discussion, "unchecked by threats either of faggots or of frowns," seemed to him the only guarantee against the possible bad consequences of human speculation and the only test of truth.[2] For more than half a century he was associated with most of the

[1]Letter of Nov. 7, 1900, Dilke Papers, British Museum Add. MS. 43916.
[2]*Rational Religion and the Rationalistic Objections of the Bampton Lectures for 1858* (Oxford, 1861), v–vi, 146.

liberal movements of the day, from the struggle for an extended franchise and the separation of church and state in nineteenth-century England to the attack on a nominated senate in twentieth-century Canada.

I

His father, Richard Pritchard Smith, was a leading physician of Reading, a man of independent means, and a director for many years of both the Great Western and the Metropolitan Railways. His mother, Elizabeth Breton, was of Huguenot extraction. Of seven children born to them only Goldwin, named for his mother's brother, lived to grow up. He was born on August 13, 1823, at 15 Friar Street, Reading, where his parents had settled the previous year, and where a plaque on the door still commemorates the family. His parents and brothers and sisters are buried nearby in St. Lawrence's churchyard. Dr. Pritchard Smith's sister was the mother of Francis Pigou, who became Dean of Bristol.

When he was nine years old Goldwin travelled by stage coach to school at Monkton Farleigh Rectory, near Bath. An early development of the solitariness and individualism so marked in his later life is suggested by a letter written to his mother from this school, in which he compared himself to a mouse scratching its cage. She died on November 19, 1833. Six years later Dr. Smith married Katharine, daughter of Sir Nathaniel Dukinfield, and in 1848 retired to a country house near Mortimer, some eight miles from Reading.

Goldwin was sent in 1836 to Eton, where at that time classics formed the whole course of study. Mathematics and modern languages were just beginning to be introduced as optional extras which no one was obliged to take. Of science, art, or music the boys learned nothing. Many years later he used to tell his friends that he started life with a very weak constitution, and that he attributed the improvement in his health and his longevity to his good fortune in having attended two extremely idle schools. An idler place than Eton in his day he could not conceive, though the assertion is not altogether borne out by the painstaking Greek and Latin verse and prose translations of his Eton notebooks, still preserved at Cornell. At any rate, on leaving Eton in 1841 he won the Newcastle Medal in classics.

He matriculated at Christ Church College, Oxford, but the next year transferred to Magdalen, on receiving a demyship there. Of his undergraduate days he always thought with nostalgic enjoyment, although his opinion of the unreformed university of his time was similar to his opinion of Eton. He kept a horse in the college stables, and one of his pleasantest memories of Oxford was riding to hounds in the Cotswolds. The students read by themselves, or with the help of private coaches. In Magdalen lived some eight of the forty Fellows, and about the same number of the thirty scholars, plus a single gentleman commoner. Two tutors made up the teaching staff of a college with an income of £40,000 a year. One of these gentlemen taught, while the other, as Goldwin Smith acidly observed, was absorbed in the theological controversy of the hour, which carried away the whole university, and turned it into a battle-field between Protestantism and the ritualism of the Oxford movement. In later years he assessed the prevalent Newmanism of that time as a movement which, though ecclesiastical and reactionary, was also in its own way revolutionary, and carried in its womb the seeds of Oxford liberalism. Tractarianism was a revolt against an old régime, which cut thoughtful minds loose from traditional moorings and launched them on a sea of speculation over which they finally floated to a great diversity of havens. Political conservatism, closely connected with Protestant orthodoxy, Newmanites attacked. The ferment of discussion led some adherents to Catholicism, but led more rebellious minds, by way of reaction, to a struggle for university reform, designed above all to free Oxford from a dominant ecclesiasticism. Into the thick of this struggle Goldwin Smith threw himself when his undergraduate days were scarcely over. Yet writing of Magdalen in after years he admitted that he "could not help feeling rather sad in applying the besom to a beloved though indefensible seat of happiness."[3]

He obtained a first class in Literae Humaniores in 1845, having won most of the possible academic laurels, including the Hertford Scholarship in Latin, the Ireland Scholarship in Greek, and the Chancellor's Prizes for Latin verse and an English essay. While he was still at Oxford his name had been entered at Lincoln's Inn, and in 1847 he was called to the bar. He went on circuit with Sir John Taylor Coleridge and later with Sir James Parke and Sir Edward Vaughan Williams, but never practised as a lawyer or seriously intended to do so. His decision to take legal training was probably arrived at by a process of elimination, in days when the gainful occupations open to gentlemen's sons were largely confined to the church, the army, and the law. Goldwin Smith was not cut out for a cleric. Although he was baptized and confirmed in the Church of England, compulsory chapel at Eton and Oxford

[3] "Magdalen College, Oxford," *Outlook* (New York), LXXXVII (Sept. 14, 1907); Goldwin Smith letter to Evelyn Abbott, May 24, 1894.

served to confirm an impatience with orthodoxy already developed by compulsory church at Reading. The army was ruled out by his extreme distaste for war. Journalism, which eventually proved his chosen profession, was in the eighteen-forties just starting to become respectable. Young men tended, however, to drift into journalism as an entertaining side line to more serious occupations rather than to select it in cold blood as work for a lifetime. Teaching he seems not to have considered. There remained the law, which, it turned out, he disliked. Few traces of legal training are apparent in his writing. His opinion of lawyers was illustrated at a dinner-party where one of the guests was extolling the attempts made by a legal luminary to simplify the law. "A lawyer simplify the law," exclaimed Goldwin Smith, "you might as well talk of a tiger cutting down a jungle."

In 1846 he was elected Stowell Fellow in Civil Law at University College, Oxford, where from 1851 to 1854 he was a tutor. "No more luminous intellect," wrote one of his students, G. C. Brodrick, in after years, "has since appeared in modern Oxford." Yet despite his ability and rare gift of expression his temperament did not fit him for life as a college tutor. Academic duties in those days were largely nominal, and from 1845 to 1858 he divided his time between Oxford and London. The summer of 1847 he spent travelling in Europe with friends, and the next year acted as a special constable during the Chartist scare. In London he had a second home in the house of his stepmother's brother, Sir Henry Dukinfield, a former rector of St. Martin's-in-the-Fields, who was an active friend and assistant of Bishop Bloomfield. Lady Dukinfield was the daughter of a diplomat stationed at Brussels in 1815, and one of the last survivors of those who danced at the ball on the eve of Waterloo. Goldwin Smith was soon absorbed in work as a journalist, as secretary for two commissions on the reorganization of Oxford University, and later as a member of the 1858 Royal Commission on Popular Education. To the report of the latter he contributed the section on charitable endowments.

II

University reform was the first of a long series of causes to which he turned his abundant energies. Oxford had been at a very low ebb during the eighteenth century, but toward its end an intellectual revival began. The statutes were revised in 1800 and a distinction made between pass and honours examinations. By the eighteen-forties standards of scholarship were rising rapidly and the effects of the liberal reaction beginning to be felt. The Prime Minister, Lord John Russell, in 1850 announced his intention of appointing a royal commission to inquire into the state of the university. This was opposed by many members in the Commons, among them the two Oxford University members, Sir Robert Inglis and W. E. Gladstone. The latter explained that he disapproved of interference with private foundations. The Prime Minister was thought to be hesitating. At this juncture five young Oxford staff members, of whom Goldwin Smith was one,[4] sent Lord John a memorandum thanking him for his proposal and supporting his stand. In addition to this direct approach, Smith wrote a series of letters to *The Times* signed "Oxoniensis," in which he called for university reform and for "open fellowships, no sinecures, and a real combination of the Professorial with the Tutorial system."[5] These letters attracted attention, were discussed in leading editorials, and were credited with having helped to confirm the Prime Minister's resolution.

Goldwin Smith and A. P. Stanley were appointed joint secretaries of the 1850-2 Commission of Inquiry into the state of the university, whose findings and report were followed by the acts of 1854 and 1856. Lord John Russell and Gladstone (who by that time had changed his mind) between them framed the bills of reform, based largely on the Commission's recommendations. Gladstone, as Chancellor of the Exchequer, took the major share in piloting the measures through the Commons, and Goldwin Smith was assigned to coach Lord Canning, who had charge of the first bill in the upper house. Many years later he confessed that he found his lordship "slow of apprehension and somewhat puzzleheaded."[6] He again became secretary of the executive commission appointed to give effect to the Oxford University Act of 1854.

The reforms effected by this act and its successor were, for the time, comprehensive and drastic. Until 1854 all who were not members of the Church of England, that is to say, more than half the inhabitants of the United Kingdom, had been excluded from Oxford. Bentham's struggle of conscience at being forced to sign the Thirty-Nine Articles when he went up in 1760 had led him to comment later that the streets of Oxford were paved with perjury. For another century the criticism was apposite. Under the act of 1854 nonconformists were admitted to lower degrees, but were still excluded from the higher, from college headships and fellowships, and from professorships. Most of the fellow-

---

[4]The others were A. P. Stanley, Benjamin Jowett, W. C. Lake, and Mark Pattison.
[5]*The Times*, May 20, 24, 28, 29, June 3, 6, 12, 15 and 22, 1850.
[6]"The Peelites," *Macmillan's Magazine*, LVI (Oct., 1887), 401-12.

ships and scholarships were opened to merit, instead of being reserved for specific localities or remaining in the gift of certain officials. The number and value of the scholarships and exhibitions were greatly increased. Two-thirds of the fellowships, however, still stipulated that their holders must take holy orders, and all except one of the headships of colleges, as well as most of the senior professorial chairs, continued to be limited to clergymen. Celibacy remained a qualification for holding college fellowships. Not until 1871 were all religious tests finally removed. The question of their complete abolition, a matter of bitter party controversy, had been carefully excepted from the issues with which the commissions of the 1850's had been asked to deal.

Goldwin Smith would have liked a secular university open to all, but realized that this was impracticable in Oxford and Cambridge where most of the colleges had been originally established as religious foundations. He particularly disliked the requirement which restricted many of the teaching posts to clerics, because he thought an adequate body of teachers should not all be drawn from one class. In a memorandum on qualifications for Oxford fellowships prepared for Gladstone in 1856, he asked "who would wish the education of the gentry of England and the learning of a great University to be confined exclusively to any one class whether upper, middle or lower?"[7] He signed a petition to Parliament asking for the abolition of tests. When one of the three bills to give effect to this proposal, which were passed by the Commons only to be rejected by the Lords, was being considered at Westminster, he sought the support of Cobden and Bright. Cobden demurred on the ground that he himself was not a university graduate, to which Goldwin Smith replied:

I understand and honour your reluctance—but this is not an academical question intelligible only to men trained at the university. It is a broad and simple question of national justice. Shall a great part of the nation be excluded from the national places of education on account of their conscientious convictions? You are as capable of answering this as the Vice Chancellor and the Proctors.

Nobody feels that the weight of the Liberal party is thrown into a movement unless you and Bright take a decided part. Your voices compared with those of the "young Academicians" in whose hand you propose to leave us, are as the sound of the cannon announcing battle to the rattle of small arms preluding a skirmish.[8]

[7]Gladstone Papers, CCXVIII, British Museum Add. MS. 44303, ff. 98–102. The Gladstone Papers contain over one hundred letters from Goldwin Smith to Gladstone on Oxford University reform and other matters.
[8]Letters to Cobden, March 8 and 11, 1864, Cobden Papers, British Museum

Bright's opinion of Oxford and Cambridge was indicated by his comment (at a meeting to support the abolition of tests on June 10, 1864, at which Goldwin Smith also spoke), that he thought of the universities as "places dedicated to dead languages and undying prejudices."

Numerous meetings of the sort were held during the next few years. Among the main speakers were Goldwin Smith, Jowett, T. H. Huxley, Bright, and James Bryce. The latter had been Smith's pupil at Oxford, and the two men remained fast friends to the end of their days.[9] Goldwin Smith's activities as a speaker and his publication in 1864 of a powerful little pamphlet, *A Plea for the Abolition of Tests in the University of Oxford*, brought him an enthusiastic review in the *Daily News*, which considered his arguments unanswerable. It also brought him into controversies with churchmen, notably with clerical members of the university staff, who naturally disliked attacks on their privileged position.[10] They may well have disliked, though they could scarcely refute, his assertion that modern Oxford, like everything connected with the Church of England, had been conservative, and was, in fact, still the citadel of the Conservative party. He dismissed as nonsense the suggestion that it was possible by compulsory orthodoxy to prevent doubt from seeping into the universities. Oxford, with her closed degrees and her open book-shops and libraries, was a city with fortified gates but no walls. "If religious scepticism is abroad in English society," he declared, "it will find its way into Oxford and Cambridge, as well as into other places. There is no help for this, unless we think that we can suspend the universities in a vacuum, or carry them back by enchantment into the middle ages; and even if we were in the middle ages we should find that irrational dogmatism would always cast its shadow of doubt. The truth is that scepticism is already here, and in an aggravated form."

In a stream of pamphlets, articles, and letters to editors, as well as through his work as secretary to both commissions on the universities, Goldwin Smith continued to attack clerical reaction and to demand reform. His obvious sincerity and capacity for expression attracted attention, and even won the reluctant admiration of the more tolerant

---

Add. MS. 43665. The Cobden Papers contain thirty-four letters from Goldwin Smith between Aug., 1862, and Feb., 1865.

[9]Bryce wrote Goldwin Smith on Nov. 19, 1904, that he would like to dedicate to him the new edition of his *Holy Roman Empire* "in remembrance of all that I have been privileged to learn from you through your voice and your books, ever since I went to your lectures in the hall of University College."

[10]Cf. H. R. Bramley (Fellow and Tutor of Magdalen College), *An Answer to Professor Goldwin Smith's Plea for the Abolition of Tests in the University of Oxford* (London, 1864).

clerics. The Rev. J. B. Mozley wrote the Dean of St. Paul's, "Have you read Goldwin Smith? The epigrammatic power is wonderful. He is, in his way, and with all his bitterness, still something of a prophet. He denounces, and with a moral weight and force not wholly wanting. He has a true perception of public sin. And the English, both Church and nation, have in him a judge who tells the truth, though savagely."[11] A conviction of public sin and a taste for denunciation remained highly characteristic of Goldwin Smith. His moral fervour bore practical results. For the eventual removal of religious restrictions at the universities he was perhaps more responsible than any other single individual. This reform, in his view, restored Oxford from the Church of England to the nation. After he settled in Canada he continued to write Gladstone about university and ecclesiastical reform in England, and to him in 1874 Gladstone confided that he felt he could even "face disestablishment if need be without alarm."[12]

III

Goldwin Smith's work on these commissions often took him to London, where through his Eton and Oxford friends and his journalistic connections he met many leading men in English public life, literature, and science. He also became acquainted with such political exiles as Louis Blanc and Mazzini, and to the latter was much attracted. He knew and liked Huxley and Tyndall, and used to meet Thackeray at *Saturday Review* dinners. Carlyle he knew and disliked, finding his talk like his books ill-considered, and his pessimism monotonous. A scathing criticism of Tennyson's "Maud," for its glorification of war, appeared in the first issue of the *Saturday Review*. Although it was unsigned, the secret soon leaked out that the author was Goldwin Smith, and Tennyson never forgave him. The poet restrained himself, however, to the extent of maintaining that he did not find Smith's presence "particularly annoying," when Lady Ashburton unwisely included both as guests at a country house party.

Through his duties with the commissions on the universities and on education Goldwin Smith came to know Gladstone, who acknowledged a real obligation for his encouragement and help during the struggle for university reform. The two men were on friendly enough terms to

[11]*Letters of the Rev. J. B. Mozley* (London, 1885), 320, letter of Nov., 1871.
[12]Letter from W. E. Gladstone to Goldwin Smith, Nov. 13, 1874, Goldwin Smith Autograph Album, The Grange, Art Gallery of Toronto.

breakfast and dine together occasionally and to discuss Gladstone's Homeric theories. These Goldwin Smith considered wild, and he tried as tactfully as possible, but with conspicuous lack of success, to moderate them. He supported Gladstone enthusiastically in more than one of his Oxford University election campaigns, and in 1859 wrote: "Young Oxford is all with you. Every year more men obtain the reward of their industry through your legislation. But old Oxford takes a long time in dying. If we have a fight, I shall fight with zeal, but I fear this place in its present condition imposes on you fetters which are a heavy weight to carry in a great career."[13] These fears were justified. On that occasion Gladstone was successful, but in 1865 he lost his seat for Oxford, and was subsequently elected for South Lancashire, to which he went, as he said, "unmuzzled." Two years later he suggested that Goldwin Smith should go into politics, but received the same reply as numerous other friends who made a similar proposal, namely that his circumstances and inclinations led him in a very different direction. Shortly before the general election of December, 1868, Goldwin Smith sailed for the United States. As he was leaving he wrote Gladstone, "May you rule England soon and long. It is the best wish that at parting an Englishman can breathe for his country."[14]

IV

His early connections in London were with the Peelite circle, although later he became associated with the Manchester School. For Peel he had profound respect, and his first journalistic experience was in 1850 as a staff member of the Peelite organ, the *Morning Chronicle*. In it appeared a series of anonymous articles attacking Disraeli, who discovered that their author was Goldwin Smith. Disraeli maintained that he bore no grudge, but although the two men never met, there was an acrimonious feud betwen them which led each to seize every opportunity for personal attacks on the other. Disraeli's opinion of Smith was not improved when the latter observed (in a perhaps unconscious echo of Mill), that "the Tories being, through some cause unexplained by political science, rather more stupid than the Whigs, have been rather more often obliged to take adventurers into their pay."

Goldwin Smith's growing reputation as a journalist received signal

[13]Letter of June 15, 1859, Gladstone Papers, CCXVIII, ff. 139–40.
[14]Letters from Goldwin Smith to Gladstone, Nov. 27, 1867, and Oct. 7, 1868, *ibid.*

recognition in the spring of 1855 when Mark Pattison sounded him about the possibility of becoming editor of the *Edinburgh Review*. He expressed surprise and gratification, but said he understood (correctly, as it turned out), that Sir George Cornewall Lewis was not giving up the editorship permanently, but was merely appointing a temporary substitute. Consequently the question of Goldwin Smith's competence for the post did not arise. Had a serious offer been made, he would have felt grave doubts about accepting it, owing to the independence of his opinions. "The appointment, I believe I may almost say the election of the Editor," he wrote Pattison, "is in the hands of the leading Whigs and the Review quite depends on that connection. So freer minds must find an opening in Oxford and Cambridge Essays, as some have done to good purpose."[15] About the freedom of Goldwin Smith's mind there was never any question. To him independent thought was always the salt without which all liberties would lose their savour, and independent journalism the only kind he found tolerable.

He had been toying at the time with the idea of establishing a joint stock newspaper, independent in politics, with a managing committee which represented all parties, and with the best possible contributors to discuss both sides of every great issue. He himself did not have the means to finance so costly an undertaking. He believed wholeheartedly, however, in the value of the project, as he was convinced that such a paper had a supremely important role to play. In semi-Ciceronian style he wrote Gladstone about the matter on May 1, 1855, urging him, as Chancellor of the Exchequer, to abolish the stamp tax on newspapers. "I need not tell you that the newspaper press is almost the sole instrument of political education to the great body of those who share political power. . . . I need not tell you that if Government is to have authority in a free country, the power of sound appreciation—only to be obtained by a good political education—in the people is as necessary as worthiness in the ruler."

At this juncture John Douglas Cook, the former editor of the *Morning Chronicle*, with the assistance of A. J. Beresford Hope, decided to start the *Saturday Review*, whose first issue appeared in November, 1855. They shared some, though not all, of Goldwin Smith's convictions on the nature of a good journal, and he accepted their invitation to become one of the original members of the new weekly's singularly distinguished staff. Among his colleagues were Henry Maine, William

---

[15] Letter to Mark Pattison, March 1, 1855, Pattison Papers, LI, Bodleian Library, Oxford.

Vernon Harcourt, James Fitzjames Stephen, and Lord Robert Cecil, Beresford Hope's brother-in-law, who as the third Marquess of Salisbury afterwards became Prime Minister. Subsequent contributors were John Morley, Walter Bagehot, T. H. Green, and E. A. Freeman. Few journals have at any one time had so many contributors destined for future eminence. It was no small compliment that Cook considered Goldwin Smith the most brilliant and trustworthy member of his staff and his "most effective pen."[16]

In the eighteen-sixties Fitzjames Stephen prophesied that English literary historians would consider contemporary journalism among the best writing of the period. He scarcely exaggerated. The ablest nineteenth-century journals were as distinguished as their forerunners in the days of Addison and Steele. According to their political predilections Englishmen could choose among the Whig *Edinburgh Review*, the Radical *Westminster Review*, and the Conservative *Quarterly Review* which, incidentally, attacked Goldwin Smith as more scourge than philosopher. The *Fortnightly*, founded in 1865 by a group of whom Anthony Trollope was one, began auspiciously with a chapter of Bagehot's *English Constitution* as its first leading article. Edited for fifteen years by John Morley, under whom it voiced the liberal rationalist ideas of the day, the *Fortnightly Review* soon became the outspoken friend of humanitarianism and labour. During Morley's régime Goldwin Smith was a frequent contributor.

Among newspapers *The Times*' influence as the Thunderer was unchallenged, but it was conspicuously the paper of the governing upper class. "No apology is necessary," said the *Saturday Review*, "for assuming that this country is ruled by the *Times*. We all know it, or, if we do not know it, we ought to know it." "The Times," wrote Cobden to Bright, "is a superstition, a mumbo-jumbo to the genteel classes."[17] In 1846 the *Daily News* was founded, with Charles Dickens for editor, as the spokesman of the middle class. Thereafter, when the Liberals were in power, the *News* became practically a Government organ. Dickens' editorship lasted only a few weeks, but his original policy of support for reform and for political and religious freedom was continued by C. W. Dilke (grandfather of Sir Charles) as manager and Eyre Crowe

---

[16]W. Robertson Nicoll, *James Macdonnell* (London, 1890), 188, letter from Macdonnell to Miss Annie Harrison, June 7, 1870. Macdonnell, who was a leader writer for *The Times*, stated in this letter that it was Goldwin Smith who used to write the merciless criticism of the French Empire in the *Saturday Review*.

[17]Letters from Cobden to Bright, Dec. 31, 1863, and Jan. 7, 1864, Cobden Papers, VI, ff. 134, 145.

as editor. Harriet Martineau and Justin McCarthy wrote much for it, and in its columns Goldwin Smith first became known throughout England by his letters advocating colonial independence.

Almost immediately the *Saturday Review*, designed to provide comment rather than news, established itself in the forefront of the weeklies. Critics dubbed it the "Saturday Reviler." Brilliant writing and pervasive cynicism were its hallmarks. It was soon being said that whereas with the generation of the Reform Bill everything was new, everything was true, and everything was of the highest importance, with the *Saturday* reviewers nothing was new, nothing was true, and nothing was of any importance. Cobden described the *Saturday*'s few thousand readers as that sceptical class who had neither faith, hope, nor charity.

All the early articles in the *Saturday*, as in most periodicals of the time, were unsigned. Consequently the majority of Goldwin Smith's contributions to it cannot be identified with certainty. Years later, when J. E. Atkinson of the Toronto *Star* asked him to name some of his *Saturday* articles, he replied that the only one he recalled definitely was the review of "Maud" in the first issue, but that he would not much like to specify what he had written there, even if he could. The *Saturday* staff worked in common, and he thought subsequent identification of certain writers hardly fair.[18] As a member of the regular staff, however, his contributions were chiefly editorials. He had a capacity for turning not only newspaper leaders but reviews and even letters to editors into literature. Most of his writing for the *Saturday* was on literary subjects, as he did not sympathize with its political views, which became increasingly Conservative, nor with its religious opinions, which in deference to Beresford Hope were High Church. *The Times*, also, before 1862, occasionally employed him as a literary critic. For many years thereafter it violently denounced him as the chief of the Little Englanders, though he was eventually readmitted to the respectable society of those who wrote letters to its editor.

His absorption in journalism, necessarily qualified by his duties on the university commissions, was checked but not halted when in 1858, at the age of thirty-five, he was made Regius Professor of Modern History at Oxford. Before accepting the post he ascertained that it necessitated neither subscription to the Thirty-Nine Articles, nor a

[18]Letter to J. E. Atkinson, Dec. 7, 1904. Unsigned *Saturday Review* articles known to be written by Goldwin Smith are "The War Passages in 'Maud'," I (Nov. 3, 1855), 14–15; "Froude's History of England," I (April 26, 1856), 520–1, and II (May 3, 1856), 18–19. Eight other articles of 1855–6 are attributed to him (on the basis of marked files of the *Saturday Review*), by Merle Mowbray Bevington, *The Saturday Review: 1855–1868* (New York, 1941), 373.

degree dependent on such subscription. Had either been required he would have declined the position. Greatly to his satisfaction, this appointment, on the nomination of Lord Derby, the Conservative Prime Minister, came unsolicited. When the Commission on Oxford University concluded its labours the commissioners had offered, in acknowledgment of his services, to recommend him for employment to the Government. This offer Goldwin Smith declined, but undoubtedly the reputation made in the cause of university reform was the main reason for his appointment to the chair. His interest in extension of the franchise had also brought him to the Prime Minister's attention. Early in 1858 Goldwin Smith had suggested to Lord Grey the advisability of appointing a royal commission to study the existing representative system before Parliament considered further measures of parliamentary reform. Impressed by the proposal, Grey asked Smith to put his ideas into a brief memorandum, which Grey sent Lord Derby. At Queen Victoria's request Derby showed this to her, and promised Grey to discuss the matter with his colleagues, though he himself doubted the expediency of obtaining the necessary information through a public commission.[19]

For three more years Goldwin Smith continued to contribute intermittently to the *Saturday Review*. He then explained that he wished to stop, and particularly to stop writing leaders, as he found responsibility for them very burdensome. He was indifferent to the payment, since he had enough without it for his limited wants. As a professor he also found some awkwardness in a connection with the political part of a journal. His reasons for resignation were interesting, in view of the fact that during his eight years' tenure of the Regius Professorship he never allowed his academic position to interfere with a spirited public defence of various reforms. Most of his energy during the next half century was directed to political journalism, yet in 1861 he explained to Beresford Hope that "it is and has long been my settled wish to retire entirely from journalism and devote myself to history. . . . I find the writing of leaders perfectly incompatible with the writing of books, especially since I have lost my interest in politics and am cut off from the sources of political information, so that the articles no longer come with ease." Hard pressed by lectures, he complained, "I have to turn from my work to produce by this evening an article on a subject for which I do not care and on which I have nothing to say. You cannot imagine a task more repulsive or more exhausting and deteriorating to the productive powers of a literary man. It is a widely different thing when

[19]Letter from Lord Derby to the 3rd Earl Grey, Grey Papers, University of Durham.

one is living in London amidst the political world and with one's head full of political information and ideas."[20] A year later, when Cobden proposed starting a new weekly, Goldwin Smith suggested that it might be wise to make the best of those already in existence. He himself, he explained, had quite renounced journalism, and simply used the correspondence columns of the *Daily News* as the most appropriate medium for advocating his opinions on certain points.

V

Nevertheless, Goldwin Smith was a born journalist, and not a born historian. Yet as he avowed, the Regius Professorship at Oxford was the desire of his heart. The chair was not customarily used by its occupants as a vantage ground for launching attacks on the ills of the world. Once appointed, however, he threw himself into his new duties with vigour sufficient to allow him to devote considerable extracurricular attention to such causes as colonial emancipation, the extension of the franchise, and the championship of the North in the American Civil War. His house in the Parks (later, as 7 Norham Gardens, the home of Professor Max Müller) became a meeting place for intellectual Oxford. In the conservative university circle party feeling ran high. At a time when to desire the abolition of religious tests was to be a Liberal and to resist this to be a Tory, Goldwin Smith was soon known as one of the ablest leaders of the party of progress. Before long the *Quarterly Review* was coupling him and John Stuart Mill as spokesmen for the new school of radicals, and indignantly asking what Goldwin Smith had done that he should dictate to all England.[21]

His inaugural lecture, delivered in 1859, made a plea for broadening the course of studies at the university, in order to train students not only in classics, philosophy, and mathematics, but also in such modern subjects as science, jurisprudence, political economy, and above all history, especially the political history of their own country. He saw Oxford's task as the education of the future rulers of England. It was therefore responsible for producing enlightened and upright governors, good landlords, and just magistrates. His views on the study of modern history as an integral part of the education of the British governing class challenged traditional concepts. They also challenged what he considered the extravagant claims put forward at the time concerning

---

[20] Letters to A. J. Beresford Hope, Oct. 15, 22, and 24, 1861.
[21] Unsigned article, "The New School of Radicals," *Quarterly Review*, CXXIV (April, 1868), 257.

the scientific nature of historical development and human behaviour. The ethical implications of historical events, not constitutional minutiae, seemed to him of primary importance. He did not believe that history was governed by necessary laws, but argued that a science of history must rest on a knowledge of causation which in this sphere was impossible. The historian, to his mind, could not be content simply to look for laws of development or effort, but must seek justice as well as order and design. Goldwin Smith's concern for moral values was such that his teaching of history interpreted men and events in the light of his own ethical judgments.

These ideas were attacked by Frederic Harrison as "a pungent apology for Christianity . . . better adapted for the pulpit of St. Mary's than the Chair of History."[22] Goldwin Smith indignantly denied the allegation, though in later years he admitted that his inaugural lecture had been given when he still lingered "within the penumbra of orthodoxy." On this as on many subsequent occasions he managed to antagonize two camps, since his enthusiasm for freeing the university from religious tests led most orthodox clerics to view him as a critic of Christianity, or at any rate of the established church, which they were inclined to think much the same thing. The controversy between him and Harrison continued, with acrimony on both sides, through letters to the *Daily News*. Eventually, however, the two were reconciled and became good friends.

His defects as an historian were obvious and naturally exposed him to criticism. To the sum of human knowledge he added little. He had no taste for painstaking research into primary sources and little capacity for objectivity. A violent partisan, he carried into the past, as Dicey once observed, the animosities of the present. He dealt freely in defence and condemnation, depending on whether he approved of those whose history he was writing. Yet he loathed Carlyle's hero worship, believing that the student of history should fix his eye on the progress of virtue, intelligence, and comfort among the masses, rather than on the efforts and characters of individuals. History, politics, and literature alike, Goldwin Smith subjected to a moral test. Against the common tendency to treat politics as an eternal struggle between classes, and history as one long record of wars and hatred, he reacted so violently that his readers were sometimes in doubt as to whether his subject was history or biography, philosophy or moral judgment. Every topic he discussed (including Conservative politics), he treated from a modern Liberal point of view, using the present to interpret the past, in a manner

[22]*Westminster Review* (Oct., 1861).

startling to more orthodox students of history. Thus in lectures on English statesmen he described Gustavus Adolphus' battle at Leipzig as "the Gettysburg of the seventeenth century," while Gustavus' English and Scottish soldiers became "the Garibaldians of their day." St. Loe Strachey thought these lectures the best and most interesting studies of modern statesmen published in that generation. An anonymous reviewer complained, however, that they were neither straight pamphleteering nor straight history, but an untenable mixture of the two, and criticized the author's "sustained tone of indignation." Whether justified or not, he suggested, indignation was of all things the least convincing and not the least wearisome.[23] It was a fair enough criticism of almost everything Goldwin Smith ever wrote. For all his ability, he too often allowed himself to be dominated by his passions.

Before a name had been invented for the comparative method of studying history, he was using one historical period to illuminate another, and in an analysis of the civil wars of seventeenth-century England he found parallels with the French Revolution. He might have done well to remember Lord Acton's observation that there are no true historic parallels, for he was always finding them—frequently most unlikely ones. He had, however, some assets as an historian, and was generally considered to have filled the chair with distinction. His style was brilliant, his concern with ideas unflagging, and his interpretation, though often prejudiced, was always challenging. An accomplished satirist, he was a master of balanced phrases and of barbed wit. The history he wrote was less a chronicle of events than a series of philosophical and epigrammatic reflections upon them. The provocativeness of his analysis and the felicity of his style fascinated students and made him an effective popularizer of history. About the permanent value of his work he was under no illusions. As he frankly observed to a friend, he wrote "more with a view to influencing contemporary opinion than to lasting reputation." Judged by the test of what he set out to do, his success was outstanding.

Among his duties as Regius Professor was giving private lectures on history to the Prince of Wales (later King Edward VII) and a select group of companions. He never pretended that he found the prince a particularly apt scholar, but he liked him as a person and appreciated his good manners in always looking interested, however bored he may

[23]*Three English Statesmen* (London, 1868), 12; letter to Goldwin Smith from St. Loe Strachey, March 2, 1896; *Pall Mall Gazette*, Aug. 16, 1867, review of *Three English Statesmen*. The *Gazette* reviewer drew an apt comparison between Goldwin Smith and Southey, who was honest, high-minded, and wrote admirably, but also was always indignant.

GOLDWIN SMITH AT ETON, AGED 18
Eton leaving portrait painted in 1841 by Margaret Sarah Carpenter. Art Gallery of Toronto, Goldwin Smith Collection.

have been by the exploits of the early English kings. Goldwin Smith considered that he was more successful in the extra-curricular activity of teaching whist to his royal pupil and euchre to a younger brother, the Duke of Albany. A certain friendship grew up between them, which continued to the end of their days. He was invited to go with the Prince of Wales's party to Canada in 1860, but thought he could not leave his professorial duties. For royalty as an institution he had little enthusiasm, and on at least one occasion his acquaintance with the prince involved him in an odd situation. "I have fallen into a curious trap," he wrote bitterly to Cobden in 1865. "I accepted what I took to be an invitation to a private dinner from the Prince of Wales, who was my pupil here—and I find I have to go in tights! What a fool I shall look." The friendship, however, survived even this disaster, and when Goldwin Smith subsequently sent the prince a copy of his *Irish History and Irish Character*, Edward wrote in his own hand that he should not fail to read it with great interest. He added politely (whether truthfully or not), that he had never forgotten the author's interesting lectures at Oxford.[24]

VI

The *Empire* letters of 1862-3, in which he advocated colonial emancipation, established him as the most effective exponent of the views of the Little Englanders, which were broadly those of the Manchester School. With delight not unmixed with surprise, Cobden and Bright found that academic men like Goldwin Smith and Thorold Rogers publicly advocated the causes of anti-imperialism, free trade, and an extended franchise. Lacking a university education themselves, they set the more store upon support from those eminent in university circles. In the summer of 1862, a few weeks after first meeting Goldwin Smith, Cobden called Bright's attention to one of Smith's *Empire* letters on Canada which had recently appeared in the *Daily News*. He thought Bright might find some parts of this too revolutionary, but would appreciate the powerful writing of "a very stout and original thinker. He is very quiet in society," Cobden went on, "—scarcely speaks at all. But in a tête-à-tête he is as forcible in conversation as with his pen. The Oxford people think he is the best writer of the day. . . . There is a charming tolerance at Oxford—Goldwin Smith does not lose caste in the slightest degree among his brother dons by his revolutionary

[24]Letter to Goldwin Smith from the Prince of Wales, Nov. 14, 1881, Autograph Album.

speculations." Cobden coupled Smith's name with that of Rogers as "men whom I know to have a vast superiority over me. . . . I bow to them with reverence."[25] He often remarked to Goldwin Smith during the American Civil War that this combination of the masses with a section of the literary and academic world was a new and significant feature in English political life. Bright, as a Quaker, had little admiration for the English university system, until he found that these two professors, at least, were willing to associate themselves with radicalism. Goldwin Smith came to be on very friendly personal terms with both Bright and Cobden. The former, in particular, he admired more than any other English statesmen except Pitt and Peel. He considered Bright the greatest speaker whom he had ever heard, and his greatest speech that delivered at St. James' Hall, London, on the Civil War. If the Northerners had been present on that occasion, he observed, they would not have thought all England was against them.[26]

A philosophic radicalism, which was the accepted creed of almost all Liberals of the age, and a common outlook on colonial and economic questions were his first bonds of union with Bright and Cobden. Their hatred of war he shared to the full. The existing links between them were more closely forged by common sympathy and joint action during the American Civil War, when as a speaker and writer Goldwin Smith supported the North, and paid a four months' visit to the United States. His confidence was somewhat shaken in 1868 when Bright took office in Gladstone's first Government. He wrote a friend that he feared Bright was "touched by Royalty which touched even Cromwell," and that as a minister he would learn to be discreet. At the same time he would probably lose his influence over the workers. "The working men will then be without a leader. Mill has their respect, but he has never quite found his way to their hearts; and for reasons to me inscrutable he has planted himself in dogged opposition to the Ballot, which to the working men and all their class is a matter of political life or death."[27]

He was more interested in political questions than Cobden, whose chief concern was with economic and fiscal reform. Cobden's enthusiasm for an extension of the franchise, as Bright discovered, was

[25] Letters from Cobden to Bright, Aug. 31, Sept. 6, and Dec. 29, 1862, Cobden Papers, VI, ff. 42, 68–9. Cf. Justin McCarthy, *Portraits of the Sixties* (London, 1903), 383, and *Reminiscences* (2 vols., New York, 1899), I, 73.

[26] "Recollections of John Bright," *Independent* (New York), XLI (April 4, 1889).

[27] Letter to Charles Eliot Norton from Ithaca, March 10, 1869, "Letters of Goldwin Smith to Charles Eliot Norton, 1863–1872," Massachusetts Historical Society, *Proceedings* (Dec., 1915), 145.

very moderate; that of Goldwin Smith was qualified. There was some difference of opinion between them on trade unions. Cobden, a master manufacturer, opposed them on the ground that individual efforts were better, whereas Goldwin Smith approved of them (though he disliked strikes), and took part in the struggle to remove the legal restrictions under which unions laboured. Neither sympathized with the violent aspects of Chartism, and both heartily disliked adulation of the aristocracy. On Irish questions, above all, they saw eye to eye. Both men inveighed against the evils of absentee landlordism, both called for disestablishment of the Irish church, and both believed that what Ireland really needed was agrarian rather than political reform. To Cobden Goldwin Smith wrote in detail about political affairs, freely expressing his opinion of Palmerston, whom he variously characterized as "the old scoundrel" and "an Irish bully." He could not forgive Palmerston's part in the Crimean War, and was seriously concerned lest he involve England in armed conflict with the United States. His only consolation in such an event would be that the war would prove the grave of the English aristocracy.

Cobden tried to persuade Goldwin Smith to go into Parliament, but as with Gladstone's similar suggestion, he flatly rejected the idea. He explained that the matter had been first presented to him when he was younger, and he had then decided once for all in the negative. He had no independent income, and thought without this no one should go into Parliament, unless, like Cobden, he was the champion of a great and definite cause. At the age of forty he considered himself "far too old to begin learning to speak. With my *pen* I will support my principles as well as I can; but I could only traduce them with my *tongue*."[28] The financial difficulty was lessened five years later, when he inherited a considerable sum from his father's estate, but he never changed his mind, despite numerous invitations to do so. His extra-parliamentary influence on public affairs, however, was significant. In addition to his work as journalist and public speaker, his letters to Cobden were full of urgent suggestions about the stand which should be taken by Cobden, Bright, and their friends on numerous issues before Parliament. He was prompt to advise on such varied questions as the cession of the Ionian Islands, the abolition of religious tests at the universities, Irish affairs, disestablishment of the church, and England's relations with the United States. Cobden's replies are missing, but their continued correspondence and unbroken friendship provide sufficient evidence that the advice was not unwelcome.

[28]Letters to Cobden, March 22 and June 11, 1863.

VII

Goldwin Smith resigned his Oxford chair in 1866 in order to nurse his father, who was suffering from mental illness as a result of an injury in a railway accident. For the next eighteen months he scarcely left his side until in October, 1867, he was obliged to leave home for a weekend business visit to the north of England. In his absence his father committed suicide. Sensitive and somewhat melancholy by temperament, Goldwin Smith blamed himself for his father's death, and it was long before he recovered from the shock. There is no suggestion, either in private papers or in published reminiscences, that he considered it a sacrifice to give up his teaching post to fulfil this family obligation. But he could not have been unaware that his decision altered the course of his life and ruined the prospect of a brilliant career confidently anticipated for him by friends like Bryce and Dicey and Morley. When he resigned his chair, Stubbs was appointed to the Regius Professorship of Modern History which for Goldwin Smith had represented "the summit of my limited ambition." His fellowship at Oriel, which expired in 1868, could not be renewed since the holder was subject to a means test. He was automatically disqualified because he had inherited from his father some £30,000. Thus, as he later observed, he found himself at the age of forty-four, "having independent means and no profession . . . rather at a loss for an object in life." He had been much attracted to the United States on his visit in 1864, had made many friends there, and had relatives in Canada. He felt the need of an occupation and change of scene, and was considering the possibility of an extended visit to the other side of the Atlantic when Andrew White invited him to join the staff of the newly established Cornell University at Ithaca, New York. Goldwin Smith promptly accepted the offer.

During the year between his father's death and his departure for America he concentrated upon the Jamaica Committee. This organization had been set up in 1865 to force an inquiry into the high-handed proceedings of Governor Eyre of Jamaica, who was charged with suppressing a negro rebellion with a severity highly unusual and allegedly unnecessary. Through his work as one of the most active members of this Committee Goldwin Smith was brought into close contact with its chairman, John Stuart Mill, whom he considered the most conscientious man he had ever known and "the most austere of patriots." Years afterward he said of Mill that "there never was a man in acting with whom you were made more comfortably to feel that you must be morally in the right."[29] Fellow members on the Committee were John Bright, Herbert Spencer, Thomas Hughes, and T. H. Huxley. A counter committee, organized to defend Governor Eyre, included Ruskin, Carlyle, Tennyson, and Kingsley. Eyre's advocates were outspoken on their antagonists. Ruskin "viewed with more than contempt" the four leading members, Mill, Bright, Hughes, and Goldwin Smith. Carlyle described them as a "knot of nigger philanthropists, barking furiously in the gutter." Violence was not confined to the press, for Mill, as the moving spirit, even received threats of assassination.

Goldwin Smith maintained that his chief concern with the Jamaica question was the protection of liberty in England, since he thought it hopeless, in the existing state of public opinion, to get Englishmen to insist that the subject peoples of the British Empire should be treated justly and receive the ordinary protection of the law. He argued that the ancient securities for public liberty had largely lost their value. Such measures as the Petition of Right and the Habeas Corpus Act were effective restraints against royal tyranny, because the Crown could not repeal an act of Parliament. As restraints on the tyranny of Parliament, however, they were far less effective, because the legislature could repeal its own acts. The tyranny of the Crown was a thing of the past, that of a majority in Parliament a very present danger.[30]

The conflict of races in Jamaica seemed to Goldwin Smith a corollary of the issue between slavery and freedom in the United States, and the one cause no less worthy than the other. At a meeting in aid of Baptist missions to the West Indian negroes, he contended that the more gifted and more civilized peoples were responsible for helping the less gifted and more backward. To his mind it was not the duty of a Christian nation to exterminate subject peoples by the unscrupulous use of power.[31] His lectures on Pym, Pitt, and Peel, later published under the title of *Three English Statesmen*, were originally delivered in the spring of 1867 in a number of cities, in order to earn the money which he had promised to the Jamaica Committee. In the end Governor Eyre was

[29]"England and the War of Secession," *Atlantic Monthly*, LXXXIX (March, 1902), 303–11.
[30]*Beehive*, Aug. 25, Sept. 8, 1866. Cf. also Goldwin Smith's letters to the *Daily News*, Aug. 6 and Nov. 20, 1866. These letters criticizing Governor Eyre provoked counter attacks on Goldwin Smith in the *Standard* (London), Sept. 3 and 14, 1866. Its editor expressed satisfaction at the news that he had resigned his Oxford chair, as his "bitter prejudices" and "spirit of class hatred" utterly unfitted him "to be the teacher of the youth of the higher orders."
[31]*Oxford Chronicle*, Dec. 22, 1866.

suspended and not reappointed. The Committee succeeded, not in having him brought to trial, but in arousing English opinion against oppression in the colonies. Goldwin Smith hoped that the publicity given the matter might "at least teach the world, and the official world especially, that the common cause of humanity is not yet abandoned, and that if a 'nigger' is unjustly put to death in Jamaica there are those in a distant country and of another race who will call for an account of his blood."[32]

The members of the Jamaica Committee were denounced by conservative imperialists as traitors to the Empire, and they were disappointed that their endeavours were not more successful. As Mill observed, however, they had done what they could to redeem the character of their country, and Goldwin Smith found to his surprise that he had acquired a reputation outside England as a friend of coloured peoples. Shortly after he settled in the United States he was invited by the negro population of Cleveland to take part in their annual celebration of the emancipation of slaves in the West Indies. He spoke to them on the conduct of England in reference to slavery, and suggested that "this chapter of the pride of race is one of the strangest in the annals of the human Lilliput, one of the most grotesque antics of the all-important pigmy, man. . . . There are two Englands," he declared, "the England of the past and the England of the future; the England of Lord Derby and the Southern Club, and the England of Gladstone and Bright; the England which has been struggling to maintain the Irish establishment, and the England which has decreed its abolition. And this latter England is prevailing over the other."[33]

VIII

Many of his friends, confident that he made a great mistake in leaving Britain, tried hard to persuade him to change his mind. They dangled before him the bait of a nomination for such Liberal seats as Marylebone and Chelsea. But he was not to be persuaded. He told Frederic Harrison that he was sure anything he could do would be better done outside the House. He thought his strength insufficient to fulfil the reasonable demands of a constituency and also leave enough freedom to devote himself to the critical questions of the day. About his health he

[32] Letter to Mrs. Hertz, Feb. 28, 1867.
[33] *England and Slavery*, a lecture given at Case Hall, Cleveland, Ohio, July 31, 1869 (privately printed).

was always apprehensive, although he lived to the age of eighty-six without a serious illness. A bad speaker, he observed to Eliot Norton, is not sorely tempted to go into the House of Commons. Furthermore he considered that he had had no training for a parliamentary career. To a man of his fastidious and retiring disposition the prospect of the hurly-burly of political life was distasteful. His private income was not large enough to cover campaign costs in most constituencies and to pay for a secretary. In any event, he was fundamentally too independent to have been a good party member, especially as the lines of party organization became more closely drawn in the latter years of the century. Invitations to stand for English constituencies were renewed on other occasions after he settled in Canada, but he never seriously considered any of them. Long after his departure his friends continued to deplore his absence from English public life. "I wish," wrote Max Müller in 1870 to Dean Stanley, "Goldwin Smith were in England—some such man is wanted now." Fifteen years later Matthew Arnold was saying the same thing.[34]

In the last weeks before he left Britain public tribute was paid to him on a number of formal occasions. He seized every such opportunity to explain that affection for America implied no weakening in feeling for his own country. "Do not believe anyone," he told an Oxford audience, "who tells you that I shall cease to be an Englishman. . . . An Englishman I am, and an Englishman I shall remain in whatever land, among whatever people I may be."[35] At a farewell meeting of the Manchester Reform Club, a speaker suggested that if there were any place in England where Goldwin Smith could expect an echo of his views upon all the great social questions of the day, it was in Manchester, among the circle of Reform Club members. He replied that he had rather been "the humble echo of the opinions of Manchester; and my part is, as a literary man, to echo those opinions with my pen, not

---

[34]"With singular lucidity and penetration," wrote Matthew Arnold of Goldwin Smith, "he saw what great reforms were needed . . . , and the order of relative importance in which reforms stood. Such were his character, style and faculties, that alone perhaps of men of his insight he was capable of getting his ideas weighed and entertained by men in power; while amid all favour and all temptations he was certain to have still remained true to his insight, 'unshaken, unseduced, unterrified.' I think of him as a real power for good in Parliament at this time, had he by now become, as he might have become, one of the leaders there. His absence from the scene, his retirement in Canada, is a loss to his friends, but a still greater loss to his country." *Civilization in the United States* (3rd ed., Boston, 1888), 149–50.

[35]*Daily News*, Feb. 29, 1868.

with my tongue. . . . If I am settled in America, so far as my humble endeavours will go, I shall . . . promote what I believe to be the best interests of both nations and cordial friendship between this country and the United States."[36] On October 26, 1868, the day before he sailed for America, he wrote Frederic Harrison, "I am afraid that you will call me a deserter; but if reaction ever makes a serious rally, you will see me again in the ranks."

[36]*The Times,* April 11, 1868.

II. THE UNITED STATES

GOLDWIN SMITH'S ENTHUSIASM for the United States developed early and proved enduring. Long before his first visit, as a British radical he had conjured up a vision of the great English-speaking republic. As an historian his sympathy and liking for the country were already apparent in an early lecture on the foundation of the American colonies. That from the beginning they had been destined for independence was to his mind obvious, but the manner of their parting, in a violent revolution which left on each side a legacy of dislike and suspicion, he thought deplorable. Not the loss of the colonies, but the quarrel, seemed to him one of the greatest disasters to the English race. He would gladly have given up such victories as Blenheim and Waterloo, if only the two Englands might have parted amicably.

He liked to remind Oxford students of the kindly reception given the first American ambassador to England by George III, who frankly confessed that he had been the last to consent to the separation. Once it had been made, however, and was irrevocable, he "would be the first to meet the friendship of the United States as an independent power." In the speech from the throne the king had declared: "Religion, Language, Interest, Affection, may, and I hope will, yet prove a bond of permanent union between the two countries; to this end neither attention nor disposition on my part will be wanting." After all, Goldwin Smith pointed out, when George III signed away his empire over America, he did not thereby sign away the empire of English law, religion, blood, language, literature, or liberty. It must be the earnest desire of every Englishman that the common and inevitable bonds between the two countries might be more closely drawn, and that in time the wound might heal, even though history could never cancel "the fatal page which robs England of half the glory and half the happiness of being the mother of a great nation."[1]

Yet his attitude toward the United States was not uncritical. He de-

[1] "On the Foundation of the American Colonies," *Lectures on Modern History* (Oxford, 1861).

plored its violent bias for democracy, which sprang from the sudden rupture with England and set up the revolutionary theory of the sovereign people. This as much as any despotic doctrine tended to retard progress by placing the will of the majority above reason and law, and taught Americans to equate patriotism with rebellion. Among American statesmen he much preferred Hamilton to Jefferson, whom Goldwin Smith considered at heart an anarchist, and whose bitterness against England he regretted. Jefferson's idea that a little rebellion now and then was a good thing made him shudder. Jefferson's faith in individual liberty and self-reliance, however, touched a responsive chord.

I

When the Civil War broke out in 1861, Goldwin Smith was among the few Englishmen intensely interested in its progress. Regarding the United States as the greatest achievement of his race, he was consumed by mingled hope and curiosity about its future, and watched the struggle with the anxiety of an American. England could not remain indifferent to the war, for the stoppage of cotton supplies from the South struck Lancashire a devastating blow. One after another the British mills, including that of John Bright, closed for lack of cotton. In the early stages of the war Gladstone and some Liberals approved the cause of the South, which they considered a nation making a legitimate and gallant struggle for freedom. Conservatives like Palmerston and Derby also sympathized with the South, as did the cotton manufacturers and many free traders, because the North stood for tariffs, and the cotton-producing South for free trade.

At first many Englishmen thought it a war to preserve the union rather than to destroy slavery, a pardonable error, since during the first year and a half this was the position adopted by Lincoln, who did not proclaim the freedom of the slaves until October, 1862. Gladstone publicly adhered to a policy of strict neutrality, but privately had a leaning toward the South understandable in a Liverpool man whose father was a West Indian proprietor and the owner of slaves. Understandable or not, it modified Goldwin Smith's early enthusiasm for him. In the beginning Smith hesitated about his own stand, because he thought it not an Englishman's business to fan the flames of civil war in another country. He was also doubtful whether the reincorporation of the slave states with the free North was desirable. His first ground of hesitation vanished, however, when Southern envoys sought to draw England into war on their side, and his second was swept away as the struggle became manifestly one between freedom and slavery. *The Times*, as the mouthpiece of the wealthier and aristocratic classes, took the position that the issue was essentially free trade against protection, and strongly supported the South. In the United States its views were assumed to be those of England, although more and more the mass of the English people sympathized with the North. Feeling ran high in Britain, where, as Cobden complained to Bright, the South was recognized as "so completely the aristocratic side that it is looked on as rather a test of gentility, and the partisans of the North are scarcely regarded as being quite fit for good society. You will hardly find a rich man within Temple Bar who does not conform to this view.—And the same spirit extends very deeply into the upper strata of the middle classes, who are little inclined to soil their gentility by espousing a low democratic cause."[2]

Once convinced that there was a clear case of right against wrong, Goldwin Smith wholeheartedly upheld the North and attacked the support given the South by *The Times* and the English governing class. In this endeavour he was allied with a small but distinguished group of British Liberals including Bright, Cobden, Mill, Leslie Stephen, and Thomas Hughes. Most of these men worked together in the 1860's, not only for support of the North, but also for extension of the franchise and for the Jamaica Committee. Within a year after he had told the editor of the *Saturday Review* that he had lost all interest in politics, Goldwin Smith turned the columns of the *Daily News* into a forum for attacks on Britain's American and imperial policies. His first letter on "England and America," under the characteristic *nom de plume* of "Anglo-Saxon," was published on November 27, 1862. To an American friend John Stuart Mill described it as "one of the most powerful and most thorough pieces of writing in your defence that has yet appeared." In this letter Goldwin Smith attacked the war which *The Times* had been labouring to provoke. The free North, he argued, was making an experiment in equality and independence which, if successful, would shake feudalism throughout the world. To his mind the Civil War was an episode in the ancient conflict between aristocracy and democracy. A few months later, in an open letter to the secretary of the Emancipation Society, he declared that the struggle was now beyond question to prevent the establishment of slavery in the midst of Christendom and civilization. "The cause of emancipation," he wrote, "is not that of the negro race alone. It is the cause of civilization, of Christian morality, of the rights of labour, and of the rights of man. It is the old and

[2]Letter from Cobden to Bright, Oct. 30, 1864, Cobden Papers, VI, f. 198.

glorious cause of England. And if a part of our upper classes and of our clergy, in their hatred of the Free States and their Free Churches, have ceased to be true to it, it still has a firm hold, I trust, on the hearts of the English people."[3]

Goldwin Smith was genuinely afraid that England might be drawn into war against the North. He first appeared on a public platform to support a political cause at a meeting held on April 6, 1863, by the Manchester Union and Emancipation Society. This was called to protest against the building and equipping in English ports of the *Alabama* and other "piratical ships in support of the Southern Slaveholders' Confederacy." In a letter to Cobden he explained that he had gone to Manchester not meaning to speak, but found they were really anxious to hear a few words by some one from Oxford, and so he had done his best. "That the 'best' was bad," he commented ruefully, "you may well believe when I tell you that I had never addressed a meeting, or made anything that could be called a speech before I found myself facing 6000 people in the Free Trade Hall."[4] His advocacy undoubtedly helped to produce the remarkable change in English public opinion, from warm sympathy with the South to an eventually even warmer support of the North. Thomas Bayley Potter, president of the Union and Emancipation Society, and for years a distinguished Liberal member of Parliament, disagreed with Goldwin Smith's own estimate of his speech at Manchester, for to it he traced the turn of the tide.

The Times, which for the past year had been fulminating against his views on colonial emancipation, had now a double reason for attacking him. Three days after the meeting at Manchester it denounced those who called on the Government to stop the outfitting of Confederate ships in English ports. Other journals followed suit, among them the *Saturday Review*, which, however, refrained from mentioning its former staff member by name when it poured scorn on the prominent Englishmen who took the side of the North. Other papers showed no such restraint. Before long Goldwin Smith was abused from one corner of the country to the other, while among the small circle of English defenders of the North he was hailed as the outstanding champion of freedom. To his critics he turned a deaf ear, and continued to state his views on American policy in letters to the *Daily News*, much less well known than

[3] *Daily News*, Feb. 3, 1863. Other letters by Goldwin Smith on the Civil War appeared in the *Daily News* on April 13, Sept. 1 and 4, Oct. 12, 1863, April 22, May 3 and 24, July 11 and 25, and Oct. 18, 1864.

Mill's letter to John Lathrop Motley, Jan. 26, 1863, is published in Hugh S. R. Elliott (ed.), *Letters of John Stuart Mill* (2 vols., London, 1910), I, 277.

[4] April 13, 1863.

his *Empire* letters, but almost equally distinguished in force and felicity of style. In these he contended that it would be a calamity for England to be involved in war with the United States. It would "put enmity for another bitter century between the two portions of the Anglo-Saxon race, one in blood, in language, in religion, in literature, in the essence, whatever may be the outward forms, of their free institutions, and one in their destined action on the future progress of mankind."[5]

Toward the end of 1863 the fortunes of war shifted, and even *The Times* began to change its tone as it appeared less probable that the South would win. To Cobden, Goldwin Smith wrote of his gratification at this turn of affairs. Despite the surface weaknesses of the American nation he thought it had shown essential greatness, and was sanguine that it would survive its trials. Although he had little confidence in the politicians produced by the American party system, he had unlimited faith in an intelligent, self-governed, and united people. Cobden wryly suggested that the success of any great reform could be ensured by three conditions: a good cause, zealous advocates, and the hostility of *The Times*.[6]

Goldwin Smith's writing on American affairs went beyond letters to the press. In a pamphlet, *A Letter to a Whig Member of the Southern Independence Association*, he argued that class interests aside, there was no reason why the people of England should fear the greatness of the English people across the Atlantic. The malignity which attacked all things American and found an organ in *The Times* was that of a party, not of the English people. Surely, he pleaded, no artificial agreement arranged by diplomats with foreign countries was worth half as much to Englishmen as their natural alliance with that portion of their race which inhabited North America. The outcome of the Civil War would make the New World new indeed, a world of new hopes and new opportunities for men.

He also published a more elaborate study, *Does the Bible Sanction American Slavery?* as a direct reply to an editorial in *The Times*, which contended that such biblical sanction did exist, and that it was the moral duty of slaves to refuse emancipation. In the controversy over university reform Goldwin Smith had already shown that he was no orthodox churchman, but this concept of religion was too much for him, and his little book launched a blistering attack on *The Times*' interpretation of

[5] Letter to the *Daily News*, Sept. 4, 1863.
[6] Open letter from Cobden to J. T. Delane, Dec. 9, 1864, *Correspondence between Mr. Cobden, M.P. and Mr. Delane, Editor of "The Times"* (Manchester, 1864); letters from Goldwin Smith to Richard Cobden, Aug. 20 and Nov. 11, 1863.

the Old Testament. Widely read not only in Great Britain, but also in the United States, it was enthusiastically discussed by Charles Eliot Norton, joint editor with James Russell Lowell of the *North American Review*.[7] A distinguished journalist and one of the founders of the New York *Nation*, Norton liked the English as instinctively as Goldwin Smith liked the Americans. Both detested slavery, and in religion both eventually rejected orthodox opinions and became professed freethinkers. Norton lived to endure as much criticism from his fellow-countrymen for attacking American expansion at the turn of the century, as was directed against Goldwin Smith by English and Canadian ultra-patriots. He considered Smith's book the best of all the publications inspired by the Civil War, and a work worthy of its author's reputation at home and abroad.

Norton's review led to correspondence with Goldwin Smith and the beginning of a close friendship which lasted for the rest of their days. Smith expressed satisfaction that his pamphlet seemed likely to do good in America, and mentioned that he hoped soon to visit the United States. Norton had noted his appreciation of American institutions. This probably arose from his being " 'an American citizen' in sympathy more decidedly than you may suppose."

I am as far as possible from desiring to see any violent revolution in this country. But, for my own part, I have fairly thought my way out of social and political Feudalism, and out of the State Church which is its religious complement; and my intellect and heart are entirely with those who are endeavouring to found a great community on the sounder as well as happier basis of social justice and free religious convictions. In my sentiments, at least in the definiteness of my sentiments, on these subjects I probably stand nearly alone among people of my own class. So that my writings, I fear, have little value as an index of English opinion. Most likely I shall be more in my element, in some respects, at Boston than I am at Oxford.[8]

Toward the end of August, 1864, at the height of the Civil War, Goldwin Smith sailed for the United States. Some weeks earlier he had written Cobden that he planned, when the war was over, to pay a more extended visit to America. Under certain circumstances he might be tempted to prolong his stay, even though this would involve giving up

---

[7] *North American Review*, XCVIII (Jan., 1864), 48–74. Norton was a cousin of President C. W. Eliot of Harvard, where he later became Professor of Fine Art, and one of the most eminent members of the staff.

[8] Letters to C. E. Norton, May 24 and July 22, 1864; to J. M. Forbes, Sept. 3, 1864. Four years earlier Bright told Cobden that he thought he would be "happier in New England than here with the supreme folly I see around me, and the gigantic pillage of the people which is practised on every side." Letter from Bright to Cobden, July 25, 1860, Bright Papers, II, f. 217, British Museum.

his professorship and (what he cared for much more) his literary undertakings in England. It would be a special inducement to him if he thought that as a writer he could throw a single grain into the scale of peace. Cobden told Bright that he would much regret losing Goldwin Smith but thought him out of time and place where he was.[9] The comment was shrewd, though whether North America proved more his spiritual home than England may be questioned. At any rate, Goldwin Smith was thus considering the possibility of settling for some time in the United States even before his first visit there and two years before he resigned his Oxford chair. In a frame of mind very different from that of a mere tourist he set out for the country he had come to regard almost as his own, believing that on its future the political and religious hopes of man rested.

Both Cobden and Bright wrote to tell Charles Sumner, chairman of the Senate Committee on Foreign Affairs, of Goldwin Smith's projected visit. From the beginning of the Civil War Cobden had kept Sumner, his friend and correspondent since 1849, informed about the real state of opinion in Great Britain. He explained that the whole nation did not support the cause of the South. Of Goldwin Smith Cobden wrote, "He needs no personal introductions, and I have given him no letters. But I need not tell you that he deserves well of your country. He is one of the few men moving in his sphere who have given a hearty and most brilliant support to your cause." Bright wrote: "He is a great friend of the North and of freedom, and is a man you will delight to know if you are not already acquainted with him."[10]

After a thirteen-day crossing Goldwin Smith landed in Halifax, and proceeded at once to Boston where he stayed with Charles Eliot Norton, paid a visit in Concord to Emerson (whom he thought more like a business man than a mystic), saw Thoreau living in a shanty in the woods, supped with Longfellow, and called upon Senator Sumner. He sampled churches of various denominations, and was struck by the church-going habit of the people. Brown University at Providence gave him an honorary degree upon the occasion of its centenary, when the president introduced him as a gentleman to whom they were "much indebted for a timely and kindly word . . . when such words were most needed by

[9] Letters from Cobden to Bright, Aug. 16, 1864, Cobden Papers, VI, f. 177; from Goldwin Smith to Cobden, April 15, 1864.
[10] Letter from John Bright to Charles Sumner, Sept. 2, 1864, Sumner Papers, Harvard University Library. Reprinted in *Massachusetts Historical Association Proceedings, 1912-13*, XLVI (Oct., 1912), 131. Cobden's letter of Aug. 18, 1864, to Sumner is quoted in J. A. Hobson, *Richard Cobden* (New York, 1919), 381-2.

America in her great struggle—uttered, too, when they were worth something and cost something."

Norton's impression of his visitor, given in letters to G. W. Curtis, editor of *Harper's Magazine* (whom he asked to give Goldwin Smith a note of introduction to both Lincoln and Seward), was that "he is as good at least as his books."[11] His appreciation of the United States and of the Northern cause was just, clear, and complete. This was Norton's privately expressed opinion, while in his public welcome he recalled what Goldwin Smith had done in England for the North: "America is not ungrateful to him who thus served her, and in serving her promotes the universal cause of liberty and justice. She pays him the tribute of heartiest gratitude; she welcomes him, not as a stranger, but as a son."

When Goldwin Smith first landed in the United States he was already well known as an outspoken friend of America and a critic of orthodox concepts of British imperialism. Even the domestic servants were familiar with his writings. While he was staying with the Nortons, the housemaid asked her mistress who this Mr. Smith was. On being told that he was Mr. Goldwin Smith, she said, "What? The one who wrote the letter to the Whig Member? I wish I had known it when I opened the door, that I might have paid proper respect to him."[12]

In Boston he gave a lecture on "England and America" which brilliantly expounded the theme nearest his heart: the relationship between these two branches of the English race. To his audience he addressed himself as a man who regarded America, not as a foreign nation alien to British political concerns, but as one of the great centres of the English-speaking peoples, estranged from Britain only temporarily and by accident. England was his country. Yet he came to America, as an English Liberal, though an alien by birth, no alien in heart. Americans and English Liberals were united by blood and by a common allegiance to the cause of freedom. Between them there should surely be "a league of the heart." Should their two countries quarrel, instead

---

[11]Letters from Charles Eliot Norton to G. W. Curtis, Sept. 6 and Oct. 18, 1864, *Letters of Charles Eliot Norton* (2 vols., London, 1913), I, 278.

[12]This incident is related in Thomas Hughes's life of *James Fraser* (London, 1887), 120-4. Fraser (afterwards Bishop of Manchester), when on a visit to the United States in 1865 wrote his mother, who lived near Goldwin Smith's father at Mortimer, that "Yankees are no respecters of persons," but "Goldwin Smith has left very pleasant memories of himself behind him here. People seem to think a good deal more of him than they do of Lord Palmerston or Earl Russell. . . . If you see Dr. Smith you can gratify him by telling him in what universal esteem Goldwin is held in Boston, and indeed everywhere I have been." Fraser added that the story about the housemaid "is further interesting as illustrating the range of reading of American domestics."

of standing together against the powers of absolutism, the hope of freedom in Europe would be almost extinguished. What would then become of the world? If the British ruling classes were against the North, British democrats were for it. With due respect he recalled that the United States, till yesterday, was the great slave power, and England, with all her faults and shortcomings, the great enemy of slavery. He reminded his hearers that

English liberties, imperfect as they may be,—and as an English Liberal of course thinks they are,—are the source from which your liberties have flowed, though the river may be more abundant than the spring. . . . It is from England that you are sprung; from her you brought the power of self-government which was the talisman of colonization and the pledge of your empire here. She it was, that, having advanced by centuries of effort to the front of the Old World, became worthy to give birth to the New. . . . It is because you are Englishmen that English freedom, not French or Spanish despotism, is the law of this continent. From England you are sprung; and if the choice were given you among all the nations of the world, which would you rather choose for a mother?[13]

His eloquent appeal initiated a three months' lecture tour of the United States, which became a triumphal progress, marked by receptions, dinners, and ovations. Goldwin Smith was received as were few foreigners, fêted from city to city, and everywhere acclaimed. In Northern circles he was regarded as an incarnation of political wisdom, and each word from his lips was reverently weighed. Southern journals, however, poured upon him abuse comparable to that to which *The Times* and its allies had already subjected him in England. As an unofficial representative of British liberalism he tried to persuade Americans that the hands of all Englishmen were not against them, and that the attitude of Great Britain was not fairly represented by *The Times*, the aristocracy, and the cotton manufacturers. *The Times*, he pointed out, was not the whole of the English press, nor the opinions of the wealthy those of all the English people. Sympathy with slaveowners was perhaps a natural error on the part of a governing class once essential to political progress as a mediator between the Crown and the people, but which had now outlived its hour. Even the Lancashire millworkers, many of whom were thrown into acute distress by the unemployment caused by the embargo on cotton, were strongly for the North. Liberal England was on their side, just as Liberal England, in the persons of men like Chatham and Burke, had been on their side in 1776. He reminded Americans that for them and with them England had overthrown France

[13] "England and America," *Atlantic Monthly*, XIV (Dec., 1864), 749–69.

and Spain on the North American continent and made it the land of the Anglo-Saxon. He called upon them to consider what the two nations had been to each other in the past, what they might be to each other in the future, what they might yet accomplish together for themselves and for the world.

From September 2 to December 14 he travelled in America, as far west as Iowa and north to Canada, seeing and learning as much about the continent as he could. Like De Tocqueville thirty years earlier, he was impressed by the widespread belief in equality and the relative absence of class divisions. In the United States equality seemed to him as much the rule of life as was inequality in Great Britain. This equality, which he considered the real essence of democracy, was not that of intellect, wealth, or influence, but of status in the community and the negation of privilege. From America he sent back letters to the *Daily News*, which made a sympathetic attempt to interpret to England the viewpoint of the North. He told his fellow-countrymen that a man must go to the United States to appreciate what a sense of security really free institutions gave, to know general prosperity, and to understand the strength of a government which no one wished to subvert, because it was the government of the whole people.[14] He was critical of the American system of an elective presidency and judiciary, but on the whole considered the country's local institutions the soundest and best anywhere, and admired greatly the political intelligence of her people. Money alone commanded less power, he thought, than in England, for in the United States wealth would not gain a man admission to the highest society. American respect for law and for intellectual distinction both impressed him. His republican sympathies were apparent in his assertion that there the greatness of a nation was substituted for individual greatness, a community for a king and his subjects, and attachment to the common good for loyalty to a crown. He liked the country's free government, free religion (the separation of church and state), and free schools. The latter he found excellent in every respect, save that they taught too many things, and he was impressed by the way in which the children of the wealthiest and of the poorest mixed together in school.

He visited Niagara Falls, Hamilton, Montreal, and Toronto where he stayed for a week with a relative, Mrs. Loring. In Canada, by contrast with the United States, he noted the lower standard of living, the absence of poor relief, the large number of poor people, and the sharp distinction of classes. He was impressed by Canadians' violent prejudice against

[14]*Oxford Chronicle*, July 21, 1866.

Americans, especially as he had found no parallel feeling against Canadians in the United States. At Toronto he visited the university and dined at the Grange with William Boulton, the former mayor, whose widow Goldwin Smith was to marry eleven years later. Among the dinner guests was George Brown, editor of the *Globe*, and the talk naturally turned to politics and to the projected confederation of the British North American provinces. His hosts explained that there was a strong and universal feeling against the political connection with Great Britain, for whose continuance no reason but sentiment remained. They emphasized, however, that there were conflicting opinions among Canadians about the political destiny of their country, and its ability to maintain itself as a nation. Their plans for a new constitution Goldwin Smith thought too slavishly based upon British models.

From Canada he returned to New York, whose citizens gave him an official welcome in the Union League Club, at a breakfast attended by some hundred people. Among those who issued the invitation were the Hon. Horace Greeley, editor of the New York *Tribune*, the Hon. H. J. Raymond, editor of the *New York Times*, Francis Lieber, professor of political philosophy at Columbia, William Cullen Bryant, the poet, and Theodore Roosevelt. President Lincoln sent a letter regretting that the exigencies of war made it impossible for him to be present. In reply to a formal welcome to the city Goldwin Smith spoke of his pleasure in finding that an Englishman who, like themselves, loved liberty and social justice, had in America a second home. "I accept this honour," he said, "not for myself, but for the great party in England of which I am an adherent, and which has followed you with its good wishes through this great struggle. Would that Cobden or Bright were here in my place."[15]

From New York he went with General Butler to Washington, where he stayed with Seward, the Secretary of State, had an interview with General Grant, and visited a hospital for Southern prisoners near Baltimore. The most memorable experience of his American visit was a meeting with Abraham Lincoln, to whom he brought messages of sympathy and support as an ambassador of the English Liberals who were friends of the North.

---

[15]*Welcome to Goldwin Smith by Citizens of New York, November 12, 1864* (New York, 1864). This breakfast meeting was described by G. W. Curtis, in his "Editor's Easy Chair," *Harper's Magazine*, XXX (Jan., 1865), 263–4. Here he spoke of Goldwin Smith as a liberal in the best sense of the word, and added, "There has been no more faithful and intelligent friend of this country in England than he, and his vigorous and eloquent vindication of the national cause has probably been not less serviceable to us than the stirring appeals of John Bright or the sagacious observations of Professor Cairnes."

On Christmas morning Goldwin Smith returned to England, confirmed in his previous theoretical belief in the vitality and general excellence of American political institutions. He wrote Cobden that family responsibilities compelled him to abandon his earlier thought of a prolonged stay in the United States, but he still hoped one day to revisit it. He had made such good friends in America that he would feel like condemning himself to exile if he did not see them again. "I have come back," he said, "more Radical—more Free Church—more against the retention of Canada—than ever. But less impatient, because more assured of the future." Cobden quoted this passage in a letter to Bright, with the comment, "His pen is a power in the state."[16]

On his return Goldwin Smith found himself in demand as a public speaker, interpreting the New World to the Old. When he lectured in the Sheldonian Theatre at Oxford it was said that his face shone like that of Moses coming down from the Mount. He was in truth, as Bagehot later remarked, "no unfavourable judge of anything American." He tried to inspire his English audiences with the concept of what he called "Anglo-Saxonry," a coming together of the English-speaking peoples of the world. This vision, which had fascinated him before his visit, was quickened by the kindliness of his reception in the United States, and by the enduring admiration which he conceived for the country of Lincoln. Much of his energy during the next forty years was to be devoted to the always delicate and usually thankless task of endeavouring to interpret Englishmen, Americans, and Canadians to one another.

In the spring of 1865, when an end to the Civil War was clearly in sight, there was some feeling in both England and Canada that the victorious North, whose claims for the depredations of the *Alabama* were still unsettled, might attack the British North American colonies, Goldwin Smith scouted the likelihood of such an eventuality (though he urged the arbitration of the claims) with the comment: "What Ireland is to England, that would a conquered Canada be to the United States."[17] In recognition of his services to their country a number of

---

[16]Letter from Goldwin Smith to Cobden, Dec. 25, 1864; letter from Cobden to John Bright, Jan. 16, 1865, quoted in John Morley, *Life of Richard Cobden* (14th ed., London, 1900), 927.

In somewhat similar terms Thorold Rogers wrote Cobden about Goldwin Smith's return to England, adding, "It is a pity that he does not however set himself to some connected work, such for instance as a practical refutation of that timid and unworthy book of J. S. Mill on Representative Government. I intend to urge on him some such labour." Letter of Jan. 2, 1865, Cobden Papers, XXV, ff. 160–1.

[17]"The Danger of War with America," *Macmillan's Magazine*, XI (April, 1865), 417–25.

American authors and publishers joined to present him with a collection of books published in the United States. These he gave to the library of University College, Oxford, to make them more widely available and to fulfil their donors' wish that they might help to familiarize English people with American literature and character.

The assassination of President Lincoln in April, 1865, shocked all England. Goldwin Smith immediately wrote A. P. Stanley, the Dean of Westminster, with whom he had formerly served as joint secretary on the first University Commission, suggesting that much good might be done if Queen Victoria would write a personal letter of sympathy to Mrs. Lincoln. He urged that this would touch the hearts of Americans as would no official expressions of condolence. He was sure that the affection of the American people for the Queen, displayed in the enthusiastic reception they had given the Prince of Wales in 1860, had never abated, despite all the bitterness between the two nations. She could not be a greater object of household veneration and love in her own dominions than she still was throughout the northern states. Dean Stanley showed this letter to Queen Victoria, who also received similar suggestions from Earl Russell, Lord Clarendon, and Lord Granville. The next day she wrote Mrs. Lincoln in kindly personal terms, and noted in her journal: "Was quite touched by a letter from Mr. Goldwin Smith (a great democrat), who was so anxious I should write, saying it would do more good than anything else, as I was so much respected in the United States."[18] This must surely have been the first and last time that Queen Victoria was happy to accept advice from a radical.

Two days after Lincoln's assassination, but before the news had reached Britain, Goldwin Smith sent Seward warm congratulations on the final victory of the North. England, as well as the United States, he prophesied, would date a new era from Gettysburg. Seward replied that he thought both countries were indeed to be congratulated, as England could not have retained her prestige had the civilization and free government she first instituted in America been extinguished. To Goldwin Smith's efforts in the cause he paid generous tribute. "Faithfully you performed your part of the duty which devolved upon Englishmen. I congratulate you upon the vindication which has crowned labors so arduous practiced under so much odium."[19]

---

[18]*Letters of Queen Victoria, 1862–78*, second series (Toronto, 1926), I, 265–7. I am indebted to Mr. Henry Pelling of the Queen's College, Oxford, for drawing my attention to this reference.

[19]Letters from William Henry Seward to Goldwin Smith, Sept. 30, 1865; from Goldwin Smith to Seward, April 16, 1865, Seward Papers, University of Rochester Library, Rochester, New York.

That autumn Goldwin Smith wrote Eliot Norton that owing to his father's illness he expected to resign his professorship the next summer and devote himself to literary work. He feared the reduction of his income would prevent another visit to the United States, yet he had a strong presentiment, perhaps springing from his strong desire, that he should see America again. If he survived his father he proposed to revisit the United States and to live there for a time, closing his literary life by writing some portion of American history.[20] When two years later his father died, Goldwin Smith thought of spending the winter of 1868-9 in Providence. He liked what he had seen of the old town on his previous visit, and hoped that his honorary connection with the university would give him an entrée to academic circles there. "I propose," he wrote an American friend, "on arriving in your country, straightway to coil myself up in my destined nest and lay in a stock of the food on which a book-worm lives."[21]

During the summer of 1868 President Andrew White was in England collecting books and scientific equipment for the new Cornell University which was to open in September. He had conceived the idea of associating with Cornell, as temporary, non-resident professors who would lecture for a few weeks or months of the year, eminent men such as Louis Agassiz and James Russell Lowell, whom he could not hope to attract permanently to its staff. White interviewed Goldwin Smith and invited him to become one of this group, as honorary professor of English and Constitutional History. He gladly accepted, on condition that he should be unpaid, with his time at his own disposal. His desire to have leisure for his own studies and to husband his strength, and diffidence about his ability as a lecturer, made him unwilling to accept a full-time salaried position. He explained, however, that he would be happy to deliver a few lectures to any students sufficiently interested in historical subjects to bear with his deficiencies. Concerned as always about his health, which had been affected by the strain of his father's long illness and death, he told White that his growing frailty was one reason for his retirement from political life in England. He looked forward, however, to his connection with Cornell, as offering him a fair chance of future usefulness, and thus of happiness.[22] Throughout the years Goldwin Smith declined to accept a penny for his services to Cornell. Although he became much attached to it, he never considered

[20]Letters to C. E. Norton, Oct. 1, 1865, Jan. 6, 1866, and July 26, 1867. "Letters of Goldwin Smith to Charles Eliot Norton, 1863-1872," Massachusetts Historical Society, *Proceedings* (Dec., 1915).
[21]Letters to J. M. Forbes, May 30, July 25, and Aug. 1, 1868.
[22]Letters to Andrew White, June 28 and Sept. 18, 1868.

himself a permanent staff member, but rather looked on the new university at Ithaca as a pleasant and interesting base from which he could write and acquaint himself further with the people and institutions of the United States. On October 27, 1868, he again sailed for America, this time, as it proved, to make his home on the other side of the Atlantic. Despite numerous subsequent visits to England, the break with his own country was lasting.

II

On a dark, rainy morning in November Goldwin Smith arrived in Ithaca, where he was welcomed by Andrew White, and taken by Ezra Cornell, the founder of the new university, to inspect its campus. He had complained to Norton before he left England that photographs which President White had sent him did not show the college or even the town, but simply the scenery. Ungratefully he had commented, "There seem to be a great number of fine waterfalls, which I abhor."[23] He was thus unprepared for what he was to see. The university consisted of one large, barrack-like structure, Morrill Hall, strategically located in the middle of Ezra Cornell's old cow-pasture. The staff and residential students lodged together, some quarter of a mile away, in Cascadilla, a building originally designed as a cure house or spa. To get to their lectures staff and students alike had to cross a wooden footbridge over a steep glen and then make their way through another smaller ravine. The less fortunate students, who lived in the town below, in order to scale the heights of learning had once or twice a day to climb a hill reminiscent of the citadel at Quebec. Luckily Goldwin Smith liked to walk, and the most inveterate hater of waterfalls could scarcely be immune to the striking beauty of the magnificent three-hundred-acre site overlooking Lake Cayuga.

The new scene of his academic labours contrasted sharply with Oxford in more respects than physical surroundings. Ezra Cornell was a self-made man, a farmer's son who had amassed a large fortune, and decided to spend some of it on founding a university to educate boys who, like himself as a young man, were poor. "I would found an institution," he declared, "where any person can find instruction in any study." Enshrined as the motto of the new university, the maxim was thereafter adhered to with remarkable precision. Cornell was determined that the institution should be built on the site of his farm, and to all

[23]Oct. 8, 1868. "Letters of Goldwin Smith to Charles Eliot Norton, 1863–1872."

considerations of Ithaca's innocence of adequate library and cultural facilities he turned a deaf ear. White's suggestion that the nearby city of Syracuse would provide a more suitable location for a university, Cornell flatly rejected on the ground that as a penniless youth he had once stood all day on a bridge at Syracuse waiting to be hired, and was then cheated out of his wages by the first man who gave him a job.

Cornell was a strong believer in the efficacy of combining mental and physical work. In the summer of 1868 he wrote a public letter to the New York *Tribune* explaining that at the new university students could support themselves by working at manual labour for half the day and pursuing their studies the other half. The result was that in September many of the four hundred prospective students who descended on Ithaca demanded remunerative employment, which the university tried to give them. President White later observed that some were successful, but most were not. It was soon discovered that it would be cheaper to put up many of the applicants at a hotel, and to employ experienced day-labourers in their stead. As an illustration of the problems which confronted him, White cited the case of a brawny young teamster who turned up from a western state, and when asked what he wished to study, replied that he wanted to learn to read. On being told that the place for that was the public school in his own district, the lad indignantly answered that the new university had advertised itself as a place where anyone could find instruction in any subject.[24]

Cornell in 1868 was as unlike Oxford as one university could be to another. When a student asked Goldwin Smith how long he thought it would take the new institution to equal Oxford, he replied, "Probably about five hundred years." It said something for his powers of adaptation that he settled down promptly, and devoted all the energy which in England he had lavished on university reform and the extension of the franchise, to building up Cornell. He wasted no time in lamenting the lack of books (it was some years before a library building was erected), but sent back to England for his private library of 3,400 volumes, which he presented as an addition to the existing nucleus, together with a large sum for its increase. To the university museum of zoology he gave a collection of British fossils. When new buildings began to rise he arranged to have stone-carvers brought from England to ornament them and roots of ivy from Oxford for their walls. He had a stone seat placed on the campus, inscribed with the quotation, "Above all nations is humanity." His purse was always open to give in-

[24]Andrew D. White, *Autobiography* (2 vols., New York, 1905), I, 344–5.

conspicuous but effective help to good students who found it difficult to finance a university education.

The Cornell authorities, for their part, did everything in their power to make him happy and comfortable, though the Cascadilla food soon compelled him to eat some of his meals at a downtown hotel. President White arranged to have a bell placed in Goldwin Smith's room, so he could call the servants without being obliged to hunt them up—an unusual concession, even for a staff member. The local *Ithaca Journal* announced his arrival in town as its leading news item, and without intentional equivocation reported his first lecture "a masterly effort." He liked the students, and they liked him. A former student later described Goldwin Smith on his arrival at Cornell as very tall, very thin, very sallow, and somewhat bent, seeming already at forty-five prematurely old. His light blue eyes contrasted sharply with his sunken cheeks, dark hair, and grizzly-black, close-cropped moustache. In his opening lecture he explained that in all his teaching he would regard complete political neutrality and abstinence from any party allusions as his most obvious duty in a country in which he was a stranger and a guest.[25] This self-denying ordinance had been urged upon him by Charles Eliot Norton, and on the whole Goldwin Smith adhered to it more faithfully than might have been expected.

He was soon on good terms with the crotchety old Ezra Cornell, who in his Quaker way called him "Goldwin" and felt a warm if somewhat surprising liking for the transplanted Oxonian. With Andrew White, who like himself was more interested in politics than in academic affairs, he had much in common, and the two became good friends. Goldwin Smith often accompanied White to neighbouring towns on expeditions made by carriage, buggy, or sleigh, which frequently floundered deep in mud or snow. He sympathized with White's ambitions for the university (not always those of Ezra Cornell), typified by his remark, "Better a splendid and complete faculty in a barn, than an insufficient faculty in a palace." White's efforts to build up a distinguished staff from nothing were remarkably successful. Among Smith's new colleagues were Bayard Taylor, who taught German literature, and G. W. Curtis, who taught English, and whose acquaintance he had made on his first visit to the United States.

Goldwin Smith remained longer at Cornell than any of the other

---

[25]"A Glimpse of Goldwin Smith," *New York Times*, June 18, 1910, unsigned article by a former Cornell student. The account of Goldwin Smith's first lecture at Cornell is taken from the undergraduate paper, *The Cornell Era*, I (Nov. 28, 1868).

non-resident professors. Andrew White found him in many respects the most attractive of them all, and was genuinely appreciative of the influence which he exerted upon the whole life of the university, entertaining the students, bringing eminent English friends to lecture there, and giving public addresses in different parts of the country.[26] When he had been two months at Cornell Goldwin Smith assured White that he never thought longingly of the halls and common rooms of Oxford; his only regret was that he could not be more useful. "I am a bad lecturer," he confessed, "and history is a bad subject for lectures. But when I come to teach a small class, I hope I shall do better; at all events I will do my best." A note of wistfulness, however, might have been detected in his comment on British politics during his first summer in America: "If I were over there I suppose I should be in the middle of the scrimmage and very hot, instead of enjoying philosophic coolness as I do in Cascadilla."[27]

His letters to friends in England vividly described his first impressions. Most of the students came from farm homes. The farming class in America was better educated and more intelligent than in England, and Goldwin Smith thought the students, despite their rough exterior, were on the whole both well-mannered and intelligent. He was surprised, "for a republic" at the semi-military discipline under which they lived in the university residence, where they were obliged to rise at six-thirty in the morning, and an inspector went around at seven to see that they had put their rooms in order. Ithaca, at that time a town of seven thousand, offered few intellectual distractions. "It will be very beautiful in summer," he wrote in mid-January during one of the hardest winters in years. "If waterfalls will make us happy, we shall be blest, for I believe we have about a score of them, of different shapes and sizes. At present we are under the siege of an almost arctic winter. . . . All the world goes about in sledges, and the little town is full of the merry jingling of their bells."[28]

In the spring of 1869 he was invited to read a paper on university education to the American Social Science Association at Albany. Here

---

[26]President White's annual report in 1885 listed various distinguished men who had been connected with Cornell. "But while all honour is due to those great men for the services which they rendered to the institution, its indebtedness has been greatest of all to Professor Goldwin Smith. . . . In any list of its founders his name will have an honored place. By counsel, by a large and timely gift when most needed, and by liberal and constant benefactions, always without a tinge of ostentation, Professor Goldwin Smith has proved himself Cornell's true friend." *Gazette* (Montreal), Aug. 3, 1885.

[27]Letters to Andrew White, Jan. 15 and July 18, 1869.

[28]Letters to William Rivière, Jan. 11, 1869; to George Waring, Feb. 8, 1869.

he suggested that a university had two functions: to teach students and to promote the advancement of learning and science. That professors should discharge both duties was, he thought, at that time more clearly recognized in the Old World than in the New. It would be presumptuous for him to pronounce on American educational problems; his mere impression was that a system of compulsory courses with its machinery of classes and degrees provided a precarious test of general culture. He had little faith in the educational efficacy of public lectures as opposed to the tutorial system, though he admitted he might be prejudiced by English customs. He thought, however, that he saw a tendency in North America toward making the university less a place of mental discipline than a repository of various kinds of knowledge "to which the student may come, choose his own department according to his inclination or destination in life, receive a certificate of proficiency in that special subject and go his way."[29] These remarks give some inkling of what Goldwin Smith found lacking at Cornell. It was indeed hardly possible that an institution devoted to providing instruction in any subject should not have awakened such reflections in his mind. They were not dispelled by the reputation which Cornell rapidly acquired for the study of practical science and agriculture.

His resolution to abstain from all intervention in political affairs was abruptly broken in the spring of 1869. Charles Sumner, in a session of the Senate, denounced the Johnson-Clarendon Convention which proposed a settlement of the *Alabama* claims, and demanded that Britain pay the United States enormous damages. His speech was widely discussed in Britain and Canada as well as in America. About the same time General Butler announced that he thought Americans would gain rather than lose from war with England. Goldwin Smith believed that as one of the few Englishmen living in America who had followed the controversy closely, he should answer Sumner's attack, which he considered an incitement to war. Accordingly, he delivered to the citizens of Ithaca a public address on the subject, prefaced by the remark that perhaps no living Englishman had more reason than himself to be grateful and attached to the United States. He concluded with the fallacious hope that he would never again speak on any controversial issue. He spoke as an Englishman who still hoped to make his home for many years in America, but he did not conceal his belief that Senator Sumner had treated England unfairly and that his attitude was provocative.[30] His speech received much publicity and aroused more

[29]"University Education," *Journal of Social Science*, I (June, 1869), 24–55.
[30]*The Relations between America and England* (Ithaca, 1869).

criticism than approval in the American press. The London *Daily News* commented that he had "made admirable use of a noble opportunity," and had acted as the friend of both the United States and England.[31] President White, like most of Goldwin Smith's American friends, supported his stand. To one of them he wrote philosophically the day after his speech, "Your newspapers are abusing me handsomely for it; but I hope it may lead some of their readers to see what they would not otherwise guess, that there are two versions of the story; and having stood all these years the paper pellets of Southerners and other Philistines in my own country, I am pretty callous to similar projectiles here."[32]

He again discussed the *Alabama* question a few months later in a speech at Cleveland, when he explained that during the Civil War he had heartily supported the English Liberals who were trying to do justice to America. Now he tried to do justice to England. He had been told that he was sitting between two stools, and would fall to the ground. His desire was not to sit upon any stool, but to stand on his own feet, and as far as he could to uphold truth and justice. To him this seemed the best homage he could pay a free people.

A month after his Ithaca address the University of the State of New York showed that all American public opinion was not against him by conferring on him an honorary degree. Thereafter he went to Canada, where he attended a University of Toronto dinner, and replied to a toast in the name, as he said, of two kindred institutions, the oldest and the youngest universities of the Anglo-Saxon peoples, Oxford and Cornell. His speech suggested that he was already considering the possibility of settling on his "own side of the line." He referred to his recent passage at arms with Senator Sumner, and to his endeavour to plead the cause of England. Thus in Toronto, where for the next forty years he was to be attacked as an inveterate champion of all things American, his first public appearance was as the interpreter and defender of England to the United States.

He spent a few days with cousins, Colonel and Mrs. William O'Brien, at Shanty Bay, Ontario, a visit which aroused mixed feelings on both sides. Mrs. O'Brien's patriotic sentiments were outraged by Goldwin Smith's views on colonial emancipation, while his own impressions were conveyed in a letter to an English friend:

---

[31]*Daily News*, June 2, 1869. Goldwin Smith was attacked by the *Hartford Post*, but supported by the *New York Times*, in editorials on May 21 and 22, 1869, and also by the *Syracuse Daily Standard*, May 21, 1869.
[32]Letter to J. M. Forbes, May 20, 1869.

I have just returned from a visit to some bush-whacking relatives on the secluded shores of Lake Simcoe in Canada. The Canadians of those districts are, as compared with their Yankee neighbours, unprogressive; but they are physically a very fine race, and kindly and courteous. They are intensely loyal and exaggerate all English habits and prejudices. Politically, when I am among them, I am in Gath of the Philistines. Socially, I get on very well, and gastronomically too, for they keep up the English, which I greatly prefer to the American cuisine. The thought of union to America is hateful to them, especially since the Fenian invasion: but it must come in time, all the commercial forces pull so strongly in that direction. I do not wish to see it hurried however. It is better that all the eggs of this Continent should not be put at once into one basket.[33]

Despite his unflattering comparisons between the United States and Canada, he felt at home on British soil, and during the winter of 1869–70 paid an extended visit to other relatives in Toronto. At Christmas he wrote back to President White: "I shall return to you . . . with the flowers and soft gales of spring. You may rely on my fidelity to Cornell, so long as I am good for anything and able to do any work. At my age . . . the possibilities of life close in, and I should be glad to anchor, even in a less happy port than this. My books are the anchor and a strong one."[34] Books, however, are a movable anchor, and Goldwin Smith was already becoming attached to his Toronto relatives and renewing his long-standing interest in Canadian problems. Nevertheless by March he was back in Ithaca, writing an English friend to keep him informed about new books, explaining that he began to feel the same interest in Cornell which he felt in Oxford, and declaring "all is sunshine to me here."[35]

James Bryce, A. V. Dicey, and Thomas Hughes visited the United States in 1870, and to Goldwin Smith's delight stayed with him for several days at Cornell, where they met the staff and students and gave public lectures. Bryce and Dicey, in particular, were greatly attracted to the country and its people. Smith had not met Dicey before, but they liked each other at once and formed a lasting friendship. Years later Dicey told Bryce that there were few days in his life more pleasant than those spent with Goldwin Smith at Cornell. "Is there any country," he wondered, "which is to any Englishman so much of a possible ideal as . . . [the United States] was to ourselves and I imagine as it had been

---

[33]Letter to George Waring, June 28, 1869. Mrs. O'Brien was the daughter of Goldwin Smith's Toronto cousin, Mrs. Loring.
[34]Dec. 13, 1869.
[35]Letters to George Waring, March 31 and July 5, 1870.

some years before to Goldwin Smith and perhaps in a different way to Cobden."[36]

Goldwin Smith's genuine enthusiasm for Cornell was undoubted. But he had never planned to settle in Ithaca for life. A variety of reasons combined to decide him to move to Toronto. One predisposing factor was the decision of the university authorities to admit women students. When Cornell opened in 1868 co-education had already been in operation at Oberlin College for more than thirty years, and for a briefer period at a number of other American universities. Goldwin Smith knew nothing of this before his arrival at Ithaca, and was horrified at the idea. After four months at Cornell he wrote Norton that he had done something to stave off, for the time being, the admission of female students, "a crotchet of Horace Greeley's." He congratulated himself too soon. The advocates of the women's suffrage movement pressed for the extension of university education to women, and in April, 1869, one of their foremost leaders, Susan B. Anthony, visited Ithaca and discussed the matter with Ezra Cornell. Of this incident she wrote succinctly: "I visited Cascadilla, smelt tobacco smoke and saw that ladies were needed there."[37] Goldwin Smith later remarked that he would never forget the meeting at which Ezra Cornell pronounced in favour of co-education, "after having had melted butter poured over his head and down his back by Susan Anthony. She ended by telling him that if he would open Cornell to women his anniversary would be regarded by posterity as equal to the Fourth of July *or* the coming of Christ."[38] The enrolment of women at Cornell undoubtedly influenced his decision to leave.

His official objection was not to higher education for women as such, but to educating men and women together, although he had in fact little sympathy for either scheme. Co-educational institutions, he complained to Norton, were never more than third-rate in scholarship, and the system resulted in a fatal relaxation of the students' energies. He believed that the Cornell faculty was almost unanimously opposed to the idea, and that it would be impossible to keep a good academic staff if the university were turned into a second Oberlin.

I hope, [he lamented] some Power of Good will intervene. I am very much attached to these students—as attached as ever I was to my Oxford pupils.

---

[36]Letters from A. V. Dicey to James Bryce, June 14, 1916, Aug. 23, 1920, Bryce Papers, Bodleian Library.

[37]Waterman Thomas Hewett, *The History of Cornell University, 1868–93*, (New York, 1905), 443–4.

[38]Letter to Andrew White, Dec. 17, 1883.

I like my colleagues. I respect Cornell's character and munificence as much as ever, and feel as strongly as ever that my life is well spent in aiding his enterprise. The people in Ithaca are as kind as possible. I do not know what I should do if I were set adrift again, for at my age the possibilities of life close in. But I do not think I could be a professor in an Oberlin.[39]

He besought Andrew White to listen to reason before it was too late. If female undergraduates were to invade Cornell, he could only say farewell to all his hopes of future greatness for the institution. If he played Cassandra, it was not because he did not love Troy.[40] His pleas were of no avail, and before the advent of women students, Goldwin Smith departed to Toronto, where the university was as yet unsullied by co-education. Two years later, despite his opinions on the subject, he accepted an invitation to deliver an address at the laying of the cornerstone of the new women's building at Cornell.

The decision to admit women was not his only reason for leaving. The climate was trying, and his doctor advised residence elsewhere, although the weather of Toronto was in fact much like that of Ithaca. At Cornell he felt increasingly cut off from the intellectual world. He also disliked the use of the university as a testing place for various experiments conceived by the fertile imagination of its founder, even if he accepted them with better grace than might have been expected. Ezra Cornell's enthusiasm for the beneficial effects of manual labour, for example, led him at one point to propose the establishment on the campus of factories for the production of chairs and shoes. Labour in these should be compulsory, he thought, for staff and students. Goldwin Smith observed philosophically that as he liked exercise he should personally not object to a "chair manufactory by way of an appendage to this seat of learning." With some difficulty President White persuaded Cornell that such an enterprise could not be combined with an educational institution without ruining both, and that the object of the university was not to enable young men to obtain an elementary education while making shoes and chairs.

Political considerations almost certainly played the major part in his decision to settle in Canada. Relations between England and the United States were very strained in 1869–70, as a result of the passions aroused by the Civil War and the *Alabama* claims. Goldwin Smith remained an Englishman, and, although personally he was treated with courtesy and kindness, he found the dislike of England so strong that the United

[39]July 17, 1870. "Letters of Goldwin Smith to Charles Eliot Norton, 1863–1872."
[40]Letter to Andrew White, July 26, 1870.

States seemed not only a foreign but a hostile country. This attitude, he told Bryce, made him feel out of place.[41] To Norton he wrote more emphatically about American politicians: "I detest the whole tribe, Republican and Democratic alike, more every day I spend here. . . . The Democratic papers began to abuse me as soon as I landed. After my speech on the *Alabama* the whole press poured on me vituperation which was to the vituperation of English papers as the contents of a cesspool are to those of a gutter. In public matters, if I mistake not, this nation is the slave of its press: no public man dares stand against the newspapers."[42] Shortly after settling in Toronto he observed bitterly that an American politician found no asset so valuable as the reputation of having insulted Great Britain. It was a moral peculiarity of New Englanders to desire the humiliation of the land of their fathers. He feared Hawthorne was right to say that Americans would regard England with cordiality only when some great calamity compelled her to implore their help.[43]

Canadians considerd Goldwin Smith pro-American, but the strength of his attachment to England was shown by his decision to live permanently in a British country rather than in the United States, although on the whole he disliked Toronto and was warmly attached to Cornell. In Ithaca he had laboured under the handicap of being a political alien, unable to participate in politics or to comment on them. Except for his public reply to Senator Sumner he had faithfully kept the vow of abstention from political discussion made when he first went to Cornell. He could the more easily do so as he found American party politics less appealing at close range than they had seemed from across the Atlantic. Participation in public issues, however, was to him the breath of life, and being cut off from political journalism even worse than being deprived of access to good libraries and many friends. As an Englishman in Canada, he need feel (and certainly showed) no inhibitions about frank discussion of public affairs.

In addition to all these considerations he genuinely liked his Toronto relatives, and to a lonely man with domestic tastes the thought of finding a home with cousins was attractive. "Do not suppose," he wrote Andrew White from Canada, "that the Canucks have seduced me. It is the home, and the home alone, that attracted me and keeps me here."[44] His

[41]Letters to James Bryce, July 7, 1869; to the Marquess of Salisbury, Jan. 31, 1870.
[42]Aug. 30, 1869, "Letters of Goldwin Smith to Charles Eliot Norton, 1863–1872."
[43]*Canadian Monthly*, II (July–Dec., 1872), 62, 553.
[44]Letters to Andrew White, June 24, 1885, Jan. 6, 1871.

interest in Cornell never flagged, and throughout his life he made frequent and generous contributions to it. On his resignation in 1871 he gave its library a valuable collection of books on Canadian history, and often thereafter presented other volumes. Nine years later Andrew White suggested that Goldwin Smith might succeed him as president. Smith, however, was not interested, and the matter dropped without any formal offer being made. He had remained at Ithaca long enough to see the university prosperously launched, and for many years returned annually to deliver one or more lectures. He continued to be listed among the Cornell faculty as a non-resident professor of English history until 1894, when he was made professor emeritus.

Three years after his departure he paid a visit to England, whence he wrote back to Andrew White: "I prize my connection with Cornell all the more when I come into contact with the odious Plutocracy, with its colossal selfishness and rottenness and its State-Church hypocrisies. What Carthage may have been we cannot tell; but since Carthage, such a domination of wealth has not been seen. . . . I see the faults and dangers of democracy, but I wonder every day how anyone can live in the Old World who has once known the New."[45] Here, undoubtedly, lay a partial answer to the question which puzzled many of his English friends: why a man of Goldwin Smith's abilities should choose to estrange himself from his own country and make his home in North America.

Oxford alone had as warm a hold as Cornell upon his affections. He delighted to revisit the Ithaca campus whenever the opportunity offered. A fine liberal arts building erected there in 1904 was given the name of Goldwin Smith Hall, so that, as President Schurman remarked, "For all time in this university the name of Goldwin Smith remains a synonym for liberal culture." Goldwin Smith laid the cornerstone, delivered the address at the formal opening two years later, and provided funds to buy books for its library. On his death in 1910 he left Cornell the bulk of his $700,000 estate, one of the largest bequests the university ever received. He was anxious that his motive should be understood. "My desire," ran his will, "is to show my attachment to the university, in the foundation of which I had the honor of taking part; to pay respect to the memory of Ezra Cornell, and to show my attachment as an Englishman to the union of the two branches of our race on this continent with each other, and with their common mother." His only stipulation was that his bequest should be used to advance liberal

---

[45]Feb. 14, 1874. To this letter President White appended, by way of comment, three exclamation marks.

studies, which he considered in some peril in a highly commercial age. This desire was appropriately fulfilled by the establishment of a number of Goldwin Smith professorial chairs. His attitude toward Cornell was shown not merely in his will but also in a letter to its president three years before his death, in which he said that among all the incidents of a chequered life there was not one on which he dwelt with more heartfelt satisfaction than his connection with the foundation of that university.[46] Cornell's attitude toward him was best expressed by Andrew White's dedication of his *Seven Great Statesmen*: "To Goldwin Smith, scholar, historian, statesman, in remembrance of his self-sacrificing championship of the American Union in its time of peril, of his inspiring teachings at Oxford and Cornell, and of his long life devoted to truth, justice, rational liberty, and right reason."

[46] Letter to President J. G. Schurman, June 11, 1907, Schurman Papers, Cornell University Archives.

III. CANADA: EARLY YEARS AND MARRIAGE

GOLDWIN SMITH settled in Canada in 1871 at the age of forty-seven. Thereafter he often returned to England for long visits, and continued to write for the British press more frequently than many journalists domiciled in Great Britain, but for the last half of his life his home was Toronto. During these forty years he never came to feel that he really belonged. As early as 1874 he told an English audience that he was "now a Canadian," and occasionally even described himself as a colonist, but he was never considered one by his new compatriots, and indeed for the most part did not so think of himself. He left his own country too late in life to become whole-heartedly attached to any other, and his adaptation to Canada was less successful than to the United States, where his position had been that of an honoured guest rather than of a permanent resident. As he himself observed, since he was middle-aged when he settled in Toronto it could not be expected that he would easily merge his character as an Englishman in his new character as a Canadian, nor see everything with Canadian eyes. The two and a half years at Cornell, when he largely abstained from political journalism, formed a peaceful interlude in a life begun in the thick of party conflicts in England and ended in frequent controversy in Canada.

He frankly accepted his position as that of a sojourner, although a sojourner for life in a country where his favourite pen-name was "A Bystander." Canadians sometimes complained that no man was ever less of a bystander, since Goldwin Smith discussed with conviction all the burning questions of the day. Fundamentally, however, he was a spectator in the sense that there was not a man in Canada to whom individually it mattered less what course political events might take. His active participation in public affairs was confined to voluntary municipal and charitable posts. No one could care less for personal aggrandizement or advancing his own interests. What he did care about profoundly was to do what he could, as a citizen and independent journalist, to make truth and justice prevail. The fact that truth as he saw it was often unwelcome in Canada never deterred him from forceful declaration of his opinions. The amused aloofness and frequent disdain with which he observed the Canadian scene, coupled with an austere rectitude and complete assurance that he had correctly diagnosed the various problems of the new Dominion, made him for many years singularly unpopular among his adopted countrymen, particularly in the conservative and ultra-loyal city of Toronto. Despite brief moments of insight he never really understood the developing spirt of nationalism which was the most pervasive characteristic of Canada in the first half-century after Confederation. Canadians, however, owed him a debt seldom acknowledged and greater than most of them realized. Goldwin Smith believed the country's eventual destiny was union with the United States, but he played his own part in turning the group of British North American colonies into a nation. His services in setting a high standard of journalism, encouraging young writers, and generally acting as a fearless and candid critic would have been rare anywhere and in Canada were unique.

I

He made his first home in Toronto with relatives, Mr. and Mrs. Colley Foster, and settled down to a more domestic life than he had enjoyed since boyhood. Mrs. Foster, formerly a Miss Morris, was a Canadian cousin to whom he was much attached, and he also liked her husband. They were not well off, and for a time Goldwin Smith practically supported the household. He found it very pleasant, he wrote an English friend, to feel that he had something like a home. In the summer of 1872 he went to Britain to see his stepmother who was ill. After her death in July of that year he told Norton that this event broke his last link with England. He would probably never cross the Atlantic again as he did not want to undergo twice the wrench of leave-taking. In any event he thought the ascendancy of wealth, worse in England than in America because it was given prestige by an aristocracy, was dragging his countrymen back to barbarism. Since he could do nothing to counteract the deplorable state of affairs in Britain he preferred to avoid the spectacle by remaining on the other side of the ocean.[1]

[1]Letters to C. E. Norton, Sept. 9, 1872; to Max Müller, Feb. 12, 1871; to Mrs. George Waring of Oxford, Oct. 9, 1871.

In November, 1873, however, he returned to England for a six months' visit, and was active in the British general election. He spoke in support of G. S. Brodrick against Lord Randolph Churchill, wrote articles on current political issues, and addressed the Trades' Union Congress at Sheffield. His friends tried hard to persuade him to remain. John Morley argued that he would be the natural leader of a disestablishment movement, and Jacob Bright urged him to stand as Liberal candidate for Manchester. All such proposals Goldwin Smith rejected on the ground that the remainder of his life was too short to be divided between two countries. In Canada, he said, literary use was made of him for a variety of odd jobs; in England he could be of no use whatever. Moreover he had formed ties with relatives in Toronto which he was unwilling to break, and was already involved in political journalism in Canada, so that if he left the country he would feel like a deserter leaving his friends in the lurch. In the Dominion even a single pen was difficult to replace. The comment was characteristic of his modesty. No one in Canada ever wrote like Goldwin Smith. To the comparative magnitude of fields of action in Britain and the Dominion he was indifferent. In Canada he found ample scope, believing that what the country lacked in importance it made up in hopefulness. England he had left in the conviction that there "plutocracy would reign till it rotted." Yet when Andrew White wrote to ask if he could suggest any Englishmen for the Cornell staff, Goldwin Smith replied that no one acquainted with British public life, except a strong radical and loafer like himself, was likely to leave England.[2]

II

Educational problems were among the first to attract his attention in Canada. The year after his arrival he lectured at McGill University and addressed a "ladies class" in Montreal. Canadians might have been taken aback to read the unvarnished account of these activities which he sent an English friend. "I have come here," he wrote from Montreal, "to take part in a movement for the intellectual regeneration of that unsatisfactory creature woman by giving lectures on English history before the Ladies' Education Class. The class consists of 200 ladies and does very well. I am lecturing at the same time to the 'University', [McGill]

[2]Letters to Andrew White, Feb. 14, 1874; to Professor Rolleston, Feb. 10, 1874; to William Rathbone, Nov. 14, 1874.

one of some eight or ten 'one horse' institutions as the Yankees call them, among which the resources of superior education in this country as in the United States are miserably frittered away."[3]

He was appointed to the Senate of the University of Toronto in 1873 and during his absence in England was chosen president of the Ontario Teachers' Association. The following year he was elected to represent the elementary and secondary school teachers on the provincial Council of Public Instruction, recently reorganized on a partly elective basis. This was the first time that under the new Ontario Education Act of 1874 the teachers were able to elect a representative. In this capacity he served for several months until the Council finally gave place to a Minister of Education. Thus at the beginning of his stay in Toronto he was assured in various ways that he was welcomed by the community. His services on the Royal Commission of 1858 on Popular Education in England were well known in Canada before his arrival. The Commission's report prepared the way for the English Education Act of 1870, and it was natural that Canadians should seek advice from a former Regius Professor with a special interest in educational questions.

Goldwin Smith's ideas on education, however, were less familiar than his general interest in the subject, and on discovering their nature Canadians did not always accept them. Before he left England he had startled the British public by suggesting that boarding schools, in which boys were largely confined to the companionship of other lads of their own age, did not necessarily provide the best type of education. When the Second Reform Act added thousands of illiterate voters to the electorate there was widespread discussion in England as to whether the government should provide public education, and if so, whether this should be compulsory and free. Goldwin Smith acknowledged the necessity of educating people who were to wield political power. He admitted the validity of the argument that if the state had to feed paupers it had a right to stop the source of poverty, and that if it had to detect and punish criminals it had a right to stop the source of crime. He supposed that it had a similar right to stop illiteracy, but he disliked centralized control, like that of France, and considered the more voluntary the school system the better. Since the various districts in England differed so much from one another, he doubted whether it would be practicable to devise a uniform system of compulsory education under the central government, suitable for the whole country.[4] Long before there was any

---

[3]Letter to Mrs. Waring, Oct. 25, 1872.
[4]Speech at Oxford reported in the *Daily News*, Feb. 29, 1868; speech at the Manchester Reform Club, reported in *The Times*, April 11, 1868. On Sept. 18, 1868, he wrote Andrew White on educational problems, "Mr. Matthew Arnold

suggestion of compulsory attendance, John Bright and his friends strongly opposed a public system of elementary education. Thus when Goldwin Smith deplored centralized state schools he was in this as in other respects following Bright. He granted the necessity of some national system of popular education, because of all tyrannies an uneducated democracy would be the worst.[5] The Education Act of 1870, however, seemed to him a vast re-endowment of the Anglican church, and this as a consistent opponent of the establishment he deplored.

These were his views on leaving England. In North America he found centralized public school systems long established. Canadians and Americans considered them well adapted to their communities. He was realistic enough to agree that the clock could not be turned back, and indeed found much to admire in the free schools of America. Their shortcomings, however, he analysed with his usual candour. He addressed the Ontario Teachers' Association in 1873, as their president-elect, on "The Moral Elements in Common School Education," by which he meant the effect of the system on character. The circumstances of their age, he suggested, were such that if education was common, it could not be religious. This was unfortunate, not because the teaching of dogma was desirable, but because education should aim to produce virtuous character. To "any slight or furtive recognition of Religion in the way of a deodorized Prayer or Scripture Reading" he attached little value. Since the school was secular, it should not presume to meddle with things to which it could not do justice. Countries like Canada, where education was considered necessary, should respect religion without undertaking to teach it. There might still be a valuable moral element in education; history alone, properly taught, could be an effective school of public virtue. Unfortunately children's history books were too often poor stuff, sawdust if not poison. The hearts of the teachers to whom he spoke must have been warmed by his comment that "the ideal Teacher,—the Teacher who is painted in all essays on Education, and whom School Trustees and parents expect to get,—may be defined as an archangel at five hundred dollars a year." The very numbers in Ontario classrooms made it impossible for a public school teacher to be a moral missionary to each child. To his way of thinking teachers

---

is always preaching the French system. But the French system, both as regards organization and subjects, is the complement of French despotism and unsuited to a free people, though Mr. Arnold being a man destitute of originality and therefore of sympathy with mental independence, is seduced by its mechanical perfection." In later years Goldwin Smith came to estimate Arnold's abilities more adequately.

[5]"The Ecclesiastical Crisis in England," *North American Review*, CX (Jan., 1870), 151–208.

could do very well without the magnetism and electricity which they were sometimes told it was almost criminal in a teacher to lack, although electricity and magnetism were not often found in either parents or trustees. He disliked the tendency to teach pupils that their chief aim was to rise in life. Too often they grew up thinking that to clamber over the heads of their fellows was the only way to respectability and happiness, so that education became a preaching of universal discontent. He had no wish to check honest ambition, but regretted that already hardly a farmer's son was content to remain quietly on the farm. The number of those who could really rise must be small, and the majority must look for their happiness to the sphere in which they were born.[6] This concern lest universal education should produce a generation unwilling to do necessary manual and unskilled work recurred frequently in Goldwin Smith's writing.

On the Council of Public Instruction he soon came into conflict with the redoubtable Chief Superintendent, Dr. Egerton Ryerson. The two men had met in England, where as early as 1857 they had been on terms of friendly acquaintance. Before Goldwin Smith settled in North America, however, Ryerson had publicly attacked his views on imperialism as those of a traitor. His genius for controversy surpassed even that of Goldwin Smith. In Toronto at first the two got on amicably enough, and on one occasion Ryerson suggested to Smith that he might succeed him as provincial superintendent, a fly to which, Goldwin Smith observed, the fish did not rise. Ryerson found his powers, however, curtailed by the reorganization of the Council, to which he became hostile. He quarrelled with one member, Professor Wilson (later Sir Daniel and President of the University of Toronto), over the latter's proposal for the abolition of the book depository which provided texts for all the provincial schools. As a Methodist minister the Chief Superintendent disliked Goldwin Smith's belief that religious education had no place in the public schools. Ryerson attacked his support, for the headship of the Ottawa Normal School, of a Catholic whose qualifications Smith thought unquestionably better than those of the other applicants. A further cause of dispute was a resolution moved by Goldwin Smith and passed by the Council, against the introduction of dogmatic matter into school textbooks. This Ryerson construed as criticism of his own work. Smith shared Wilson's lack of enthusiasm for the book depository's monopoly in school textbooks, and served on a committee to inquire into the system. Ryerson in return suddenly attacked him at a meeting

[6]Goldwin Smith's speech is reprinted in J. George Hodgins, *Documentary History of Education in Upper Canada*, XXV (Toronto, 1908), 217–22.

of the teachers' association at which Goldwin Smith was presiding as chairman, and then wrote the press, defending his action. He accused Smith of conspiring against him and the public school system, and of wishing to further his own interest by the sale of certain textbooks—a charge patently absurd. Goldwin Smith denied the allegation, but refrained from public controversy on the subject.[7]

III

In Canada, as in England, a political career was inevitably urged upon Goldwin Smith. His reiterated refusal sprang from real conviction and was undoubtedly wise. A strong independent, with emphatic views, opposed to party in general and to caucus control in particular, could scarcely have made a success of public life anywhere. In Canada, unlike England, political differences were commonly turned into personal feuds with a maximum of vituperation; here the chances of success were negligible. Nevertheless on at least two occasions he toyed with the idea of entering provincial politics. The first was in the spring of 1874, when he had lived less than three years in Toronto. He was then seriously interested in serving for a session or two in the Ontario legislature in order to get some practical insight into Canadian politics to use in his writing.[8] In England his lack of political experience was not a serious handicap, because almost from boyhood he had been thrown among public men, a fact which helped to compensate for the want of first-hand parliamentary experience. His idea of going into politics to improve himself as a journalist was characteristic, one among many evidences that Goldwin Smith rated the contribution of the journalist above that of the statesman.

Six months later, however, he wrote Edward Blake, who had promised to use his influence to obtain him a nomination, that he had dismissed the idea. George Brown was then violently attacking in the *Globe* both Smith's and Blake's nationalist views. Under the circumstances Goldwin Smith thought he had little chance of election. With the *Globe* against

---

[7]*Leader* (Toronto), Aug. 14, 21, 23, 24, 26, 27, 31, Sept. 3, 4, 7, 10, 17, 18, 1875. Cf. *The Public School Candidates, Professor Goldwin Smith and Dr. Sangster* (Toronto, 1874), 12–13. This incident is discussed by Professor Sissons in his biography of *Egerton Ryerson* (Toronto, 1947), II, 632–7.

[8]Letter to Charles Lindsey, April 18, 1874, Lindsey Papers, Public Archives of Ontario. Lindsey was for a time editor of the Toronto *Leader*. He married a daughter of William Lyon Mackenzie, and subsequently wrote a life of his father-in-law.

him he could not have stood as a Liberal, and would have had to come out as an Independent. Moreover he was anxious to avoid any ill effect his possible defeat might have had upon Blake and the Canada First movement, in which they were both involved.[9] Also on closer view Canadian provincial politics looked uninviting and the prospect of a backwoods campaign in the wintertime anything but attractive.

When in 1874 the National Club was founded, Goldwin Smith was chosen as its first president. He told a dinner meeting of its stockholders that, although he had lived only a few years in Canada, no native Canadian could be more loyal or more interested in its future. He appreciated the kind reception given newcomers like himself who meant to cast in their lot with the country. Such courtesy was doubtless the more welcome to him by contrast with the *Globe*'s persistent personal attacks, caused partly by his opinions on the emancipation of colonies and even more by his example of fearless journalism, which seemed to threaten the *Globe*'s "long reign of literary terror" under the autocratic aegis of George Brown. Goldwin Smith believed the independence of the Canadian press, rather than any political ideas, was attacked in his person. When during his absence in England in the spring of 1874 the *Globe* was denouncing him as a renegade, a different Canadian attitude was illustrated by an editorial comment in the first issue of the *Nation*.[10] The writer suggested that with the possible exception of D'Arcy McGee, no one had done more than Goldwin Smith, in his comparatively brief residence, to arouse a feeling of nationality in the country and to stimulate its intellectual progress. Hence the *Nation* warmly welcomed his decision to settle permanently in Canada.

IV

On September 30, 1875, he married Harriet Elizabeth Mann Dixon, the widow of William Henry Boulton, at whose home Goldwin Smith had been entertained on his first visit to Canada in 1864. He had renewed his friendship with them after he settled in Toronto, and a year after Mr. Boulton's death in 1874 his widow and Goldwin Smith decided to be married. This, he observed, put a happy end to all his wanderings. It found him at a distance from England, but could not sever or weaken

---

[9]Letters to Edward Blake, Oct. 5 and Nov. 27, 1874, Blake Papers, Public Archives of Ontario. Goldwin Smith's connection with Canada First and his views on the political destiny of Canada are discussed in Chapter xi.

[10]April 2, 1874.

the tie which bound him to his own country. His wife, two years younger than he, was born at Boston, Massachusetts, and was the daughter of Thomas Dixon of Amsterdam, who had been consul for the Netherlands in Boston. Her brother, Benjamin Homer Dixon, was in his turn consul-general of the Netherlands in Toronto. Goldwin Smith wrote Eliot Norton to tell him the news. "The 30th of this month will, I hope, see the friendship which has long united me to Mrs. Boulton of this City converted into a companionship for life. It is of course a different union from yours,—a union for the afternoon and evening of life. But it promises its own kind of happiness."[11] He was then fifty-two; thirty-four years of unusually happy married life lay ahead.

In many ways they were an oddly assorted pair. Mrs. Goldwin Smith was kindly and pleasant, ran her large household smoothly, and was a gracious and hospitable hostess. Completely devoid of any intellectual interests, she was devoted to her husband, whom she considered a great man. All this Goldwin Smith found eminently satisfactory in a wife. The chief sorrow of his life was her death a few months before his own. In an unpublished draft for his reminiscences he jotted a note on his settling in Canada. "Probably I might in the end have gone back to England, my connection with which remained unbroken and whence I was still receiving invitations political and academical. But I was finally bound to Canada by the happiest event of my life. Whatever might happen to me outside I was supremely blest in my home."

Although his wife had many relatives in the United States, whom Goldwin Smith henceforth adopted as his own, he thought it would be a wrench for her to leave Canada. He was unwilling to ask her for his sake to move either to the United States or to England. They visited Great Britain a number of times, and she thoroughly enjoyed meeting his friends (especially when they happened to be prominent), but he felt that she would not easily become accustomed to a new life in a strange land. He admitted the truth of his friends' reproaches that he lacked ambition. To a public career he preferred family affection, domestic pleasures, and tranquil privacy. "My life here, with that of my dear wife," he wrote an English friend a decade after his marriage, "glides in a quiet stream of uneventful happiness." The latter half of it was largely shaped by two decisions governed by family considerations. On his father's account he had not hesitated to resign the one position he wanted in England, at the top of the academic profession. For his wife's sake he gave up with equal cheerfulness all prospect of returning permanently to Britain, where a brilliant career in journalism certainly

[11]Sept. 23, 1875.

awaited him, if he preferred this to academic or public life. His dislike of England's class society, based on a wealthy landed aristocracy and an established church, doubtless also influenced his decision. And for a man more interested in the English-speaking peoples than in any other subject, Canada provided a promising observation post.

V

His marriage brought the one thing he most valued, a completely happy home. After the death of her first husband his wife had continued to live in the old Boulton house, the Grange, and here Goldwin Smith joined her. Built by D'Arcy Boulton, the Solicitor-General of Upper Canada, about 1817 when Toronto was Little York, the house was reputed to be the oldest in the city, and certainly was of historic interest as an early centre for United Empire Loyalists. Toward the end of his days Goldwin Smith commented ruefully that although the Grange was only half a dozen years older than he, it was considered one of the most venerable landmarks in Canada. He liked to recall that it had seen the time when a bear attacked a carriage horse in the garden, when Indians strolled in unannounced, and when a British officer lost his way in the surrounding bush. Here the "Family Compact" had met in the second and third decades of the century. The house had originally stood in a hundred-acre estate outside the town, but by 1875 the grounds had dwindled to ten acres and one of the most fashionable quarters of the city had grown up all around them. The great fir-trees and elms in the park, dark and mossy with age, still suggested the primeval forest and provided effectual privacy. In the summer when the leaves were out all that could be seen of the surrounding town from the front door was a church spire. Here, as Goldwin Smith observed in his *Reminiscences*, fortune had made for him almost an England of his own in Canada. The Georgian Grange, "an antiquity among mushrooms," with its encircling grounds, broad lawns, and sunny tennis courts, was the counterpart of the little mansions familiar on the outskirts of English towns. It was the only English house, Goldwin Smith often commented, that he knew on this side of the water. Here he lived the life of an English country gentleman, with the traditions and customs of his class, and delighted to entertain friends from all over the world.

Most of the interesting people who passed through Toronto, from governors-general and prime ministers to visiting journalists, called at the Grange. If English aristocrats were warmly received, no less hearty a welcome awaited Canadian farmers and trade union representatives. The lists of tea and dinner-party guests in the butler's pantry books read like a roster of the great of the earth: Lord Lansdowne, Prince Leopold, Duke of Albany, who was Queen Victoria's youngest son, Prince Kropotkin, and many others. The presence of such guests sometimes made Canadians think Goldwin Smith a social snob. Nothing could have been further from the truth, as anyone familiar with his publicly reiterated opinions of the aristocracy and of "flunkeyism" would have realized: "plutocracy with a coronet" was one of his kinder phrases. The most distinguished visitors to the Grange were usually old friends from England, where as a Saturday Reviewer and later a Regius Professor he had moved in political and literary circles. As perhaps the ablest English-speaking journalist of his day he was inevitably known, by reputation at least, to the readers of numerous British, Canadian, and American newspapers and periodicals, to many of which he contributed for some fifty years. He could not help knowing most of the people who shared his interest in the political problems of the British Empire and the United States. An inveterate letter writer, he combated the isolation of his position at Toronto by lively correspondence with friends in widely separated parts of the earth, and by welcoming at his house any who chanced to visit Canada.

When friends like Matthew Arnold and John Morley were undergoing the rigours of a North American lecture tour they found a welcome refuge at the Grange. Arnold spoke appreciatively of "that delightful old house at Toronto; we found nothing so pleasant and so like home in all our travels." Before starting off from New York on a cross-country journey in the autumn of 1883, Arnold wrote Goldwin Smith, "This lecturing is an odious necessity, but if it succeeds it will enable me at least to take my retiring allowance and cease at last from school-inspecting, so I thought it worth attempting. But I never set about any task so unpleasant, and I do not feel at all confident of success, though Lowell and others, who ought to know, are sanguine. But I am glad of an opportunity to see this country, at any rate—though at present I find it a very *tiring* country indeed. But the newspaper people cannot go on calling for ever." These misgivings about his American tour were not unjustified, for incautiously critical remarks at Chicago concerning philistinism on that side of the Atlantic led many Americans to think Arnold a hubristic Britisher. After his return to London he wrote Goldwin Smith about the unfavourable notices of the Chicago incident which had appeared in the American press: "Surely one cannot imagine a like supposed deliverance of Holmes or Howells about London or Edinburgh society causing a similar storm, or causing anything but the very faintest of ripples."[12]

John Morley's experience in the United States was more fortunate, no doubt because he approached the country in a different frame of mind. On his way there he stayed at the Grange, and later wrote back from Chicago to Goldwin Smith: "As I foresaw I have a hundred points that I should now like to put to you. The whole spectacle of this country interests me even more than I had expected, but it needs interpretation by a man of vision and experience, and here your position is unique. Perhaps I may write you from Washington. . . . I look forward to it with some unwonted excitement of mind. . . . Your conversation was a stimulus to me, and I shall not let my sense of your kindness grow dull."[13]

In the autumn of 1898 A. V. Dicey went to Harvard to deliver lectures, destined to become famous, on the relation of law to public opinion in England. Before returning to Britain he visited Goldwin Smith in Toronto. The two men had much in common, including a strong dislike of Irish Home Rule, votes for women (which Dicey like Smith had earlier supported), and old age pensions. In a letter to his wife Dicey gave a graphic description of life at the Grange.

Here one is suddenly set down in an old English house, surrounded by grounds, with old four-post beds, old servants, all English, and English hosts. I declare, not as a joke, but as a simple fact, that if you were brought here blindfolded in the evening and dined here, as I have, you would never doubt for a moment that you were in an English mansion in some English county. It is, I believe, the very last of a set of houses built on the English model in what you may call the old colonial days. Goldwin Smith and his wife . . . make the most charming hosts. The course of life is very regular, and to me very pleasant. Breakfast regularly at 9. Then Goldwin Smith, who has a first class secretary, retires to his library and works all the morning till luncheon . . . at 1.30; often some one to lunch with us. In the afternoon Mrs. Goldwin Smith has taken me out in the carriage, except when I have gone somewhere with Goldwin Smith. Tea at 5. Dinner if we are alone at 7. A game at whist, over which Goldwin Smith is somehow grimly amusing. . . . At 9.30 the ladies retire, and I may go to my room or my bed or stay up as I please. . . . The very house which has received so many much more eminent friends of Goldwin Smith gives one a sort of prestige.

Dicey talked to a political science class at the University of Toronto, and told his wife, "The plain truth was that they wanted to see me

[12]Letters from Matthew Arnold to Goldwin Smith, May 2, 1884, Oct. 24, 1883, Autograph Album, The Grange, Art Gallery of Toronto.

[13]Letter from John Morley to Goldwin Smith, Nov. 8, 1900, Autograph Album. Quoted with the consent of the executrix of the late Guy Morley.

because they had read the *Law of the Constitution*. One thing only made the speaking rather formidable. Goldwin Smith went with me, and his habitual command of absolutely perfect language made me sure he must feel at every turn the imperfection of my expression. However I put this aside as well as I could."[14]

The household at the Grange included a domestic staff of nine, whose married members lived on the grounds with their children in four picturesque cottages. Goldwin Smith's will provided that they should continue to live there during their lifetime, and that each should receive a legacy of $500 or more. The secretary, Arnold Haultain, declared that his servants were all devoted to Goldwin Smith. He and his wife were both anxious that the Grange should be not merely a place of domestic employment, but a united household in the best English tradition, bound together by mutual regard. In achieving this relationship they were singularly successful.

Goldwin Smith's shy and reserved disposition, coupled with a somewhat forbidding appearance, were apt to discomfit those who met him casually. In Canada he had many acquaintances, but few if any intimate friends. Yet his formal manner completely belied the warmth of his relationships within the circle of his own household and his real interest in others. His sympathy for underdogs ranged from attacks on imperial policy toward the Boers to criticism of alleged ill-treatment of an elephant in the Toronto zoo. An officer of the Humane Society, he would not allow his coachman to use a bearing-rein, nor permit his horses' tails to be docked. On daily visits to the stables he regaled his horses with tidbits of sugar and carrots. A tap was kept running on the front lawn of the Grange to provide water for thirsty birds. Its owner managed to combine a liking for birds with an even greater liking for cats. He prided himself on the familiarity with which he was treated by the household pets, and would cheerfully take a hard seat rather than disturb a kitten which had usurped his comfortable arm chair. One of his rare verses was written to Flossy, a Skye terrier he gave his wife shortly after their marriage, which for years was the pet of the family.

To one wing of the house he built on a study, lined to the ceiling with books. At the end was a huge fireplace, and carved above its mantel his favourite quotation from Cicero: *magna est veritas, quae facile se per se ipsa defendet*—"great is the power of truth, which can easily defend itself by its own force"—no bad motto for his life. In this library he spent much of his time, as a rule seeing no one but his secretary until

[14]Quoted in Robert S. Rait, *Memorials of Albert Venn Dicey* (London, 1925), 164–7.

his day's work was over. An extraordinarily hard worker, he worked for several hours and read all the newspapers before breakfast, and by 9.15 was in his library, where he wrote, dictated, and read until 1.30. Fifteen minutes sufficed to dispose of a lunch of pudding and tea, and by 1.50 at the latest he was back at work. After tea he played tennis or bowled with friends, or went for a drive. Late afternoon callers often found him reading aloud to his wife as she sat at her sewing. If there were no guests for dinner he spent the evening playing whist or cribbage, or reading.

Isolated as the Grange was by its spacious grounds from the surrounding city, Goldwin Smith was even more isolated by his tastes and temperament and by the unpopularity of his opinions. Essentially lonely in Canada, he must often have missed the companionship of the senior common rooms in Oxford. Perhaps at his best as a conversationalist, he much enjoyed entertaining a select group of friends at lunch or dinner. The elaborate receptions and crowded tea parties beloved by Toronto hostesses he cordially disliked. In a review of Pepys' diary he observed that those who lived at that time, despite their predilection for cock-fighting, could give some lessons to modern society. They did not "crush all the people of their acquaintance at once into a hot room, and make them stand there for hours talking against the buzz to people to whom they did not want to talk, on subjects which they did not want to talk about."[15] Toronto journalists in the nineties described Goldwin Smith as the central figure of their limited intellectual world. At times the limitations of colonial society were more apparent than the intellect. On one occasion he asked Martin Griffin, the librarian of Parliament, for some bibliographical material, and apologized for the work involved. Griffin promptly sent the information requested, with the comment, "Pray do not think anything I can do, the least trouble to me. I serve so few men who really take an interest in history or literature that [it] is a pleasure to serve those who do."

When Goldwin Smith first settled in Toronto, cows grazed along rural Dundas Street at the edge of the Grange grounds, and the lost and found columns of the local newspapers contained such notices as: "Lost—a roan cow—horns inclined inward; last seen on Queen street east yesterday." On the island in the bay stood one lighthouse and a solitary bungalow. Sunday was strictly kept, though the strong Sabbatarians had failed to have passenger boats forbidden on Sundays. By the eighteen-eighties there was agitation for running Sunday streetcars. Goldwin

[15]Review of *The Diary of Samuel Pepys* in the *Nation* (New York, LVI (June 22, 1893), 457–9).

Smith suggested that a reasonable compromise would be to allow trams to run during the summer months after the hours of morning service. But like others he clung not only to the Sabbath respite from labour but also to its accustomed quiet and repose. The godly *Globe* strenuously opposed running streetcars on Sunday. The Sunday concert, the Sunday theatre, and the Sunday saloon, it prophesied, would all ride in on the Sunday tram, not to mention the Sunday newspaper, whose publication would be nothing short of a national calamity.[16] In 1897, however, after two decades of discussion, Toronto succumbed, and the Sabbath quiet was shattered by the clanging of horse-drawn streetcars.

By the turn of the century the population of the city and costs of living had both trebled. Apartment houses wreathed in smoke from factories were beginning to replace private homes on tree-lined streets. The red coat of the English fox-hunter was still seen in the countryside on a fine day, although as Goldwin Smith remarked, it was not to be supposed that foxes could be "preserved among democratic hen roosts or freely chased over democratic farms."[17] The English tinge about Toronto society began to disappear with the departure of the British regiments and the replacement of Englishmen and Scots by native Canadians in leading business and professional positions. As early as the eighteen-seventies British Canadian society was already that of the New World rather than the Old, obviously democratic in character, although tempered by distinctions of income and position. Colonial customs began to seem outmoded, but the new country was as yet too young to have developed traditions of its own. The rawness of a community where few possessed much education or leisure, and wealth was often mistaken for culture, was commonly condoned under the guise of respect for pioneer values.

Whenever Goldwin Smith revisited Britain he was struck afresh by the sight of "the lovely garden which unlimited wealth expended on limited space has made of England." He could not repress a wave of homesickness for his own country when he returned to Canada, with its tropical summers and long arctic winters. To an English audience he described it as "a land just redeemed from the wilderness, with all its untrimmed roughness, its fields half tilled and full of stumps," with "snake fences and charred pines which stand up gaunt monuments of forest fires."[18] Ottawa, which Laurier talked of making a capital of

[16]*Globe*, Nov. 24, 1885, Dec. 18 and 24, 1890, Dec. 2, 1891, April 6, 1895.
[17]*Canada and the Canadian Question* (Toronto, 1891), 43.
[18]*Oxford Chronicle*, Nov. 30, 1877; *Weekly Sun*, Aug. 12, 1896; "Toronto: A Turn in its History," *Canadian Magazine*, XXVIII (April, 1907), 523–5.

literature, art, and science, was the "nearest lumber village to the North Pole" turned into a political cockpit, an embryo capital among the polar solitudes.[19] Yet he was not indifferent to the beauty of the country, with Muskoka as a summer paradise, and he made strong if ineffectual pleas for the preservation of the Canadian forests. "Yesterday," he wrote an Oxford friend in December, "Canada was in the perfection of her winter beauty—snow on the ground, with a brilliantly clear atmosphere, gorgeous sunset, and splendid starlight. To-day comes a snowstorm from the east, with some blockades on the railways and nuisances of all kinds. To a bookworm, with plenty of pabulum, and in a warm house, it is pleasant to look out on the storm. But I always wonder that poor people ever emigrate to cold countries."[20] For English journals he pictured the changing Canadian seasons, the hot, short summers which ripened the "paragons of apples," the autumnal brilliancy of the northern woods, and the brief spring, less a season in itself than a sudden break-up of winter, and a rush of green shoots into buds and leaves. In more gloomy moments he spoke of "that last and hardest kick of winter called the Canada spring."[21]

IV

Goldwin Smith's reputation rests on his journalism. He made his mark as a political commentator, not as a professor of history. His primary interest was the present, not the past. A controversialist by temperament, he was usually in opposition, championing the unpopular cause, fighting with rapier wit successive rearguard actions, always profoundly convinced that he was right and the rest of the world wrong. A journalist by preference and profession, he preached the virtue of a charitable attitude, but practised the precept little. Historians and contemporary statesmen alike received short shrift at his hands. He paid lip service to the ideal of presenting an opponent's opinion by setting up a straw man, only to knock it down with devastating dexterity. Yet as the Canadian correspondent of *The Times* commented: "We have no other such journalism on this Continent. . . . No other man who writes on Canadian affairs can so measure a politician in a sentence or so endow a gibe with the quality of eternal justice."[22]

[19]*Bystander*, I (Feb., 1880), 86; I (April, 1880), 178; II (June, 1881), 305–06.
[20]Letters to Mrs. Hertz from Toronto, Dec. 4, 1882, Nov. 18, 1878.
[21]Letter to C. E. Norton, June 29, 1888; review of Mrs. Traill's *Pearls and Pebbles*, in *Illustrated London News*, March 16, 1895.
[22]*Times Weekly Supplement*, Sept. 3, 1909.

That his writing was evanescent he was well aware. "I have produced nothing," he said frankly to a friend, "but what is purely ephemeral." The president of Cornell once asked whether he would care to have any of his books noted in a tablet commemorating his connection with that university. Goldwin Smith replied that despite an author's partiality he could not name one which he thought likely to survive him or to command respect in the future if mentioned in an inscription. He suggested only that his writing might perhaps have produced some collective effect during his life.[23] Candid friends inquired why he spent time on journalism, instead of writing books. He granted that perhaps it was true that he had set out to write books. He supposed this was his manifest destiny, but it was not fulfilled. In England he had become a journalist almost by accident. He came to Canada to make his home with relatives, not to write for the press, but was drawn into Canadian journalism by the political and intellectual currents of national life which developed after Confederation. Probably he could not help himself. A journalist by instinct, like all great journalists, he simply had to write.

It is perfectly true that the works of a journalist are ephemeral [he said at a Canadian press banquet in his honour]. They go into the nether world of old files and are forgotten. But does not the same fate befall a good many books? Look at the book shelves of any great library. What a necropolis of the immortals is there.... The fact is, that to be immortal you must not only have an undying genius, but an undying subject.... We all wish to survive our ashes in a certain sense, but not to one in millions is it given to be really immortalized by literature. If you look at the works of Harrington, Hobbes, or Locke, or at those of any other great writer, what are they but the current thought of the time worked up into a permanent shape? And it is ... the journalists that have the largest share in making the current political thought. ... Writing an editorial is not the easiest matter in the world, but there are many who think they can do it until they try. The writer of an editorial is not producing an immortal work, but he is trying to produce a distinct effect at the time, and to do that he must be master of an art. He must be able to give his work a certain unity, form, and finish.[24]

Goldwin Smith considered himself a journalist or nothing. In the latter half of the nineteenth century—the golden age of editorial journalism—he believed that the power of the press was increasing; that to it from legislative assemblies the real debate had been transferred; and that parliaments did little more than record conclusions. Hence men who wanted to discuss frankly the great political, religious, and social ques-

[23]Letters of Nov. 29 and Dec. 7, 1905, to President Jacob Schurman, Schurman Papers, Cornell University Archives; to Mark Pattison, Nov. 25, 1875, Pattison Papers, Bodleian Library.
[24]As reported in Rose-Belford's *Canadian Monthly*, VII (July, 1881), 102–6.

tions of the age probably found a more appropriate sphere outside the House of Commons. The danger was not that the press should lack power, but that its independence should be impaired.

His inaugural lecture at Cornell maintained that in a country like the United States the proper education of the journalist was as important as the right education of princes in a monarchy. The power of journalists in the contemporary world was immense, and their responsibility equal to their power. They needed, above all, training in philosophy and history, for a man so trained "to the point where the eye and the heart take in humanity, will not find it quite so congenial to him to wallow in the mire of party fanaticism or of scurrilous personalities." Cornell was dedicated to practical knowledge. Surely, Goldwin Smith argued, political studies based on history were eminently practical in a country where all men had political duties and where any man might be called to be a statesman. For the future journalist they were not only practical, but a necessary part of his professional training. The day might come when society would demand some more expert and more responsible guidance than that of the journalist. But for the time being journalism reigned, and by its extra-constitutional power had reduced congressional and parliamentary debates to relative insignificance.

These were Goldwin Smith's views of the journalist's calling when he first settled in Toronto. It was common at that time to complain about the poverty of intellectual life in Canada. Common also was the assumption that almost everyone was interested in politics and devoured newspapers with avidity. This national peculiarity had been noted as early as 1852 when the newspapers of the British North American colonies were described as a strange mixture of politics, abuse, religion, and general information which Canadians could as little get on without as Americans without their tobacco.[25] At Confederation D'Arcy McGee had criticized the Canadian press for egotism and provincial narrowness. He deplored its servile dependence for opinions on leading British and American journals, and "the absence of a large and generous catholicity of spirit, both in the selection of its subjects and their treatment." The deficiencies of Canadian newspapers were the more serious because they formed much the largest part of what people read. McGee estimated that probably half the men were regular newspaper readers, and that those who saw only one journal were largely what their favourite editors made them. The responsibility of the editor was proportionate, since to

---

[25]Susannah Moodie's *Mark Hurdlestone, the Gold Worshipper* (2 vols., London, 1853), I, xx-xxii, cited by James J. Talman, "Three Scottish-Canadian Newspaper Editor Poets," *Canadian Historical Review*, XXVIII (1947), 166.

hundreds or thousands of readers he stood in a relationship as intimate as that of the physician to his patient or the lawyer to his client. The editor served as counsellor, director, and teacher. His task was to cut away prejudices, enlarge sympathies, and make his readers lovers of truth and justice. Only the priest or minister occupied a position more honourable, more responsible, and more powerful for good or evil.[26]

At the inaugural dinner of the Royal Colonial Institute in London, a Canadian politician, the Hon. W. Macdougall, observed optimistically that the British North America Act, then two years old, had proved a perfect success. Dissatisfaction of course prevailed in some quarters, but it was difficult to prevent this in a country like Canada where every man read a newspaper, and almost every man thought he could write one.[27] Some years later a member of the Canadian Commons remarked with pride that he had never been anywhere—in the United States, England, or other parts of the world—where every woman and child seemed to take such an intense interest in politics, or to be so well posted on them as in Canada.[28] About this ground for self-satisfaction Goldwin Smith expressed certain doubts. It was often said that Canada produced more politics to the acre than any other country. He feared that the more politics there was, the less public spirit, and the more afraid men were to be in a minority, even for a good cause.[29] On the widespread influence of the Canadian press, however, and the general interest in public affairs there was only one opinion. By 1870 some 432 newspapers were published in Canada, more than half of them in Ontario. A decade later, with a population of about four million, the Dominion had 465 newspapers, of which at least fifty-six were dailies. Hardly any important village in the country lacked one or more weeklies.[30] An independent press, however, was almost unknown at Confederation. The newspapers were either Conservative or Liberal, and were strongly partisan. A ready-made audience existed for the enterprising journalist who had something to say.

When Goldwin Smith arrived in Toronto plans for launching a new periodical, the *Canadian Monthly*, were already under way. He declined the editorship, but promised to give any advice and help that he could.

[26]D'Arcy McGee, "The Mental Outfit of the New Dominion," *Gazette* (Montreal), Nov. 5, 1867.
[27]Royal Colonial Institute, *Report of Proceedings, 1869–70*, I (London, 1870), 44.
[28]Canada, H. of C. *Debates*, 1885, II, 1407.
[29]*Canada and the Canadian Question* (Toronto, 1891), 178.
[30]J. G. Bourinot, "The Intellectual Development of the Canadian People," Rose-Belford's *Canadian Monthly*, VI, (Jan.–June, 1881), 118–19, 230.

The first editor was a young Scot, G. Mercer Adam, who afterwards for several years served as business manager of the *Bystander,* and later contributed to the *Week* when it was under Goldwin Smith's control. Smith assisted the *Canadian Monthly* both with money and with his pen. His first essay signed "A Bystander" in the issue of February, 1872, was an analysis of Ontario's provincial politics singularly astute for a newcomer. This was followed by other articles on political affairs, and in December of that year he began to contribute a monthly section on current events, which continued until the end of 1874. Although unsigned, these articles were all written by Goldwin Smith with the exception of those which appeared when he was in England from November, 1873, until the next May. He interpreted current events broadly, discussing the contemporary scene not only in Canada, but in the United States, Great Britain, and the major European countries.

The *Canadian Monthly* was the nearest equivalent to such British periodicals as the *Fortnightly* and *Contemporary Review.* In its ten years' existence it gave a literary expression to the spirit of nationalism signalized by Confederation. A national magazine, Goldwin Smith explained to friends in England and the United States, was a step toward nationality in Canada, where newspapers and periodicals were almost the only reading of the people. The sponsors of the *Canadian Monthly* hoped to stem the process of Canada's intellectual annexation to the United States, then going on through the flood of American magazines. He was interested in aiding this attempt by writing for this "small journal through which my small lucubrations are published to a small public."[31]

He was first attracted to the *Canadian Monthly* by its avowed independence in politics. He soon found, however, that the independent journalist was as unwelcome as he was unusual in the Canadian newspaper world. The Ontario press had long been dominated by the allegedly Liberal *Globe* under George Brown, editor from 1844 to 1880. Party policy has often shaped newspaper opinion. The *Globe* reversed the usual order (especially when the Liberal leader was the somewhat pedestrian Alexander Mackenzie), through its influence upon the policy of the Liberal party. This state of affairs Goldwin Smith criticized. The Grits were singular, he observed, in being the party of a newspaper, whose editor manipulated the party in accordance with his own opinions and dislikes, and virtually chose its parliamentary leaders. This might not be surprising, when the editor was himself a former party leader, but it was bad for the party and for Liberal statesmen, as would be increasingly apparent when they were no longer in

[31]Letters to Andrew White, April 19, 1875; to Max Müller, Sept. 4, 1871.

opposition. No nation could regard with pride or complete confidence a government which was not thought to be its own master.

George Brown was not the man to allow such comment to pass unrebuked. Through the *Globe* he renewed previous personal attacks on Goldwin Smith for opinions expressed in unsigned articles. The *Canadian Monthly* protested, in the interests of Canadian journalism at large, against such personal denunciations. The common disregard of editorial impersonality in North America as contrasted with England, it considered a principal cause of the different character of journalism in the two countries. The *Monthly* deplored the violation of anonymity "either from the vulgar love of personalities, or under the influence of that tyrannical petulance which cannot endure an honest difference of opinion, but upon the slightest contradiction breaks through all rules of justice and courtesy to get at the object of its spleen."[32] For its part it aimed to be "the organ of nothing but perfect freedom of speech," and intended to do its best to guard against all attempts to muzzle discussion, or to establish in the press a narrow tyranny of opinion.

As Prime Minister Sir John A. Macdonald felt the need of a Conservative newspaper in Toronto to challenge the sway of the *Globe*. Hence he provided the impetus and raised much of the money necessary to launch the *Mail*. When its prospectus appeared Sir John wrote the editor, T. C. Patteson, "The only doubt I have is whether you do not go at the Globe too strongly. You call G[eorge] B[rown] a bully and a tyrant. He is both, but is it wise to throw down the gauntlet so early and so offensively? I have however no strong opinion in this, and do what you think best." A month later, in April, 1872, the first issue was published. Sir John congratulated the editor, but by this time was ready for the fray. "The first number," he said, "is a good one—*for a first number*. You must assume an appearance of dignity at the outset. The sooner, however, that you put on the war paint and commence to scalp the better. It must be done in first rate style, with the skill of a Tecumseth, . . . but scalps must be taken. This is my sentiment."[33]

The *Mail* thus started as a Conservative organ, but was also a general newspaper purporting to be reasonably independent in its views. As such Goldwin Smith welcomed it, if only for its promise of rescuing Ontario from the journalistic despotism of the *Globe*. In 1873, however, at the time of the Pacific Scandal which eventually swept the

---

[32]"Current Events," *Canadian Monthly*, III (March, 1873), 225; (Feb., 1873), 141.

[33]Letters from Sir John A. Macdonald to T. C. Patteson, March 5 and April 2, 1872, Patteson Papers, Public Archives of Ontario.

Conservatives from office, the *Mail*'s devotion to party was more apparent than its independence, for it strongly supported the Government. Goldwin Smith sadly observed that its "literary ability has been almost quenched by the fetid stream of party invective and personality. It has ... saved us from a dictatorship, though much as we might be saved from typhus by having the smallpox. In other respects it has been a calamitous disappointment. From the very outset it became the tool not only of a clique, but almost of a single politician. . . . Instead of raising, it has lowered the standard of public manners."[34] He wondered why the tone of the Toronto press need be so much lower than that of Montreal. There the leading journals joined vigorously in party warfare, and one often saw in them things with which one disagreed, but never anything which might not have been written by a gentleman.

Within three years of his arrival in Canada, by his plain speaking against Liberals and Conservatives alike, Goldwin Smith managed to estrange himself from both parties. The breach thus early created was never completely healed, despite his amicable personal relations with Macdonald and to a lesser degree with Laurier. As he found to his cost, friendly social relations between political opponents, while common in England, were rare in Canada. When Colonel George Denison, an ardent Conservative and imperialist, was about to visit England, Goldwin Smith, who disagreed with him on every conceivable subject, gave him a letter of introduction to the Marquess of Salisbury.

> Colonel Denison [he wrote impishly] has written with distinction on military subjects, and it is an enterprise connected with that sanguinary department of literature that now takes him to England. He is an ultra-loyalist and a good Tory, and proposes to settle all political problems by a charge of light cavalry drawn up and armed in some improved fashion. I think you cannot fail to like him personally, as well as to concur in his opinions. Since I last wrote to you I have married and settled down; but, my head being out of your reach and that of Lord Beaconsfield, I am "unreconstructed" and as Radical as ever.[35]

Years afterwards Denison repaid his introduction to Salisbury by a vitriolic personal attack on Goldwin Smith as a traitor. Smith never recovered from a feeling of outrage that the unpopularity of his political opinions should involve social ostracism, as for years it did, in the intensely loyal capital of Ontario.

Before his departure for a six months' visit to England in November, 1873, a complimentary dinner in his honour was given by a group of

[34]"Current Events," *Canadian Monthly*, VI (Nov., 1874), 459-60.
[35]Letter to the Marquess of Salisbury, Oct. 10, 1876, published in Arnold Haultain (ed.), *Goldwin Smith's Correspondence* (Toronto, n.d.), 56-7.

professional people, lawyers, bankers, merchants, and public men of both parties, in acknowledgement of his services to Canadian journalism during his two years in Toronto. At the dinner Goldwin Smith referred to himself as "a literary loafer," a description from which the *Canadian Monthly*, in its report of the occasion, sharply dissented. To his ever ready advice as well as to the contributions from his pen its editor attributed much of the new journal's success. At the sacrifice of both leisure and personal advantage, he pointed out, Goldwin Smith had furthered the cause of a national literature in the new Dominion.[36]

VI

When he returned to Canada the following spring a new weekly, the *Nation*, had already been started by Edward Blake and his friends, as an organ of the nationalist movement known as Canada First. Goldwin Smith had nothing to do with founding this journal (described by Lord Dufferin as a cross between the *Spectator* and *Pall Mall Gazette*), but had much sympathy with its objects. He became one of its most active sponsors and contributors, and in 1874–5 almost every week wrote leading editorials for it in addition to articles and reviews. In December, 1874, in order to devote more time to the *Nation* he severed his connection with the *Canadian Monthly*, which by that time was well launched. On it he had expended much labour and not a little money. His last article on current events again criticized the extra-parliamentary influence exercised by Brown and the *Globe* upon the nominal leaders of the Liberal party at Ottawa and Toronto, Alexander Mackenzie and Oliver Mowat. It called for "an avowed and responsible leadership—a leadership in Parliament and not in a Journal Office," as the great change which the country desired from the party of reform.[37] Goldwin Smith probably exaggerated Brown's political power after 1867 and the extent to which Mackenzie, as Prime Minister, was his puppet, although Smith's views on this matter were shared by the Governor-General. Brown's influence on his party remained considerable until the failure, in 1874, of the reciprocity negotiations which he conducted, yet it undoubtedly declined after Confederation. About the importance of his influence on the press, however, no two opinions were possible.

When it was announced that the principal writer of current events in the *Canadian Monthly* had joined the staff of the *Nation*, the *Globe*

[36]*Canadian Monthly*, IV (Dec., 1873), 547–8.
[37]*Ibid.* (Dec., 1874), 550–1.

again attacked Goldwin Smith for writing anonymously, and declared that he could not expect to enjoy at one and the same time the advantages of publicity and the immunity of anonymity. The fact was that his articles in the *Nation* could usually be identified, even when unsigned, by a quality and style which no other Canadian journalist could hope to emulate. In them he dealt faithfully with the various sins of the two old parties. Unused to an independent press, Canadian public men bitterly resented this criticism and naturally looked askance at the Canada First movement, which for a time seemed likely to offer a serious threat to both Liberals and Conservatives. Hence the vials of party wrath were poured out upon Goldwin Smith. If possible George Brown disliked even more Edward Blake, as a maverick Liberal, and violently attacked him also in the editorial columns of the *Globe* until Blake decided to abandon Canada First and return to the orthodox Liberal fold. Brown's method of opposing those who dared to differ from him was illustrated in numerous editorials. He referred to Goldwin Smith by name as "a dreamer, not a statesman," a "covert traitor" too insignificant for a traitor's doom, too thin-skinned and too cowardly for a popular leader.[38] Brown alleged that the *Nation* had been established as Goldwin Smith's organ, and paid no attention to the denials immediately made both by the *Nation* and by Smith, who through the correspondence columns of the *Liberal* appealed "to all genuine Liberals . . . . against those who, in violation of the first principle of Liberalism, seek to crush political independence by personal slander."[39]

The *Nation* in return attacked the *Globe*'s habit of heaping personal

[38]*Globe*, Nov. 7, 1874, Jan. 4, June 14, and July 24, 1875. Goldwin Smith's opinion of Brown and the *Globe* was made plain in a review of Alexander Mackenzie's highly laudatory life of George Brown, published in the *Bystander*, III (Jan., 1883), 70–8, three years after Brown's death. Smith here described Brown as the power behind the throne on which Mackenzie briefly sat, and referred to the revulsion of feeling since Brown's death against his bitter and partisan style of journalism. "Those who thwarted Mr. Brown's will," he wrote, "or incurred his enmity, were not merely assailed with the abuse which is bandied in our party frays, and often shows more heat than malice; they were systematically hunted down. Misrepresentation and distortion were applied constantly and without scruple to hold them up not only to political but to social and personal odium. If they were journalists, all the rules and privileges of the Press were disregarded in the determination to destroy them. No journal ever did more to poison the heart of society; the most virulent of party organs, the most scandalous of society papers, would not have wrought practically so much harm. Thanks to the ability with which the *Globe* was managed, and to the failure of its rivals, there arose a literary despotism which struck without mercy. . . . Few men were bold enough, or sufficiently independent in circumstances, willingly to brave the tiger. Mr. Mackenzie is fully warranted in saying that public men were made, and he might have added unmade, by the *Globe*."

[39]Letters to the *Liberal*, Feb. 19 and March 11, 1875.

abuse on those whose views it disliked, imputing discreditable opinions to opponents, and murdering reputations through its despotic control of the press. The *Canadian Monthly* made similar complaints about the difficulties of independent journalism in Canada and the absence of independent thought in a country where the penalty was attack by sages stricken with "a horrible doubt as to the prospects of party government should the practice of telling the truth in the papers ever become at all general."[40]

The *Mail* wrongly attributed to Goldwin Smith an anonymous criticism of that journal in the *Nation*. As a result it violently attacked Smith, although the *Nation* denied that he had written the paragraph in question, or seen it before it was in print, and pointed out that as he was not the editor he could not be held responsible. Most of the Ontario press joined in the three-cornered contest between the *Globe*, *Nation*, and *Mail* from 1874 to 1875, with Goldwin Smith as the principal target. To the attacks on him by the *Globe* as a would-be "dismemberer of the empire" the *Nation* retorted that the *Globe* used this pretext to cloak its real aim to stifle independent journalism. Its desire to dominate the newspaper scene had certainly aroused the antagonism of local editors. Many of the smaller papers all over English-speaking Canada and a few of the larger ones supported the *Nation* in this dispute. Although some of them disagreed with Goldwin Smith's political views, they stoutly upheld the journalist's right to say what he thought.[41] The little Brockville *Recorder* expressed a general opinion when it observed that the root of Smith's offence was that he had ideas which conflicted with those held by Brown.

Early in 1875 Edward Blake sounded out Goldwin Smith about becoming editor of a new daily, the *Liberal*, which Blake had recently established. Smith declined on the ground that he was not prepared to tie himself for the rest of his life to a daily newspaper; he found his commitments to the weekly *Nation* bad enough.[42] The post was accepted

---

[40]"Old and New in Canada," *Canadian Monthly*, VII (Jan., 1875), unsigned, *not* written by Goldwin Smith; *Nation*, Nov. 26, 1874, June 11, 1875.

[41]The *Nation* was supported by the principal Montreal papers, the *Gazette*, *Star*, and *Witness*, and by such local journals as the Hamilton *Times*, the Stratford *Herald*, the Sarnia *Observer*, the London *Advertiser*, the Woodstock *Review*, the Orangeville *Advertiser*, the Galt *Reformer*, the Markham *Economist*, the Orillia *Packet*, the Kingston *News*, the Belleville *Intelligencer*, the Cornwall *Gazette*, and the Halifax *Reporter and Times*.

[42]Letter to Edward Blake, Nov. 27, 1874, Blake Papers. Among the Blake Papers are fourteen letters from Goldwin Smith. All Blake's replies appear to have been lost. Goldwin Smith said that he contributed a few articles to the *Liberal*, but these have not been identified.

by John Cameron, who later, as editor of the *London Advertiser* and from 1883 to 1890 of the *Globe*, was one of the best-known and ablest journalists in Ontario. The *Liberal* was an intelligent paper, but proved too good to live and survived only four months. From the beginning it had financial difficulties, and in June, 1875, ceased publication after Edward Blake had accepted office as Minister of Justice in Mackenzie's cabinet.

After the demise of the *Liberal*, Blake and Smith discussed the possibility of starting another newspaper. "I shall be ready," Goldwin Smith wrote, "to do what I can again—that is if I stay here."[43] A few weeks later he told Blake that his friends were eager to start a daily, and he agreed as to the importance of the venture, since this offered the only hope of emancipation from the existing state of affairs in the newspaper world. David Mills would like to see the *Liberal* revived, and so would he, if defeat would not cling to its name, as he feared might be the case. He wanted to begin, however, only on a thoroughly sound basis, since a second failure would exhaust their spirit as well as their resources. He envisaged a considerable financial outlay, estimating that not less than $100,000 was required. A sound basis might, he thought, be attained if a junction could be effected between Blake's forces and his. Anxious that Blake should understand his point of view, Goldwin Smith wrote, "You know my mind. I do not want the paper to advocate my opinions. I do not want to meddle with its politics or management in any way whatever. So long as I can be pretty well assured that it will be independent and decent, and that it will live, I am ready for my part to lay down my money." He anticipated no serious difficulty about politics, and stressed the necessity of leaving a large daily in the hands of a good editor, who would run it with a view to commercial success. The first step, in his opinion, was to find the right editor. Some of his friends, unversed in journalism, were disposed to trust Providence to produce one, but he knew better.

Blake's return to an active career in federal politics made him doubtful about launching another newspaper, and he finally decided not to act in the matter. Under these circumstances Goldwin Smith agreed to help found an evening paper to be run on usual commercial lines. He advanced a sum of money, keeping clear of partnership or ownership, but stipulated that he should choose the editor. Under these auspices the *Evening Telegram* began publication in April, 1876. William

---

[43]Letter to Edward Blake, July 7, 1875, Blake Papers. This is the only suggestion in Goldwin Smith's papers that he seriously considered not staying in Canada. At the time he was doubtless weary of the personal attacks on him which the *Globe* had been persistently making for more than a year.

Houston, who had been on the staff of the *Liberal*, was Goldwin Smith's first preference for editor. When he was not available the appointment fell to a young Canadian, John Dent, who had for some time been employed on the Boston *Globe*. The proprietor of the *Telegram* was John Ross Robertson, former business manager of the *Nation*. "He is believed," Goldwin Smith wrote somewhat doubtfully to Blake, "to be much improved in character and is certainly an excellent hand at his trade."[44] Of all Smith's numerous journalistic ventures in Canada, the *Telegram* was the only daily newspaper catering to the popular taste, and perhaps for that reason the only one which survived. He never directed its editorial policy, nor wrote anything for it except occasional letters in the correspondence column. Its proprietor said he hoped always to keep the paper's policy in line with Goldwin Smith's convictions.[45] The *Telegram* soon became, however, a conservative and imperialistic newspaper reflecting completely contrary ideas.

Blake's return to the political scene at Ottawa left Goldwin Smith with an unsought burden, as the moving spirit behind the *Nation*. With Blake's default the Canada First movement, which the *Nation* had been started to promote, collapsed. In the autumn of 1876, weary of continual controversy, Smith planned a protracted visit to England. On September 30 he wrote to tell Blake that the *Nation* was to cease publication that week. It had become, he said, "practically a question between my chaining myself to the oar and the withdrawal of the paper; and to chain myself to the oar, and such an oar, I had no inclination." He hoped to leave the *Telegram* on a good footing, but whether it should sink or swim must be determined by those more interested in the matter than he.

In later years Goldwin Smith looked back with some bitterness on his connection with Edward Blake, though he never lost all his admiration for the man he once described as the most eminent guardian of Canada's political morality. He deplored Blake's lack of a clear policy, his failure to emerge as a strong Liberal leader, and his persuasion of the Canadian Commons to pass resolutions supporting Irish Home Rule. To Blake's high-mindedness, political purity, and eloquence he paid warm tribute. On Blake's subsequent career as an Irish National member of the British Parliament, Smith observed, "no one was ever better qualified to win a Chancery suit or less qualified to lead men."[46] Long afterward he told John Willison that when the *Liberal*'s affairs were in

---

[44]Letters to Edward Blake, Feb. 17, 1876, July 25, 1875, Feb. 8, 1876, Blake Papers.
[45]Letter from John Ross Robertson to Goldwin Smith, March 31, 1909.
[46]*Weekly Sun*, April 29, 1897; *Week*, May 8, 1884.

a critical condition he had offered Blake for its support "fully as large a sum as my patrimony could afford. In return he left me to the tiger. What he lacks as a leader of men is not only *manner* but *heart*. The Browns, thinking me a safe mark, turned their attacks and boasted that they could drive me from the country." At the critical juncture, however, Goldwin Smith had been more sympathetic. "Poor Blake!" he wrote Charles Lindsey, "I suspect he has suffered quite as much from the perplexities of his position as from hard work. He wanted a grain more of resolution to make him a firstrate man. When he set up the 'Liberal' against the Globe he had crossed the Rubicon, and he ought to have marched on Rome."[47] Goldwin Smith was not the first or last person to find Edward Blake an enigma.

VII

Despite ample private means he made a point of being paid for his contributions to well-established journals, although his own immediate wants might have been supplied by the salary of his footman. He thought it unfair for writers who had to earn their living to face competition from a man with access to literary circles who wrote for nothing. For struggling Canadian periodicals, however, he not only wrote without payment, but constantly contributed large sums of money to keep them on their feet.

His connection with the Canadian Press Association began early and was always cordial. He became a member in 1875, when he spoke at the association's meeting in Hamilton, in reply to a toast in his honour. The next year, at their convention, he urged the importance of giving journalism the tone and character of a regular profession. The newspaper, to his mind, was now "the boast and terror of the world," with an influence which increased as that of the individual member of Parliament waned. A good article or letter was worth as much as a good speech. He doubted whether it was desirable for journalism to be a stepping-stone to a political career, but was sure that the first day of public life should be the last of journalism. The functions of the statesman and the political critic were distinct, and could be combined only with detriment to both. Without mentioning George Brown he declared

---

[47]This letter, in the Lindsey Papers, is dated only Feb. 13, but was almost certainly written in 1878. Goldwin Smith's letter to Sir John Willison, on April 24, 1903, is published in A. H. U. Colquhoun, *Press, Politics and People* (Toronto, 1935), 120.

his own belief that an editor who ran for Parliament was lost. Thereafter he ceased to be an observer and critic, and became a party to the fray. Since such a man wrote with his own candidature in view, it was a waste of time to read his editorials. The influence of the journalist had become so great that it was difficult to understand why anyone who did not want office should desire a political career, unless he had easy access to Parliament and abundant leisure. For those who valued the reality above the appearance of power, the formation through the press of the public opinion which parliamentary votes only reflected, afforded a position of more genuine importance. The relationship was of course reciprocal, since the newspaper must take its hue from society as well as society from it; thus the journalist and his constitutency acted and reacted on each other. People would probably see the ideal paper when they saw the ideal community and the ideal man. All this, however, did not lessen the responsibility of the individual journalist, at a time when sensationalism was the disease of the age and when the newspaper was almost the only instructor of the masses, even inheriting a great portion of the influence which in earlier days belonged to the pulpit. An evil of the party system was that journalism tended to be prostituted in its service and the difficulties of the independent journalist multiplied.[48]

On this theme Goldwin Smith spoke with a conviction born of experience. His faith in independent journalism and his lack of faith in party met and blended. To his mind the office of the press was to make government by the people a government of intelligence. He suspected that the future of both Canada and England would lie to a large extent in the keeping of their press.

He and his wife left Toronto in October, 1876, and spent the next eighteen months in Britain. Before his departure it was rumoured that he thought of returning permanently to England. If this report were true, commented one of the smaller Conservative papers in Ontario, it would be a great loss to Canada.[49] With this unaccustomed tribute ringing in his ears Goldwin Smith departed to the serener air of England.

[48]As reported in the *Evening Telegram,* June 30, 1876; cf. also *Week,* Oct. 16, 1884.
[49]Cobourg *Sentinel,* Sept. 30, 1876.

IV. CANADA: JOURNALISM AND PUBLIC AFFAIRS

DURING THE SUMMER of 1877 Goldwin Smith and his wife visited John Bright, who deplored his intention to return to "voluntary exile," but acknowledged that a wife and home in Toronto were real reasons for doing so. "All your English friends regret it," he wrote, "but we will not set our judgment against yours, and we admit the force of the new tie which binds you to Canada."[1] During the past twenty years Goldwin Smith had admired Bright almost to the point of reverence, but he began to see flaws in his idol. To an American friend he commented that Bright was "apparently restored to health and shows no signs of intellectual decay. But time and perhaps social influences have mellowed the Great Tribune. He made a good speech against war at Bradford the other day; but in Parliament he has been silent and apparently apathetic."[2]

Despite strong pressure from the constituency of Leeds, Goldwin Smith declined an invitation to stand as its candidate at the forthcoming general election. "Say yes if you possibly can," urged a local Liberal, "you ought to be in the House."[3] Although he rejected a parliamentary career, he promptly immersed himself in writing for the British press. His friend John Morley, then editor of the *Fortnightly Review*, enlisted him, with James Bryce and Robert Lowe among others, in a journalistic attack on Disraeli's foreign policy.[4] To Goldwin Smith no enterprise could have been more congenial.

[1]Letter from John Bright, Jan. 15, 1878, Goldwin Smith Autograph Album, The Grange, Art Gallery of Toronto.
[2]Letter to G. W. Curtis, Aug. 26, 1877.
[3]Letter from Robert Kell of Bradford, July 1, 1878.
[4]F. W. Hirst suggests that three unsigned articles entitled "The Political Adventures of Lord Beaconsfield," which appeared in the *Fortnightly* about this time, were probably written by Goldwin Smith. Cf. Hirst's *Early Life and Letters of John Morley* (2 vols., London, 1927), II, 50. I doubt this. The style is unlike that of Goldwin Smith, and there is no manuscript of these articles among his papers.

I

When in June, 1878, he returned to Canada, a group of working-class electors in West Toronto who were weary of both parties asked him to stand as an independent in the federal election. Sir John A. Macdonald even tried to persuade him to run as a Conservative. Despite Goldwin Smith's earlier outspoken criticism of ministerial corruption in the Pacific Scandal, he and Macdonald remained on friendly terms until 1886, when they were permanently estranged by differences of opinion on the political future of Canada. Both invitations to run for Parliament he declined, explaining to Macdonald that the library was now his proper sphere. If there was any promising young man, however, whom Sir John would like to bring into public life, he would be glad to help defray the election expenses, regardless of the candidate's political views, and would think himself amply repaid by the interest of watching a youthful career. Sir John next tried to persuade him to run for the Ontario provincial legislature, a proposal he rejected with equal firmness.[5]

A main plank in the Conservative platform in the 1878 election was an increased tariff. This ingeniously christened National Policy Macdonald originally defended as a means of reducing the high duties imposed by the United States against Canadian goods. Although a moderate free trader, Goldwin Smith was prepared on these grounds to vote for Sir John, because he was not impressed by the past four and a half years of weak Liberal rule at Ottawa under Alexander Mackenzie. He conceded that in a country like Canada something might be said for a temporary tariff to foster young industries, provided that their infancy was not prolonged. Too often, he cautioned, such infants when mature, instead of casting off their swaddling clothes, took the community by the throat. Before the election, however, he tried to dissuade Sir John from committing himself to much protection.

After the Conservative victory Goldwin Smith both congratulated and warned Macdonald:

Your main difficulty will be the exaggerated expectations formed in some quarters of the benefits to be derived from the National Policy, though your own language, so far as I have seen, has been perfectly guarded. I do not doubt that the Tariff is capable of useful revision. . . . But the only measure which can materially increase the commercial prosperity of Canada is one

[5]Letters to Sir John A. Macdonald, Aug. 22 and Sept. 1, 1878, Macdonald Papers, vol. 266, Public Archives of Canada.

which will give her free access to the markets and other commercial advantages of her own Continent. . . . You and I differ widely in our general view: you regard Canada as a part of the British Empire, I as a community of the New World. . . . But I do not permit my theories as to the future to blind me to the exigencies of the present. I have no doubt that it is the best thing for the country that you should be at the head of the government, and I trust you will remain there for many years to come and receive that general support which good government receives from every reasonable man.[6]

A more diffident and less independent newcomer to the country might have hesitated to constitute himself so soon an unofficial mentor to the Prime Minister.

Goldwin Smith's free trade proclivities were well known, and he was twitted with inconsistency for supporting the National Policy. He retorted that he was no protectionist and had never voted for Macdonald on protectionist grounds, but solely in the hope of obtaining good government. The Prime Minister's views on external affairs and fiscal problems were evidently very different from his own. In a tariff war with the United States he saw little hope for Canada, since the weaker contestant usually suffered. He doubted the feasibility of building up from Cape Breton to Vancouver a Chinese tariff wall which could prevent smuggling. The country was suffering from depression, and defeat in a fiscal war would hardly improve Canada's commercial or diplomatic position.[7]

If he was a lukewarm supporter of the Conservatives, he was even less enthusiastic about their opponents. Consequently his sympathies, or as he more accurately preferred to say, his antipathies, were divided. The Liberal administration at Ottawa may have been honest, but its connection with the proprietors of the *Globe* struck Goldwin Smith as humiliating and equivocal. Alexander Mackenzie's strong point as a political leader was that he had been a stone-mason; his weak point was that he remained one. The Liberals, Smith argued, could not form an adequate party platform out of intolerance, clannishness, and boasts of purity. To his mind they showed no affinity with true liberalism; Gritism merely applied to politics the Scottish Calvinists' doctrines of election and predestination. Thus he contended that Macdonald's government could not possibly be more reactionary than the concealed influence of George Brown. In some respects it would probably be more progressive, it would certainly be far abler, and it would have the great

[6]Letters to Sir John A. Macdonald, Oct. 4 and Sept. 12, 1878, *ibid*.
[7]Letter to the Montreal *Herald*, Oct. 12, 1878.

COLUMNED PORCH AND GABLE OF "THE GRANGE"
From the etching by Owen Staples by kind permission of Mr. Herbert Staples.

advantage of being a parliamentary government as opposed to one directed by a newspaper from outside the House.[8]

When the Liberals led by Oliver Mowat were returned to power in Ontario in June, 1879, Goldwin Smith wrote gloomily to Macdonald: "We are in for four years more of the Grit régime, with all its pharisaic and insolent intolerance. It is a comfort to think that it does not extend to the Dominion." He urged Sir John and Lady Macdonald to visit the Grange in the autumn, promising a complete rest from politics, unless the Prime Minister cared to provide a little information for the political history of Canada which he hoped some day to undertake. Eleven years later in his *Canada and the Canadian Question* Goldwin Smith attacked Conservative policy, and drew a singularly pessimistic picture of Canadian development. Fortunately he did not possess second sight, and in 1879 he tried to persuade Macdonald that his occasional presence in Toronto would be useful to his friends. The Grits were rapidly getting Ontario back into their hands, and he feared that once successful there, they might win the Dominion. His own plans remained unchanged. Political life in any form he had renounced, although he renewed his former offer to help launch some able young man in public life. "But for myself," he declared firmly, "I remain as I am."

Three years afterward he congratulated Macdonald on his re-election as Prime Minister, but once again offered a caution. "Who reigns at Ottawa," he wrote from England, "is a question which affects me as little as any man in the Dominion, yet I welcome the tidings which we have just received of your victory in the election. . . . Do not forget that you have received a good deal of non-party support, given in the broad interest of the country." Two months later, after his return to Canada, he wrote again in his self-appointed role of friendly critic: "Believe me, what you want, to make your party victorious, is a stronger set of men."[9]

Goldwin Smith was attracted by Sir John's ability, engaging manners, and amusing conversation. He knew and liked him better than any other Canadian, but saw his faults clearly. He considered Macdonald unscrupulous where Conservative interests were at stake, and thought that the bribery used to cement his party debauched the political character of Canadians. Sir John, he observed, was a skilful debater and

---

[8]"Papers by a Bystander," Rose-Belford's *Canadian Monthly*, II (Jan., 1879), 114–15.
[9]Letters to Sir John A. Macdonald, Aug. 23, 1882, Oct. 3, Nov. 2, 1879, June 22, 1882. Joseph Pope (ed.), *Correspondence of Sir John Macdonald* (Toronto, n.d.), 262, 269–70, 290–1.

a clever fisher for votes, but only a palpable flatterer could maintain that he had raised the standard of public life. Yet if Macdonald had been the political corrupter of others, his bitterest opponents must allow that he was himself incorruptible. Much had been forgiven Walpole because he faced the difficulties of a disputed succession; not a little, he suggested, might be forgiven the Prime Minister who had to deal with Canadian Confederation.[10]

A decade after Macdonald's death Goldwin Smith sketched his character in a paragraph in the *Weekly Sun*. Unquestionably, he wrote, Sir John

> was the paragon of party leaders. He possessed in perfection all the qualities which that business requires. He combined life-long experience with consummate tact. He thoroughly understood the characters, the aims, the weaknesses, and, where there was venality, the price, of all the men with whom he had to deal. He had singular attractiveness of manner, with a playful wit. He had great social versatility. Cultured himself, though not very deeply, and capable of taking interest in serious discussion he could talk to men of culture in their own style at one end of the table, and to men not of culture in a very different style at the other end. He was a thorough man of the world, with nothing about him narrow or fanatical; in this a very pleasant contrast to his enemy, George Brown. That he could stoop, and stoop low to conquer, he showed too well in the affair of the Pacific Railway scandal. . . .[11]

II

Since he did not wish to enter public life, Goldwin Smith devoted most of his energies to journalism. Experience had made him wary about having no outlet in Canada save as a contributor to papers whose editorial policy he did not control. Years earlier he had told Professor Rolleston of Oxford that he preferred, in general, to write to a friendly audience and to contribute to a journal with whose opinions he agreed. He had added, however, that he looked on them all as platforms, any one of which it was legitimate to use to address the listeners immediately surrounding it. To a degree he adhered to this view. Throughout his life he wrote for a multitude of British, American, and Canadian newspapers and periodicals, which represented a wide variety of opinions. Few writers have with such catholicity taken all publications for their province. In addition, however, he liked a platform of his own to print whatever he wanted to say. This was the more necessary

---

[10]"Current Events and Opinions," *Week*, Dec. 25, 1884.
[11]Dec. 12, 1900.

because his ideas were usually those of an unrepentant minority, and he was impelled by a missionary zeal to preach to the unconverted. As he once observed in a moment of self-revelation, he was "unblushingly heterodox." By the end of 1879 he was writing G. W. Curtis of *Harper's* to announce the imminent advent of the *Bystander*, "a little monthly journal which I have just started on principles pretty much the same as those of Harper's—I wish I could add, in the same style."[12] The competition from English and American publications, he explained, made it difficult to maintain a magazine in Canada, but he thought there was an opening for something different from the daily papers. He wanted to say a word at the right time on continental as well as Canadian questions, and the *Bystander* would give him an opportunity to be completely independent.

In January, 1880, the first number appeared, with the characteristic motto, "not party, but the people." The name was an obvious choice. Since 1872 "A Bystander" had been Goldwin Smith's favourite pen name, although he often sent letters to the press under other pseudonyms, such as "Liberal," "Equity," and "Radical." The little magazine was a tour de force in more ways than one. No periodical in Canada either before or since approached its quality. It was Goldwin Smith's journal in a special sense: he wrote every word of its sixty-odd pages. The *Bystander* announced itself as "a monthly review of current events, Canadian and general." Devoted primarily to political comment, it also discussed social, economic, and cultural issues, not in Canada alone, but in the United States, Great Britain, the Empire, and Europe. Books were reviewed not only as literary works, but as "events and landmarks in the history of opinion." In such reviewing Goldwin Smith was particularly interested, and from the beginning he tended to enlarge the literary sections at the expense of the political, and would have gone even farther in this direction but for the remonstrances of friends. Modelled on the best English and American periodicals, the *Bystander* had in Canada no serious competitors as an independent journal written in lucid and inimitable prose. It contained some of his best writing, for in its pages he was usually more objective and less polemical than in his books and other contributions to the press. The three volumes remain invaluable to Canadian historians as a brilliant if biased source of contemporary comment on the ideas and events of the eighteen-eighties.

The journal was better received than Goldwin Smith had dared to hope. He thanked Curtis for a friendly notice in *Harper's*. "The little

[12]Letter to G. W. Curtis, Dec. 25, 1879.

thing is doing wonderfully well," he wrote, "considering what a bad time its principles have hitherto had in Canada. A commercial success of course it is not expected to be: it is sold at the lowest possible price that it may get into the hands of the people, and I am well content if I do not lose much beyond my labour."[13] He might be forgiven modest pride in the fact that before the *Bystander* was a year old it had attained a far larger circulation than any previous Canadian periodical. This achievement was the more surprising since through its pages Goldwin Smith persistently advocated his favourite but unpopular doctrine that the country's manifest destiny was union with the United States.

The *Bystander* was soon known from one corner of the country to the other. A New Brunswick editor remarked that whatever Goldwin Smith wrote was read and admired for style, thoughtfulness, and honesty, even by those who differed widely from his views. He considered the discussion of public questions in the *Bystander* (then just a year old) among the finest specimens of political writing which had appeared in the Dominion.[14] The clerk of the House of Commons, Sir John Bourinot, hailed its publication as an event in the political and literary annals of the country.[15] Canadians would have been surprised to know how far the little journal's influence reached. Among its British readers were the Duke and Duchess of Albany, their private secretary Sir Robert Collins, and Lord Coleridge, Chief Justice of England. When it ceased publication Bryce wrote from London to say that many people there greatly regretted its disappearance. From it "we learnt what we most desired to know about Canadian affairs."[16] Here was a practical refutation of Goldwin Smith's common complaint that the confines of Ontario represented the limits of the literary field open to a writer in English-speaking Canada.

The first series of the *Bystander* was brought to a close in June, 1881, by Goldwin Smith's departure for a year to England. Before he left, the Press Association gave a dinner for him, mainly as an evidence of sympathy with what he had suffered in fighting the battle of free speech. It was also a tribute to the man himself, for his contribution to journalism, and for the impetus he had given literary development in Canada. In his comments on this occasion Goldwin Smith said simply that to Canadian journalism he had brought the best he had, the fruits of a life largely spent in historical and political study and among statesmen. He

---

[13]Letters to G. W. Curtis, Oct. 23 and 27, 1880.
[14]*Daily Telegraph* (St. John, N.B.), Dec. 28, 1880.
[15]J. G. Bourinot, "The Intellectual Development of the Canadian People," Rose-Belford's *Canadian Monthly*, VI (Jan.–June, 1881), 232.
[16]Letter to Goldwin Smith, May 15, 1884.

hoped he had also done the little in his power to encourage the growth of a Canadian national literature without distinction of opinion or party.[17]

III

He and his wife stayed in Britain from July, 1881, until the next June, and again from the spring to the autumn of 1886. On each return he renewed old acquaintances and former connections with British journalism and public life. In 1881 he visited Gladstone at Hawarden and the Duke and Duchess of Albany at Claremont. Some of his friends wanted to submit his name for the Mastership of University College, Oxford, which was shortly to be vacant. Others urged him to accept a nomination for the House of Commons. Despite his unabated interest in English affairs, Goldwin Smith declined both proposals, on the ground that it was too late to make such changes, and that his "lot was cast on the other side of the Herring Pond." Less permanent commitments in Britain he willingly accepted. He spoke in Chelsea on parliamentary reform, addressed various Liberal gatherings at Grantham, Lewes, and Bradford, and in Manchester attacked the opium trade with China. In Nottingham he discussed technical education before working men and addressed the students of Nottingham University College. In Oxford he spoke to a congress of delegates from co-operative societies.

At the Oxford encaenia in June, Robert Browning and Goldwin Smith received honorary degrees, and were Jowett's guests for the occasion. Smith enjoyed meeting Browning, but thought his poetry "out of my welkin." He himself, he suspected, had been given the degree at Jowett's suggestion, in recognition of his earlier work for university reform.

On his return to Toronto in 1882 he did not at first intend to revive the *Bystander*, and told his friends that he was disinclined to touch Canadian literature or public affairs again.[18] He might have known himself well enough to suspect that he would change his mind. Less than six months later, in January, 1883, the *Bystander* reappeared, this time as a quarterly, because he found a monthly issue too constant a tie, and too frequent an interruption of other work. The second series was

[17]*Canadian Monthly*, VII (July, 1881), 101–6.
[18]Letter to John Cameron, editor of the *London Advertiser*, July 19, 1882. Cameron had much in common with Goldwin Smith. He was friendly to the Patrons of Industry and gave their activities a good deal of publicity. He favoured a low tariff and closer trade relations with the United States, but believed in Canadian independence rather than union between the two countries.

concluded in October of the same year. Taking leave of his readers in the last issue Goldwin Smith explained that the reception given the *Bystander* seemed to warrant a larger experiment in independent journalism. He rejoiced in the end of his own labour and in the appearance of a more adequate organ of Canadian opinion. This was the *Week*, "an independent journal of politics, society, and literature," which first appeared in December, 1883. Goldwin Smith was part proprietor as well as founder, and until the beginning of 1885 besides numerous signed articles wrote a "Bystander's" weekly comment on events and opinions. The first editor was twenty-four-year-old Charles G. D. Roberts, whose own poetry appeared from time to time in its pages, as did that of such writers as Archibald Lampman, Bliss Carman, Wilfrid Campbell, Charles Mair, and Pauline Johnson. One of the chief contributions of the little weekly was the outlet it provided for young Canadian writers at a time when few such opportunities existed.

It is not surprising that Goldwin Smith found burdensome the task of writing the whole of the *Bystander*. His explanation that he wanted uninterrupted leisure for other work was more accurate than his apologetic comment that he grew lazy with advancing years. Laziness was not one of his attributes. He never had enough time for all the articles, pamphlets, and letters to the press which he wanted to write. Before the *Week* was a year old he told friends that he would like to slip his shoulder from the wheel altogether, but there was a real place in Canada for an independent periodical, and he was the only person who could afford the financial loss involved. His weekly section, however, would henceforth cease, since the journal was now fairly established. "It is doing wonderfully well," he wrote cheerfully, "for a paper of its class in this little country—and I feel at liberty to leave it in other hands."[19]

The *Week* was never his mouthpiece in the same sense as the *Bystander*. From the beginning it was made clear that the opinions in the section on current events were not editorial, but those of an individual writer. People with opposite views were invited to advocate them in its pages, as the special object of the *Week*'s founders was the provision of "a perfectly free court for Canadian discussion." The sincerity of this declaration was proved when after 1889 the *Week* became one of Goldwin Smith's critics. In the interim, however, Charles G. D. Roberts had resigned as editor owing in part, at least, to differences with the founder on political issues.

From the end of 1885 all Goldwin Smith's contributions to it

[19]Letters to G. W. Curtis, Dec. 3, July 8, and Dec. 17, 1884.

appeared under his own name. Almost every week during the early months of 1886 he wrote a signed editorial, usually on the iniquities of Gladstone's Irish policy. Finally his sentiments on the subject became so strong that he could no longer content himself with journalistic comment from across the Atlantic. From April until October of that year he was in England, where he threw himself into the general election campaign as an ardent Unionist, but made time to send back to the *Week* at least every fortnight long editorials on English and Irish politics.

This journal also had distinguished British readers. Matthew Arnold made its acquaintance when he stayed at the Grange. On his return home he wrote from the Athenaeum, inquiring whether Goldwin Smith had found a new editor for the *Week*. "If you have, and you are satisfied with him, and continue to write in it yourself, I must get them to take it on here." Arnold's opinion of newspapers in the United States, as of many other things in that country, showed little of his enthusiasm for the *Week*. "I think the American press, the great danger of the nation," he wrote Goldwin Smith, "grows worse and worse from all I can see. The Times, Standard, Post, Manchester Guardian, Leeds Mercury, Scotsman, and so on, are real causes for satisfaction here in Great Britain, and forces of conservation."[20] At the time Smith's enthusiasm for conservative forces was less than Arnold's, but as he grew older he valued them more. It would have been difficult, however, for Arnold or anyone else to prize more than Goldwin Smith the independence of the press. Both agreed that the censorship of the mob might be no less inimical to the free expression of truth, less narrowing, or less degrading than that of autocratic rulers.

IV

During the British election of 1886, Goldwin Smith declined an invitation to stand for Parliament against a member of Gladstone's cabinet. To the Unionist cause, however, he wholeheartedly devoted himself, contributing to its campaign literature and speaking throughout the country against Home Rule. In this crusade he was not pleased to find himself allied with Joseph Chamberlain, whom he heartily detested. After the Unionist victory Lord Lingen, the party organizer, expressed warm thanks for his services during the election.

[20]Letters from Matthew Arnold, Jan. 13, 1886, Goldwin Smith Papers; May 2, 1884, Autograph Album.

His longstanding interest in Ireland dated from 1861, when he had spent the summer at Phoenix Park with Edward Cardwell, then Irish Secretary, collecting material for a book on *Irish History and Irish Character*. This early study showed more sympathetic understanding of the country's problems than his later writings, and won him some reputation as an expert on Irish affairs. Its defence of British policy, however, irritated certain readers. Among these was Friedrich Engels, who told Marx that he had "nicely caught Monsieur Goldwin Smith," with whose "assertions in extenuation of the English" he had no patience. "But," he concluded with satisfaction, "I shall get the fellow."[21]

Twenty years later Goldwin Smith had revisited Dublin, and come to the surprising conclusion that since the disestablishment of the Irish Church in 1869, no serious political difficulty remained. He was convinced that Ireland needed economic and agrarian, rather than political reform. The Irish people needed bread. To his mind the best solutions for their difficulties were land reform and emigration. The two possible political alternatives were legislative union with Britain or complete separation. Anything, he thought, was better than Gladstone's plan for Home Rule and a vassal parliament always struggling to be free. Despite his usual enthusiasm for colonial emancipation, Goldwin Smith had little sympathy with the cause of Irish independence because he feared the danger to the United Kingdom of a hostile republic on its flank. Independence, he argued, was possible only for a united nation, which Ireland, divided into the Protestant North and Catholic South, was not. His attitude was reflected in a comment to an American friend: "You fought for your Union against Slavery; we are fighting for ours against Savagery and Superstition."[22]

In Canada as in England he vigorously supported the Unionist cause. In Toronto he was chairman of the Loyal and Patriotic Union, formed to "defend the integrity of the Empire against Home Rule," and addressed its members on "Dismemberment No Remedy." When in the eighteen-eighties the Canadian Parliament passed resolutions in favour of Irish Home Rule, Goldwin Smith promptly protested against unwarranted interference by the Dominion in imperial affairs. While he had little enthusiasm for the rancorous spirit of the Orange Lodges which flourished in Ontario as nowhere else outside Ulster, he spoke briefly at a celebration of the two hundredth anniversary of the Battle of the

---

[21] Letter to Karl Marx, Nov. 29, 1869, Karl Marx and Friedrich Engels, *Correspondence, 1846–1895* (London, 1934), 276.
[22] Letter to G. W. Curtis, Feb. 11, 1886.

Boyne, when Toronto's annual Orange walk on the twelfth of July was unusually magnificent.

In later years he wrote much on Ireland, with ever increasing bitterness, and attacked Gladstone as "that unspeakable old man." Toward the end of his life, however, he was assailed by some doubts. He once referred to English policy toward Ireland, "pursued with almost undeviating perverseness for seven hundred years." On a few isolated occasions he even showed some sporadic sympathy with Home Rule, though he still thought the happiest state for both islands was complete union. At the turn of the century he commented to Bryce that the Boer War would put new life into Home Rule, and that if there was no other way of stopping the career of jingoism, he would be inclined to become a Home Ruler himself. Then, however, he would favour outright and immediate independence. To Justin McCarthy he wrote in 1903 that in view of the strong spirit of nationality which the protracted struggle had developed in Ireland, he believed he would vote for the one feasible measure of Home Rule, namely the independence of Ireland, in the hope that a peaceful parting might lead eventually to reunion with the United Kingdom.[23] This sanguine hope reflected little credit on his grasp of political realities.

V

Shortly after his return to Canada in the autumn of 1886 he was invited to stand as candidate for Lisgar, Manitoba, at the forthcoming federal election. This was the last time that he seriously considered an active political career. The Northwest interested him more than any other part of the country except Ontario. He visited it four times between 1870 and 1889, and was present at the opening of Manitoba's first provincial legislature. The project of extending the new Dominion from sea to sea had at first seemed to him wildly impractical, and he strongly opposed the building of the Canadian Pacific Railway. He was not the only person in Canada to wonder how the line could pay its way, with only sixty thousand white inhabitants on the prairies west of Winnipeg. When he saw the Northwest, however, he was much impressed by its beauty, agricultural possibilities, and the sturdy character

[23]Letters to Justin McCarthy, April 2, 1903; to James Bryce, May 18, 1900, May 17, 1903, Oct. 18, 1906; "The Irish Question," *Contemporary Review*, XXI (March, 1873), 503–28; *Bystander*, I (Nov., 1880), 605; I (Dec., 1880), 642–3; II (March, 1881), 141–3; letter to the *Daily Telegraph*, May 6, 1886; *Weekly Sun*, Jan. 28, 1902.

of its people. He early advocated that the federal government should give the Northwest control over its own natural resources, in order that the settlers might reap the full benefit from a bountiful land. This special interest in the prairies, as in rural Ontario, partly sprang from his belief that farmers were the group most apt to support closer trade relations with the United States.

When Goldwin Smith was suggested as a possible candidate for Lisgar, Macdonald wrote that he would like to see him in the Commons. This was one of Sir John's typical acts of generosity, for the *Bystander* and *Week* had strenuously attacked both the National Policy and Conservative corruption. Nor could anyone expect a man of Goldwin Smith's lively conscience and quixotic independence to be a comfortable ally in Parliament. He replied that it had never occurred to him that Sir John could countenance his candidature. He was an independent, not a Conservative, though with some slight exaggeration he protested his entire friendliness to the Government. Reasonably enough he pointed out that he could hardly throw himself into the arms of a Conservative constituency, nor, if he did so, feel sure that he would be cordially supported. He might possibly have run for the Ontario legislature as an anti-prohibitionist had not the *Mail* embraced prohibition.[24] Owing to illness, he finally declined the nomination for Lisgar. He helped, however, in 1890, in founding the Winnipeg *Tribune*, to provide an independent newspaper in the West.

VI

No single individual did as much for journalism in Canada as Goldwin Smith. Many would have considered the amount he wrote for the Canadian press a full-time occupation, even if he had not concurrently been producing histories, biographies, and verse translations from the classics, as well as numerous pamphlets. All these, however, formed only a fraction of his output, even when he was publishing the *Bystander* singlehanded. From the eighteen-sixties until well after the turn of the century a steady flow of articles by him on political, literary, or social problems appeared in numerous English and American periodicals. His efforts to direct by letter the politics of Britain and Canada on occasion provoked glancing gibes even from the journals in which his pronouncements appeared.[25] Yet it was a rare editor who hesitated to

---

[24]Letter to Sir John A. Macdonald, Dec. 11, 1886, Macdonald Papers, vol. 266; *Week*, Sept. 18, 1884.

[25]Cf. *Athenaeum*, Dec. 2, 1893. "It is always a pleasure," remarked *The Times*

publish anything he cared to write. Willison of the *Globe* merely voiced the opinion of most British and American editors when he said, "I know what value a letter of yours has to the paper that is fortunate enough to get it."[26] C. P. Scott, in thanking him for the letters which he often sent the *Manchester Guardian,* praised them as a powerful incentive to the better sort of Liberals, and a stimulus to recall the party to its bearings. Smith's gift of a subscription to the *Weekly Sun* Scott acknowledged with the comment, "I shall now know where to look for sound opinions on Canadian affairs. . . . Your letters to us have been a constant source of interest and distinction."[27] The managing editor of the *New York Times* expressed his appreciation for a letter from Goldwin Smith on reciprocity. "Perhaps it is hardly necessary," he wrote, "to say that we shall be very happy to print anything you may care to say at any time on any topic."[28]

Goldwin Smith contributed for years to the New York *Nation,* first under the editorship of Wendell Garrison (a biography of whose famous father he once wrote), and later under that of E. L. Godkin. He was among the thirty-four distinguished men of letters whose names appeared as prospective contributors to its first issue in 1865. His death in 1910 left Henry James the sole survivor of the group. Much of his best writing remained unknown in numerous book reviews for the *Nation* from 1869 to 1884 and in the decade after 1890.[29] The six years' hiatus from 1884 to 1890 was caused by a quarrel with Godkin. Goldwin Smith had worked with him on the Anti-Imperialist League of New York which, among other activities, distributed at Smith's expense many copies of his pamphlet on *Commonwealth or Empire.* The friendship broke over their differing views on Ireland. Godkin was an ardent Home Ruler, who with some reason considered Goldwin Smith's opinions on the subject "a mixture of those of a Tory squire and a London-

---

magisterially, "to read Mr. Goldwin Smith's utterances, even when, as generally happens, we are unable to agree with them. He is certain to write with grace, dignity, and a certain nobility of style." May 23, 1902, in a review of his *Commonwealth or Empire,* with very little of which *The Times* found it possible to agree.

[26]Letter from J. S. Willison in 1895.

[27]Letters from C. P. Scott, Oct. 31, 1905, and Dec. 5, 1903. The *Guardian* was one of the few English papers which criticized Britain's part in the Boer War. Scott's biographer, discussing contributors to the *Guardian,* wrote that "Freeman and Goldwin Smith brought the distinction and authority of an older generation." J. L. Hammond, *C. P. Scott* (London, 1934), 53.

[28]Letter of Jan. 24, 1907.

[29]Since these reviews were unsigned, they would be impossible to identify had they not been marked in Goldwin Smith's own file of the *Nation,* acquired from his secretary by the Cornell University Library.

derry Orangeman."[30] Both men expressed personal opinions of each other better left unprinted, but after a long estrangement they were eventually reconciled.

The Toronto *Mail*, founded as a bulwark of Conservatism and a rival to the *Globe*, gradually became more independent. Until 1882 it was strongly Conservative, but it differed from the party over the execution of Riel, and violently opposed ultramontanism in Quebec at a time when Macdonald was trying to bring French- and English-speaking Canadians closer together. By 1887 when the Conservative federal Government and Liberal Opposition were both toying with the political advisability of closer trade relations with the United States, the *Mail* came out strongly for commercial union. From 1882 to 1894 it welcomed contributions from Goldwin Smith, who wrote not only letters to its correspondence column but many editorials advocating the abolition of customs barriers between the two countries or attacking the Jesuits' Estates Act.[31] As a counter to the *Mail*'s manifestation of independence, in 1887 a new Conservative organ, the *Empire*, was launched in Toronto. Eight years later it was bought by the *Mail*, and the two fused under the name of the *Mail and Empire*. The *Empire* never so far forgot its own origins as to falter in a consistent policy of personal attacks upon Goldwin Smith. As the *Mail* became more independent the *Week* became more loyal and imperialist in sentiment, until it too was denouncing him as a traitor with little less violence than the *Empire*.

In 1889 the *Mail* decided that commercial union was a lost cause, and began to attack it. Goldwin Smith promptly revived the *Bystander* to provide an organ for this movement, which would otherwise have received a scant hearing in the Canadian press. The third series was published monthly from October, 1889, until the next September. The Toronto *Saturday Night* welcomed the *Bystander*'s re-establishment, noting that since its last appearance its author had been writing for many of the city papers with which he had not been entirely in sympathy. As a statement of fact rather than criticism, the editor added: "Goldwin Smith is not entirely in sympathy with anything or anybody."[32]

In the last issue of the *Bystander* he reaffirmed his position. He had

[30]*New York Daily Tribune*, May 31, 1884. Godkin's "An American View of Ireland," *Nineteenth Century*, XII (Aug., 1882), was countered by Goldwin Smith's "Great Britain, America, and Ireland," *Princeton Review* (Nov., 1882).
[31]Goldwin Smith was the writer of editorials on commercial union on May 20, June 18 and 21, Sept. 1, 9, 17 and 23, Oct. 1, Nov. 5, Dec. 7 and 24, 1887, Feb. 1 and 24, March 16, June 8, July 13, and Nov. 10, 1888. He also wrote the editorials on the Jesuits' Estates question published on Jan. 26, Feb. 5 and 9, March 2, 9, 11 and 13, May 18 and 25, June 22 and 27, and July 6 and 13, 1889.
[32]Oct. 5, 1889.

revived the journal to fill a serious gap in the advocacy of a commercial policy desirable in the interests of Canada as a whole, and absolutely vital to those of the Northwest. For the general objects which the *Bystander* was originally intended to promote, independent discussion of public affairs and interest in literary matters, more provision was now made.

Whatever political destiny may be in store for us [he concluded], whether Ontario is always to remain apart or to be united with the English-speaking race of this continent, there is no reason why she should not be made and always remain a centre of intellectual life. Those who have been unsparing in their efforts to bring this about may fairly plead that they have shown patriotism in their way, albeit their way may not be that of the Jingo. One at least, though perhaps not the most important of the elements of nationality, they have done what was in their power to produce.

The charges of "treason" so often levied against him were a sore point with Goldwin Smith. He remarked to a friend on how difficult it was, in the limited constituency of English-speaking Canada, to keep alive any literary and non-partisan publications. If expenditure of money and labour, and the sacrifice of other work to make Toronto an intellectual centre was any proof of patriotism, he thought he could scarcely be found wanting in loyalty to his adopted country.[33]

VII

Financial problems caused by a small circulation have always made it difficult to establish good periodicals in Canada. The *Canadian Monthly* at one time managed to make ends meet, but it was helped by unpaid contributions. The *Nation*, as much literary as political, was barely balancing its accounts when the departure of its two moving spirits, Edward Blake and Goldwin Smith (both of whom had been unpaid), compelled its withdrawal. The *Bystander* achieved a reasonable circulation, but could not long have continued as a purely commercial venture.[34] When a reference was made to its costs, Goldwin Smith shrugged the matter off with the comment that though his journalism always cost him something, a yacht would have cost more.

In the nineteenth century as in the twentieth the dearth of good Cana-

---

[33]Letter to F. C. Ware of Winnipeg, Aug. 12, 1890, *Goldwin Smith's Correspondence*, 224–5.
[34]These facts are cited in a letter from Goldwin Smith to the *Week*, Aug. 31, 1894, entitled "What is the Matter with Canadian Literature?"

dian books formed a perennial subject for discussion. Goldwin Smith forthrightly declared that what was needed to produce a national literature was a nation: the voice of an infant community was sure to be infantile. With his usual disregard of Canadian susceptibilities he maintained that no such thing as a Canadian literature existed or was ever likely to exist, because Canada was a literary expression without literary unity. There could only be the literature of Ontario and Montreal, a field too small for indigenous growth. An Ontario writer had hardly any constituency outside his own agricultural province with its two million inhabitants. Even if the English-speaking population of all the provinces could be reached, it would still provide a small audience for a really able writer. From the American market Canadian authors were practically excluded unless they published in the United States, since otherwise they could not obtain American copyright. Canada, Goldwin Smith pointed out, had no great publishing firms or printing offices and scarcely one first-class bookshop. There were few men of leisure with intellectual tastes, and business men for the most part read little. As for trying to exclude foreign literature from the country, they might as well try to keep out the south wind.[35] At the beginning of the twentieth century he was more optimistic. Considering that there were only about four million Canadians who spoke English, and that they had not yet finished clearing the land, they perhaps produced as much good writing as could be expected.[36]

When the Royal Society was formed in 1881 Goldwin Smith declined to join it because he thought such an institution artificial and premature. He had similar doubts about the proposal at the turn of the century to form a Canadian Authors' Society, but consented to act as its president because it was trying to secure a specific end which he approved, namely reform in the unsatisfactory Canadian copyright law. He had little personal concern in the matter, since he published in London and New York simultaneously works which, being scholarly rather than popular, were in no danger of Canadian appropriation. He felt keenly, however, that authors were entitled to the protection of copyright, and went to Ottawa to discuss the problem with the Prime Minister, Sir Wilfrid Laurier. No man of the time worked harder to develop literary taste in Canada and to encourage young Canadian writers, but he was disheartened by his qualified success.

Yet despite the attacks of the *Empire*, the *Week*, and the imperial

[35]*Ibid.*; *Bystander*, III (Jan., 1883), 67; "Literature in Toronto," *Week*, Sept. 9, 1892.
[36]*Weekly Sun*, Feb. 14, 1906.

federationists, only the most violent political antagonists could ignore or minimize Goldwin Smith's contributions to Canadian letters.[37] His arrival in Toronto inaugurated a new era in Canadian journalism, previously considered the last resort of the destitute and dishonoured in all other professions. His reputation, independence, and style aroused healthy emulation and quickened the intellectual pulse of the country. These contributions won increasing recognition, although so fearless and formidable a journalist could scarcely receive the credit he deserved while his pen had free play.[38] Canadian journalism alone, however, to say nothing of other branches of letters, owed him a debt which it could never wholly discharge.

VIII

With literary activities he combined a lively interest in local government and public welfare. In his attitude toward social reform there was nothing of the bystander. He had an Englishman's conviction that a primary responsibility of municipal governments was to make cities pleasanter and healthier places in which to live. This doctrine, seldom the view of Canadian local authorities, Goldwin Smith forcefully expounded over some forty years. After two decades' residence in Toronto he commented bitterly on the municipal government's sins of omission. "We all pay for our own roads, sidewalks, drains and water. We shovel our own snow and care for our own boulevards. The relief of the poor is left to private charity and there is not even a city officer for its superintendence. A city government could hardly do less for the inhabitants."[39]

When he first settled in America he had been struck by the corruption of municipal politics in great cities like New York. This to his mind belied the hopes of those who put their faith in a multitude of elective institutions. Vast city mobs were a far cry from the direct democracy of the original New England parishes, and were neither seen nor fore-

[37]The *Week* changed hands in 1894, and began to support the cause of a united empire. On Sept. 7, 1894, it attacked Goldwin Smith in an unsigned article as "hopelessly out of touch with everything Canadian, and . . . constitutionally and mentally unable to understand the country and the aspirations and genius of its people." There was some truth in the charge.

[38]Appreciative estimates of his services to Canadian letters were made by W. Blackburn Harte, "Some Canadian Writers of ToDay," *New England Magazine*, new series, III (Sept., 1890), 21–40, and John King, in a review of Goldwin Smith's *Bay Leaves* in the *Week*, Aug. 15, 1890.

[39]*Bystander*, new series, (Jan., 1890), 113.

seen by De Tocqueville.[40] In Toronto he served as chairman of a citizens' committee on civic reform, which at the turn of the century brought in a report on a new system of government for the city. The one-year term for the mayor, council, and municipal aldermen he repeatedly attacked, as certain to focus city officials' primary attention on the next election and thus make almost impossible sane long-range policies. Nothing was less responsible than an annually elected body. Government by popular election was to his mind a failure in large cities because it involved use of political machinery for what were essentially questions of expert business management. Elective civic governments at their worst were dens of thieves, at their best administrative nuisances. If the citizens wanted an elective legislative body, they should at least provide for skilled and permanent administration, which would be stable, systematic, and responsible. He preferred either the Washington commission system or the city manager type of government. Among the drawbacks of elective local bodies he cited the difficulty of getting good candidates to run for the city council and of the ordinary voter obtaining accurate information about those who did stand. He himself was reduced to seeking advice from a member of his household who knew more about the candidates than he did. Thus for some years he had voted his butler's straight ticket.[41]

When the city fathers or the University Board of Governors proposed to sell off large sections of park land for building lots, he protested indignantly that one of the best investments of municipal funds was to give children facilities for harmless play, at whatever cost. Catching and punishing culprits, young or old, were expensive operations. Surely cities would some day be wise enough to try the experiment of prevention on a thorough and systematic basis. Prohibitionists were given to arguing that drink was the cause of crime. Goldwin Smith pointed out that crime varied with factors unconnected with drink, such as the abundance of employment and the cheapness of food. Juvenile delinquency was not combated by piecemeal destruction of Toronto parks and abolition of the breathing spaces and safety-valves of city life.[42] These beliefs he put into practical form in 1872 by giving the town of Orillia several acres of land for a park, an opera house, and a new market. The pleasant grounds of the Grange were always open to convalescents in the neighbourhood who cared to enjoy its lawns and flower beds, and Goldwin

[40]Letter to George Waring from Ithaca, in 1869.
[41]*Globe*, Dec. 23, 1902; *Canadian Monthly*, VI (July, 1874), 74; *Week*, Oct. 30, 1884; *Sun* (New York), Nov. 17, 1901; *Mail and Empire*, July 11, 1903.
[42]*Week*, July 18, 1890; *Bystander*, n.s. (Aug., 1890), 350–1.

Smith made a habit of stopping to chat with any casual guests who took advantage of this invitation.

The beneficial effects of free lending libraries seemed to him more doubtful than those of parks. He was unenthusiastic when in 1883 Toronto imposed a tax to support a public library. There was much more to be said, in his opinion, for establishing a good reference library with a reading room, than for encouraging the taste for novels, which hardly needed stimulation from public funds. "A novel library," he tartly observed to Andrew Carnegie, "is to women mentally pretty much what the saloon is physically to men."[43] He saw no more justification for the free circulation of second- or third-rate novels than for free theatre tickets, though he had no objection to the enjoyment of really good fiction. Despite these doubts, once the citizens of Toronto decided that they wanted to use taxes for such a purpose, Goldwin Smith did what he could to help. He participated in founding a public library, donated books every year, and co-operated enthusiastically in plans to increase its efficiency. When Bruce Mines, a tiny village in the wilds of Algoma, asked if he would give some books to its newly established little library, he willingly did so. He had small sympathy, however, with Andrew Carnegie's endowment of either libraries or universities. Of the former he held that three-quarters of the books circulated would be inferior novels; with regard to universities he was convinced that there were already far too many students at college. His views on these matters showed little of the enthusiasm for popular education felt by most liberals of the day.

During the last thirty years of the century Canada was rapidly becoming industrialized, although as late as 1901 Goldwin Smith could still contend that Ontario was and was likely to remain predominantly agricultural. One familiar with the manufacturing centres of the English "Black Country" naturally felt qualms about the beginning of a similar transformation in a new land. He granted that the factory system had to come, and that it had vastly added to the productivity of the country and consequently to its material well-being. He agreed that Canada, like other lands, must have its fair share of manufactures and desire their prosperity, but he disliked the endeavour to increase their growth artificially by tariffs designed to protect infant industries. A factory hand seemed to him not much more than a human spindle or hammer, spending his days in monotonous repetition of the same uninteresting task, without ever seeing the finished product. Where factories existed, how-

[43]Letter to Andrew Carnegie, Dec. 29, 1906; *Week*, Dec. 13, 1883; *Weekly Sun*, Nov. 5, 1902.

ever, he thought their regulation by law only sensible and the protection of women and children in factories no more socialistic than their protection from maltreatment elsewhere.

The social problems of industrialization were particularly marked in Canada where the transformation from a rural economy, in older countries spread over half a century or more, was concentrated into the decades of the eighteen-seventies and eighties. Throughout much of this time there was acute depression. A minor symptom of the new industrial age, the scarcity of domestic servants, was already a much discussed problem when Goldwin Smith first settled in Toronto. Even then it seemed unlikely that in the democratic society of the new world the personal subordination of the kitchen to the parlour would be restored. Girls left domestic service to crowd into the factories, and the old-fashioned type of household with a domestic staff attached to the family for life and remembered in their master's will had departed with the conservative and quiet society to which it belonged. It lingered longer at the Grange than in most places in Canada.

Goldwin Smith's enthusiasm for political reform showed concern for humanity in the abstract. Love for mankind, however, is not always accompanied by a real interest in the problems of flesh and blood individuals. About his sympathy for people in trouble there was nothing abstract. He repeatedly emphasized that wealth carried with it social obligations to the community, and few wealthy men have more actively practised their precepts. His private papers abundantly illustrate his grave courtesy toward all classes of the community and the kindly help he gave, as inconspicuously as possible, to numerous unfortunate men and women. He was noted for his habit of lending money, at very low interest, to people of moderate means in order to help them buy homes of their own. He said he never lost any money in this way, and he liked to help people help themselves. He owned a great deal of real estate in Toronto, and among those who had cause to appreciate his generosity as a landlord was John King, father of the future Prime Minister, Mackenzie King, who in his turn became one of Goldwin Smith's grateful admirers.

One of Toronto's largest and most unostentatious contributors to a multitude of good causes, he devoted a considerable portion of his income to charitable work, on which he spent thousands of dollars every year. He gave $1,200 toward the education at St. Andrew's College of a boy known to him only through the recommendation of the headmaster. Prejudiced though he was against Catholics and Jews, he regularly supported the St. Vincent de Paul Society, and gave a generous donation toward the building of a new synagogue, at whose opening he was present. A cheque sent one day to the Irish Protestant Benevolent Society would be followed the next by another to the Sacred Heart Orphanage. At the dedication of a new wing of the Catholic House of Providence, the archbishop thanked representatives of various charitable organizations for attending, particularly "Mr. Goldwin Smith, who is always impartial in his charity and generosity, who knows no creed or race and sets up no barriers in the direction of his good work."[44] He contributed largely to work among the poor of the neighbourhood carried on by the Beverley Street Baptist church which (although a member of the Church of England) he sometimes attended. Countless appeals from the Salvation Army, the St. George's Society, nursing missions, labour temples, boys' clubs, orphanages, and old people's homes all met with a ready response.

To the relief of distress and to the more difficult constructive attack on the causes of social problems he gave not only his money, but what he valued much more, his time. One of his first public lectures in Toronto was given to help raise money for a newsboys' home. The social welfare activities in which he took part were remarkably varied. He sponsored penal reform,[45] chaired meetings of the Toronto Women's Christian Association, served on the governing boards of hospitals, and was the chief financial supporter of an athletic club which provided recreational facilities for young men. In recognition of his public services and his particular interest in charitable work he was elected vice-president of the National Conference of Charities and Correction.

Together with J. E. Pell, secretary of the St. George's Society, and John Bailie of the Irish Protestant Benevolent Society, he founded the Associated Charities of Toronto.[46] This body acted as a clearing house for existing social agencies, gave outdoor relief, and provided the city council with information on which to base its grants to charitable agencies. To the Associated Charities alone Goldwin Smith customarily gave an annual subscription of $1,000, and for many years served as its president. But while he thought it desirable to link together individual charities in an organization of this sort, he was convinced that in a large city like Toronto all outdoor relief should be distributed from

[44]*Catholic Register*, May 28, 1896.
[45]He expounded his progressive views on this subject in an address to the National Prison Congress, reported in the *Week*, Sept. 15, 1887.
[46]The Associated Charities represented the following organizations: the Ladies Relief Society, the St. George's Society, the St. Andrew's Society, the Irish Protestant Benevolent Society, and the St. Vincent de Paul Society. The city relief officer was also included after provision was made for this office in 1893.

a single centre under a municipal board, leaving the private agencies free to do their own specialized work.

In a presidential address on social problems to a conference of the combined city charities in 1889, he expressed regret that the city gaol was still used as a place of confinement for the mentally ill, but satisfaction that at least it no longer served as a poorhouse for sick and destitute labourers, committed on purely nominal charges of vagrancy. The changing temper of the times was apparent in his stress on the manifold causes of destitution, such as lack of work, individual misfortune, illness, old age, and accidents, in addition to the traditional explanations of indolence, improvidence, and vice. In this address he touched on many questions still vigorously debated by social workers in the middle of the twentieth century: the types of service which should be carried on under private as opposed to public auspices, the place of public assistance, and the underlying causes and proposed remedies for poverty.[47]

Goldwin Smith was early involved in what proved a lengthy and difficult effort to persuade Canadians in general and Torontonians in particular to recognize that public welfare services were needed even in a young country whose pioneering days were not yet over. He understood the reluctance to concede the need of permanent provision for the poor, but pointed out that, since poverty was among them, its problems, however unwelcome, could not be evaded simply because they were difficult. In the last resort responsibility for people in want must rest somewhere, and it could scarcely be laid with propriety on even the most devoted volunteers. When in 1881 a leading man declared that no one in Canada who was willing to work could want bread, Goldwin Smith retorted that unfortunately this was a dream of the past. He was impatient with the common assumption that poverty sprang largely from personal inadequacies of character. In any event a Christian nation could not allow anyone, however culpable, to starve. Despite Canadian unwillingness to adopt a poor law, it seemed to him inevitable that some public and regular provision for the poor must come. Although only in the Maritime Provinces was such provision then made (under legislation similar to the Elizabethan Poor Law), the Toronto House of Industry, which received a subsidy from the city, was in fact scarcely distinguishable from a poorhouse. Goldwin Smith argued that Canada had outgrown the period when casual want could be adequately relieved by private charity. It was surely futile to talk of making the churches the agents of charity. How, he demanded, was one to inquire into the church

[47]*Social Problems* (Toronto, 1889), 4–5, 13–19.

membership of a waif who presented himself late at night and famishing at the door?[48]

The depression of the eighteen-eighties revealed an unsuspected amount of hopeless and friendless destitution for which nothing but state aid could provide. Beggars began to besiege the gates of the Grange, and people without work thronged to the mayor's office, asking for lodging in the city gaol. On a single night three hundred men and women sought shelter in the town's police stations. Under these circumstances Goldwin Smith redoubled his efforts to persuade the reluctant citizens of Toronto that it was necessary to appoint a public welfare officer who would both relieve distress and help to prevent the waste of charitable donations to the clamorous but undeserving. No one familiar with the subject could doubt the superiority of expert and regular to casual and inexpert alms-giving.

To say that the substitution of such an officer [he wrote in the *Week* for December 13, 1883] for the half organized visiting, the blind benevolence, and the ridiculous employment of the chief magistrate of the city as a superintendent of tramps, which constitute our present system, would undermine the independence of our people, is surely absurd.

Age and infirmity were no crimes, and prisons no proper refuge for the old and helpless. Ten years later he put the case for a municipal relief officer in a succinct letter to a Toronto alderman.

Without such an officer devoting his whole time to the subject and conversant with the characters of the city, you cannot expose imposture, direct the unemployed to employment, collect and record the necessary information, act or set the authorities in motion when authoritative action is required, meet urgent cases, forward waifs to their destination, or keep the different charities mutually informed and prevent them overlapping each other and encouraging the growth of pauperism with which we are threatened.[49]

When, largely owing to his efforts over two decades, a city welfare officer was at last appointed in 1893, his salary for the first two years was paid by Goldwin Smith. This official controlled the grants of money given by the city to various social agencies, and was responsible to a charities commission appointed by the mayor. Smith was a member of this body and frequently chaired its meetings. He repeatedly attacked the idea that public relief pauperized, arguing that what really demoralized was assistance given unwisely, as private charity was too apt to be. What, after all, was free education, he asked, but a vast system of public

[48]*Bystander*, I (Jan., 1880), 25; II (May, 1881), 246-8; III (July, 1883), 206-7.
[49]Letter to Alderman Burns, Sept. 21, 1893.

relief, for the most part received by those not in need? A good outdoor relief system, providing information, guidance, and observation as well as assistance, he considered no less necessary than good sanitation and a good police force. By the strength of this argument, long accepted in England, half a century later most Canadian local authorities remained unconvinced. The primary requirements, in Goldwin Smith's opinion, were strict investigation and adaptation of the assistance given to the need of the individual. In an early plea for professional social work he contended that investigation could be effectively performed only by trained visitors or by those who had abundance of time as well as special aptitude for such tasks.[50]

Public employment bureaux seemed to him as essential as public relief. He urged that every Canadian city and town should provide a labour exchange. In the eighteen-nineties there were few proponents of the right to work. Goldwin Smith argued that in a land of plenty and industry it was both just and feasible to ensure that no one able to work should suffer from lack of opportunity to do so.[51]

During the depression of the previous decade there was much criticism in Canada of the unselected immigration encouraged by the federal government and the railway and steamship companies, with the enthusiastic co-operation of English charitable agencies. Goldwin Smith wrote bitterly:

Four hundred and ninety-five applicants for a night's shelter at a single police station in one month, more than eighteen hundred families relieved by two private associations in Toronto in the course of the winter, the street outside the House of Industry blocked by a destitute crowd, and men by scores sent to the city gaol to save them from starvation are surely signs of danger not to be disregarded.[52]

At the request of the Toronto social agencies, overburdened by demands from large numbers of unemployed, many of them newcomers to Canada, he wrote English papers suggesting that as work was scarce, prospective immigrants would be wise to satisfy themselves in advance that openings would be available. Only able-bodied farmers and domestic servants found employment easy to obtain, and trade unionists were protesting against bringing skilled workers into the country. This letter provoked the wrath of the *Empire*, which delivered a series of editorial blasts against "our domestic enemies . . . the calumnious letter of Pro-

[50]Letter to the *Evening Telegram*, Nov. 7, 1901; *Canada and the Canadian Question* (Toronto, 1891), 45–6; *Globe*, Oct. 13, 1893.
[51]*Week*, Nov. 14, 1890.   [52]*Ibid.*, June 12, 1884.

fessor Goldwin Smith and the insulting misrepresentation of some members of the Associated Charities."⁵³ It made no attempt, however, to refute the statement that four per cent of the population of Toronto was dependent on private charity: the allegation which had particularly incensed government spokesmen. Unfortunately for the men and women out of work, their plight was used by politicians of both Canadian parties as a stick with which to beat their opponents. The Liberals declared that Sir John A. Macdonald's high tariff was largely responsible for shutting out cheap American goods and thus for provoking a recession of trade. Conservatives countered that the National Policy helped to protect industry and that without it business would have been much worse off that it was. The unresolved argument occupied energy which might better have been devoted to constructive attack on the problem of unemployment.

Goldwin Smith gave only qualified approval to the immigration of the Doukhobors, sponsored by his friend Professor Mavor of the University of Toronto and commended by Kropotkin. Many Canadians, he granted, would prefer British immigrants, yet the Doukhobors were welcome. Exiles for conscience' sake were sure to be religious, and likely to be moral and industrious. They might be good farmers, yet it would not therefore follow that they would be good citizens or good social and political material for a new British community. He feared they were socially uncongenial and politically blind. Surely it was a mistake to suppose that mere increase of population without regard to quality was necessarily a sign of prosperity. When the Doukhobors had been several years in the country and seemed likely to prove less than model settlers, Goldwin Smith counselled patience. They could not be blamed for induging their eccentricities, since it was avowedly to indulge at least some of these (such as refusal to undergo military service) that they had come to Canada in the first place. He thought it time, however, by the beginning of the twentieth century, to limit the importation into the Northwest of the waifs of Europe. He questioned whether the Government's policy of encouraging such immigrants was as good for the country as it undoubtedly was for the railway companies and speculators in land. Some of them had admittedly proved hard workers and in this way good additions to the population. But it would probably take generations for them to become assimilated in character and customs and to make good Canadian citizens. Even the digestive power of the United States, which Canada could not aspire to equal, had begun to

⁵³*Empire*, Feb. 5, 21, and 24, 1890.

flag. In his opinion the best settlers were connections of British immigrants already established in the Dominion, Americans, and Canadians who could be persuaded to return from the other side of the border.[54]

Within a few months of the time that the *Empire* was abusing Goldwin Smith roundly as a traitor whom the great majority of Canadians regarded with deserved loathing and contempt, the Associated Charities Conference presented him with an address of appreciation. This referred in warm terms to the courtesy, ability, and kindness with which he had presided over their deliberations, and to his sympathy and generosity toward the sick and needy. Such an acknowledgement was a pleasant change from constant criticism by Canadians who disliked his political views. A Toronto newspaper commented that the tribute was well deserved, as the time and services he had given the Associated Charities were invaluable. Whatever the merits or demerits of his political ideas, there was "but one opinion as to the deeds of generous Christian charity which are one of the governing impulses of his private life and kindly nature."[55]

His active concern to attack social problems was the more impressive since his major occupation was that of a political journalist and literary man. The belief that those for whom the lines had fallen in pleasant places had a responsibility for the less fortunate, a view always more prevalent in England than in Canada, was among his strongest convictions. It was early apparent in one of his lectures at Oxford, where he maintained that society was the necessary medium of man's moral development, and that morality required the individual to give active service to the community. Such a concept of ethics, which regarded man as essentially a social being, bore hardly on indolent wealth, on sinecurism, and on all who lived by the labour of others. Greed viewed in this light, although it might not violate the law, was still robbery of the common store, at once immoral and fatuous.[56] Throughout Goldwin Smith's long life his thought and actions were dominated by this consciousness of *noblesse oblige*.

[54]*Weekly Sun*, Feb. 1, 1899, Sept. 17, 1902, Sept. 23, 1903, May 18, 1904, Aug. 16, 1905.
[55]*Sentinel*, June 14, 1890; *Mail*, June 10, 1890.
[56]*Lectures on the Study of History* (Oxford, 1865), 107, 116–17.

V. CANADA: LATER LIFE

AS HE GREW OLDER Goldwin Smith sometimes spoke of retiring from political journalism. Actually he never did. But while he could still embalm an enemy in an epigram, he began to weary of continual controversy, and turned for relief to literary and historical studies. During the last fifteen years of the century he wrote all his biographies, his principal histories, and most of his verse translations from the classics. He exercised his patience, as a friend once remarked, more on polishing his periods than on meticulous research, and relied on wide reading in secondary rather than primary sources. To his patience the numerous scorings, revisions, and rewording of his manuscripts bear abundant witness. English letters, always the resource of his leisure, became more and more his latter-day hobby. Despite his liking for and familiarity with literature, he was not a successful critic. "Taste," he once said, in a revealing definition, "is aesthetic common-sense."[1] His best writing was in reviews for the New York *Nation* and his own *Bystander*, and these were essentially journalism rather than literary analysis. Both as biographer and historian he was mainly interested in human motives and character.

I

A Trip to England appeared in 1888. Although primarily intended as a guide book for North American tourists, it attempted a bird's-eye view, not only of places of historical interest, but of the social and political problems of contemporary Britain. The success of this endeavour was indicated by Ostrogorski's reference to "this very remarkable tiny volume."[2] Goldwin Smith published a book on Cowper in 1880, on Jane Austen ten years later, on William Lloyd Garrison in 1892, and

[1] "Burke," *Cornhill Magazine*, I (July, 1896), 17–29.
[2] M. Ostrogorski, *Democracy and the Organization of Political Parties* (London, 1902), I, 618.

on *Shakespeare: The Man* in 1899. *My Memory of Gladstone*, a little study expanded from two long review articles on Morley's *Life of Gladstone*, appeared in 1904. Of these works the short life of Garrison was the most effective, dealing as it did with a leader in the American crusade against slavery in which Goldwin Smith had taken so active an interest. Between Garrison and his biographer there was a natural affinity: both were journalists, both controversialists, and both haters of slavery. Smith's book painted an attractive portrait of a man whom he greatly respected.

Cowper and Jane Austen, as social satirists, were congenial subjects for a master of satire. His studies of them were commissioned: *Cowper* for the English Men of Letters series, and *Jane Austen* for the Great Writers series. In comparison with his best work, both read like potboilers, as in a sense they were. The less successful of the two was *Jane Austen*, which consisted largely of synopses of her novels, little biographical material being available. He appreciated her quiet irony, and aptly compared her to a miniature painter. But the lives of the "genteel idlers" whom she portrayed he found "necessarily somewhat vapid," although he admired her capacity to hold a mirror up to one small facet of human nature. His comment that she was not interested in politics or social problems suggests merely what Goldwin Smith found lacking in Jane Austen. As literary critic and political journalist he assessed people, less on the basis of what they did or tried to do, than on how far they met or fell short of his own preconceptions of conduct and character.

His life of *Cowper*, as the *Westminster Review* with some justice observed, was the least successful among the English Men of Letters series. The *Saturday Review* thought it hardly calculated to increase the reputation of either the author or his subject. Cowper was, however, a better subject than Jane Austen for Goldwin Smith, who painted the poet against the background of the social, political, and religious movements of his day. The effect of such influences on Cowper's work was what most interested him. More biography than literary criticism, the study gave a sympathetic treatment of Cowper's mental illness, a subject of which Goldwin Smith's experience with his father had given him some understanding. Cowper, however, was a poet. His biographer liked his poems only when their ideas coincided with his own.

In poetry his taste tended toward the rhythmic and robust. Despite his early strictures on *Maud*, to which he objected less on poetic grounds than because it glorified war, he enjoyed Tennyson. He not only liked the beauty of the Poet Laureate's language and the melody of his verse, but approved of his ideas. Tennyson to him was the perfect mirror of contemporary English society. To speak of him as a great teacher was absurd, said Smith, because he had no settled opinions to teach. He was the poet of doubt, with *In Memoriam* reflecting the religious uncertainty of the day. Here Goldwin Smith had a natural bond with Tennyson, for he himself was deeply concerned with ethical and religious problems. With the current enthusiasm for a latter-day mediaevalism, illustrated in the work of both Tennyson and Morris, he was too practical to be sympathetic, and doubted the success of such attempts to revive the past. The student of history, in his view, must recognize the moral interest of the Middle Ages, as an artist recognized their aesthetic interest, but the mould was broken, and nineteenth-century mediaevalism seemed to him an enfeebling dream. He feared that a pining for the past might make men unjust to their own age, and lessen their interest in a practical attack on current problems. A schism between aesthetic Oxford, for instance, and industrial Lancashire would be bad for both.[3] Goldwin Smith clearly had little flair for aesthetics, yet in the hey-day of the Pre-Raphaelite movement his criticism showed some perspicacity.

Of Scott's poetry he never tired, though he thought it by no means equal to the "incomparable fiction." His writing on Scott, unlike his study of Cowper, came from the heart. To begin with, he approved of Scott as a man—"that paragon of pure-minded and noble-hearted gentlemen"—and for Goldwin Smith this was a *sine qua non* for real appreciation. He could imagine no better antidote to depression than the rousing lines through which readers breathed the air of the Scottish hills. "One might almost as well," he wrote, "try to argue a man into or out of love for a woman as into or out of taste for a poet. Boys will be boys, and will persist in venerating Browning and loving Scott."[4]

Philosophizing in poetry had for him little appeal, and he confessed his inability to understand, and therefore to appreciate, Browning, "that philosopher in verse with Browning societies to interpret his poetry." Obscurity, in Goldwin Smith's opinion, was perhaps permissible in metaphysics, but not in poetry. The great modern poets and all the great writers of every age were clear. A twentieth-century reader may be forgiven some satisfaction at his forthright declaration that "if it is the writer that is obscure, the obscurity may safely be set down not to the depth of the stream but to its muddiness."[5]

His favourite hobby was translating classical poets into English verse,

[3]Address delivered to the Oxford School of Science and Art, published in the *Oxford Chronicle*, Nov. 30, 1877.
[4]"Scott's Poetry Again," *Atlantic Monthly*, XCV (March, 1905), 300–2.
[5]Lecture at Cornell on "The Future of Poetry," published in the *Sun* (New York), May 14, 1899; "English Poetry and English History," *American Historical Review*, X (Oct., 1904), 28–40.

an exercise in which he had excelled at Eton and Oxford. He read Greek and Latin as easily as English, and when travelling liked to take Homer or Ovid with him for relaxation. When the students at Cornell or Toronto asked him to write something for their undergraduate journals, his usual contribution was a verse translation from Horace or the Greek Anthology. *Bay Leaves*, a little volume of translations from the Latin poets, was privately printed in 1890 for informal distribution to friends. Three years later he published two volumes of translations from the Greek dramatists, *Specimens of Greek Tragedy*. In the preface to *Bay Leaves* he suggested that it was hardly possible for anything but a free translation of poetry to give the spirit of the original. The general idea and mood were all a translator could usually hope to reproduce, since the more literal he strove to be, the more fetters he imposed on himself. Works like those of Plato and Tacitus, whose principal excellence lay in their style, could not be adequately translated. Great poets could not be translated at all, and great orators only imperfectly. Furthermore a gulf of thought and feeling between the ideas of the original and of the translator imposed almost insuperable difficulties. In the case of Homer the only solution was a prose translation. "The translation of Homer into verse," he wrote in his study of Cowper, "is the Polar Expedition of literature, always failing, yet still desperately renewed." Such remarks check criticism of the writer's own translations. Goldwin Smith would have been the first to admit that his own attempts were among the polar expeditions. He had sense enough to realize that he was no poet. His verse translations, like those of many another classical scholar, were merely ingenious exercises for his own amusement. As such they fulfilled their purpose.

History and politics, like life itself, he considered pre-eminently schools of morality. He himself was less an historian than a pamphleteer, though, in the phrase he applied to Burke, a prince of pamphleteers. Adept in marshalling arguments to support his own views, he found it difficult to be fair to those with which he disagreed. His history of the United States, published in 1893, was generally acclaimed, although Southerners disliked its pro-Northern bias in treating the Civil War. The book was primarily designed to interpret American history to Englishmen, a task its author had first begun at Oxford, some thirty years earlier, in his lectures on the American colonies. His use of history as a vehicle for his own moral judgments as usual irritated critics. Among the reviewers was Woodrow Wilson, then a young staff member at Princeton, who asked with some acerbity whether the author was writing homilies or history.

Lord Acton thought that Goldwin Smith discussed men's motives and character far oftener than befitted an historian, and suggested that a more painstaking study of original sources might have saved him from mistakes in fact and judgment. His real interest, Acton rightly observed, lay in politics rather than history. Lord Acton himself, however, made many moral judgments of men and events, and held strongly the view that history is a study in ethics. As editor of the projected *Cambridge Modern History* he asked Goldwin Smith to contribute one or more chapters on any part of the eighteenth or nineteenth century. Had his *United States* not already been published, Acton wished that it might have been kept for a much larger volume in the *Cambridge Modern History*. He would, he wrote, be especially grateful for a contribution large or small "in memory of the days when you made Regius Professorships of Modern History illustrious."[6]

Goldwin Smith's major work on English history, published in 1899, when he was seventy-five years old, was *The United Kingdom*, a study intended to interpret Great Britain to the United States. Like its predecessor, the book sold widely on both sides of the Atlantic. Its lively running commentaries on events were not objective, but showed its author's old capacity for brilliant writing. His early belief that the study of history was the study of politics reappeared more clearly than ever, with primary emphasis placed on the theory, development, and practice of the state. Social and economic problems were not ignored, but their significance in comparison with political issues tended to be underestimated. Goldwin Smith here made no more effort than in earlier books to conceal his own strongly marked personality, and once again displayed a lack of sympathy with the mental attitude of other times than his own. But critics were disarmed by the confession in the preface that the friends who had urged him to undertake this task knew that it was performed by the hand of extreme old age.

II

In his adopted country he grew steadily more unpopular, owing to his persistent and public advocacy of commercial union between Canada and the United States. In 1891 he delivered to the Young Men's Liberal

[6]Lord Acton, "Mr. Goldwin Smith on the Political History of England" (review of *Three English Statesmen* in the *Chronicle*, Aug. 31, 1867), reprinted in *Essays on Church and State* (London, 1952), 406–10; letter to Goldwin Smith, Dec. 25, 1896, Autograph Album, The Grange, Art Gallery of Toronto.

Club three addresses published under the title of *Loyalty, Aristocracy and Jingoism*. These speeches, as he later explained, were intended to be defensive not aggressive, an answer to Conservative attacks at the preceding general election on the loyalty of Canadian Liberals. The *Globe*, reporting one lecture almost verbatim, observed that the pleasure of its readers would be accompanied by regret at the speaker's decision that this was his last political utterance. Such a tribute from the same paper in which George Brown had earlier abused him was explained by the fact that the *Globe* and Goldwin Smith had become allied supporters of unrestricted reciprocity. Regrets about his abstention from political comment proved premature.

Despite the sanguine expectations of the *Globe*, some Torontonians did not receive his speeches with pleasure. Among these was Colonel George Denison, who made them the occasion of a violent personal attack on Goldwin Smith and his views.[7] Denison was among the most imperialistic and loyal citizens of an imperialistic and loyal city. He had supported the South and slavery during the American Civil War, and had won a prize offered by the Russian Czar for the best cavalry manual ever written. Although a local police magistrate, he did not carry on controversy by rational argument, but proposed to attack with his sword any advocate of union between Canada and the United States.

Some years later, at the Upper Canada College prize day, Goldwin Smith was asked to present the award in classics, as he had done for the past two decades. Colonel Denison, also on the platform, seized the opportunity to attack (without mentioning names) "the intrigues of a few men who were trying to place their country under the flag of the United States . . . and who should be behind prison bars instead of here in this room."

Another encounter with Colonel Denison occurred in 1895, when Goldwin Smith was invited to propose a toast to Canada at a Press Association dinner. Colonel Denison promptly announced that in Russia a man like him would long since have been sent to the mines of Siberia, in France to a convict settlement, and in the United States to a lynching gang. This attack created a public furore. At the press banquet the Prime Minister, Sir Mackenzie Bowell, and other speakers were well received, but Goldwin Smith was given an impressive ovation. Brief and non-controversial, his address concluded with the comment that he had never been afraid to say what he believed. He was sure that Cana-

[7]In a lecture on "National Spirit," delivered at Toronto, Dec. 17, 1891, and published as Appendix B to Denison's *Struggle for Imperial Unity* (London, 1909).

dians could look confidently to the future, whatever it might bring, for Canada's destiny was in her own hands.

The press treated the incident as a question of free speech. Many editors of small newspapers in little Ontario towns, regardless of whether they shared Goldwin Smith's political views, supported him as the protagonist of independent journalism against the strictures of Colonel Denison and the *Empire*. The Hamilton *Herald* declared that the calm assumption of a few imperial federationists that they monopolized loyalty in Canada was a "cool piece of cheek." The reception given Goldwin Smith, the little *Dundas True Banner* observed, was a protest against attempts to prevent citizens from expressing their own opinions.[8] In this newspaper debate, where the honours were won by the defenders of free speech, Goldwin Smith himself took no part.

He was also involved in an acrimonious controversy with the St. George's Society, a social and benevolent organization, formed to promote friendly intercourse among its members and to provide relief for poverty-stricken British families in Toronto. Goldwin Smith had been elected a life member in 1879, when his political opinions were already well known. For some ten years he was one of the most generous contributors to its charitable funds, and was active in its work. Toward the end of this period a number of the members began to criticize him for his political views. As a result he practically retired from the Society, but did not resign his membership.

When in 1893 Goldwin Smith and his wife were visiting the United States, Castell Hopkins, a member of the editorial staff of the highly Conservative *Empire*, moved at a meeting of the St. George's Society that "in view of his advocacy of the annexation of the Dominion of Canada to the United States, his position as President of the Continental Union Association of Toronto, and the treason to his Sovereign, to England, and to Canada, involved in these conditions, this body of loyal Englishmen request Mr. Goldwin Smith to tender his resignation as a life member of the St. George's Society." This was the first and last time that Castell Hopkins was active in the Society, and it turned out that he was technically disqualified from making the motion, since he had not paid his fees. He was, however, secretary of the Imperial Federation League, whose president happened also to be president of

---

[8]Feb. 7 and Jan. 17, 1895; Hamilton *Herald*, Jan. 15 and 18, 1895. Similar views were expressed by the *Globe*, Jan. 15, 18, 19, 22, and Feb. 1, 1895; the Goderich *Signal*, Feb. 7, 1895; the Port Hope *Evening Guide*, Jan. 17, 1895; and the Mitchell *Recorder*, Jan. 25, 1895. Goldwin Smith was attacked by such Conservative papers as the *Empire*, the Stratford *Evening Herald*, and the *Hamilton Spectator*.

the St. George's Society. Hopkins was finally persuaded to agree to a somewhat milder statement, which was carried. "The Society desires emphatically to place on record," it ran, "its strong disapprobation . . . and its extreme regret that the Society should contain within its ranks a member who is striving for an object which would cause an irreparable injury to the Dominion, would entail a loss to the mother land of a most important part of the empire, and would deprive Canadians of their birthright as British subjects."

The local newspapers enthusiastically joined the controversy. Despite the *Globe*'s frequent differences with Goldwin Smith, it considered that an English scholar known all over the Empire ought not to be denounced and lampooned for his opinions.[9] Goldwin Smith for his part pointed out that independence for Canada, to which many people, including the Premier of Ontario, looked forward, would mean severing the link with the British Crown quite as much as would union with the United States. He had no intention of allowing the St. George's Society to interfere with his convictions as a man or his conduct as a citizen. Six months later he resigned his membership.

Thirty years earlier, in England, Goldwin Smith's opinions on the need for colonial emancipation had conflicted sharply with the views of the conservative governing classes whose mouthpiece was *The Times*. In Toronto it was inevitable that his dislike of imperialism and war, his admiration for the United States, and his ideas about the political destiny of Canada should collide with those of local Tories. Colonel Denison and his friends took enormous pride in their United Empire Loyalist stock. Their forbears had made a virtue of refusing to help build the United States as an independent nation, and had come to Canada in the eighteenth century because they would not support revolution against Great Britain. The descendants of these early Loyalists were traditionally conservative, strongly colonial in outlook, and deeply convinced that to be pro-English meant to be anti-American. With them loyalty to Britain was a fetich. In the British North American colonies they formed the nearest approach to a governing class. Often better educated than other members of the community, they considered themselves, and were generally considered, a social élite. In practice, however, their pretensions were limited by the uncongenial atmosphere which the New World provided for aristocracy. To the exploits of their Loyalist ancestors they looked back with the nostalgic pride of the

---

[9]Feb. 7, March 3, 6, 8, and 10, 1893. The *Empire* supported Hopkins in a series of editorials. Typical among these was one on March 3, under the caption, "The Disgraced Professor."

GOLDWIN SMITH
From a charcoal drawing by F. Sandys in the White Library,
Cornell University.

modern Afrikaner for the Voertrekkers. To them the United States was a nation of raw democrats, whose grandfathers and great-grandfathers had been traitors to England. "Traitor," the worst epithet in their repertory, was the only appropriate description for renegade Englishmen who admired America and its republican institutions. Insult was added to injury when the advocacy of closer relations between Canada and the United States and more flexible relations with England emanated from the Grange, the former home of the Family Compact. There were Canadian nationalists who were not Empire Loyalists, and who, although attached to the British connection, were primarily interested in building a new nation. These naturally disagreed with Goldwin Smith and said so, but for the most part they respected his integrity and considered him entitled to his erroneous opinions. Outside of the Maritimes, however, Toronto was the centre of United Empire Loyalism, as it was also the centre of a grim Ulster Orangeism. A less congenial atmosphere for a man of Goldwin Smith's views cannot be imagined.

For his part, accustomed to the English practice of allowing men like Bright and Cobden to advocate Little England doctrines as freely as they chose, he was puzzled and resentful at being attacked as a traitor in colonies more vociferously loyal than Britain itself. By this time over seventy, he had little taste for personal controversy. With a sense of relief he bade farewell to the vituperation of Toronto, and in the autumn of 1893 departed with his wife for a seven months' visit to England.

III

Goldwin Smith's interest in education, shown early in Britain, continued throughout his life in Canada. He was among the first and most persistent advocates of federation to solve the problems of Ontario's struggling universities. A federal solution had been discussed before he settled in the province, but he did much to help win acceptance for it. Shortly after his arrival, he proposed that all the institutions of higher learning should federate into one university, modelled on Oxford, in which the colleges retained their own identity, but admissions and examinations were controlled and degrees conferred by the university. At Oxford he had known such a scheme at first hand, and at Cornell had learned much about the problems of competing colleges, poor in every sense of the word.

He was anxious that Ontario should avoid "the calamitous dispersion of resources and the equally calamitous prostitution of degrees," which friends of higher education deplored in the United States. A small university, he insisted, could mean only an inadequate and underpaid staff, a poor library, inferior scientific equipment, depreciated degrees, and a feeble intellectual life—in short, inferior education. He believed that a small university was necessarily a bad university, narrow in outlook and ineffective in achievement. Unfortunately, the weaker the college the more likely it was to cling to its isolation and to its untrammelled facilities for graduation. Nothing was more destructive of high standards than the American system of "one-horse" colleges, with staffs whose training and numbers were more appropriate for secondary schools than for a great university. Such institutions were not competent to teach everything they professed to teach, and wasted the time of students who, not being taught thoroughly, were not really taught at all. Ontario's resources were inadequate to maintain more than one first-class university. A non-sectarian university, with denominational colleges giving religious instruction and moral discipline, met the reasonable requirements of religion, while it also secured the best education. He hoped that the provincial government would soon lead the way in this reform.[10] A generous gift of money, conditional on its removal to Toronto, eventually helped to persuade Victoria College to migrate from Cobourg. Goldwin Smith was among the speakers at its formal opening in the city in 1892, and three years later delivered the convocation address. A decade later Trinity followed Victoria's example in becoming a federated college within the University of Toronto. Principal Grant's decision that Queen's University should remain independent in Kingston, Goldwin Smith proclaimed an unfortunate mistake. His practical interest in the University of Toronto was shown by his establishment of a scholarship in classics, his contributions to new buildings, and his bequest to its library of his own books, reputed to be the finest private collection in the city.

When in 1895 certain frictions arose between staff and students, five commissioners were appointed to inquire into the university's affairs. At the request of the Chancellor, Goldwin Smith consented to confer with them, although he disapproved of settling such matters by a public commission, and thought they might better be handled privately within the university. His main recommendation, which was not adopted, was that the university should administer itself and be made completely independent of the provincial government. He believed wholeheartedly in the English system which entrusted to universities responsibility for

[10]*Canadian Monthly*, III (March, 1873), 234–5; VI (Oct., 1874), 358–9; "University Questions in England," *Princeton Review*, Nov., 1879, 451–70.

their own government, thus placing them beyond the reach of political control. Ten years later a step in this direction was taken by providing a separate Board of Governors for the university, whose members, however, were appointed by the provincial government.

In 1896 the nominating committee of the University Senate proposed that the honorary degree of LL.D. should be conferred on Goldwin Smith, and the recommendation was unanimously approved by the Senate. Thereupon one of its members, Mr. Justice Falconbridge, resigned, on the ground that the atmosphere of the Senate was no longer congenial to him as a British subject and the holder of a commission from the Queen. He thought it unnecessary to say why he found fault with conferring an honorary degree on Goldwin Smith, as everyone loyal to the Crown would understand his motives. He predicted that the university's grotesque decision would prove disastrous, since thousands of parents would ask themselves whether it was safe to entrust to such an institution responsiblity for moulding the characters of young men. His letter of resignation, published in the local newspapers, promptly aroused a lively controversy. The proposal to give the degree was attacked by the *Week* and the *Mail and Empire*, and eleven law graduates petitioned the Senate to refrain from honouring a man who advocated the severance of Canada from the British Empire. The editor of the *Mail and Empire* wrote to Goldwin Smith: "You trade on the clemency shown to traitors at the end of the 19th century. In what we call the good old times you would have been hanged, Sir."[11]

The *World* published an indignant letter from Colonel Denison, declaring that Canada never had a more bitter and active enemy than Goldwin Smith. If the Senate persisted in honouring such a person, Denison requested that his name should be struck off the list of university graduates. Somewhat similar sentiments were expressed by Principal Grant of Queen's.[12] It was reported that the Vice-Chancellor

---

[11] Letter from T. C. Patteson, June 23, 1896, copy in Patteson Papers, Public Archives of Ontario; *Week*, May 22, June 12, July 24, 1896; *Globe*, June 9 and 13, 1896; *Mail and Empire*, June 10, 1896.

The conferring of the degree was warmly supported by academic men like Professor James Mavor and Chancellor Burwash of Victoria College. The latter, who was also to be given an LL.D., asked to withdraw his name when he heard that Goldwin Smith had done so.

[12] G. M. Grant, "Canada and the Empire," *National Review*, XXVII (July, 1896). This was an attack on Goldwin Smith's views about the union of Canada and the United States. Smith replied in a personal letter to Grant on Aug. 19, 1896, and in an article in the *Canadian Magazine*, VII (Oct., 1896). The next month Grant published a rejoinder in the same journal. Grant's attack was criticized by the Winnipeg *Tribune* (which opposed annexation) in an editorial on "Dr. Goldwin Smith and Dr. Grant," Oct. 19, 1896.

declined to preside at the convocation when the degree was to be conferred. Two days after the publication of Colonel Denison's protest, the *Mail* printed the following letter from Goldwin Smith to the President of the university:

MY DEAR PRESIDENT LOUDON,

When, in pursuance as you said, of the unanimous vote of the University Senate, you offered me an honorary degree you were probably not aware that there would be any opposition or manifestation of ill-feeling in other quarters. For myself, accustomed to the manly and generous habits of English gentlemen, who make it their rule to lay aside political enmity in social life, I could not anticipate that in a matter so remote from politics as the bestowal of an academical degree political antipathy would find an occasion for its display. It is now evident that I was mistaken, and that this little compliment paid to me as a scholar is likely to bring on the university more annoyance and disturbance of its proper dignity than anything of the kind can possibly be worth. I will therefore beg to withdraw my acceptance of the honorary degree of Toronto University and rest content with that which has already been conferred upon me by my own University of Oxford.

Let me at the same time assure you and the Senate of my undiminished gratitude for the intended honour.

After the honorary degrees had been conferred at the convocation, the students who crowded the top gallery called for cheers for Goldwin Smith, which were lustily given. President Loudon rose to express his

extreme regret that the gentleman for whom you have just given three cheers is not here to receive the honour which the Senate of the university unanimously decided to confer upon him on this occasion. The reason for his absence is doubtless known to all present, as his letter of explanation is published in this morning's papers. Professor Smith's reputation as a scholar is so high, and the academic distinctions conferred upon him by other universities so marked, that it would have been a great honour to this university to have enrolled him among our list of doctors of law.[13]

These comments received another enthusiastic outburst of applause.

The furore aroused in Toronto over the LL.D. brought the university much criticism, although, as President Loudon pointed out, protests against giving the degree were made by less than a score out of a Convocation of more than four thousand. The Senate promptly passed a resolution regretting Goldwin Smith's withdrawal of his name, and recording its disapproval of the attacks which induced him to do so. Professor Clark of Trinity declared publicly that if any man alive would bring honour to any university in the world by accepting its degree, it was Goldwin Smith. The Toronto Trades and Labor Council, usually uninterested in university affairs, rallied to his support, although, as

[13]*Globe*, June 13, 1896.

they noted, they frequently disagreed with his views on economic questions. Goldwin Smith replied appreciatively: "If as a political economist I am somewhat conservative, perhaps my years may plead my excuse. But I sincerely trust that I shall never prefer the interest of any class or section of the community to the material welfare of the whole people, or shrink as a member of a class from any economical change, by which the welfare of the whole people may be promoted. When I do, I shall be false to the faith of the political school in which I was bred, as well as to the dictates of my own heart."[14]

The London correspondent of the *New York Times* observed that the little group of bigots at the University of Toronto might have stopped to reflect if they had realized how England, whose honour they professed to defend, would regard their stupid insult to Goldwin Smith. It simply would not occur to anyone in Britain to allow dislike of a man's political opinions to prevent a tribute to him as a journalist and scholar.[15] Seven years afterward the University of Toronto conferred an honorary degree on Goldwin Smith. On this occasion the only public expression of opinion was prolonged applause when he was presented by the President. Some time later a friend mentioned that the University proposed giving an LL.D. to Lord Milner, whereat Smith (who loathed Milner's South African policies) commented that they would give a degree to the devil if he had a title.

When in 1905 a Royal Commission on the University was set up, Goldwin Smith was appointed a member, together with Sir William Meredith, Byron E. Walker, Joseph (later Sir Joseph) Flavelle, Canon H. J. Cody, D. Bruce Macdonald, and A. H. U. Colquhoun. Owing to increasing deafness Goldwin Smith declined to serve as chairman, but invited the Commission to meet at the Grange, where in a five-month period it held over seventy sessions. His appointment as commissioner was publicly criticized by his old antagonist, Castell Hopkins, but otherwise met with unanimous approval.

The Commission recommended that the university should have its own Board of Governors, appointed by the provincial government, and that responsiblity for purely academic policies should be vested in the Senate. The University Act embodying these recommendations took effect in June, 1906, when most of the members of the Commission, including Goldwin Smith, were appointed to the first Board of Governors. He remained a member until his death four years later. Of his labours on the Commission he wrote Frederic Harrison, "I began with a University Commission. With a University Commission I am end-

[14]*Ibid.*, June 19, 1896.
[15]*New York Times*, June 14, 1896.

ing. . . . The English University has hitherto been a finishing school of culture for a wealthy class and for the clergy. But what the New World demands is an emporium of the knowledge which will lead to wealth. We must try to keep a little culture, while we yield, as yield we must, to the utilitarian tide."[16]

One of the Board of Governors' first tasks was to find a new president for the university, a duty complicated by a variety of conflicting opinions as to the qualifications desired. After months of discussion Goldwin Smith observed wearily to the provincial Premier, James Whitney, "I am greatly bewildered. There is an objection to a stranger, an objection to a clergyman, an objection to one of the present staff on account of connections with cliques and quarrels. What is left?"[17] The choice finally fell on a Maritimer, Robert (later Sir Robert) Falconer, who for many years was to serve the university with distinction.

IV

Goldwin Smith's last major enterprise in Canadian journalism was the *Weekly Sun*, an agricultural paper in which he bought a controlling interest in 1896. W. L. Smith, the former editor of the Toronto *News* (a strong supporter of Canada First), who was currently employed by the Orange *Sentinel*, was secured as editor. Until 1903, however, most of the editorials were written by Walter Dymond Gregory, a Toronto lawyer active in the cause of continental union, who shortly became president of the *Sun* board. The journal had originated, under the name of the *Farmers' Sun*, as the organ of the agrarian movement known as the Patrons of Industry. It generally opposed the Liberal Government of Ontario, and as until 1898 the Patrons were influential in a number of provincial constituencies, the *Sun*'s support was for the most part welcomed by Conservatives. Under Goldwin Smith it was independent in politics but championed the interests of farmers and advocated the views of the Continental Union Association. When he first took it over monthly deficits were usual, and his expenditures on the paper, including the original purchase price, totalled about $30,000—an outlay which he never regretted. Some years before his death he made over his stock in the *Sun* to Gregory and two other members of the board of directors.

[16]Letter to Frederic Harrison, Feb. 20, 1908, *Goldwin Smith's Correspondence*, 495.
[17]Letter to James Whitney, Nov. 5, 1906, Whitney Papers, Public Archives of Ontario.

Gregory found collaboration with Goldwin Smith a liberal education. He was impressed by Smith's care about everything he wrote and by his desire to avoid controversy with other journals. "So long as they are your friends," Goldwin Smith sagely observed, "they will quote you. When you differ from them, do it without naming them; when you agree with them, name them." A paper should be careful, he insisted, not to antagonize before it had built up a strong position. Hence he counselled, "First build your pulpit. Then you can speak from it."[18] This policy was vindicated by the fact that for a time the *Weekly Sun* was more widely quoted than any other newspaper in the province and even found readers to cite it in England. Subscribers often commented that Goldwin Smith's articles alone were well worth the price of the journal, and an English friend remarked on the oddity of finding in a remote and unknown Canadian agricultural weekly, political writing of a calibre which would have won immediate acclaim in any leading British paper.

Goldwin Smith himself thought perhaps his most significant intervention in Canadian public affairs was the help he gave the farmers' movement in Ontario, after the collapse of the Patrons, by rescuing the *Sun* from extinction. His interest in a paper which circulated almost exclusively in rural Ontario was solidly based. If any section of the Canadian community might be expected to support lower tariffs and closer trade relations with the United States, it was the farmers. They formed the most receptive audience for his cherished scheme to abolish barriers between the two English-speaking nations of North America. Moreover he came increasingly to believe that there was much value in the country press, under the influence of the farmers, as opposed to the city press, under the influence of wealthy business interests. Rural journals were more likely to be independent, fair-minded, and wholesome.

From August, 1896, until November, 1909, except for brief intervals when he was out of Canada, Goldwin Smith wrote each week for the *Sun* "Comments on Current Events by a Bystander." In these, as in his earlier articles for the *Canadian Monthly*, the *Week*, and his own *Bystander*, he discussed public affairs in Canada, the United States, Great Britain, and the world at large. The front page of the *Weekly Sun* was devoted to these comments and to editorials, many of which he also wrote. The rest of the paper was typical of the better farmers' magazines, in which the recorded milk yields of prize Jerseys competed for space

---

[18]These details are cited on pp. 115–18 of W. D. Gregory's unpublished autobiography, which is among the Gregory Papers in the Douglas Library at Queen's University, Kingston.

with suggested remedies for diseases in pigs and chickens, or with advice on modern methods of pruning orchards. When Goldwin Smith became proprietor of the *Weekly Sun* he was seventy-three. During the past twenty-five years his receptivity to new ideas had not been marked, and it did not increase with age. As a young man he had found much to condemn in the world around him, and as he grew older he perceived the faults of society more clearly than its virtues. Nevertheless his writing on public affairs gave the *Weekly Sun* a distinction lacked by many wealthy city newspapers with large circulations. The most intelligent farmers of Ontario all hailed its arrival as the event of the week. Without his assistance they felt their voice would scarcely have been heard amid the clamour raised by business interests.

When Goldwin Smith bought the *Sun*, the *Week* was violently attacking him. He wanted some organ to express his views and deliver his cannonades, for he had lost none of his old faith in the virtues of independent journalism, even on such a diminutive scale. Among other causes, the *Sun* championed the Ontario Agricultural College at Guelph, and did much to secure public confidence in it. When the cornerstone of its library was laid, Goldwin Smith delivered the address. The *Weekly Sun* was almost the only paper in English-speaking Canada to support the Boers, not only in the preliminary stages before war was declared, but throughout its course. By so doing it became very unpopular. After the war ended, however, it regained its former position, and in Goldwin Smith's opinion ultimately profited from this proof of its unquestioned independence. As he told Henri Bourassa in 1901, it drew heavily on his purse and his labour, but he wanted to "try to keep it going so long as it can do good. Its constituency, though limited, is attached and has convictions."

In a notice on E. L. Godkin's death Goldwin Smith declared that the journalist no longer feared the monarch's frown or the censor's scissors. The two modern dangers were secret influence and popular passion. Independence entailed sacrifice, which few journalists were willing to make, as they could scarcely hope for compensation. "Nobody," he dryly observed, "who has shared the delusion is ever grateful to the monitor who told the unpalatable truth. From that sacrifice Mr. Godkin never flinched."[19] He here made handsome amends for his quarrel with Godkin, but his comments also applied to his own career as a journalist.

[19]*Weekly Sun*, May 28, 1902. It has been possible to identify Goldwin Smith's unsigned editorials in the *Weekly Sun* from a scrapbook of them made by his secretary, Arnold Haultain, which is preserved among the Goldwin Smith Papers at Cornell.

During the previous four years he had steadily faced unpopularity by criticising the public enthusiasm for war.

There are necessary wars, as we are all aware [he wrote]. There are also unnecessary wars, made by men or parties for the objects of their ambition, gainful to the authors of the war, costly to the people in bread as well as in blood, destructive of industry, poisonous to national character, and subversive of the general interests of humanity. Such was the war of the United States with Spain. . . . Such was this South African war. . . . To oppose such wars in the interest of the people, however much the people may be misguided, is the plain duty of the honest journalist. It is a duty . . . the reverse of lucrative or pleasant; but a duty it is, and in these columns it has to the best of the writer's ability been done.[20]

With increasing concern Goldwin Smith watched newspapers develop the traits of large businesses. He reiterated a warning that one of the greatest dangers of the hour was the secret control of the public press by unscrupulous wealth. By the beginning of the century this seemed to him the most serious question of the day. He deplored the way in which leading newspapers fell into the hands of capitalists who cared little for political principles or for anything but circulation, and their own personal and commercial aggrandizement. Such men made the editor simply an instrument of their designs. With this state of affairs he contrasted the custom of earlier days when the editor of a paper was its owner, who owed nothing to anyone's favour save that of the reading public, and was a literary statesman with a personal sense of political responsibility. The proper function of a journalist, he insisted, was not that of a diplomatist or mere politician; what he owed the public was a fair judgment on the merits of the case before him. His role was the more important, since the pamphlet had almost disappeared, and the newspaper had largely replaced the book. Journalism was not a profession with set qualifications, analogous to those for a legal or medical degree. Hence Goldwin Smith was sceptical about special courses of training for it. The general information necessary for a journalist could be learned at universities; the knack of writing editorials could hardly be taught anywhere, except in the newspaper office. No professional training could provide independence, integrity, and patriotism.[21]

After John Willison became editor of the Toronto *News* in 1902, Goldwin Smith congratulated the journal on its force in braving popular prejudices. Shortly after, in his study of *Sir Wilfrid Laurier and the Liberal Party* Willison commented that Smith's influence had been

[20]*Ibid.*, June 25, 1902.
[21]*Ibid.*, Aug. 26, 1903, Feb. 8 and Sept. 20, 1899, Nov. 19, 1902, Sept. 28, 1904, Aug. 28, 1907.

minimized by his persistent assertion of unpopular opinions. To this Goldwin Smith retorted: "Without 'persistent assertion of unpopular opinions,' to what would the world have come? We might now be worshipping Thor and Woden. No opinion could be more unpopular in its day than disbelief in witchcraft."[22]

The constant public attacks to which in middle life he had been subjected gave way in later years to even more general—and better deserved—plaudits. It became a custom for Toronto newspapers to publish on his birthday appreciative editorials on the "Sage of the Grange," a sentimental sobriquet which Goldwin Smith would certainly have disowned if he could. Among letters received on his eightieth birthday was one from John King, expressing gratitude for his services to independent journalism in Canada. "For this alone," wrote King, "although there is very much more that might be mentioned, you deserve all the honour and reverence that will be paid you publicly and privately to-day." On the same occasion the *Globe* remarked editorially that Goldwin Smith had made his pen-name of "Bystander" as much a household word as his own proper name. It would be difficult, it suggested, to overrate the influence on Canadian journalism of his matchless style, moral courage, and inflexible independence.[23] Three years later its editor, J. A. Macdonald, wrote asking Goldwin Smith to autograph a picture. "May I be permitted," he said, "as a young man to a veteran, to express my personal debt to you and your work. If I am able to hold The Globe true to essential principles against party pressure it is to a degree due to your example and inspiration. More than this no man can do for another."[24]

An editorial writer in the London *Daily News*, commenting on a letter from Goldwin Smith published in the same issue, described him as "the most powerful writer of the English language in the new world or the old."[25] Almost forty years earlier his *Empire* letters to the same paper had brought his first and perhaps most enduring claim to fame as a journalist. Another English newspaperman, W. Robertson Nicoll, considered Goldwin Smith "out of sight the most wonderful journalist of his day." It was nearly half a century, he recalled, since Smith joined the original staff of the *Saturday Review*, "to which he was the most brilliant contributor." A recent number of the Toronto *Weekly Sun* had carried columns by Goldwin Smith, including a review of Worsfold's

[22]*Ibid.*, May 6, 1903.
[23]*Globe*, Aug. 13, 1903.
[24]Letter from J. A. Macdonald, Feb. 5, 1906.
[25]*Daily News*, Nov. 29, 1901.

THE GRANGE IN 1896
Attributed to Owen Staples, and reproduced by kind permission of *The Telegram*, from John Ross Robertson's *Landmarks of Toronto*.

recent book on Lord Milner. "I am the last man to disparage the ability of British journalists," said Nicoll, "but I am sure that they would agree that none of them all wields a pen so powerful as this veteran of eighty-four. In the very best of our papers this review by Goldwin Smith would shine out conspicuously, and attract universal attention."[26]

The *Weekly Sun* announced on November 10, 1909, that Goldwin Smith had decided to retire from journalism. Unsigned articles were no longer to be attributed to his pen. The shock of his wife's death two months earlier, rather than his eighty-six years, brought him to this decision. The immediate regret at the news expressed by journals all over Canada and by some in the United States proved premature, although he discontinued his regular weekly column in the *Sun* and relapsed into what the *Financial Post* described as his "now comparative silence on public questions."[27] Comparative silence, for Goldwin Smith, meant that in the last seven months of his life, during half of which he was prostrated by a fatal illness, his writing was largely confined to brief letters to the *Weekly Sun*, the *Spectator*, and the New York *Sun*. Editorials in the *Weekly Sun* on December 8, 1909, and February 9, 1910, were also from his pen. Comments on his retirement indicated that Canadians' abiding respect for him was not diminished by their frequent disagreement with his views. Every article supposed to be written by him, as a Montreal journalist observed, was the stronger for the supposition, and it was difficult for the man with the best prose style in Canada to preserve his anonymity.[28]

Goldwin Smith's primary interest was politics. But about historical, social, and religious questions he was only less keenly concerned. His lively intelligence ranged readily over a wide gamut of the ideas, problems, and vagaries of the British peoples. His readers and his writing were to be found all over the English-speaking world, but he liked to be considered a Canadian journalist. In Canada he wrote all his biographies, most of his histories, and the majority of his political pamphlets, articles, and letters. In Canada he founded his own periodicals, took a leading part in establishing others, and contributed to yet more. He was always ready to lend a sympathetic ear to the problems of struggling young journalists and literary men. Canadians, like Englishmen, on occasion had reason to think his views perverse. His enemies were likely to consider them wilfully perverse. Yet to his influence more

[26]"Rambling Remarks" by "A Man of Kent" (W. Robertson Nicoll), *British Weekly*, Feb. 28, 1907.
[27]Feb. 5, 1910.
[28]Montreal *Chronicle*, Nov. 12, 1909.

than to any other single cause was due the fact that at the time of his death invincible partisanship was almost as rare in the Canadian press as was independence of party when he first arrived in the country. His own estimate of his work was modest. "I practised journalism at Toronto on a small scale," he wrote in some rough notes for his reminiscences. "My success . . . was small; less than small in a pecuniary point of view. But I had my little constituency, and my interest was kept up in the events and movements of the age."

V

The last decade of his life was uneventful. Among the trials of his later years was the death of many friends. As he saw them drop off one by one he was constantly reminded that his generation belonged to the past. On his early connection with the Manchester School and the Philosophical Radicals he observed, "I am one of the last sere leaves left fluttering on that tree, and I am not ashamed of the tree on which I grew."[29] Frederic Harrison wrote to express his appreciation of a letter from "one who is now, I believe, far the senior survivor of the mid-Victorian intellectual forces. . . . I am in my seventy-seventh year, and am still striving to keep alive the torch of social morality, justice, and honest thought, which you—now, alas! alone of the comrades of Bright and Mill and Darwin and Spencer—remain to applaud."[30]

The greatest sorrow of his life was his wife's death, after a few days' illness, on September 11, 1909. Goldwin Smith was already frail himself, and he never fully recovered from the shock. Some years before they had discussed what disposition should be made of the historic Grange, which belonged to Mrs. Smith, and which she was anxious to bequeath for some public purpose. They agreed that the grounds should be left to the city for a park, as otherwise they would probably be divided up for building lots. They were in some doubt, however, as to what should be done with the old house, until one day Byron E. (later Sir Edmund) Walker suggested that it might be left for use as a gallery to the Art Museum of Toronto, which had been incorporated in 1900, but still lacked a permanent building. They gladly fell in with this proposal, and Goldwin Smith told Walker that he was pleased to have the matter settled. "I have often felt some compunction," he said, "at having this place, in the midst of a great city, given up to the sole en-

[29] *New York Times*, Sept. 10, 1905.
[30] April 23, 1908, published in *Goldwin Smith's Correspondence*, 498.

joyment of two old people. I shall now feel that compunction no more."[31]

In February, 1910, Goldwin Smith broke his hip. Edward VII cabled the Governor-General to express his concern and ask for news of his "old friend." Among the many who called at the Grange to inquire were the Prime Minister, Sir Wilfrid Laurier, and Sir John Gibson, the Lieutenant-Governor of Ontario. To the end public affairs were uppermost in Goldwin Smith's mind. In Britain he was concerned about the constitutional crisis between the Lords and Commons, and in Canada about the Ontario act which gave the newly constituted Hydro-Electric Commission power to regulate the rates charged by competing companies. The Governor-General, Lord Grey, agreed with his views on this latter question, and after visiting Goldwin Smith wrote Laurier about this "horrid arbitrariness," suggesting that disallowance might be appropriate. Grey painted a vivid picture of the old man "lying on the bed from which he will never rise except to descend into the grave, and occupied with only one care—namely the well-being and honour of Canada. . . . The old Sage of Toronto feels," he told Laurier, "as if a rat were gnawing at his heart, the penalties about to overrun Ontario and the Dominion for legislative and executive crimes. His refrain is 'They have opened the gates of confiscation and closed the doors of Justice.' . . . I wish Goldwin Smith were 50 years younger."[32]

He died on June 7, 1910, in the library of the Grange, where over the years he had spent innumerable hours writing and talking with friends. Goldwin Smith's death removed from the scene one of the most controversial figures in Canadian history.

[31]Letter of May 25, 1903, Sir Edmund Walker Papers, Public Archives of Ontario.
[32]Lord Grey to Sir Wilfrid Laurier, April 10, 1910, Laurier Papers, Governor-General's Correspondence, ff. 206676–94, Public Archives of Canada.

PART II—IDEAS

VI. LIBERAL CREED

NINETEENTH-CENTURY LIBERALISM comprises an amorphous blend of ideas, which may be loosely grouped under the general heading of revolt against authority in the political, religious, and economic spheres. Liberals attacked restraints they found irksome, and in so doing from time to time shifted their ground in response to changing situations. Within the broad confines of liberalism there were many mansions, and a generous latitude for differences of opinion.

Goldwin Smith liked to call himself a Manchester liberal. Many of his most deeply held convictions were typical Manchester doctrine: his hatred of military expeditions and "foreign entanglements," his enthusiasm for the republican institutions of the United States, his dislike of aristocracy and plutocracy and in general of a privileged governing class, his hopes and fears concerning extension of the franchise, his distrust of parties as apt to reduce politics to a trade, and his fearless concern for what he believed to be the dictates of public morality. Bright and Cobden were his close friends, but on many points he differed from them. To social and labour legislation he was far more sympathetic. On economic questions he was a qualified, not doctrinaire, free-trader. He shared Bright's desire to widen the franchise, but considered Disraeli's Second Reform Act too radical, and Gladstone's Third Reform Bill frankly demagogic. He advocated colonial emancipation and deplored pride in empire, but his imperial creed was more positive than that of most Manchester men. He was profoundly interested in the development of colonies as independent nations and seed-beds for transplanted British traditions. Thus while he sympathized with the Manchester faith in internationalism, he cared more than most of its exponents about the future of new nationalities. On education his views were close to those of John Bright and John Stuart Mill: he believed in popular education, but considered its provision a private rather than a public responsibility. He was, in short, a strong individualist. Among the tenets of Victorian liberalism he adopted some, rejected others, and added new elements of his own.

In an age of sects and parties he was above all the publicist of a highly individual liberalism. Frequently he was in a minority, even among liberals. Sometimes he was in a minority of one, and like John Stuart Mill was accused of exalting eccentricity into a virtue. Yet to Goldwin Smith the adoption and defence of independent beliefs in itself seemed an important element of liberalism. When critics attacked him for persistently advocating unpopular ideas, he countered that liberty of opinion was the most precious of all freedoms and the safeguard of every other. Liberalism consisted in thinking independently oneself and encouraging independent thought in others. Independence of mind was the basis of the liberal character and the primary article of the liberal creed; the frank avowal of honest beliefs was the most effective protest against political cowardice and the best tribute a private citizen could pay his country. Liberalism meant not anarchy, but the ascendancy of laws ordained by the community over the will of the individual. Nevertheless modern institutions rested on the assent of public reason, and the test of that assent was free discussion. Liberty of thought and speech was not the promoter of violent revolution, but its surest antidote. Under a despotism everyone was tongue-tied, and everyone conspired.[1]

Within Goldwin Smith's memory England was transformed from an aristocratic society to a modern democracy and her working people from an uneducated mass to literate voters. He was in his forties when Disraeli declared, "We do not . . . live—and I trust it will never be the fate of this country to live—under a democracy." More than a decade later Queen Victoria told Gladstone that she could not and would not be queen of a democratic monarchy. The final transference of power from the Crown and aristocracy to the cabinet, Commons, and electorate, the development of a highly organized modern party system, the rise of a professional civil service, and the growth of socialist thought, all took place during his lifetime. The change in public opinion may be illustrated by contrasting the *Saturday Review*'s comment in 1856 that "to a great extent every Liberal is now a Conservative" with Sir William Harcourt's dictum three decades later that "we are all socialists now." The Whig supporters of the 1832 Reform Act and the Liberal upholders of the Lloyd George budget of 1909 stood on very different ground. That Goldwin Smith found himself unable to move with enthusiasm from the advanced views of the second quarter of the nineteenth century to those of the first decade of the twentieth, and that in some respects his liberalism became outmoded, is scarcely cause for wonder. Four

[1] Presidential address to the National Club, reported in the *Nation* (Toronto), Oct. 15, 1874.

years before the outbreak of the First World War he died, content to describe himself as a liberal of the old school, and to rest with the judgment of posterity his claim to have been all his days on the side of liberal progress.

I

Nominally a Liberal, Goldwin Smith was simply liberal. Despite his intense interest in politics, he preferred independent criticism to party orthodoxy. He was no personal follower of Gladstone, he averred, or of any other man in public life. His faith was in principles and policies, not men. In much the same spirit John Stuart Mill declared he was not a follower of Bentham, on the ground that no independent thinker could be any man's follower.

It has never been easy at a given moment to define precisely what Liberal or Conservative orthodoxy involves. Nineteenth-century Liberals themselves were not always agreed on what principles they supported. At the beginning of the eighteen-seventies Goldwin Smith complained to the secretary of the Reform League that much apathy, timidity, and even positive reaction lurked in England under the guise of Liberalism.[2] A decade later, speaking at Chelsea on parliamentary reform, he was at once more specific and more optimistic when he answered his own rhetorical question, "What is the Liberal party?" by declaring, "It is the nation, less the Tory aristocracy, with its retainers on one side and the Fenians on the other. The nation at large has accepted the great principles of Liberalism; it has renounced reaction, privilege, monopoly, intolerance; and though all may not be for advancing at the same pace, all are for going by the same way . . . the way of ordered progress."[3] Beside this statement may be placed Gladstone's comment that "the principle of Liberalism is trust in the people qualified by prudence; the principle of Conservatism is mistrust of the people qualified by fear." Lord Rosebery told the Liberal League in 1904 that Liberalism was "the readiness to accept the best ideas of the time and to apply them with honesty." All three explanations are party manifestoes which attempt to annex for the Liberals a monopoly of concern for ordered progress. Disraeli, on the other hand, tried to persuade the electorate that Conservatives alone took an intelligent interest in both order and progress.

[2]Letter to George Howell, May 19, 1871, Howell Collection, Bishopsgate Institute, London.
[3]*Pall Mall Gazette*, Nov. 2, 1881.

The maintenance of order had always been considered a respectable, indeed essential, function of government. By the eighteen-seventies it was becoming clear that belief in progress, a characteristic Victorian tenet, formed a good campaign slogan for any party.

The Conservative victory of 1874 Goldwin Smith interpreted as a defeat of the Liberal party rather than of Liberal principles, whose continuing hold on the country was out of proportion to their representation in Parliament. The Tories had adopted much of the Liberal creed: humanitarianism, public education, an extended franchise, labour legislation, and local government reform.[4] His assessment was to be re-echoed by latter-day Liberals confronted by a series of defeats in the twentieth century.

II

Goldwin Smith's conception of liberalism may be illustrated by his views on free trade and political democracy. As the nineteenth century advanced, unquestioning faith in laissez-faire was more honoured in the breach than in the observance, though probably few Englishmen realized how qualified was even Adam Smith's support for the doctrine often associated with his name. In his early days Goldwin Smith showed true Manchester School enthusiasm for restricting the function of the state to a minimum. One of the things he most admired in America was the comparatively slight need for government. State action involved compulsion, the need for which was in inverse proportion to the intelligence of the people. Thus in the eighteen-sixties he came close to agreeing with Tom Paine that the best government is that which governs least. If he did not go so far as to foretell with the Marxists and anarchists the ultimate abolition of the state, he yet suggested that the role of government was destined to decline as religious feeling increased, and as the need for coercion was replaced by brotherly love and a general willingness to co-operate for the common good. "The more a community can afford to dispense with government," he declared, "the more Christian it must be, and no great country has yet been able to dispense with government so much as America."[5] As he grew older, however, this faith in the inactivity of governments was shaken.

His belief in free trade was reflected in his opinion that Peel, Bright, and Cobden were the three nineteenth-century statesmen who had done

---

[4]"The Defeat of the Liberal Party," *Fortnightly Review*, XXII (July, 1877), 5–6.　　[5]*The Civil War in America* (London, 1866), 11.

most for the English people. A member of the Cobden Club from its foundation in 1866, Goldwin Smith was the author of its motto: "Free Trade, Peace, Goodwill among Nations." The phrase occurs in a lecture where his tendency to assume a certain divine merit for what he believed, and to interpret history in the light of the present, are both illustrated by the comment that "in the mind of Pitt, as in that of Adam Smith, as in that of Cobden, as in the counsels of Providence, free trade was connected with a policy of peace and goodwill among nations."[6] Despite this comprehensive tribute, his belief in laissez-faire was not strong enough to make him an uncompromising advocate of free trade, though he never altered his opinion that it was, as a rule, the dictate of plain common sense, and a natural adjunct of political liberalism. He was not a purist, he explained, but a moderate free-trader, who held that there might well be practical exceptions to a practical principle. Fiscal and economic questions were not matters of inflexible law, but of expediency, to be settled according to the merits of the particular case.

III

If his support for free trade, or at least low tariffs, numbered Goldwin Smith among the Manchester Liberals, he was at heart an independent. He once observed that his political consciousness (and he might have added, his social conscience) was early awakened. It did not slumber until his death at the age of eighty-six. His ideas on political democracy reflect the combined hopes and fears of many other liberals in the mid-nineteenth century. At that time democracy was unpopular and something less than respectable among the middle classes of both Great Britain and Canada, as the Canadian Confederation Debates, among other examples, abundantly illustrate. More prescient thinkers, like Mill and Bagehot and Goldwin Smith, considered democracy inevitable, and, on the whole, good. Yet their intellectual approval was tempered by an instinctive dread of the dangers of popular government. Again and again Goldwin Smith stressed the fact that democracy had its own special vices: corruption, popular passion, the ostracism of merit, and the oppression of classes not numerically strong. Above all he loathed the tendency of the sovereign people to self-worship. As appropriate safeguards against these perils he proposed public education and strong local institutions. Apparent inconsistencies in his attitude are explained

[6]*Three English Statesmen* (London, 1868), 122–3, 143.

by the conflict in his mind between the good which he hoped would eventually spring from democracy and the evils which initially followed it.

One reason why he objected to the continued dependence of the colonies was that England thereby not only retarded their political development but actually misdirected it along extravagantly democratic lines. Their nominal subjection to the British Crown concealed the absence of conservative elements in their institutions and encouraged them to "plunge with impunity into all the excesses of universal suffrage."[7] The effect of popular institutions on personal liberty was as yet undetermined. It remained to be seen whether democracy would be authoritarian or liberal. There was certainly no reason to believe that the will of the masses, necessarily half-informed on matters of state, was divine. Equally illusory he considered the belief that good government could be assured by given political institutions and mechanical divisions of power, apart from the qualities of those who served as statesmen and public servants.

Goldwin Smith's hopes for democracy grew dimmer with advancing years, and his fears of its excesses more lively. When in 1893–4 he paid a seven months' visit to the United Kingdom, journalists asked for his impressions of the changes in the British political scene since he was last in England. The monarchy, he replied, had almost ceased to exercise any real political force, and the House of Commons had taken unto itself not simply all the legislative power but also the virtual appointment of the executive. The majority in the Commons had become not only radical but revolutionary, responsive to the will of the wage-earners who, having secured political power, were now inclined to use it to effect industrial and social change. England had been transformed into a democracy unawares, fancying all the time that she had a monarchical and autocratic constitution. What she had in reality was the most unbridled democracy in the world, with a government subservient to "the ephemeral creature of the caucus, which upon the first reverse would fall"—an unfortunate forecast, based on his dislike of parties. How affairs of state were to be carried on after the adoption of universal suffrage and payment of members he professed himself unable to tell. If the British artisan had any political convictions, he was a socialist, loyal not so much to his country as to his trade union and the labour movement.

[7]*The Empire: A Series of Letters, Published in "The Daily News," 1862, 1863* (Oxford, 1863), 3.

A decade later he suggested that if the Liberal party could agree on nothing else it could surely agree on the defence of parliamentary government against encroachment by ministers of the Crown so serious that the legislative liberty of the Commons was in peril. He deplored the dwindling importance of private members, and the fact that nearly all initiative in debate as well as the introduction of most legislation was now undertaken by the Government of the day. Parliamentary democracy seemed to him seriously threatened by the growing power of the cabinet over the Commons, when according to constitutional theory the cabinet derived its authority from the support of the House.

The secret conduct of foreign policy he considered indefensible. When the Anglo-Japanese agreement was concluded in 1902, he protested that treaties binding the nation to go to war should be submitted before ratification to Parliament, which would ultimately have to assume the responsibility and vote the money. Despite the practical difficulties occasioned in the United States by Senate control over treaties, he approved this aspect of American politics. There the people's representatives had the final say in a matter vitally affecting the lives of citizens. Surely, he argued, parliamentary control over the making of treaties which might involve the country in war was the essence of real responsible government. Half a century earlier John Bright had made a similar plea, and hoped that a wider franchise would bring the change he advocated. In matters of foreign policy, Bright told an audience in 1858, "you are no longer Englishmen; you are no longer free; you are recommended not to inquire. If you do, you are told you cannot understand it . . . that the matter is too deep for common understandings like ours."[8]

At new constitutional conventions, developed since the days of his youth, Goldwin Smith looked askance. He could not reconcile himself to accepting as an established usage the practice that a Government beaten at the polls should resign without waiting to meet its inevitable defeat in Parliament. With more justification he attacked the custom of leaving constituencies unrepresented for weeks or even months in order to further party ends.[9] Such departures from the conventions in his youth made him increasingly gloomy about the prospects of democracy, though he still liked to quote Bacon's maxim, "That which man changes not for the better, time, the great innovator, changes for the worse."

[8]Quoted in G. M. Trevelyan, *The Life of John Bright* (London, 1913), 277–8. Goldwin Smith's views on the matter are given in a letter to the *Manchester Guardian*, Jan. 21, 1907.
[9]"The Impending Revolution," *Nineteenth Century*, XXXV (March, 1894), 356–66; interview with Goldwin Smith, *Mail*, May 16, 1894.

IV

These general criticisms of popular government may be illustrated by charges which he brought against democratic institutions. The main target of his attack was the party system, which in good eighteenth-century style he commonly described as faction. To him it seemed not a necessity of political life, but an accident of English history, born of the conflict between the adherents of the Stuarts and those of the House of Hanover. That conflict over, party broke into cabals. Parties appeared to clash with individual action in politics, and Goldwin Smith was pre-eminently an individualist. Moreover the first half of his life was lived before the development of national party organizations placed an increasing premium upon orthodoxy and discipline. Many of his liberal contemporaries shared both his dislike of parties and his underestimate of their utility. John Stuart Mill published in 1861 his famous essay on representative government in which parties were barely mentioned. In the eighteen-eighties Sir Henry Maine, discussing popular government, linked together as twin phenomena party and corruption. Lord Acton considered that Goldwin Smith, for all his vehemence against parties, if anything understated the case against a system whose effects on the elected were no less disgraceful than on the electors, and which taught otherwise honourable men to say what they knew to be false and to advocate what they believed to be wrong. Acton thought, however, that Smith's proposal for the abolition of party was chimerical.[10] Mill, Maine, and Acton were, of course, theorists. The practical liberals who shaped political change, like Gladstone, Morley, and Bryce, all accepted parties as inevitable.

Goldwin Smith contended that parties were justified when they were divided by real issues of principle, but that in the absence of such issues, as for instance in Canada, the system degenerated into a mere struggle for power between the ins and the outs. The ordinary voter he thought incapable of deciding upon the general policy of the country, since he had not the leisure, even if he had the knowledge and ability, to make an adequate study of the complex questions placed before him. The elector, transformed from a subject to a participant in sovereign power, was reduced to voting a straight party ticket. Nowhere but in politics was it proposed to thrust upon men a duty which they could not discharge intelligently. The notion that people were divided by nature into Con-

[10]Lord Acton, review of Goldwin Smith's *Three English Statesmen* in the *Chronicle*, Aug. 31, 1867, reprinted in Acton's *Essays on Church and State* (London, 1952), 406–10.

servatives or Liberals might best be relegated to comic opera. They were doubtless so constituted as to differ, at least until discussion brought them to agreement. The shades of temperamental differences, both political and otherwise, however, were numberless, melting into each other by imperceptible degrees. There were as many natural parties as there were individuals; the same man was quite likely to be conservative on one question and radical on another. To divide all the world into two parties by the constitution of their minds was preposterous, "the bisection of a rainbow, the demarcation of a wave."[11] Burke's famous definition of party as "a body of men united for the purpose of promoting by their joint endeavours the public interest, upon some principle on which they are all agreed," struck Goldwin Smith as a satire on actual parties. He only wished that Burke had had an opportunity to attend an American national party convention.

On many occasions he attacked the caucus system invented by the Liberal organizer, Schnadhorst. The attention paid his opinions by English statesmen was illustrated by a letter which Joseph Chamberlain wrote him in 1882. He deprecated criticisms Goldwin Smith had expressed in a recent article, and enclosed a couple of papers which he himself had written for the *Fortnightly Review*.[12] The English caucus, Chamberlain pointed out, was quite different from the American, being merely the simplest possible machinery to elicit a full expression of opinion from all the electors. The officers of such an association were the servants of their constituents, not the managers of a machine. In any large English borough wire-pulling would be fatal to success. Chamberlain hoped that in this and other questions he and Goldwin Smith might be able to work together. His ingenious explanation suggested his concern to deflect Smith's attack, and if possible to win his approval and support, though it would have taken more than a tactful letter to change Smith's opinion of Chamberlain and all his works.[13] Goldwin Smith granted, however, that English Liberals had some justification for

[11]"Current Events," *Canadian Monthly*, III (Feb., 1873), 140; letter to *The Times*, Jan. 17, 1899.

[12]Joseph Chamberlain, "A New Political Organization," *Fortnightly Review*, XXII (July, 1877), 126-34; "The Caucus," *ibid.*, XXIV (Nov., 1878), 721-41.

[13]Chamberlain's letter is in Goldwin Smith's Autograph Album. In an unpublished draft for his *Reminiscences* Goldwin Smith summed up his opinion of Chamberlain in one impressive sentence. "I saw the career of Mr. Joseph Chamberlain from its start, at which he drove everyone with the slightest taint of Conservatism out of the city of Birmingham, threatened to make property pay a ransom for its existence, and advocated the disruption of the United Kingdom, to the close, at which he was heading the party of reaction, militarism and imperialism, courting the smile of royalty, vehemently opposing Gladstone on Home Rule, and making the Boer War."

imposing party discipline because they had to fight a class organization more compact and more coercive than any caucus ever devised by party tyranny. Nothing could exceed the social pressure exercised by the British governing class. Although the Conservatives had no formal caucus, disobedience to their party whips in the Commons was almost unknown. Party organization had its evils, but Liberals were compelled to choose between it and weak opposition to the cohesive unity of a landowning plutocracy.[14]

The theory that the sovereign people would elect the best men seemed to him an illusion, since even in the improbable event that they were willing to do so, the best men would not allow themselves to be elected. Among other things, they could not afford it. Yet he was never reconciled to the payment of members in Great Britain, thinking that this merely invited "a swarm of adventurers" who desired public office for the wrong motives, though after living in Canada he regretfully concluded that in a frontier community, without a wealthy leisured class, some payment was necessary. He conceded that any country which wanted people to do hard work must pay them or they would pay themselves. So it would be, he wrote of municipal government, "at least till the Angel Gabriel is Mayor, with a city council of seraphs."[15] But their reward might be either money, or dignity as in England, and of the two he vastly preferred the British system.

On party, as on other matters, he found the role of a destructive and doctrinaire critic easier and more congenial than that of a constructive reformer. His only solution for the ills of the party system was to recommend that it be abolished, that the members of the legislature be elected like those of any other board, and that they be allowed, as in Switzerland, to nominate certain of their own body to serve for a fixed term as an executive council. Such a plan would ensure adequate support and necessary stability to governments. Many of his friends as well as his opponents argued with him concerning his stand against parties, but they all had the same experience as Bryce, who declared that he was never able to extract from Goldwin Smith, for all his political acumen and mastery of history, how parliamentary democracy could be carried on without them.[16]

As a scholar and independent journalist, he felt himself above party, and proudly asserted that he did not speak its language. To Lord Rose-

---

[14]"Papers by a Bystander," Rose-Belford's *Canadian Monthly*, II (March, 1879), 366.
[15]*Weekly Sun*, Feb. 26, 1895.
[16]James Bryce, *Modern Democracies* (London, 1929), I, 138, n. 1.

bery he suggested that the party system had outlived its usefulness. Rosebery agreed that the system was decadent, but did not agree that the end of party government was at hand. He granted that British parties had become mere husks, embodying only a name, and separated as a rule by very few distinctive issues, but added that most people saw no alternative to them.[17] To this realistic argument of men like Bryce, Acton, and Rosebery, Goldwin Smith never produced an effective reply.

V

His deep distrust of parties modified his approval of the cabinet system, for he realized that cabinet government necessarily rests upon party alignments. The tendency of new democracies to fashion themselves after the British model struck him as a serious error. Commenting on political unrest in France and Italy, he prophesied that "some day the . . . architects of Europe will discover the absurdity of reproducing as a universal constitution the combination of historical accidents and hypocrisies called British Party Government." The political clothes of England would not fit the whole world. The British constitution was too essentially English to be exported to any country, as though it were a universal specific like Morrison's British pills. Goldwin Smith believed, with Mill, that constitutions are not made, but grow, and that if they are to be strong and win respect, they must be developed out of national circumstances and character, not imposed from above. "Free institutions," he wrote in 1890, "will not make free natures, and small is the number of those who are by nature free. Most of us crave for a sheepfold and a shibboleth."[18]

His enthusiasm for the political institutions of the United States led him to favour a set time for elections and for the duration of Parliament. In later years he consistently minimized the importance of the distinctions between cabinet and presidential government, probably because their significance was commonly stressed by opponents of his favourite project for union between Canada and the United States. Although he realized the weaknesses of the American checks and balances he was convinced that democracy needed a bridle. The safeguards of the separation of powers in the United States, the presidential veto, an indirectly elected Senate, and a written constitution interpreted by

[17]Letters from Goldwin Smith to Lord Rosebery, Feb. 17, 1909; from Lord Rosebery to Goldwin Smith, March 3, 1909.
[18]*Bystander*, n.s. (Jan., 1890), 109.

a supreme court, he contrasted with the defenceless and perilous position of Great Britain, with no bulwarks against revolution but an ancient and powerless monarchy and a doomed aristocracy. The only really effective check in the United Kingdom was the non-payment of members of Parliament, and this he foresaw would not last long. He concluded that England needed a written constitution, interpreted by a court of law, since informal traditions and understandings might be adequate as long as government was vested in statesmen with similar ideas who walked in ancestral paths, but did not command the same respect under totally different social conditions.[19]

The power of an American president, he noted shrewdly, was greater than was commonly supposed, and if the constitutions of England and America were compared as to substance instead of form, it would be found that the English came closer to an aristocratic republic and the American to a popular and elective monarchy. The elected ruler of the United States had infinitely more power than the British constitutional sovereign. In England democracy had penetrated beneath the mantle of the old feudal constitution, although people fancied that power still resided in its monarchical and aristocratic forms. There is a suggestion here of the distinction earlier made by Bagehot between the dignified and efficient parts of the constitution, and more than a suggestion of his famous comment that "a republic has insinuated itself beneath the folds of a monarchy."

Yet there were times when Goldwin Smith criticized American political practices, and spoke enthusiastically of the unique capacity of the unwritten British constitution to adapt itself freely to the exigencies of progress. On such occasions he granted that the English system had a vast advantage over other constitutions, notably the American, which had become obsolete in many ways, was far too difficult to amend, and practically precluded the training of statesmen. He tried to persuade an American Congressman whom he knew that the House of Representatives should have a longer term, since no man could make himself a statesman in two years. The Senate, which gave the small states equal representation with the large, no more represented the American people, in Goldwin Smith's opinion, than the unreformed Parliament returned by rotten boroughs had represented the people of England. He would like to have seen it replaced by a new upper house with members selected on a different basis.[20]

---

[19]"The Canadian Question," *Independent* (New York), Feb. 23, 1888.

[20]Letters to Bourke Cockran, April 19, 1904, and Oct. 12, 1907, Cockran Papers, New York Public Library; *The Civil War in America*, 54; "The Conflict with the Lords," *Contemporary Review*, XLVI (Sept., 1884), 13-21.

VI

Despite his fears as to what might be expected of the ordinary voter, a wider suffrage was one of the causes he first espoused. He ignored or did not realize the fact that an extended franchise would lead to increased state functions. From the beginning, however, he viewed the prospect with some apprehension. "No one," he wrote Cobden in 1862, "can be more sensible than I am of the risks and evils attending a great and sudden transfer of political power: yet I see the absolute necessity of struggling for a great measure of Parliamentary reform, as the indispensable condition of every other measure of improvement and justice." The risks must be faced to achieve a good otherwise unobtainable. "It is not the mere denial of political rights under the present system which calls for redress: *it is the wretched and hopeless condition of great masses of the people.*"[21]

The Second Reform Act was passed in 1867, the year before Goldwin Smith left England. In the agitation which preceded its passage he took part both as a speaker and writer. Like his friends Bryce, Dicey, and Leslie Stephen, he contributed to an influential little volume of *Essays on Reform*. In a democracy, he argued, justice demanded some representation for all classes. It was unfair to exclude five-sixths of the English people, since no one had as great a stake in the country as the working man.[22] He saw no remedy for Britain's class government save one which gave to all alike political rights and freedom to promote and defend their own interests by constitutional means. Hence he called for a free Parliament, arguing that those who thought that a fair distribution of political power would result in anarchy, and that order could be secured at the expense of justice, vastly underrated the good sense of the ordinary man. Eventually, he told a cheering Brighton audience, they would have universal suffrage with equal electoral districts.

Goldwin Smith twice declined (in 1865 and 1866) an invitation to become a vice-president of the Reform League, but addressed many public meetings under its auspices. Before he left England the council of the League expressed its gratitude, at a time when the predominant state of feeling at the universities and among the governing upper classes was "lamentably anti-Liberal," for his services to political progress and parliamentary reform. His close association with this latter cause led Lord Elcho to denounce him in the Commons as an advocate of republicanism and a strange occupant of an Oxford chair. Lord Elcho suggested that many Liberals who fought for the Reform Bill were

[21]Letters to Cobden, Oct. 27, 1862, April 13, 1863.
[22]*Oxford Chronicle*, July 21, 1866.

mainly interested in cheap notoriety, since "there is no such easy way of obtaining popularity as by taking up the Constitution and giving it a good shake."[23] In his opinion every man had a right, not to a vote, but to proper government. The English constitution was based on representation not of individuals but of classes.

One of Goldwin Smith's last public appearances before he left England to settle in the United States was at Sheffield, where, during Mundella's election campaign, he spoke on the duties as voters of the town workers enfranchised by the Reform Act of 1867. Here he set before working men, not a millennium of cheap tobacco and short hours, but the prize of a high political calling. He wished simply to describe the advantages which friends of parliamentary reform anticipated from a wider suffrage.

We hope it will give us reduced taxation, because when the people themselves are the government costly armaments are no longer needed to protect the government against the people, and because the desire of the people everywhere is not war with other nations, but peace. We hope it will give us a better system of popular education, because on popular education, not on bayonets, social order must rest for the future. We hope it will improve our local institutions, the only sure foundations of public liberty. We hope it will revise other parts of our institutions, especially the House of Lords, which is now almost the only relic of the purely hereditary system in Europe. . . . We hope it will give us the benefit of all that science and better sanitary administration can do to improve the health of the people and to mitigate the ghastly contrast between the streets of palaces inhabited by the rich, and the foul, noisome, and plague-stricken dwellings of the poor. We hope, above all, that in its ecclesiastical legislation it will take away every obstacle that stands in the way of man's pursuit of that which is his first need and the primary condition of his social being—religious truth. But all this and more than all this is summed up in these words, that government shall henceforth be the government not of a class, or of a balance of classes, but of the nation.[24]

This eloquent address, interlarded with skilful thrusts at Disraeli and Lord Derby, would seem to refute Goldwin Smith's belief that he was too poor a public speaker to embark on a parliamentary career.

The reasons for Mill's opposition to the secret ballot he could not comprehend, and he distrusted proportional representation as apt to result in torpid compromise. He professed himself at a loss to under-

---

[23]*Hansard's Parliamentary Debates*, Third Series, CLXXVIII, May 3, 1865, 1403–5. To this personal attack Goldwin Smith retorted that he hoped he served the university with as much zeal as he could if his political views had the happiness of meeting with his lordship's approbation. Open letter to the *Daily News*, May 6, 1865.

[24]*Sheffield and Rotherham Independent*, Oct. 16, 1868.

stand the object of compulsory voting, which Edward Blake at one time proposed for Canada. Goldwin Smith considered that those who would not take the trouble to vote had generally not thought about the issues involved, and hence were better at home. University representation, like that which existed in England and was suggested for Canada, he opposed, believing that if the universities were worth anything they would make their influence felt in politics, yet it was undesirable that they should be directly involved in party struggles. Theirs should be neutral territory in a serener air.

An educational test for the franchise seemed to him indispensable. On this one point he agreed with Lowe that "we must educate our masters." Disraeli's Second Reform Act he attacked as merely a stroke of party strategy, intended to "dish the Whigs" rather than improve the government of the country, and likely to arrest progress by swamping intelligence. Its author Goldwin Smith publicly characterized as "the plagiarist of reform." Similarly he criticized the Third Reform Act, partly because it enfranchised the illiterate, and partly because it gave increased weight to the Irish vote. In later years he argued that everyone capable of using it well should have political power. But it was undesirable that people totally incapable of making a good use of power should possess it. "If the government of the people is to be government of ignorance and irresponsibility, it will fall. To stand, it must be government by the intelligence of the community in the interest of the whole." He agreed that every man had a natural right to justice and fair treatment. But the idea that he had a natural right to political power, regardless of whether he used it for the benefit of the community, or knew anything about the question on which he was to vote, ought in Goldwin Smith's opinion to be "relegated to that limbo near the moon to which reason has now sent the Jeffersonian generalities of the preamble to the Declaration of Independence." While as early as 1866 he believed that all adults would eventually have the right to vote, this was a consummation for whose postponement he devoutly hoped. In a moment of disillusionment caused by the high tariff under the McKinley Act of 1890, he wrote a friend that "the government of the world has by the extension of the suffrage been taken, for the time at least, out of the hands of intelligence; and narrow-minded cupidity, worked upon by political intrigue, is undoing the work done for humanity by Turgot, Pitt, Peel and Cavour."[25]

[25]Letter to Mrs. Winkworth, Oct. 20, 1890, *Goldwin Smith's Correspondence*, 227; letters to the *Daily News*, May 6, 1865, Sept. 24, 1866, to *The Times*, June 17, 1867.

He was little more enthusiastic about the results of manhood suffrage in England, where, in his opinion, supreme power had become centred in an assembly elected by vast masses of gullibility, ignorance, and blind passion. No other journalist so clearly mirrored the combined political hopes and fears of the Victorian era. His views on the franchise in particular illustrate the uncertainties and confusions widespread among intelligent Liberals. There were, of course, consistent and confident reformers, but Goldwin Smith reflected the views of the doubters who oscillated between faith in and despair of democracy. Joseph Howe, for example, warned Lord Stanley in 1866 that in Nova Scotia an extended franchise (based not on possession of property but on payment of rates) had been tried for two elections and then abandoned by general consent. Knowledge of the United States had convinced Howe that the franchise there was too wide, and that the superior classes in America would like, if they could, to follow the British example and limit the right to vote.[26] Sir Henry Maine was similarly dubious about popular suffrage, even with the spread of education. He feared the omnipotence of mass prejudice, with legislation and policy based on a dead level of commonplace ideas. Since most people were unprogressive, the end result, he foretold, would be the evils of ultra-conservatism rather than of ultra-radicalism. Goldwin Smith admired Maine's *Popular Government*, but would not agree that mankind was naturally conservative. Nor did he consider democracy merely a form of government. To him it seemed rather a phase of society and of public opinion to which the form of government corresponded.[27]

In an unguarded moment he had signed Mill's petition for extending the terms of the Second Reform Act to give women the suffrage. Of this early indiscretion he later, like Bright, bitterly and publicly repented. He gave as one reason for his change of heart that he had not then "seen the public life of women in the United States," and that he had since found that the most sensible women of his acquaintance viewed the prospect of the franchise with great mistrust. He believed that women would not be improved by politics, nor politics by women. Women had already invaded some of the male professions, and intended to invade the rest. They had usurped man's headgear and ulster, had made their way to the smoking-room, and had mounted the bicycle. He deplored politicians' readiness to make capital out of the revolt of women "against

[26]Letter from Howe to Lord Stanley, Aug. 21, 1866. Howe Papers, IX, ff. 100–8, Public Archives of Canada.
[27]Sir Henry Maine, *Popular Government* (London, 1885), 36–41; Goldwin Smith, "The Moral of the Late Crisis," *Nineteenth Century*, XX (Sept., 1886), 305–21.

the natural limitations, duties and delicacies of their sex." This revolt must in the end be repressed if domestic life was not to be thrown into confusion, and the relations between the sexes completely revolutionized. Theoretically he believed in equality of the sexes, but argued that perfect equality was compatible with diverse abilities and functions. Conservatives should remember that the most active female politicians were sure to be radicals, since conservative women would stay at home. Even worse, the political woman would be an authoritative radical, prone not only to sentimental but to arbitrary legislation. With gusto he cited the dreadful example of a Utah woman who had run against her husband in a contest for the state senatorship, and beaten him. Goldwin Smith understood that she favoured polygamy as well as female suffrage. To his way of thinking, women were not an unrepresented class, but a sex, whose interests were completely identified with those of their husbands, brothers, and sons. Moreover, government rested ultimately on force, and force was male.

This argument that government rests in the last resort on force, in contrast with T. H. Green's view that will, not force, is the basis of the state, recurred in many of Goldwin Smith's discussions of votes for women. On other occasions he argued that the essence of political liberalism was a frank recognition of the elective principle, and the national will the only conceivable basis for government. Yet he was troubled by the thought that it was government by the reason rather than the will of the people which was needed, and this, popular representation could scarcely be trusted to ensure.[28]

A common dislike of votes for women was one of many bonds between him and James Bryce, although the latter was actively associated with the movement for higher education for women, and tried to obtain for mothers the right to guardianship of their children. When a clause in the Third Reform Bill providing limited female suffrage was being discussed at Westminster, Bryce wrote Goldwin Smith for information on the women's franchise movement in Canada and the United States, and used this ammunition in a parliamentary debate. He was unable, Bryce observed bitterly, to understand the fascination such a project had for certain usually judicious statesmen.[29]

Goldwin Smith's anti-feminist zeal never flagged. When in 1889 a proposal to give the vote to unmarried women property owners was

[28]"Female Suffrage," *Macmillan's Magazine*, XXX (June, 1874), 139–50; "Conservatism and Female Suffrage," *National Review*, X (Feb., 1888), 735–52; "Woman's Place in the State," *Forum*, III (1890), 515–30.

[29]*Hansard's Parliamentary Debates*, Third Series, CCLXXXIX, June 12, 1884, 166; letters from James Bryce to Goldwin Smith, May 15, June 29, 1884.

before the British Commons, he wrote *The Times* asking, "To the denationalized factory hands, the ignorant farm labourers, and the rebel Irish, if you add the irresponsible emotions of the woman, what sort of a constituency will you have and in what hands will England be?" On this the *Pall Mall Gazette*, a strong supporter of both Home Rule and female suffrage, commented: "Burke refused to draw an indictment against a nation, but Mr. Goldwin Smith has grown so hardened to drawing indictments against Ireland that he now thinks nothing of impeaching one half the human race." *The Times*, however, for once agreed with him, and published another letter in which he deplored the levity of the debate at Westminster as inconsistent with the gravity of the situation. A decade later when votes for women were again being discussed in England, Goldwin Smith wrote gloomily to Bryce: "The thing is inevitable, I suppose. If party continues to reign, the Dutch auction will go on, the two parties bidding against each other for votes, till you get to universal suffrage of both sexes, when probably the end will come."[30]

VII

Republicanism had its advocates in Great Britain at the beginning of the eighteen-seventies, partly owing to criticism, after Prince Albert's death, of Queen Victoria's prolonged retirement from the duties of public life. Chief among these protagonists was Sir Charles Dilke, who sympathized, however, with the widowed queen's desire for privacy. For a time Joseph Chamberlain was numbered in their ranks, though he was too astute politically to allow his name to become prominent in an unpopular cause. Frederic Harrison believed England's ultimate adoption of republicanism was "as certain as the rising of to-morrow's sun."[31]

Goldwin Smith's detractors, who in later years were wont to criticize him for undue conservatism, would have been surprised to learn that in 1870 he had written from Ithaca to George Howell, secretary of the Reform League, suggesting the expediency of forming in Great Britain an avowed republican party. He admitted that such a proposal would have been useless when he left England two years before, but during the interval he thought he detected a change in public opinion, which had

[30]Letters to Bryce, April 4, 1897; to *The Times*, Jan. 3, 1889, Feb. 3, 1897; *Pall Mall Gazette*, Jan. 3, 1889.
[31]Frederic Harrison, "The Monarchy," *Fortnightly Review*, XI (June, 1872), XIII (Jan., 1873).

been strengthened by the recent overthrow of the Empire in France. Aristocracy and plutocracy seemed to him to have triumphed too completely at the recent English elections, with the result that the Parliament at Westminster did not really represent the democratic party. At the same time he thought he saw a growing sense of community of interests among all nations. Hence it appeared less chimerical "to propose a general European effort for the deliverance of all countries from dynasties and aristocracies and for the inauguration everywhere of industrial and pacific government." He realized that anything he might write on the subject would have the disadvantage of being attacked in England as the work of an exile, ignorant of the real state of politics at home, but it might at least help to kindle public discussion. Despite obviously serious difficulties, a well-conducted republican movement might gather strength in England and in the end prevail. It would need to have links with republican parties in other countries, for the force and dignity of the movement would lie in its European character. Although he had struck deep roots in North America, the turn of events made Goldwin Smith wish himself once more among his English friends. When he left his country in 1868 he felt he could derive no satisfaction from spending the rest of his life in a struggle whose sole object was to put Whig oligarchs in power instead of Tories. "But if I am invited," he wrote in the spring of 1871, "by a respectable (I do not mean genteel) republican organization to become one of its members and devote my pen to the assistance of its cause, I am not sure that I should resist the invitation."

A cautious reply from Howell, suggesting that English opinion might not yet be ripe for such a movement, gave Goldwin Smith pause. "My words," he wrote back, "were the expression of a momentary feeling of enthusiasm caused by the apparent unfurling of the flag which I had always longed to follow; and perhaps they had better have been left unwritten." He was still confident, however, that a republican movement had already begun in England, and that some reputable organization would have to be formed to keep it in the right course and save it from extravagances.[32]

No one could be less of a revolutionary than Goldwin Smith. He spent his life working for various causes in which he believed, but he never wanted to see any change, from disestablishment of the church to the formation of a republic, brought about by other than strictly constitutional means. He was a republican in the sense that he considered

[32]Letters from Goldwin Smith to George Howell, Oct. 24, 1870, April 6 and May 11, 1871, Howell Collection.

hereditary monarchy and aristocracy had outlived their usefulness, that he admired the democratic institutions of the United States, and that he believed England to be, for all practical purposes, already a republic. This *de facto* state of affairs he thought it reasonable to recognize by appropriate legal changes in the constitution.

When in 1871 Sir Charles Dilke, in a speech at Newcastle, criticized the civil list, he was at once attacked by *The Times* and by most of the other powerful journals in the country. But he received supporting letters from both Goldwin Smith and Chamberlain—probably the first and last time that they found themselves in agreement. Chamberlain went beyond anything Dilke had said or even believed, when he wrote him, "The republic must come, and at the rate at which we are moving it will come in our generation." Dilke stated frankly that his abstract preference was for a republican rather than a monarchical form of government, although he had not, like Fawcett, joined republican clubs. He pointed out, however, that to think and even to say that monarchy in Western Europe was a somewhat cumbersome fiction was not the same thing as declaring oneself ready to fight against it at a barricade.[33]

The Liberal party as a whole never espoused republicanism, but Dilke like Goldwin Smith prided himself on the fact that party ties sat lightly on him. The two were old friends, and had both supported the cession of the Ionian Islands and the cause of the North during the American Civil War. Dilke, however, was a Home Ruler, and advocated votes for women because he believed in universal adult suffrage. W. E. Forster commented in 1874 that the republican party in England had little life left in it. "He may be right," said Goldwin Smith, "but if, in the great plutocracy, speculative Republicanism is weak, the Republicanism of misery is strong, and the wider becomes the gulf between the extremes of wealth and poverty, the stronger it is likely to grow."[34]

For occupants of thrones, as involuntary captives, he felt a certain sympathy, yet he discussed royalty almost as frankly as Bagehot, and far more frankly than is fashionable today. Queen Victoria was "a Stuart upon a Hanoverian throne." Enthusiasm for such a piece of tinsel as the title "Empress of India" on the part of one who wore the crown of Alfred struck him as a conclusive example of littleness of mind. On his return from the United States at the time of the Civil War he declared in an open letter to the press that only once in his life had he felt the sensation of loyalty—when he stood in the presence of Abraham

---

[33]Sir Charles Dilke, "Political Memoir" (unpublished), Dilke Papers, British Museum, ff. 176–7, 181, 191–3.
[34]"Current Events," *Canadian Monthly*, VI (Nov., 1874), 462.

Lincoln. A quarter century later he referred to "blind and spaniel-like devotion to the person of the king" as an unattractive example of political fetichism. For Edward VII he had the personal liking of an old tutor for a former student. Discussions of plans for his coronation, however, led Goldwin Smith to reflect how well Britons concealed from themselves the secret that real government by hereditary kings belonged to the past, and that the prime minister was now an uncrowned king.[35] The English monarchy had undergone revolution and become at least semi-democratic. To him it seemed also to have become provisional, simply serving to secure order during a critical period and to facilitate an inevitable transition.

VIII

Goldwin Smith's impatience with monarchy was modified by the fact that although hereditary kings and queens still reigned in England, at least they no longer ruled. The Crown, moreover, symbolized the unity of the nation. These mitigating circumstances did not apply to the aristocracy, in a country which still possessed a House of Lords, and for it he had no good word to say. It was merely a privileged class, subjected to the corrupting influences of luxury, wealth, and a social position assured without exertion. The manners of young English noblemen he criticized on the ground that the only real school of manners is equality. Nor was he prepared to marvel, with Matthew Arnold, that human beings in a position so false should on the whole be so good. Since public virtue was not hereditary, he saw no reason why titles should be. To him they seemed nothing but baubles—badges of distinction without merit—breeding a false presumptuousness in their wearers, and in others humbug and sycophancy. The British aristocracy struck him as the most formidable existing enemy to progress and happiness in England, and "colonial flunkeyism" in the New World little short of a crime. Surely, he suggested, there should be some limits to the fatuous worship of people who, as Macaulay said of George III, had "no merits but abstinence from adultery and a preference for roast mutton."[36] As a product of Eton and Oxford Goldwin Smith had grown up on terms of easy familiarity and frequently of friendship with members of the ruling class. By temperament he was himself an intel-

---

[35]*Weekly Sun*, July 24 and Aug. 28, 1901; letter to the *Manchester Examiner and Times*, March, 1868; *Loyalty, Aristocracy and Jingoism* (Toronto, 1891).
[36]Letters to G. W. Curtis, Dec. 2, 1876, July 3, 1877.

lectual aristocrat. But he fully shared Mill's hatred of the class government which to him also seemed in mid-nineteenth-century England to usurp the name of democracy. Class lines were so sharply drawn that most members of the aristocracy knew little and cared less about how the great mass of the people lived, or what they thought. Government by such an élite, unconnected with industry and living apart from the people, Goldwin Smith condemned. In foreign affairs particularly, he thought it likely to result in complete misdirection of the policies and energy of an industrial nation.

His desire for the extension of the franchise in the early eighteen-sixties sprang principally from a passionate conviction that, in a country which ostensibly enjoyed representative government, to allow the aristocracy indirect control over the House of Commons in addition to exclusive power in the House of Lords was a glaring injustice. He had the Manchester School's whole-hearted belief that the aristocratic class was no longer capable of leading the nation. Whatever it might have been in Norman times, its day of usefulness was past. It had now become "an august nullity . . . a thing of feudal shreds and patches that can neither rule nor dazzle any more."[37]

The notion that the peers had acted as the sober second thought of the nation, correcting the rashness of the popular House, he dismissed as pure fiction. Why, indeed, should a young lord be less rash than an old commoner? Against the House of Lords he appealed, not to abstract theory, but to the historical record. In the past four hundred years the peers had done nothing but block all change, as far as they dared, in their own interest. They had delayed or prevented not only parliamentary reform, but religious toleration, freedom of the press, personal liberty, and such humanitarian legislation as the reform of the criminal law and the abolition of the slave trade. They had never initiated any major improvement, and in the case of the First Reform Act had finally succumbed to fear only when the nation had been brought to the verge of revolution. In his history of the United Kingdom Goldwin Smith wrote of this incident: "Thus the great oligarchy passed to its long account in history. . . . The golden age had begun." When the peers dared not throw out reforms they mutilated them, but never seriously considered any popular measure. In no single instance had they impartially revised precipitate legislation.

As early as 1860, when reform of the Commons was widely discussed, Goldwin Smith wrote an article entitled, "Why Not the Lords Too?" His avowed object was conservative, although he admitted that

[37]*Bystander*, I (Jan., 1880), 43.

the means proposed and some of the expressions used might appear revolutionary. Only by bold reform of the House of Lords, he argued, could a conservative element in the constitution be restored. He suggested that the second house should be made more representative (so that it might divide with the Commons the allegiance of the people), by appointing to it outstanding men from the great corporations, the universities, and the professions. Haste, he urged, was essential, before successive extensions of the suffrage rendered the Commons a complete reflection of the will of the sovereign people. That once done, it would be too late to attempt to impose any curb.[38]

For a democratic House of Commons to work in harmony with a purely hereditary House of Lords, he argued in 1868, was impracticable. The second chamber could not hope to stand if it attempted to vote against measures passed by the Commons. Yet unless it was different from the lower house, it was futile. By 1881 he thought conflict between the aristocracy and the nation imminent. The House of Lords was not a real second chamber or senate, but an estate of the realm. In any constitution a check on hasty legislation was essential, in the same way that quiet reflection on personal decisions was necessary for individuals. To be useful, however, such a check must be both rational and impartial. The House of Lords was neither. The peers seemed to him an invitation to revolution rather than a bulwark against it, since they dammed up the waters of progress until they became a flood. In the last quarter of the century he thought he could discern a change in attitude toward the aristocracy. Sensible men began to dread peerages for their sons, though fools still coveted them. Was there in a House of Lords, he demanded, any higher wisdom or morality which could afford a better guarantee of rational action than public opinion enlightened by general education? The combination of a court of appeal with a legislative assembly was a relic of the time when legislative, executive, and judicial functions were all exercised by the monarch. Under modern conditions such a fusion of powers could only be described as an anachronism. His chief count against the peers, in addition to their obstruction of change, was that they had given the general policy of England a class bias.

[38]"Why Not the Lords Too?", *Fraser's Magazine*, LXI (Feb., 1860), 290–300. This article is signed only with the initials G. S. Goldwin Smith expanded these views in a letter of March 27, 1860, to the 3rd Earl Grey, which is among the Grey Papers at the University of Durham. Cf. also his letter to the *Daily News*, March 5, 1868; "The Decline of Party Government," *Macmillan's Magazine*, XXXVI (Aug., 1877), 298–306; "The Machinery of Elective Government," *Nineteenth Century*, XI (Jan., 1882), 126–48.

These opinons about the House of Lords reflected a general belief that bicameralism was indefensible. Goldwin Smith had in fact arrived at this position before he left England, though he realized that public opinon would not yet support it, and that consequently it must for the time being remain purely speculative. When he left England at the end of the eighteen-sixties he was convinced that the danger of increased power concentrated in one chamber would be more than counterbalanced by the increased responsibility of a single legislature. After fifteen years' residence in Canada he still attacked second chambers and considered abolition easier than reform. Under elective institutions there could be no real power save that which rested in the votes of the people. Conservative checks were necessary, but he looked for them, not in a futile second chamber, but in a properly constituted lower house. Experience favoured a single assembly, in which all the best elements, conservative as well as progressive, might find a place, and temper each other by mutual interaction.[39]

From the time, however, when the Lords rejected Home Rule for Ireland (thereby in Goldwin Smith's opinion preserving the unity of the kingdom and performing their first useful act in centuries), his conviction of the worthlessness of second chambers altered, and he began to examine ways of mending rather than ending them. Like most other men he was more radical and more optimistic, doubtless more radical because more optimistic, when he was young. As he grew older he placed greater value on checks to democracy, and perceived at least one valid argument for retaining the House of Lords: namely the difficulty of devising anything to put in its place. To this endeavour he consequently bent his attention, as he became more convinced that no defects of an upper house could be as bad as an uncontrolled Commons. An assembly prepared to grant Home Rule might do anything. He favoured indirect election of the second chamber, by the county councils in England and by the provincial legislatures or electorates in Canada. Such a plan might be expected to produce a rationally conservative body, a real organ of national opinion, instead of a mere representation of landed and commercial interests. He proposed abolition of the hereditary principle in the Lords and the substitution, in both countries, of a set term of office for life tenure. A suspensive veto seemed to him precarious and inadequate.

By the end of the century he was convinced that no responsible person, however liberal or progressive, would wish to be left absolutely

[39]*Bystander*, I (Feb., 1880), 603, III (July, 1883), 189–90; *Week*, July 31, 1884.

at the mercy of a democratic or socialistic House of Commons, elected by universal suffrage. Only a whole-hearted believer in democracy could deny the need for a second chamber or its equivalent. "Wisdom herself must sometimes be beholden to a second thought. Moreover the rivalries of class, now becoming marked, call for mediation. There must be something to prevent injustice being done by the class that has many votes to the class that has few." Goldwin Smith thought the House of Lords should be considered not simply an obstacle to be removed, but an essential part of the constitution, with a purpose of its own. What was wanted was not only that it should cease to do evil, but that it should positively do good, that it should be characteristically a house of statesmanship as the Commons was characteristically a house of reformers.[40]

Despite his eventual belief in the need for an improved second chamber as a conservative check on rash innovation, he was suspicious of all proposals for reform other than his own. Campbell-Bannerman's plan to reduce the revising power of the upper house to a suspensory veto Goldwin Smith criticized in a letter to the *Manchester Guardian*, on the ground that this would be no real check, but only an irritant. An editorial in the same issue agreed with his own suggestion that his liberalism was perhaps a little timorous, although "Professor Goldwin Smith carried with him to Canada one of the finest traditions in English politics of the last century." The writer observed that the reformed second chamber which Smith desired as a real check on the Commons would be a much more powerful irritant than the existing house, because it would be stronger. Even Conservatives did not venture to plead for an effective check, but nowadays always defended the House of Lords on the ground that it expressed the real will of the people, not that it imposed a brake upon this will. The *Guardian* granted that some check was needed, but argued that this could be provided in only one way—by the people themselves. Any other method was fatal to the whole theory of democratic government. What was wanted was truer representation of the popular will; it was on misrepresentation, not representation, that checks were needed.[41] Even Goldwin Smith was realistic enough to admit that a genuine reform to increase the influence of the upper house would not meet the views of radicals in the Commons any more than those of Conservatives.

[40]"The Organization of Democracy," *Contemporary Review*, XLVII (March, 1885), 315–33; "The House of Lords: Reform by 'Resolution,'" *Nineteenth Century*, XXXV (April, 1894), 539–46.
[41]*Manchester Guardian*, Nov. 1, 1907.

As the controversy between the two houses became more acute during the last three years of his life, from 1907 to 1910, his concern about their relationship deepened. He not only bombarded English journals with his opinions, but arranged to have them brought to the attention of his old pupil, Edward VII. The king's private secretary wrote to explain that His Majesty had read with great interest Professor Goldwin Smith's views on the reform of the House of Lords. Bryce, writing from the British Embassy at Washington, thoroughly agreed with his friend's stand. To cripple the Lords by leaving its composition unchanged, while its powers were limited, was in his opinion virtually to abandon the chance of a really useful reformed upper house. To Goldwin Smith's suggestion that the house might be half nominated by the Crown, half elected by the Commons, Bryce replied that he favoured a majority of elected members. He thought most people agreed there was need for a second chamber different from the House of Lords and with restricted powers. But how it should be reconstituted and what authority it should have were questions which had not been thought out, even within the ranks of the Liberal party.[42]

When the Lloyd George budget was brought down in 1909, Goldwin Smith asked Lord Rosebery whether, if wealth was to be openly confiscated in the manner proposed, it would continue to be sought and stored. Rosebery answered that he thought the Lords had a moral right to deal with the budget, because its purpose was revolutionary, and its effect would be to infringe the salutary principle of no taxation without representation. He considered the finance bill "a wild catalogue of ill-digested schemes borrowed from socialism," designed to sweep away both the landed gentry and the House of Lords. The lack of an outburst against it in the country at large he attributed to the fact that wealth was always unpopular and always timid. However, as the Chancellor of the Exchequer knew nothing about finance and still less about his own proposals, Rosebery hoped that he might be exposed in Parliament, to the edification of the electorate. By August, 1909, he was still confident of the Lords' constitutional right, whether by precedent or common sense, to reject the budget, but thought it as yet too early to say what they ought to do. "The nation is now very different," he observed sadly, "from what it was when you and I first remember it. It thinks very little, derives its impressions from a cheap and wild press; it seems singularly lacking in discipline and ideals. That perhaps is so all over

---

[42]Letter from Goldwin Smith to Bryce, Aug. 31, 1907; letters from Bryce to Goldwin Smith; April 13 and Sept. 4, 1907, Jan. 20, 1908, Aug. 8, 1909, March 22, 1910.

the world. But it is not very easy for a nation of this kind to guide an empire." Rosebery's grasp of constitutional realities led him eventually to the conclusion that the Lords should pass the budget. He saw clearly that if they rejected it, an election would follow on grounds very favourable to the Government, which would probably be returned to power with an increased majority. The risk of renewing the Liberals' power, which they would undoubtedly use for socialistic purposes, he thought too great to run. Furthermore it might be salutary, if bitter, for the nation to have a brief experience of the disruption of trade and immediate increase of unemployment which he was sure the budget would produce.[43] Unfortunately for the peers, Rosebery's counsel of moderation did not prevail.

Goldwin Smith continued, like Rosebery and Dicey, to criticize the budget as a partisan political and socialist measure, disguised as a financial bill. It has so long been taken for granted, in the twentieth century, that a budget is an important instrument for effecting the purposes of the party in power that it is difficult to realize how much contemporary support existed half a century ago for such criticism. There was more shrewdness in Goldwin Smith's suggestion that the ultimate result of death duties would be the substitution of "ante-mortem donation for post-mortem bequest." The conflict between the Lords and the Commons, he observed, placed old radicals like himself in a strange position. "No radical, old or new, wishes to retain hereditary legislation. . . . At the same time no one whose Radicalism stops short of revolution wishes to see absolute power vested in a single chamber."[44] In a letter to Lord Channing, speaking of Lloyd George and Winston Churchill, he declared: "I can conceive nothing worse befalling the country than its getting into the hands of such men, with an infuriated Socialism behind them. The certainty that they would presently share the fate of the Girondins would not be a great consolation."[45]

Fortunately he did not live to see the passage of the Parliament Act. At the time of his death in 1910 he was oppressed by the fear that England was in great peril. Without a written constitution or other adequate safeguards against sudden changes, the country was exposed to unknown dangers from the whims of an ignorant electorate. His early Manchester School distrust of aristocracy was later modified by his fears of universal suffrage and of the newly formed Labour party.

[43]Letters from Lord Rosebery to Goldwin Smith, Jan. 2 and Dec. 27, 1908, Feb. 1, April 13, June 6, Aug. 25, Sept. 13 and Oct. 3, 1909; letters from Goldwin Smith to Lord Rosebery, Feb. 17 and May 4, 1909.
[44]*Weekly Sun*, June 30, May 5, 1909; letter to the *Spectator*, May 29, 1909.
[45]Oct. 11, 1909.

Viewed in the light of such developments there seemed more reason for an effective second chamber, if not for a governing class. His comment that most people were conservative on some points and radical on others applied with peculiar force to himself, and he had a genius for being radical where most Canadians were conservative and conservative where they were progressive. To the end of his days he presented an odd study in contrasts, an enigmatic compound of liberal and conservative beliefs. His temperamental inconsistency was accentuated by his living into an age very different from that in which his mind had matured. But from one liberal tenet he never deviated, a passionate faith in liberty, above all in freedom of opinion.

IX

Goldwin Smith clearly wore his liberalism with a difference. A Little Englander, he yet looked forward to the coming together of the English-speaking peoples of the world in a wider and freer union than that of the nineteenth-century British Empire. An adherent of the Manchester School, he yet voted for Sir John A. Macdonald's National Policy. An advocate of colonial emancipation, he was a violent opponent of Irish Home Rule. A Liberal Unionist, he was a bitter critic of absentee Irish landlords and preached incessantly that dependencies were destined to become independent. Nothing ever convinced him that Home Rule would be good for Ireland or that independence within the Empire was seriously possible for Canada. He believed in an extended franchise, but not for women; he supported the removal of restrictions upon trade union activities, but abhorred strikes and class bitterness; he favoured the free development of creeds and cultures, but deplored those of French Canada. There was some truth in a contemporary critic's description of him in 1894 as "an arrested Liberal," who retracted nothing, and had not even become timid, but had simply stood still for the past twenty years. He was indeed a liberal who lived too long, and whose reputation would have stood higher had he died in his forties instead of in his eighties. At heart half Peelite, half Radical, and the last of the early Victorians, his liberalism was permanently moulded by the time he left England in 1868 to make his home on the other side of the Atlantic.

He was then forty-five, an age at which most men's opinions have become set. Moreover the England of the era after the 1867 Reform Act was very different from the England which preceded it, and of this later Britain, despite frequent return visits, Goldwin Smith had little first-hand knowledge. His home was in Canada during the last three decades of the century which saw the reform of the civil service, the completion of manhood suffrage, and the rise of the labour movement. Had he lived in England while these developments were taking place he might have understood them better, and hence have shown more sympathy with them. A temperamental pessimist and sceptic, his cynicism was sharpened by contact with the less attractive side of North American democracy, though at the same time he was quick to admire its virtues.

In the eighteen-seventies he called himself a republican. He certainly went farther than most Liberals in detesting the aristocracy and in placing a low value upon the monarchy. Ten years later he thought he deserved the name of radical, but protested that no Conservative could be more opposed to revolution. With a touch of wistfulness he said in 1890 that "a loyal Englishman and a Unionist who is not a jingo, a Liberal who is not a Socialist or Revolutionist, is now a nondescript, for whom hardly any haven of refuge is open in the press." "An old-fashioned Liberal," he later lamented, "who is satisfied with political and social justice, national independence, and the full measure of individual liberty consistent with law, finds himself out of touch with his age and regarded as a political and social mastodon." An English reporter's description of him in 1907 as "a well-known exponent of Canadian Conservative opinion" must have been equally startling to Goldwin Smith and to Canadian Conservatives. But he was pleased when, two years before his death, a friend spoke of him as one who had kept the traditions of the old Radicals. An old Radical, he affirmed, was the designation he meant to give the porter at the gate of heaven.[46]

[46]"The Invitation to Celebrate the French Revolution," *National Review*, XI (Aug., 1888), 729–47; letters to the *St. James Gazette*, June 4, 1890; to the *Manchester Guardian*, Feb. 3, 1908; *Weekly Sun*, Sept. 10, 1902; interview with Goldwin Smith, *Sheffield Daily Independent*, Aug. 16, 1907.

VII. STATE AND INDIVIDUAL

INTELLECTUAL DOUBT and economic unrest, during the last thirty years of the nineteenth century, accompanied militant imperialism and commercial prosperity. Thoughtful people began to question the inevitability of progress, instead of taking it for granted. "We live," wrote Goldwin Smith in 1897, "in a highly civilized, highly restless, highly anxious and highly sensitive age."[1] Among its typical maladies, he noted, were an increase in suicides and in mental illness. John Stuart Mill was the outstanding proponent of individual liberty, yet before his death in 1873 he had moved to what he described as a position of qualified socialism. He cared as much as ever for freedom, but had come to define it in terms different from those of his famous earlier essay. Between Mill, who stood at the end of the distinguished line of English individualists, and Hobhouse, who at the beginning of the twentieth century bridged the gap between liberalism and socialism, there was little fundamental difference of opinion. Both resolved the intellectual dilemma by a belief that individualism and collectivism were complementary, not antithetical, since every group is composed of individuals and every individual is a member of a community.

With the views of Mill and Hobhouse Goldwin Smith agreed more than he was always willing to admit. His inaugural lecture of 1858 discussed the great questions of social and political philosophy which confronted the age. No period, he suggested, had to deal with more important issues than the rights of the labouring population, the education of the people, and the distribution of political power among all classes of the community. As a liberal humanitarian confronted by the social problems of the day, he was concerned to examine the relation of the state to its citizens and the proper function of government. An individualist no less passionate than Mill, he feared quite as much the tyranny of the majority but was less willing to move from his original position and to grant the need for widening the sphere of the state. Both were convinced of the merits of the instructed few and of the probable

[1]*Weekly Sun*, Jan. 14, 1897.

inherent virtues of a minority—a natural enough position for temperamental dissenters. Yet Goldwin Smith attacked the contention of extreme exponents of laissez-faire that such measures as factory acts were an unjustifiable interference with individual freedom. Popular suffering, he reiterated, was the spur to socialism. His views on the functions of government as on many other questions were too advanced for the timid, too cautious for the radical. Thus he pleased neither camp, and the very independence of his position lessened his practical influence. To the unpopularity of his views he was supremely indifferent, although he cared much about shaping opinion and the course of public affairs.

In a period when most liberals, as well as conservatives, considered poverty a natural retribution for incompetence and vice, Goldwin Smith inveighed against the vulgar worship of success which led men to look upon the material misfortunes of others as the judgment of heaven. Two decades before the Fabians he was arguing that poverty sprang from many sources, general as well as personal: not from indolence and intemperance alone, but from old age, ill health, the decline of trade, the failure of harvests, and the growth of population beyond the means of subsistence. A very large proportion of crime, he assured a Manchester audience in 1866, was the offspring of want, and could be effectively removed only by giving the people bread. At that time such a doctrine, while perhaps acceptable in the stronghold of the anti-corn law movement, was for the most part highly unpopular.

To Goldwin Smith social hatred seemed a bad reformer. He detested all conspiracy, whether that of Ignatius Loyola or of Karl Marx. Unlike many of his contemporaries he read Marx, and underestimated him less than did most nineteenth-century British liberals. Early in the eighteen-eighties he was confident that the influence of Bakunin, Lassalle, and Marx had not died with them. Thirty years later, however, he made the unfortunate prophecy that Marx seemed to be rather falling into the background. The goal of Marx and his followers seemed to him a dictatorship, political, moral and social, exercised in the spirit of Robespierre, although avowedly in the interests of the proletariat. From this class all those who worked with their brains instead of their hands were by definition excluded. If Marx had been willing to include all labourers, both by hand and brain, Goldwin Smith would have been prepared to agree with his dictum that everything rightly belonged to labour. The first problem for communists to solve was how to find a government sufficiently wise and impartial to justify entrusting it with the functions of a political autocrat, an omniscient taskmaster, and a universal proprietor. He concluded that communism, as a movement, was a mistake, but that a kind of communism was deep-rooted in every good man, which made him feel that "the hardest of all labour is idleness in a world of toil, and that the bitterest of all bread is that which is eaten by the sweat of another man's brow."[2]

I

Then as now it was easier to attack or defend socialism than to define it. Nineteenth-century writers who were apt to assume that such words as democracy and liberty needed no definition, because everyone knew what they meant, were more interested than their twentieth-century successors in trying to assign a precise meaning to the new concepts of anarchism and socialism, and to distinguish between their different varieties. Goldwin Smith believed that socialism proper was a vision of felicity and equality in a world of suffering and inequality, a vision presented in its most appealing and least practical form in the Utopia of Sir Thomas More, and in a guise somewhat less appealing and more practical by such men as Robert Owen, Saint-Simon, and Fourier. The practicality of Fourier's picture of a lemonade sea, inhabited by anti-whales, which washed the shores of a land populated by anti-lions instead of ordinary lions, is, however, open to question.

Belief in abstract equality such as that enshrined in the Declaration of Independence seemed to Goldwin Smith little less visionary. The author of the dictum "all men are created equal," he pointed out, was himself a slave-owner. With due deference to Jefferson, he considered the statement a self-evident fallacy. All men had an equal right to justice, but there, in his view, their natural equality ended. Surely they were created, not equal, but infinitely diverse, mentally, physically, and morally. Inequality of capacity inevitably meant inequality of opportunity, though he agreed that there were inequalities of fortune far beyond any differences of capacity and merit. Yet if it were possible today to wipe out all distinctions by rolling humanity flat, he had no doubt that by tomorrow the differences would reappear. He hazarded the hope that the inequalities of happiness were less great than the inequalities of wealth, but granted that it was understandable that the unhappy should be apt to take inequality for injustice. In a discussion with Cobden on the French Revolution, Goldwin Smith attacked its denial of political and personal liberty and of freedom of thought. He himself, he insisted, desired equality, but a more genial and less envious equality, the offspring of reason and social duty, not of the guillotine.[3]

[2]"The Labour Movement," *Canadian Monthly*, II (Dec., 1872).
[3]Letters to Cobden, Jan. 28, 1863, Cobden Papers, XIX, ff. 160–1; to the *Sun*, Nov. 4, 1906, Sept. 29, 1901.

Differences of capacity and character, he maintained, led naturally to differences in success and position in life. Hence arose class divisions which might be mitigated but could scarcely be abolished. Henry George's contention that progress and poverty went together was no more true than Marx's dictum that the rich were becoming richer and the poor poorer. Both were dangerous fallacies, disproved by history. Goldwin Smith had no sympathy with the luxurious life of the idle rich, whom he considered the most dangerous of all classes, since by the vulgar ostentation of wealth they excited among the people at once envy and contempt. But he was impressed by the amount done in England during the course of his long life and still being done to improve the condition of the labouring poor. Only a man blind to the facts of social history, he thought, could fail to recognize this. Karl Marx and Henry George did not write history from an impartial analysis of the facts. Had they done so, their economic doctrine would have had less effect. Goldwin Smith agreed that much remained to be done and commented bitterly on the fearful inequality in the distribution of goods. But he found the chief cause less in the imperfections of social and political institutions than in the accidental advantages of health and intellect meted out by nature on no principle of distributive justice. Civilization tended to mitigate such distinctions.

Yet the thought of the difference between rich and poor must press upon the heart of every rich man who has one, especially if he is a follower of Jesus of Nazareth, and dispose him not only to relieve distress and avoid that ostentatious use of wealth which adds bitterness to poverty, but to give a ready ear to any theories which promise to render the condition of men more equal. He will only ask that the theory shall bear the stamp of goodwill, and not of envy and hatred, for of envy and hatred neither truth nor justice can come. Some show of practicability may also be reasonably required.[4]

Goldwin Smith practised what he preached, for he was always ready to consider seriously any proposals, including those of socialists, which were designed to improve economic conditions. Like Hobhouse, however, he believed that some types of socialism were defensible, but others were not. Marxism he rejected on the ground that arousing class hatred and conflict was no way to usher in a régime of brotherly love. He put his finger on one weakness of communist theory when he pointed out that socialism of this sort, while looking to the goal of a classless society, fed to a remarkable extent on class bitterness. He could see no

[4]*Bystander*, II (May, 1881), 269-70.

sense in denouncing a whole class as robbers and tyrants when most of them, in fact, were nothing of the kind. The vision of More and Owen, no matter how impractical, was at least that of a social paradise. Modern revolutionary socialism, which taught class hatred and applauded the bomb-thrower, even if combined with a dash of idealism, seemed to him a vision of a social hell. Municipal ownership of public services, which in the eighteen-eighties began to be described as gas-and-water socialism, he considered not socialism at all, but probably the most satisfactory system of administration, providing confidence could be placed in the public authorities. It was simply a question of what could be done best by individuals, and what by the community. Much depended on the quality of the government. Some limits to public ownership he thought necessary, and cautioned devotees to remember that political management might bring political jobbery in its train. Services such as water, lighting, transportation, and telegraphs should clearly be run by public authorities, but he saw no reason for transferring other industries to state control.

Socialist views neither surprised nor shocked Goldwin Smith, who simply considered them natural products of human inequalities. He did not deny that the dream of the socialist might be in some measure fulfilled, yet a dream he thought it must remain until certain specific questions were answered. Above all he wanted to know where the human material for fashioning an earthly paradise was to be found, what were to be the guarantees for the integrity and wisdom of the socialist state, how its autocracy could be reconciled with freedom, and how without freedom progress could endure. His own position, he wrote at the age of seventy, was that of "a Liberal of the old school as yet unconverted to State Socialism, who looks for further improvement not to an increase of the authority of government, but to the same agencies moral, intellectual, and economical, which have brought us thus far."[5] After all, on the old lines society was advancing, though slowly, toward equality and fraternity as well as toward liberty. Within his own lifetime there had developed an increasing belief that property had duties as well as rights, an enthusiasm for philanthropy, and a sense of social brotherhood. The more equal distribution of political power through an extended franchise brought some security against oppression. All these were of recent birth and were effecting a great change, though not a sudden transformation. Any abortive attempt at such a transformation would wreck reasonable hopes for lasting improvement.

In a review of *Man versus the State*, published in 1884, Goldwin

[5]Preface to *Essays on Questions of the Day* (Toronto, 1893), v.

Smith showed a certain sympathy with Herbert Spencer. He agreed that the radicalism of the eighteen-eighties was really a new toryism, restraint being a conservative doctrine as opposed to the true liberal principle of relaxing restraint. Had not liberalism of late tried to pursue its ends through the coercion of law instead of through the removal of restrictions? For him, however, Spencer's uncompromising enthusiasm for complete laissez-faire went too far. He granted that the functions most proper to government were national defence, the maintenance of public order, the protection of property, and the repression of crime. But he could not agree that the actions of government should always be limited to these. The state

> must sometimes become paternal; it must, as in the case of children employed in factories, take care of those who cannot take care of themselves; it must enforce regulations which, though interferences with private habits, are essential to public health or comfort; it must sometimes interpose to save people from the consequences of their own misconduct, and prevent them from dying of hunger on the street, though their destitution may be the consequence of their own faults and the penalty affixed to such faults by nature. Strictly to define the duties of a government is impossible; they must vary with the circumstances, with the character of the nation and the stage of civilization which it has reached. Government is the organ of the community for such purposes as it may be found, from time to time, expedient to effect by common action. But unless we have renounced our faith in liberty and its fruits we must all hold that the narrower is the range of coercion, the wider that of free action, the better for each man and the community it will be.[6]

Here is no pure doctrine of the Manchester School, no stand-pat adherence to the *status quo*. The passage foreshadows, well before Hobhouse, the distinction between society and the state so important in the definition of democracy.

Goldwin Smith detested the habit of apostrophizing the state as a fictitious being, a kind of earthly vicar of God, when in fact it was nothing but an abstract entity. The only political body with a real existence was the government, with its attendant institutions, which merely enjoyed such rights and duties as the community assigned it. The leading politicians of the hour were not archangels but men. The government to him was simply one of the great associations within the community, created by human beings to perform certain tasks. Other fundamental associations, such as the family, had their own rights and obligations. He disliked systems of public education because he thought they transferred to the state one of the proper responsibilities of parents. In his

[6]*Week*, Jan. 31, April 3 and 24, 1884.

view, the family was ultimately more important than the state, and a greater source of character and happiness. So long as its integrity was unimpaired, it had power to regenerate the state, whereas the state had none to regenerate the family. Hence he sympathized with Spencer's fears of a bureaucracy in which the arch-bureaucrat became master, not only of the state but of such other associations as the family, the church, and the school.

While he conceded that government must sometimes become paternal, Goldwin Smith was concerned about certain aspects of paternalism which seemed increasingly to threaten individual liberty.

Government [he commented gloomily] is in some quarters encouraged to become the universal educator, sanitary guide, purveyor of literature, and provider of amusements for the people, as well as the reliever of every kind of distress. . . . Socialism, the ultimate consummation of the system on which the world seems now disposed to enter, would actually, as Mr. Spencer says, be a revival of Slavery, since each man in the army of workers would be compelled to render absolute obedience to the command of the officers appointed to set each his task. Then liberty and progress at once would cease.

He feared many hard-won liberties might be lost unless philanthropic drill-sergeants could be persuaded that there was a moral limit to the prerogatives of the ballot as well as of kings. "The fate of society," he suggested, "would be hard if, after emancipating itself by centuries of struggle and suffering from the tyranny of monarchs, it were doomed to fall under the more searching tyranny of crotcheteers."

II

No political or social problem of the day failed to interest Goldwin Smith, but to him the most important was the relation between labour and capital. Few doctrines irritated him more than that of class war. In a period when Bryce and Dicey were inclined to define democracy as simply the rule of the majority, which might well lead to collective mediocrity, Goldwin Smith insisted that its more fundamental characteristic must be a common faith in the essential unity of the interests underlying class divisions. In the eighteen-sixties this conception had few upholders. There was novelty in his argument that the consciousness of a real community of interests must ultimately survive all class distinctions, and end the conflict between labour and capital, not by making one the slave of the other, but by establishing between them mutual good will, founded on justice and intelligence. The attainment of such a community seemed to him the aim of all social effort and the goal toward which society must press. "Pass from the dwellings of the rich to those of the poor," he wrote, "and you will own, that though we may be a great and powerful nation, a community in the full sense of the term we are not. . . . Though man does not live by bread alone, he must have bread to live. . . . The removal of physical misery staunches the greatest source of crime."[7]

Most of his contemporaries thought social war unlikely, despite such signs of the times as Chartism, the Social Democratic Federation, and the development of the labour movement. Goldwin Smith was less sanguine about the immediate future, though more confident that modern democracy was ultimately based on an underlying harmony. Who, he asked, thought civil war possible till it came? As early as 1877 he commented on the danger of the widening social distance between classes in England's new industrial society where the old personal relations between an employer and his workmen were fast disappearing. Yet he argued that in a Canadian community, at least, there was no such thing as class in the strict sense of the term. Gradations of property and social status there were and would continue to be, but the overriding and tyrannical caste structure which the socialist conjured up was purely a figment of his own disordered brain. The Marxist, Goldwin Smith pointed out, thought of nothing but the workingman and the millionaire. To what class would he assign the independent farmer, the storekeeper, and the small business man? How could a sharp line be drawn between classes when there was a perpetual interchange of personnel among them?

To the decline in religious faith he attributed much of the semi-communism which was beginning to appear even at the universities. He found natural enough the determination to get here and now the good things which people no longer were confident of securing hereafter, since they had ceased to believe in a future state wherein Dives and Lazarus would change places. It was not the impatience of the unfortunate, but their patience, which roused his wonder. After all, the poor were freshly possessed of political power and wanted to use it to secure change. They were just in that twilight of education, warned Goldwin Smith, in which chimeras stalk. That a religious basis for socialism was possible he seemed to have no inkling, despite the importance of religious motives in the development of the English labour

[7]*England and America* (Manchester, 1865), 13; *Letter to a Whig Member of the Southern Independence Association* (Boston, 1864), 8–9.

movement. The Christian Socialism of men like Maurice and Kingsley he discounted as of no significance. The Oxford student's heart leapt up at socialism, he wryly observed, as in his own undergraduate days in the eighteen-forties it had leapt up at neo-Catholicism, and as tomorrow it would leap up at whatever the bright vision of the day might be.[8]

Socialists denounced more violently than other men all existing governments as untrustworthy and incompetent, yet proposed to invest the socialist state with powers more searching and more absolute than any ever exercised by emperor or dictator. Goldwin Smith would not join the socialists till he knew how they proposed to obtain this all-wise and just state. That socialism should increase, however, as men grew more sensitive and more thoughtful, he considered natural. Indeed he regarded this growth with qualified satisfaction on the ground that the socialist at least had the happiness of mankind at heart, and meant to be loyal to freedom, though the tendency of his theory was against it.

In the last twenty years of the nineteenth century socialism seemed to him the only strong force in the political field against militant imperialism. He liked it the better of the two, and suspected that it would be the more enduring. Yet he discerned with uneasiness signs of an approaching conflict, unlikely to terminate in a ballot box, between civilization and anarchism. At the turn of the century he noted that liberalism was everywhere losing ground. For the moment conservatism seemed to be gaining, but socialism was gaining still more. It looked as though extremists and moderates would ultimately be left to fight for control of the political world, in a struggle between some form of socialism and the principle of individual liberty.[9]

Yet socialism, even when defined as public ownership of the means of production and distribution, was in his view a sign of the times. He believed that it probably had salutary lessons to teach, at least to the idle rich, and he fully admitted its right to perfect freedom of discussion, so long as it kept within the bounds of law. When in 1906 the Canadian Postmaster-General banned an American socialist journal, all Goldwin Smith's liberal instincts against censorship were roused, and he argued that written matter should be refused admission only if it incited to violence.

In the latter half of the nineteenth century most Englishmen took it for granted that political and civil liberties had been so firmly established that henceforth they would rest on an unshakeable foundation. Goldwin

[8]Report of an address at Shipley, *Bradford Observer*, Sept. 28, 1877; "England Revisited," *Macmillan's Magazine*, LIV (Oct., 1886), 401–12.
[9]*Weekly Sun*, June 27, 1900, July 10, 1901.

Smith was less confident, believing that the holders of power might yet try to extirpate revolutionary opinion. The tolerance of the sceptical eighteenth century, which had ended wars of religion, was in his view based partly upon indifference to religious issues. A similar indifference would scarcely prevail in the political sphere if those interested in the existing state of things were menaced with the confiscation of their property and the destruction of their social institutions.

For the anarchist doctrines too often confused with those of socialism, he had no sympathy. Coupling the two was a libel upon socialists, who for the most part sought their ends by peaceful means. Between revolutionary communism and anarchism he saw more affinity. Both were phenomena of discontent, but whereas communism desired to confiscate and level, anarchism wanted permanently to destroy the state, to produce chaos out of which a new world might be born. He took pains, however, to stress the marked difference between the dagger and dynamite anarchism of Bakunin and the idealistic anarchism of Tolstoi and Kropotkin, who would soon be disillusioned by a short experience of a country without government or police. The gentle anarchism of the lamblike Kropotkin and the evangelical enthusiasm of Tolstoi were speculative and visionary, based on the belief that human nature was so good that all compulsion might be abolished. Tolstoi's proposal to forbid private ownership of land was impractical, since what the Russian peasant really wanted was to own land himself. But Goldwin Smith sympathized with Kropotkin's argument that co-operation and mutual aid were as important as competition and the struggle for existence.[10]

Writing of Russian nihilism at the beginning of the eighteen-eighties, he foretold that revolution was coming in Russia. Since the country lacked the makings of democracy, the change could scarcely be democratic. The Russian masses were unripe for anything but benevolent autocracy. As violent revolutions tended to result in military despotisms rather than free governments, Russia was unlikely to produce another model of the British constitution. Nihilism paralysed genuine reform. It perpetuated the tyranny and corruption of the government by making impossible the objects at which reform ought to aim: free discussion, reduction of bureaucracy, and diminution of military power. Russian socialism was all too reminiscent of French Terrorism, and a Russian

---

[10]Letter to the *Sun*, Sept. 23, 1900; *Weekly Sun*, April 24, 1901, Aug. 9, 1905.
When Kropotkin visited Toronto in 1897 to deliver two papers at the meetings of the British Society for the Advancement of Science, he dined at the Grange with Goldwin Smith, who later commented that if all anarchists were like Kropotkin he would be one himself. James Mavor, *My Windows on the Street of the World* (2 vols., London, 1923), II, 133.

revolution too likely to result, not in a glorious millennium of freedom, but in autocratic government run by Cossacks. He thought Russia urgently needed reform, but feared lest revolutionary feeling there might only breed an equally murderous counter-repression, and that between them they might well wipe out such civilization as the country enjoyed. "There is in fact," he wrote in 1904, "no saying what might be the consequences to Europe of a Russian revolution."[11]

III

The metamorphosis, at the turn of the century, of English liberalism into liberal socialism profoundly disquieted Goldwin Smith. From the eighteen-eighties his letters reflected growing uneasiness. He was horrified at Gladstone's conversion to Home Rule, scandalized by the Newcastle Programme of 1891, and concerned about the internal struggles for leadership of the disunited Liberal party. To him Lord Rosebery's 1894 ministry was a "Home Rule and Socialist Government," and both the Eight Hours Act and the Employers' Liability Bill interference with liberty of contract. Though the party from which such measures emanated retained the name of liberal, he held that it was, in truth, no longer liberal, but socialistic. Members of Parliament hardly kept up the pretence of voting according to their conscience, but obeyed the dictates of the caucus, till they were reduced to the status, not merely of delegates, but of political messengers. Lacking any effective check, he feared that an English Parliament might overnight change fundamental institutions, dismember the realm (i.e., grant Irish Home Rule), or pass sweeping measures of agrarian confiscation.[12]

What struck him most on his return to England in 1894 after several years' absence was the decline of the landed gentry, once a great power in the country, but now impoverished, and the advance of semi-socialism. An old Liberal like himself found different principles attached to the name from those in which he was brought up. "Then we wanted to restrict government to its necessary functions, and leave the rest to individual initiative and decision. Now the tendency is greatly to enlarge the sphere of government, and extend it even to private and domestic matters. It may be, of course, that they are right and I am wrong, but

[11] *Weekly Sun*, Dec. 21, 1904.
[12] "Problems and Perils of British Politics," *North American Review*, CLIX (July, 1894), 13.

all I want is that if they are going to place all these matters in the hands of 'government', they should tell us what their government is to be."[13] He congratulated Canadians and Americans on their relative immunity to the semi-socialism which was infecting Britain. This he attributed to the fact that every North American either possessed or hoped to possess property; hence self-help and independence were still the native American creed. To try to light the flame of nationalization in a country of freehold farmers was like throwing a match into the Hudson.

Goldwin Smith's concern about the condition of affairs in Britain was sharpened by the views of many English friends of his own age. Lord Selborne, his contemporary at Oxford, wrote bitterly:

We are certainly in a most critical state here politically. Gladstone is morally insane: and under his management the party which used to glory in the name of Liberal has become demoralized to an extent which bodes ill for the future of this country. I do not like to play the part of Cassandra: and it is impossible to say, what recuperative power may yet remain to us. But the system of political bribery, not improperly described . . . as "putting up the institutions of the country to auction," brings out all the selfish cupidity of which classes or individuals are capable.[14]

The accession to power, a decade later, of Campbell-Bannerman's Liberal ministry, and its triumph at the polls in 1906, when fifty-three Labour members (including the trade union supporters of the Liberal Government) also secured seats, was not calculated to allay such doubts. By this time over eighty, Goldwin Smith was unlikely to welcome reforms far in advance of those he had supported forty years earlier. His political thinking had been shaped by the ideas and conditions of the mid-Victorian era. In the new century he was acutely disturbed by fresh currents of thought and opinion. In letters to friends he advocated a general combination of moderates to make a stand against socialism and revolution. Asquith might, he granted, be able, but his party was no longer entitled to call itself Liberal when it was in fact a jumble of liberalism, Home Rule, radicalism, labourism and socialism.

His apprehension about labour as a political force was shared by his friend, James Bryce, who held office in the Liberal Government as Chief Secretary for Ireland from 1905–7, and afterwards as British ambassador to the United States. "The rise of a so-called 'Labour party,'" Bryce wrote from London, "whose most active spirits are practically socialists, seems the most ominous cloud on our horizon. Sound economics have

[13]Interview with Goldwin Smith, *Illustrated London News*, March 24, 1894.
[14]Letters from Lord Selborne to Goldwin Smith, Oct. 7 and Nov. 22, 1893, Easter Day, 1894, Autograph Album, The Grange, Art Gallery of Toronto.

been sadly forgotten in England." The Labour party, he thought in 1906, had not so far proved dangerous. Half of those who bore the name were

really no more than advanced Liberals, who render a general and valuable support to Liberal measures. The other or "Independent" half contains a few socialists, perhaps five or six, and a certain number of rather ignorant and rather irresponsible persons. But only a few show ignorance of principles and what may be called the revolutionary temper. However a larger Labour party, with a strong leader, might become dangerous. Indeed any new party aloof from the two old-fashioned ones, and perhaps holding the balance between them, as in Australia, must spoil the working of our Constitution.

Two years later Bryce was still uneasy, though he thought the Labour party as yet too weak to be likely to win over the English working man. But he dreaded its effect on democratic political institutions, as a development which threatened the cabinet system and might demoralize politics.[15]

Lord Rosebery considered socialism less dangerous in Britain than elsewhere. Its root cause, he wrote Goldwin Smith, was "a desperate sense of the misery of the world and a clutching at any new remedy, however wild." In a subsequent letter he dealt acidly with a recent newspaper statement that the Liberal party's task must be the redistribution of property in order to correct existing inequalities. "If one could be astonished at anything," he observed, "one would be surprised to find so many sane people talking so glibly of the right of the State to limit and apportion wealth.... Individualism shrinks and shrinks ... and a hungry collectivism seeks to appropriate and administer everything."[16] Goldwin Smith agreed.

IV

Despite his fears of socialism, he always prided himself on being a friend of labour. He liked to mention that he had appeared on a platform with Joseph Arch, the organizer of the English agricultural workers, and had supported the effort to free British trade unions from

[15]Bryce letters to Goldwin Smith, Dec. 23, 1905, June 16, 1906, Oct. 17, 1908; Goldwin Smith letters to General J. H. Wilson, June 15, 1908, to Sir Robert Mowbray, March 7 and Oct. 8, 1906, Jan. 11, 1907.
[16]Letters from Lord Rosebery to Goldwin Smith, Dec. 4, 1907, May 25, 1908.

legal restrictions. He had never failed to cast a vote for "a respectable labour candidate with any chance of success." He sincerely believed that to be secure society must show that it was trying to be just. But he deprecated as immoral a resort to strikes purely in the interest of strikers, without regard for the general well-being of industry and the community; a point of view remote from that of the more radical union organizers. He had, however, some understanding of the workman's attitude, and granted that it was difficult to distinguish between the conduct of men who struck against a reduction of wages and that of employers who combined to lock them out. Goldwin Smith could not accept class war as inevitable, and considered strikes a barbarous and wasteful means of settling differences of opinion. Picketing and forcing a man to join a union against his will seemed obvious infringements of individual liberty, and voluntary conciliation and arbitration preferable to the compulsory systems of Australia and New Zealand.

In Canada he was in much demand as a speaker at union meetings. He contributed occasionally to labour journals, gave the newly established Toronto Labour Temple a collection of books as the nucleus of a small library, and delivered the address at its opening. During the Ontario provincial election campaign of 1902 he supported a labour candidate, on the ground that no legislative assembly was complete without a representative of labour. Every great interest, he declared in a vein reminiscent of Mill, ought to have a vote, and no one could speak for labour as well as working men. Six years later, at the age of eighty-four, he contributed $100 to the Independent Labor Party's Ontario campaign fund. During periods of unemployment and depression he made generous contributions to the Labour Temple for unemployed trade unionists and their families, and to it his will bequeathed $1,000. When the Toronto Lithographers' Union was engaged in a dispute with their employers they asked Goldwin Smith to act as an unofficial conciliator. To Mackenzie King, then federal Minister of Labour, he expressed his conviction that the only solution for labour difficulties lay in some form of industrial partnership between labour and capital.

In all these activities, as in his friendship with John Burns, there was a hint of the benevolent aristocrat. The truth is that Goldwin Smith and labour representatives never managed to feel wholly comfortable with each other. There was a gulf between them which good will on both sides did not bridge. Two decades after the Education Act of 1870 he thought the English people had been educated just up to the point at which scepticism and socialism found access to their minds. He was concerned because trade unions, despite their undoubted merits, served as nurseries of antagonism between employers and employed. He criticized the British Trade Disputes Act of 1906, which reversed the Taff Vale decision that unions were liable for pecuniary losses to companies caused by strikes. "I wish well to the unions," he wrote a friend, "and have no doubt that they were necessary to justice. But this truckling to them in the British Parliament is shameful and disastrous; disastrous it will probably be in the end to the unions themselves."[17]

Trade unionists, for their part, regarded with caution, at best, his advice that employers and workmen should co-operate instead of looking upon each other as natural enemies. They did not easily sympathize with his insistence that if democracy was to endure the community must in a real sense be one, not two antagonistic classes. Nor did they always grant the justice of his contention that when industrial disputes affected the public, its welfare must come first. Goldwin Smith denied that public utility employees should be permitted to strike, on the ground that it was unjust for one section of the community, providing a vital service, to inconvenience other citizens who were not parties to the dispute. Workers could scarcely be expected to share his fear that society was "in danger of being crushed between the upper millstone of accumulated capital and the nether millstone of labour unions," nor to agree that the movement for a closed shop resembled the guild tyranny of the Middle Ages.

Yet on both sides good will did exist. Goldwin Smith really believed that working men should be represented in the legislature, in municipal councils, and on boards of education, and gave practical effect to this belief by contributing toward the campaign expenses of labour candidates. He also thought that labourers should have decent homes and adequate wages. When he addressed a meeting of the Trades and Labor Congress in 1905 he received an ovation as, in the words of the chairman, "the most sincere friend of labour in Canada." A year later he told the annual convention of the Plasterers' International Union that he saw nothing socialistic in the public ownership of public utilities, of which, indeed, he thought everyone would approve "provided there is no public robbery committed in the transfer."[18] On his death Toronto journalists commented that probably no other man outside the ranks of labour was as popular with Canadian trade unionists.

[17]Letter to the 4th Earl Grey, Dec. 5, 1906, Grey Papers; *Weekly Sun*, July 9, 1902; "The Invitation to Celebrate the French Revolution," *National Review*, XI (Aug., 1888), 729–47.
[18]*Tribune* (Toronto), Sept. 29, 1906; *Globe*, Sept. 19, 1905.

V

Like most liberals of the day, Goldwin Smith supported some social legislation and some state intervention in economic affairs. But income taxes, succession duties, minimum wages set by law, and old age pensions all seemed to him indefensible. He considered an income tax unfair, demoralizing, inquisitorial, and socialistic. He was critical of the accumulation of vast fortunes by a few multi-millionaires, but equally critical of what to him was a confiscatory inheritance tax on estates of $100,000 and over. He inveighed against a Toronto municipal by-law which forbade city employees to be paid less than fifteen cents an hour, and suggested that the first step to provide work for the unemployed during a period of depression was to repeal this enactment. Labour could not be given value by an act of the legislature, nor a price beyond its real worth be set on any commodity. Every man had a right to whatever his labour would fetch, but minimum wages merely prevented the natural distribution of employment at a time of need.[19]

Similarly he rejected legislative limitation of working hours. He favoured the general objects of those who pressed for the early closing of shops and for a nine hours' working day, since free time should be within the reach of all, not merely the few. But leisure should be obtained by negotiation between employers and employed, not by state action. If it were true that as much or more work would be done in shorter hours, then presumably the employer would see what was for his own interest and free contract would produce the desired result. Yet Goldwin Smith, like Cobden and Bright, made some exceptions for children, although the suggestion that children of poor parents should be given free meals at school struck him as "demagogic confiscation." He regretted that the federal factory bill of 1883 remained abortive, since the government did nothing socialistic or beyond its rightful sphere in protecting those unable to protect themselves. "That children are for the purposes of a Factory Act the wards of the State," he wrote in the *Bystander* for July, 1883, "nobody denies, nor does anybody question the terrible effects of setting them to work beyond their strength, for too long a time, or in unwholesome air. . . . It would be hard if, while the master manufacturer is protected against the community, the community were to be debarred from protecting the health of its women and children against the selfishness of the master manu-

[19]Letters to J. V. L. Pruyn, Jan. 27, 1866; to the *Mail*, Nov. 23, 1894, Dec. 7, 1895; "The Labour Movement," 531.

facturer." It was good Manchester School doctrine that protective legislation for children should not be applied to adults, or at least not to men.

With the proposals for old age pensions in England at the end of the nineteenth century and in Canada early in the twentieth, Goldwin Smith had little sympathy. As an alternative to the poorhouse there was much to be said for pensions for old people, but the scheme seemed to him open to many dangers, and he was convinced that if those who stood to benefit from social legislation possessed political power, their pressure for increased grants would be steady and irresistible. Fifty years earlier, as a member of the Royal Commission on Popular Education in Britain, it had been his special task to inquire into the operation of charitable endowments. He had then been impressed with the tendency of almshouses and doles to breed improvidence among the poor. To the end of his life he never ceased to fear that large-scale systems of what he considered public almsgiving would invite thriftlessness. From this defect the poorhouse, being penal and deterrent, was largely free. He emphasized a view still prevalent in twentieth-century French Canada, in expressing fears about the effect of "mechanical distribution of alms by the State upon the Christian duty and grace of charity." Private beneficence discriminated, as state pension lists did not, and had the additional advantage of creating a kindly feeling between classes.[20]

When in 1907 and 1908 the British Parliament was discussing non-contributory old age pensions at seventy for those who would otherwise be destitute, Goldwin Smith attacked the scheme in English journals, notably in the *Spectator*. Its editor, J. St. Loe Strachey, thoroughly concurred with this criticism, and declared he meant to fight the proposal "to the last ditch." Both agreed that the Lords made a great mistake in not immediately rejecting the measure, and the full editorial weight of the *Spectator* was thrown behind an endeavour to persuade the upper house to retrieve this error.[21]

Goldwin Smith's pleas that the House of Lords should justify its existence by throwing out the old age pensions bill were too much for the saner members of the second chamber, although most of them disliked the measure as much as he did. The Lords adopted the more conciliatory course of amending the bill in committee, rather than rejecting

[20]*Weekly Sun*, Dec. 19, 1906, Feb. 27, 1907, Oct. 7, 1908; letter to the *Spectator*, March 7, 1908.
[21]Letters to Goldwin Smith from J. St. Loe Strachey, Dec. 31, 1907, Jan. 30, March 10, June 9, and Aug. 3, 1908.

it outright on second reading. When the Commons declined to accept these amendments, on the ground that the measure was a money bill, the peers yielded. The reasons for their action were carefully explained in a letter from Lord Rosebery to Goldwin Smith.

In various articles in the eighteen-nineties he had dismissed Rosebery's claims to the Liberal leadership as those of "a showy man of talent," and "a thorough-going opportunist," whose ambition exceeded his ability, and who possessed neither settled opinions nor strong character. Such a man, he complained, was out of place as leader of a radical party, because he lacked radical sympathies and convictions.[22] Naturally he disliked Rosebery's aggressive imperialism. All this, however, did not deter him, a decade later, from writing numerous urgent letters telling Rosebery precisely what he ought to do to save the country and redeem the reputation of the House of Lords.

Toward the end of his days Goldwin Smith grew more and more out of touch with Great Britain, where in the opening decade of the twentieth century public opinion was well in advance of mid-Victorian liberalism. Rosebery was no longer influential in British politics, but to Goldwin Smith's proposals, which ranged from biased to wild, he replied seriously and with unfailing courtesy. "If you will not save the State," Smith demanded in 1907, "who will? There is not a really strong man on either side of the House. . . . No measure could be more thoroughly demagogic than this of Old Age Pensions. . . . Payment of members, universal suffrage, and female suffrage will probably follow. Then where will you and your Empire be?"[23]

Even Rosebery's aplomb was shaken when Goldwin Smith's hatred of party led him to make the extraordinary suggestion that the country should be saved by rallying a non-party ministry around Edward VII. "We are no doubt as you say," replied Rosebery, "in great danger from the fact that the present majority, in combination with the Socialists, support the view that everybody should be supported by somebody else. This agreeable doctrine has been furthered by the Old Age Pensions Bill. But I see no hope except in the British common sense that has usually pulled us through, in experience and in expense. But the middle class, which should govern, is everywhere timid and apathetic." Rosebery confessed himself staggered by the suggestion that the King

[22]*Bystander*, n.s. (Jan., 1890), 127; *Globe*, May 19, 1894; *Weekly Sun*, Oct. 14, 1896.
[23]Letter to Lord Rosebery, Dec. 20, 1907, *Goldwin Smith's Correspondence*, 491–2.

should form a non-party ministry. If it could be formed, which he greatly doubted, it would not last an hour. Both parties would successfully combine to defeat it, and would thus inflict a crushing blow on constitutional monarchy.[24]

Unique among Goldwin Smith's English friends in supporting old age pensions was Sir Francis Channing, who stoutly maintained that they were simply a kind of outdoor relief, necessary under existing conditions for a large number of old people, and free from the demoralizing aspects of public relief. He would be astounded if old age pensions, far from fulfilling the forebodings of gloomy prophets, did not turn out to be "the most natural and best stimulus to thrift and hope and good conduct."[25] Goldwin Smith, however, having long since made up his mind on the subject, remained unaffected by such arguments.

VI

Goldwin Smith was not really inconsistent in attacking combination acts, but deploring strikes, in supporting factory legislation for children but not for grown men, in accepting public relief for the poor, but not old age pensions. He was merely acting in accordance with his own reiterated belief that what the state ought to do was a matter not of abstract principle but of common sense in the particular circumstances at issue. The answer to the question whether something could be best done by the government or by the individual citizen must in his opinion, as has been shown, vary with the problem involved and the character of the community.

About one kind of state intervention he had no doubts. Mill himself was not more contemptuous of proposals to make men moral by acts of Parliament. Probably few communities have tried as hard to achieve this end by legislative action as the province of Ontario, whose Lord's Day Alliance organization struck Goldwin Smith as a cross between the ridiculous and the tragic. The provincial legislature, he suggested, was in danger of passing an act for hating Sunday. He saw no connection between Christianity and the restraint of innocent enjoyment, was horrified when Toronto citizens were haled into court for playing golf on Sunday, and deplored the city's reputation for being "gloomily Sabbatarian and otherwise repulsively austere"—a reputation which in fact he thought not altogether deserved. Since policemen did not hold

[24]Letters to Goldwin Smith from Lord Rosebery, May 25, Aug. 16, and Sept. 10, 1908.
[25]Letter from Sir Francis Channing to Goldwin Smith, Jan. 1, 1909.

the keys of conscience, he did not see how they could be qualified to enforce conscientious observance of the Lord's Day.[26]

On an American demand that Zola's works should be banned as immoral, Goldwin Smith commented with vigour. He disliked Zola's naturalism, but was too good a liberal to support censorship. Nor did he believe that people who liked bathing in cesspools would be made much dirtier than usual by being allowed to indulge their taste.

His chief wrath, however, was reserved for prohibitionists. He himself drank little, but Canadian ideas on the subject appalled him, and during the eighteen-eighties he took an active part in the journalistic campaign against the Canada Temperance Act. The term "temperance" particularly irritated him, because of the implication that all consumption of liquor, no matter how moderate, was by definition intemperate. He argued that the act was frequently broken and left unenforced, that it had been repealed in many districts, and that it simply substituted an illicit for a licensed and regulated trade, while it filled the community with law-breaking and perjury. No law unsupported by the moral conviction of the citizens could be carried into effect. That it was a crime to drink a glass of wine or beer could scarcely be believed by anyone, certainly not by anyone who took Christ or St. Paul as standards of morality. Canada was not sinking into an abyss of drunkenness, but was a temperate country, steadily growing more so. Goldwin Smith rejected the whole attitude of mind which held that government might properly be used to inculcate private opinions. The government was no more a physician than a theologian, and could regulate the diet and taste of its citizens with no more propriety than their religion. For his part he would as soon pay ship-money to the Stuarts as allow his private life to be invaded by a coercive inquisition. He quoted with satisfaction Abraham Lincoln's remark that legislation of this sort was both impolitic and unjust—impolitic because it was not much in man's nature to be driven, still less to be driven to that which was his own business. Statutory virtue was on a par with the cloistered virtue of which Milton was so contemptuous. Extreme prohibitionists would "not be able, without a police stronger and more inquisitorial than any free country will maintain, to compel all men, in obedience to their fiat, and that of a bare majority, to drink nothing but cold water. . . . Society has set itself free by centuries of effort from the single-handed tyranny whose instrument of coercion was the sword: it does not want now to fall under a many-headed tyranny whose instrument of coercion will be the ballot."[27]

[26]Toronto *Evening Telegram*, May 30, 1895; *Weekly Sun*, May 20, 1897, July 4, 1906. [27]*Week*, Oct. 9, 1884.

At bottom Goldwin Smith was a convinced but apprehensive democrat, fearful of the possible tyranny of the majority. He would set fairly wide limits to the functions of the state, and did not demand that its boundaries be drawn in a given place. Indeed he deplored any attempt to do so, because circumstances change and public opinion changes with them. He saw dangers both in leaving everything to the individual and in leaving everything to the state. Unrestricted competition was likely to mean unlimited selfishness. State action, on the other hand, posed the problem of corruption, bureaucracy, and official dislike of change, and might teach the people to depend too much on bread and circuses. At the end of the nineteenth century he thought he saw excessive zeal to renounce liberty as selfish isolation, and to invoke the paternal despotism of the state. By reasonable legislation the government, he granted, could do and had done much for its citizens. It could defend the worker against fraud or culpable carelessness on the part of his employer, improve his housing conditions, provide parks for his recreation, and protect his wife and children against overwork. Goldwin Smith no more worshipped individual liberty than state interference. But so long as government consisted at best of ordinary men and at worst of demagogues, he preferred to confine its activities to matters with which it alone was competent to deal.[28]

He was, in short, friendly to many ideas which his contemporaries considered socialistic. He certainly believed that the chief authors of revolution were not the intemperate friends of progress but its blind obstructors, who in defiance of nature tried to avert the inevitable and to recall the irrevocable. No man ever enjoyed more his pleasant life in a comfortable house set in spacious grounds and staffed by devoted servants. Yet he told friends that his "semi-communistic feelings" sometimes gave him a twinge when he thought how much labour was wasted over him. "I shall leave the world,—political, social and theological," he wrote in his seventy-second year, "in a considerable ferment, and I hardly know whether to rejoice that I shall be out of the fray or grieve that I shall miss the fun."[29] He liked to recall that justice to labour was among the traditions of the Radicals, with whom he had early thrown in his lot and gone through good and evil report. "At the age of eighty-seven," he wrote shortly before his death, "one is too old for a great leap. This it may be that keeps me from taking the leap from Labour to Socialism. . . . You will not be surprised if while I claim to be a staunch Labour man I cannot pretend to be a Socialist."[30]

[28]"The Political Necessity," *Pall Mall Gazette*, April 26, 1894.
[29]Letters to Andrew White, Dec. 7, 1894, April 18, 1879.
[30]From a fragmentary jotting among his unpublished papers.

VIII. CRITIQUE OF IMPERIALISM

THE BRITISH CONCEPT of imperialism has been many-sided, variously interpreted for the past three hundred years by a succession of statesmen, economists, historians, and political theorists. Few discussed it with more brilliance or more vigour than Goldwin Smith, although on few subjects were his ideas less popular. A Little Englander of the Little Englanders, he was concerned, unlike many of this group, not only with the emancipation of the colonies, but also with their development as independent nations. In his vision of a free association of the English-speaking peoples of the world, linked by common bonds of language, literature, and law, he was a prophet of the modern Commonwealth of Nations.

I

The opinions of the Little Englanders were never more ably expressed than in his provocative letters on colonial emancipation written for the *Daily News* in 1862–3 and subsequently published in book form as *The Empire*. These letters immediately roused the wrath of *The Times*. In scathing editorials it attacked the renegade who demanded "the renunciation of that position and that destiny of which the nation is proud, the world envious, but of which Mr. Smith speaks contemptuously as a mere sentiment." In reply Goldwin Smith freely voiced his ideas, not only on the colonies but on "that eminent organ of wealth and its privileges which aspires to shape British public opinion."[1]

His letters distinguished between the dependencies which he thought England should keep, like India, those which should be emancipated, like Canada, and those which should be ceded to other countries, like Gibraltar and the Ionian Islands.[2] Garibaldi, who regarded the return of

[1]"The Revolution in England," *North American Review*, CVIII (Jan., 1869), 221–54; *The Times*, Sept. 20, 1862.
[2]Two years later, in 1864, the Ionian Islands were returned to Greece. Of Goldwin Smith's influence on this outcome John Elliot Cairnes commented in

these islands to Greece as a step toward national unity, wrote to express his approval of such views. In a letter to Cobden Goldwin Smith described himself, with obvious satisfaction, as "both a Cobdenite and a Garibaldian." To Cobden's urgent plea that *The Empire* letters should be published as a book he finally yielded, despite previous refusals on the ground that they were merely fugitive productions.³

This advocacy of the cession of Gibraltar and the Ionian Islands provoked the ire, not only of *The Times*, but of Disraeli, who neither forgot nor forgave the critical articles Goldwin Smith had written a decade earlier for the *Morning Chronicle*, and who also disliked Smith's attacks on the law of entail. Colonial policy, Disraeli declared in the Commons, was the affair of statesmen, not professors and rhetoricians; the destiny of the British Empire must not be left to "prigs and pedants."⁴ He described his adversary as a "wild man of the cloister," an "itinerant spouter of stale sedition," and in *Lothair* pilloried him under the guise of a professor noted as a "social parasite."⁵ Replying in an open letter to *The Times*, Goldwin Smith briefly dismissed "the stingless insults of a coward."

His deep-rooted faith in colonial emancipation did not extend to either India or Ireland. Britain's position in India, he argued, was one from which retreat was difficult, without abandoning the country to anarchy. The principle of colonial emancipation did not apply, because India was a conquered land, not a colony. In it the British were alien and unbeloved, trampling in the pride of superior race and conquest upon what they considered an inferior people. Between ruler and ruled a great gulf was fixed. The conquered might respect the conqueror, but

---

his *Political Essays* (London, 1873), 56–7: "Professor Smith may congratulate himself upon a triumph speedier and more complete than often falls to the lot of political innovators. Before six months had passed, the Ionian Islands, if not in deference to his teaching, at all events in perfect conformity with the policy he had just propounded amid the all but universal protests of the Press, were conceded to Greece among the not less general applause of the nation. This, it must be owned, is a singular testimony to political forecast; and the whole course of events in the two years that have since elapsed has served but to strengthen it. . . . Many statesmen and even his quondam enemy, *The Times*, adopted his opinions."

³Letters from Goldwin Smith to Richard Cobden, Oct. 27 and Dec. 23, 1862.
⁴*Hansard's Parliamentary Debates*, Third Series, CLXIX, 1863, 96.
⁵On this incident Mrs. Humphry Ward commented that "it would be difficult to find two words in the English language more wholly and ludicrously inappropriate to Goldwin Smith" (than social parasite), though she thought his letter on the subject to *The Times* might better have been left unwritten. *A Writer's Recollections* (London, 1919), 250. *Lothair* was published in 1870, when Goldwin Smith had been two years at Cornell. There was thus no truth in the legend that Disraeli's attack drove him out of England.

could scarcely be expected to love him. The ability and beneficence of British administration in India, although unmatched in the annals of conquest, could not overcome the fatal defect of government by a stranger, in which liberty had no place. To those who, like Lord Roberts, spoke of the Indian Empire as the brightest jewel in the British crown, Goldwin Smith rejoined that one might have supposed its brightest jewel was Great Britain herself. In a letter to John Bright he described the empire in India as "a splendid curse." But he differed from Cobden, who thought it would be a happy day when England no longer held a single acre in Asia. Cobden argued that it was natural for the Indians to prefer misgoverning themselves to being well governed by aliens, and that England could not rule India with advantage to the people of either country. Since Catholics and Protestants could not live together in Belfast save under an approximation to martial law, Cobden wondered whether the British were really the people to teach Christian charity and toleration to the Hindus.

Goldwin Smith wished that England had never acquired India, but since she had he thought she should continue her work there, which she stood pledged before the world to perform. On this matter he never changed his mind, but in after years foretold that the triumph of democracy in Britain would endanger the Indian Empire. A democratic state, whatever its blessings, could not govern an empire.[6] Yet he never wearied of quoting his favourite historian, Macaulay: "There are triumphs which are followed by no reverses. There is an empire exempt from all natural causes of decay. Those triumphs are the pacific triumphs of reason over barbarism; that empire is the imperishable empire of our arts and our morals, our literature and our laws."

For the Irish point of view Goldwin Smith showed even less understanding than for the Indian. His prejudices were deep, and on few subjects was he more prejudiced than on Catholics (though he favoured the disestablishment of the Irish Church), and on Celts, an ethnic group of which he thought the Irish the least attractive example. He described them succinctly as "an amiable but thriftless, uncommercial, saint-worshipping, priest-ridden race." After all that had happened he thought Ireland could scarcely be an independent nation living on terms of ordinary friendship with England.

It was not surprising that critics called Goldwin Smith inconsistent

[6]*The Empire: A Series of Letters, Published in "The Daily News," 1862, 1863* (Oxford, 1863), 8, 21, 138, 296; letter to John Bright, Sept. 10, 1882. More than twenty-two hundred years before, Cleon had told the Athenian assembly that a democracy was incapable of empire.

when he supported independence for countries like Canada and New Zealand but bitterly opposed Home Rule for Ireland. He retorted indignantly that there was no real parallel. Canada was a distant land, friendly to the mother country, and satisfied, not with Home Rule, but with practical independence. It was right to give freedom to a country three thousand miles away, but not to an integral part of the United Kingdom.[7] The explanation hardly carried conviction. The fact was that he regarded the British settlement colonies as on a completely different footing from less fortunate parts of the Empire. His views on Ireland and India formed marked exceptions to his usual liberalism and reiterated belief in colonial emancipation. In the eighteen-eighties his Unionist sympathies were to set him apart from the leading Liberals, most of whom supported Irish Home Rule, although a few middle-class intellectuals unconnected with politics, like Goldwin Smith, opposed it.[8] Despite these exceptions, his genuine belief in colonial freedom not only inspired the early letters to the *Daily News* which first brought him fame, but remained a basic tenet of his liberalism.

When *The Empire* letters first appeared they provoked widespread criticism. Viewed in retrospect, they contain much good sense. England, they argued, had long promised herself the honour of becoming the mother of free nations. Was it not time for this promise to be fulfilled? The Province of Canada was a good place to begin, since this and other settlement colonies were actually free countries dependent on Great Britain only in name. The sole way to defend Canada against possible aggression was "to fence her round with the majesty of an independent nation." Goldwin Smith was not the man to ask himself whether Canadians wanted to be emancipated when he thought they clearly should be. Accordingly, when some Canadians objected to his views on the colonies in general and on Canada in particular, he pointed out that England had already given them the essence of her constitution: free legislation, personal liberty, ministerial responsiblity, and trial by jury. This stress on the links of heredity and culture which bound the colonies to the mother country had been partly counterbalanced in his inaugural lecture as Regius Professor. Here he contended that since for the most part the colonists came from the more progressive and enterprising sections of English society, in them and their institutions the mother country could discern the prophecy of her own future.[9] England

[7]Letters to Earl Grey, March 30, 1886; to *The Times*, Sept. 29, 1892, and June 13, 1899.
[8]Among these were Tyndall, Huxley, Matthew Arnold, Froude, and Jowett. This point is noted by Sir Philip Magnus, *Gladstone* (London, 1954), 346.
[9]*Lectures on the Study of History* (2nd ed., Oxford, 1865), 14–15.

was aristocratic, whereas in Canada the whole frame of society, to which political institutions must conform, was democratic. The English governing classes would be not only high-minded and sensible, but more than men, if they could like a society based on equality. How could they be good foster-fathers of what they did not like?

Goldwin Smith's opinions on these matters, though unpopular in many circles, were not novel. The authority of *The Wealth of Nations* could be cited to support the view that colonies which contributed neither revenue nor military assistance to the mother country were not really provinces at all but rather appendages: in Adam Smith's words, "a sort of splendid and showy equipage" of an empire which existed in imagination only, "not an empire but the project of an empire, not a gold mine, but the project of a gold mine." The dry tones of the economist could be recognized in the conclusion that a project impossible to complete ought to be abandoned. Almost three-quarters of a century later Sir George Cornewall Lewis argued that the British Empire was necessarily self-liquidating, since "a self-governing dependency is a contradiction in terms."

The loss of the American colonies led many Englishmen to believe that an empire was subject to the law of rapidly diminishing returns. Since England was more interested in trading with the world than in dominating it, they looked forward with equanimity to the disintegration of an ungrateful empire wherein mercantilism was dead. Responsible government, a necessary precursor of independence, was advocated by colonial reformers like Durham, Buller, Wakefield, and Molesworth. In the mid-nineteenth century, when free trade doctrines had become sacrosanct in the mother country, the colonies began to outrage economic decency by imposing tariffs, not only on the goods of foreigners, which would have been bad enough, but even on those of Great Britain herself. Assessed purely in cash terms, as was then customary, they seemed obvious liabilities rather than assets. Even Disraeli incautiously expressed the opinion in 1852 that England's wretched colonies were "a millstone around our necks," and in a few years would all be independent. As late as 1866 he wondered publicly what was the use of "these colonial deadweights which we do not govern." The day of jubilees and jingoes was yet to come.

Like Cobden and Bright, Goldwin Smith thought of free trade, peace, and the emancipation of colonies as interconnected. Free trade would loosen the bonds of the colonial system, and a major cause of wars— the desire for colonies as sources of raw materials and protected markets —would thus be removed. Adherents of the Manchester School held that rivalry between nations based on isolation as well as on economic interest must be destroyed before there could be universal peace. Their belief in colonial independence led them to believe also, like Mazzini, in a romantic concept of nationality, as inherently a liberal force. Disillusionment naturally followed, when in the latter part of the century nationality was often transmuted into an aggressive and illiberal nationalism. Goldwin Smith shared the Manchester weakness of underestimating in international affairs the realities of power. Even after the rise of Bismarck and the partition of Africa he still hoped that free trade among nations would eliminate power politics, produce mutual interdependence, and hence secure lasting peace.

He refused to write off colonies as nothing but deadweights upon the mother country. He did indeed argue that "this expensive and perilous connexion has entirely survived its sole legitimate cause," and asked what was the use of continuing it if Great Britain and her colonies were to do nothing for each other. But when taxed with being against the colonies, he retorted: "I am no more against Colonies than I am against the solar system. I am against dependencies when nations are fit to be independent." He was the chief member of the Manchester School to picture England surrounded by independent daughter nations. Coupling the views of the Little Englanders with Disraeli's contempt for "those wretched colonies" provoked his instant protest. Contempt for the colonies, he maintained, was neither felt nor expressed by the Manchester School. English Liberals never thought any such thing. They never wished to make England little but simply wanted her to be the first country in history which freely granted independence to a daughter state. They opposed the continued subservience of adult colonies, capable of governing themselves, because they believed a community could not be both a dependency and a nation. To them ultimate autonomy seemed a higher ideal for the colonies than perpetual dependence.

For voicing these sentiments Goldwin Smith was accused of lacking common patriotism. His object, he avowed, was not to show patriotism, but to appeal to those who valued the abiding springs of their country's greatness, and were as unwilling as himself to keep in leading-strings such free nations as Canada, which were dependent only in name. To them England had given all that she had to give: her language, with its wisdom and beauty, her national character, and her commercial energy. Ties of affection and illustrious traditions linked them with the mother country. These bonds with the colonies to him seemed the significant and essential part of England's greatness: not the bonds of trade or military fealty, but of blood, ideas, and sympathy, which would not be affected by political separation. He refused to admit that colonial emancipation would reduce England to an insular position. She would differ from other islands by being the centre of a great confederacy of nations of her own race. Each would be independent and contribute its experience to the political progress of the whole, while all would be united by sympathy, by alliance, and perhaps by mutual citizenship. And when the colonies became nations in their own right, "something in the nature of a great Anglo-Saxon federation may, in substance if not in form, spontaneously arise out of affinity and mutual affection." England should recognize that the world had changed since her Empire was formed, should be willing to take practical note of this change, and should realize that her true greatness lay not in empire but in herself. Far from attacking the colonies, Goldwin Smith contended that there was nothing of which Englishmen had more reason to be proud.

To the curious complaint that on colonial questions he neglected considerations of sentiment, and looked only to material gain, he countered that if political associations were to endure, they must be based on reciprocal advantage. "None by a cynic would despise sentiment: none but a fool would build on it."[10] When in 1869 a Canadian paper attacked him as anti-colonial, he wrote to the *Daily News* in protest:

I have argued, not against the foundation of colonies, but in favour of their timely emancipation. It is impossible for any human being to be more profoundly convinced of the value of British colonies, or more sincerely proud of them, than I am. I rate these monuments of our powers of organization and self-government far above all the other trophies of our greatness. I avow my belief that it is as the parent of communities which are propagating the British language, character, and institutions over the globe, that this little England of ours will in future times retain her place of honour in history, and that it is mainly as the preparation for her great work of colonization that her own history has an interest above that of other nations.[11]

At the time such views on colonial emancipation attracted more criticism than support, but their candour and independence won recognition. The *Spectator*, which disagreed with them, nevertheless approved of making the English public consider ideas not their own and re-examine the grounds of their political faith. Holding with John Stuart

---

[10]*The Empire*, 97; "The Empire," *Essays on Questions of the Day* (Toronto, 1893), 149; "The Proposed Constitution for British North America," *Macmillan's Magazine*, XI (March, 1865), 416.
[11]*Daily News*, Oct. 5, 1869; *The Empire*, 36.

Mill that the chief weakness of British public opinion was uniformity, the editor congratulated Goldwin Smith, whose brilliant exposition of unpopular opinions enlarged the horizons even of those who thought him the most dangerous political writer in England.

While the force of his arguments and felicity of his style placated some Englishmen hostile to his views, it did nothing to placate the outraged loyalty of Canadians who declined to be emancipated. Joseph Howe (not the least independent of colonials), in a speech at Niagara on September 18, 1862, indignantly rebutted the allegation that Canadians were cravens who refused to defend their country. Premier Tilley of New Brunswick had recently asked him whether he had read Goldwin Smith's letters and whether Nova Scotia was prepared for independence. Howe replied that he had not read Goldwin Smith, but was prepared for anything. Nova Scotia would float, if the devil himself cut the tow-line. He wondered how Goldwin Smith would like to see the mother country cut off from British America, and left without a harbour on the North American continent into which her ships could put for a spar or a ton of coal. If England should ever decide to cast off these provinces—which Heaven forbid—it would be a sadder day for her than for British America.[12] Howe's frank faith in "the empire one and indivisible" naturally led him to regard the Little Englanders' colonial policy as dismemberment.

He was not the only Canadian whom it irritated. At the Quebec Conference two years later John A. Macdonald insisted that despite the Manchester men and Goldwin Smith he believed the British people wanted to maintain their Empire.[13] Christopher Dunkin, the chief critic of the Quebec Resolutions, however, argued during the Confederation Debates of 1865 that in both British North America and the United Kingdom there were those who supported the proposed union as a step toward severing all ties with the mother country. Independence for Canada, he prophesied, would necessarily lead to her early absorption by the United States. If the desire for separation did not dominate British opinion, it was at least entertained by many prominent public men. When challenged to give names, Dunkin replied that he spoke of

---

[12] J. A. Chisholm (ed.), *Speeches and Public Letters of Joseph Howe* (2 vols., Halifax, 1909), II, 372, 381. Some six years later Howe turned to Goldwin Smith for help, when he went to London to plead for Nova Scotia's secession from Confederation. Smith arranged for Howe to meet a group of leading British Liberals, to whom he made an able, though ultimately unsuccessful, presentation of his case.

[13] Oct. 11, 1864. Joseph Pope (ed.), *Confederation Documents* (Toronto, 1895), 55.

"the Goldwin Smith school," which included such influential Manchester Liberals as Cobden and Bright.

Fuel was added to the fire when some weeks later, in an able analysis of "The Proposed Constitution for British North America," Goldwin Smith argued that the English Parliament was incapable of performing maternal functions for colonists who were far away, and at least as fitted for self-government as the members of the British House of Commons. Even if the political connection with England were dissolved, all the really effective ties of kinship would remain. A year later Egerton Ryerson expressed the hope that no future professor of history in any university would imitate Mr. Goldwin Smith in his "morbid enmity against the higher classes and cherished institutions of his country, in his revolutionary ardour for the dismemberment of the Empire, in his pandering to the lowest anti-British spirit of American democracy, in his misinterpretation of historical facts, and in his sacrificing to passion and party the higher claims of patriotism, reason and truth."[14] The charge of sacrificing truth to party was an unfair body blow, in view of Goldwin Smith's intense dislike of the party system and party politics. It was small cause for wonder that shortly after he settled in Toronto he became involved in controversy with the Reverend Mr. Ryerson.

Despite his lively interest in the fortunes of Britain's overseas possessions, it was thus apparent long before he left England in 1868 that his ambitions for them were not shared by most of those closely concerned. The opinions of men like Howe, Dunkin, and Ryerson about the relationship between England and British North America undoubtedly represented the views of a considerable number of Canadians. Goldwin Smith admitted that the doctrine of colonial independence progressed more at home than abroad, and attributed the change of heart among English public men less to theoretical conviction than to a practical sense of the liabilities of empire. He himself had no doubt that Canadian Confederation was the forerunner of independence. Although many English statesmen publicly repudiated such a possibility, he was convinced that in their hearts they accepted it as inevitable.[15]

In the colonies themselves, however, there appeared no desire to end the British connection, but much irritation at Goldwin Smith's Olympian pronouncement that this was the dictate of destiny. Canadians were

[14]A Canadian, *Remarks on the Historical Mis-Statements and Fallacies of Mr. Goldwin Smith, in His Lecture "On the Foundation of the American Colonies," and His Letters "On the Emancipation of the Colonies"* (Toronto, 1866), ii.

[15]Letter of July 31, 1865, from Goldwin Smith to J. D. Lang, Lang Papers, Public Library of New South Wales, Sydney, Australia.

particularly annoyed by his confident prophecy that they would soon join the United States, as a step toward an amicable confederation of all the English-speaking states of North America.[16] They had reason, after all, to be primarily concerned in 1867 about their own Confederation, an outward and visible sign of an inner spirt of nascent nationalism which Goldwin Smith, for all his belief in national independence, never really understood.

Early in 1870 *The Times* reiterated its conviction that the colonies were of the greatest value to Britain, and ought to be retained. The maintenance of an honourable connection need not involve keeping helpless people in leading-strings. Should Mr. Goldwin Smith renew his dogmatic proposals for emancipation, it promised to combat them as vigorously as in the past. This article was cited with approval by the Montreal *Gazette*, which had long attacked his views on the colonies. With premature satisfaction its editor noted that Professor Goldwin Smith seemed to have become dumb, and rashly concluded that residence in North America had taught him how little he really knew about the colonies when he first discussed them. Knowledge, the *Gazette* suggested hopefully, had made him, as it made most men, more modest and reticent.[17] Goldwin Smith was to spend the next forty years combating imperial sentiment in Canada with the same weapons of satire which he had directed against Disraeli's imperialism in England.

II

Toward the end of the eighteen-sixties the tide of opinion in Great Britain began to turn from a widespread belief that the sooner the colonies went their own way the better, toward a romantic and aggressive concept of a far-flung empire. By 1872, when Disraeli explained that the preservation of the Empire was a major tenet of conservatism, it was clear that a professed devotion to the colonies had become a political asset. Only six years earlier he had been speculating as to their possible utility. His astute change of front and his skill in annexing belief in the Empire for the Conservative party presaged the victory of the jingoes over the Little Englanders in the last quarter of the century. Yet despite the professions of party politicians, the colonial policy of

[16]"The Case of the Alabama," *Macmillan's Magazine*, XIII (Dec., 1865), 162–76; *The Civil War in America* (London, 1866).

[17]*Gazette* (Montreal), Jan. 19 and 22, 1867, Jan. 24 and Feb. 11, 1870; *Montreal Evening Telegraph*, Feb. 4, 1870; *The Times*, Jan. 7, 1870.

every English statesman, whether Liberal or Conservative, as Goldwin Smith shrewdly noted, was still laissez-faire. "No one," he wrote from Toronto in 1873, "thinks of meddling with us; our destiny is absolutely in our own hands."[18]

An early sign of the change in British public opinion was the founding in 1869 of the Royal Colonial Institute (later the Royal Empire Society), as a centre for the intellectual defence of the Empire and for accurate information on colonial affairs. At its inaugural dinner Gladstone extolled "the noble tradition of the unity of the British race," and the chairman, Viscount Bury, lamented that hitherto it had been no one's business to defend the Empire, while there had grown up a whole school of politicians devoted to its attack and dismemberment. He regretted that the doctrines of that school had been enunciated from a professorial chair in Britain's oldest university. Goldwin Smith's brilliance made him all the more dangerous. The very existence of such a school of thought as the Little Englanders was of itself, in Lord Bury's opinion, sufficient reason for the establishment of the Colonial Institute. Its members deprecated independence for the colonies, arguing that at all hazards the integrity of the Empire should be maintained.[19]

British imperial policy during the last quarter of the nineteenth century, the era of the jingoes and the partition of Africa, involved more than maintaining the integrity of the Empire. Darwin's fashionable views on evolution were extended by analogy to struggles between nations. Herbert Spencer's comfortable conviction that it was a beneficent private war which leads each man to strive to climb upon the shoulders of his neighbour was less surprising that the assumption of a sober analyst like Bagehot that the victorious nations were proved by the test of war to be also the best. The nineteenth-century belief in progress and in the amalgamation of smaller political units into larger wholes seemed to support the doctrine of the white man's burden and the civilizing mission of a superior race. In the successful progress of this new concept of empire the earlier belief in colonial emancipation was submerged. By 1884 the *Pall Mall Gazette* announced triumphantly that "the school of Mr. Goldwin Smith is as extinct as the megatherium, the contraction of England has not one articulate advocate left in the daily press, and Liberals and Radicals vie with Conservatives in professions of enthusiastic patriotism."

Goldwin Smith, for his part, was not convinced that his cause was

[18]"Current Events," *Canadian Monthly*, III (April, 1873), 329-30.
[19]Royal Colonial Institute, *Proceedings*, I-II (1869-70), (London, 1870), 53, 68-73.

lost. To him the reaction in favour of imperialism seemed a wave, not a tide. Every jingo was not a ruffian, but it might almost be said that every ruffian was a jingo.[20] Like a true Victorian he largely accepted the doctrine that the white (though not the Anglo-Saxon) peoples were superior. But he loathed the theory of a struggle for existence. The belief that strong countries were destined to devour first the weak and then each other, until at last the community of nations was reduced to one colossal beast of prey, seemed to him a curious and melancholy theory of human destiny. He agreed with Kropotkin that Darwinism (or rather a misinterpretation of Darwinism) was running mad, and that human beings advanced by mutual help, not by butchering and devouring their kind. The man who excelled in moral and intellectual power was fittest to survive. Britain's rapidly expanding empire in Africa was a vast fabric of iniquity, reared by greed and ambition. Yet though the victors trampled down the vanquished and for a time might even trample down public opinion, they did not write history.

He continued to hope that his countrymen would wake from their dream of conquest to remember that against the glories of empire must be set its responsibilities as well as its effect on other countries. England's untenable and irritating claim to rule the seas was a standing affront to other nations and a constant provocation of warlike feeling. If the white man wanted a burden, it lay at his door. A member of the British Parliament need only step out into Whitechapel or Houndsditch, and see how in his own country the woolcomber, the white lead maker, and the alkali worker lived. The English, he prophesied, would come again to their senses, and realize that "enormous and unnatural agglomerations of territory are not really and permanently conducive to wealth, strength or happiness." The modern process whereby nations became more closely linked together was simply a continuance of a development through which the family expanded into the tribe and the tribe into the nation. To him this heralded, not the rise of vast imperial units, but the gradual transfer of men's allegiance from the nation state to humanity as a whole. Some day, perhaps, a way might be found to prevent the powerful countries from working their will upon the weak, and to bring great and small states alike before the supreme tribunal of world public opinion.

The arbitration movement, which led to the establishment of the Hague Tribunal, Goldwin Smith viewed with distrust. He thought it tended toward a compact of the strong to keep their hands off each other while they all preyed on the weak. To him the great security for peace

[20]Letter to Henri Bourassa, March 16, 1900, Gregory Papers, Douglas Library, Queen's University.

in North America was its independence of European powers and their wars.

He recalled the sinister effect of empire on freedom, pointing out that the more democratic England herself became, the more difficult she would find domination over colonies. "To proclaim Democracy," he declared in 1894, "is to renounce Empire."[21] Military aggression and political liberty, imperialism and liberalism, were incompatible. Morality was not the handmaid of empire. If jingoism prevailed, freedom would die, and the coming century reverse the moral progress made in the last. Despite all the contemporary evidence of material improvement, people seemed to him to be living in a backstream of civilization, surrounded on every side by the reaction against humanitarianism, and by a fancy for returning to the robustness of the barbarian. It would be a relief if the jingoes would stop talking about the Bible, Christianity, and civilization, and simply emulate Captain Kidd, who said what he meant and took what he wanted, without talking flummery about his mission.

In the eighteen-seventies and eighties it required prescience as well as stubbornness to oppose aggressive imperialism, though in retrospect Little Englandism seems more realistic than Disraeli's flamboyant concept of empire. The last thirty years of the century saw the partition of Africa, the extension of British interests to Egypt, the Boer Wars, and the birth of American imperialism under McKinley. Goldwin Smith inveighed against them all alike, holding that in the end the fabrics reared by ambition and cupidity would be cast down, and man discover that he could not build his own happiness on the misery of his fellows. No nation was sufficiently moral to be able to govern other peoples for the benefit of the governed. In a letter to John Bright he inquired bitterly how long it had been part of the Liberal creed that Englishmen should make war in order to improve the governments of other countries. He doubted whether the worst government in the world could do anything much worse than what was done by war.[22]

His enthusiasm for the United States was so great that he was the more disillusioned, at the end of the century, when she emerged as an imperial power. He wrote wistfully to an American friend that he could not imagine any political connection with Cuba that would not be bad for the United States, for democracies could not govern dependencies— a reiteration of his earlier criticism of British imperialism. To President Jacob Schurman of Cornell, who had been commissioner to the Philip-

[21]"The Impending Revolution," *Nineteenth Century*, XXXV (March, 1894), 360; "The Expansion of England," *Contemporary Review*, XLV (April, 1884), 524–40; letter to Alexander MacGregor, Feb. 28, 1905; letters to Bourke Cockran, April 13 and May 12, 1904.
[22]Letter to John Bright, Oct. 15, 1882.

pines in 1899, he confessed that he was not sanguine about the possibility of one nation being trained by another for self-government. "There is no saying what might be the result if Boston were to migrate to the Philippines and take the political nursing in hand; though even then there would be the barriers of race, language, and religion. But the nursing fathers will probably be of a very different class." President Roosevelt was reported to have "generous impulses." So, according to the story books, he believed, had Dick Turpin. When in 1904 Roosevelt was re-elected for a second term, Goldwin Smith doubted whether even Hearst would do as much harm. Probably there were worse men than Roosevelt, but at that juncture he thought there could scarcely be a worse candidate for President. The American people had suddenly changed their character and become devotees of swagger and a big stick. He supposed it was all part of the advance toward materialism and the retreat from the Sermon on the Mount.[23]

For the time, at least, the policy of McKinley and Theodore Roosevelt delivered a crushing blow to his former enthusiasm for union between Canada and the United States. No Canadian, he thought, would desire incorporation with a negro and Malay empire. In American expansion he could see nothing but naked aggrandizement and a departure from Jeffersonian principles, destined to bring ruin upon victors and vanquished alike. To Andrew Carnegie he commented: "England is slaughtering the Zulus, a very fine and promising race; Germany is slaughtering the native races in Central Africa; Belgium is slaughtering the native races in the Congo; the United States are slaughtering the Philippines—this is the work of 'civilization.' All the wild-stocks of humanity are being destroyed, with doubtful advantage to humanity."[24] The Philippines could be no possible use to the Americans save as a trophy, a political adjunct or barnacle, neither salutary nor suitable for a republic. If the Americans wished to bear their share of the white man's burden, he suggested dryly, a noble field of endeavour was open to them within their own borders, where some nine million negroes were as degraded and downtrodden as any race could be.[25] Yet his longstanding faith in the character and good sense of the people of the United States was not wholly destroyed. He told Bryce, who shared his

[23]Letters to Bourke Cockran, April 19, 1904; to General J. H. Wilson (then commanding officer in Cuba), Jan. 14, 1897, Jan. 4, 1899; to President Jacob Schurman, Feb. 17 and May 4, 1902, Schurman Papers, Cornell University Archives.
[24]Letter to Andrew Carnegie, July 26, 1898.
[25]"Imperialism in the United States," *Contemporary Review*, LXXV (May, 1899), 620–8; "The Perils of the Republic," *North American Review*, CLXXXIV (March, 1907), 464–74.

enthusiasm for that country, that he was sure more Americans were opposed to the Spanish war than actually spoke out against it. "You know," he added, "that it is not in the American Republic that opinion is most free."[26]

Empire-building was one bond of union between the United States and Great Britain which he deplored. "The world is in a lively state," he wrote in 1902, "Imperialists, Socialists, Anarchists, pacific or militant, Tolstoi Humanitarians, advocates of Beneficent Feudalism, advocates of Anglo-Saxon supremacy, Anglo-Israelites and Utopians of all sorts are struggling at once to cast us in a new mould." Of all these schemes "the most curious is the proposal . . . that Great Britain should enter into partnership with the United States, and that the two conjointly shall dominate the world for its good. That the world might object to being dominated, and show its objection in a lively form, is what no author of schemes of this kind seems to suspect." He had done what he could to promote cordial relations between England, Canada, and the United States, but failed to comprehend how any right-minded person could desire co-operation in aggression.[27]

III

Goldwin Smith, with Cobden and Bright, hated war, holding that unless absolutely necessary it was a crime. He was thus unconvinced by arguments for an empire of conquest, based on considerations of trade or strategy. Yet he considered visionary the pacifism of the Quakers and the Christian nihilism of Tolstoi, which would sweep away all restraints against violence. His original feeling on the subject had been intensified by the lasting impression made on him during the American Civil War when he visited the Northern troops, saw army hospitals, and talked with newly returned prisoners. Only the historian, he thought, could appreciate the enormous waste of war and its terrible effect on the progress of civilization. How could any question of right be settled by force? No British war seemed to him so unjustifiable as the South African. This he violently attacked, although the *Weekly Sun*, in which he held a controlling interest, and which was almost the only journal in English-speaking Canada that consistently opposed the war, thereby lost half its circulation. G. M. Trevelyan, writing of Bright's and Cobden's opposition to the Crimean War, rightly commented that in a

[26]Letter to James Bryce, June 30, 1898.
[27]*Weekly Sun*, Sept. 10, 1902.

modern democracy to attack the wisdom and justice of a popular war while it is still in progress requires most unusual political courage. Such courage Goldwin Smith possessed. One of his chief counts against statesmen like Palmerston, Disraeli, and Chamberlain was their light-hearted readiness to involve England in war in order to increase her prestige and indirectly their own.

Just before the Boer War broke out Goldwin Smith announced his belief that British troops were being sent to the Cape, not to rectify the Transvaal franchise but to establish British ascendancy and mask the financial designs of Cecil Rhodes. He loathed Rhodes and everything he stood for, including the Rhodes scholarships and the directions for "his unspeakable tomb." The idea of linking Oxford with such a man outraged him. Ironically enough, however, he and Rhodes shared a common ideal—a passionate belief in the English-speaking peoples of the world. The jingoes, Goldwin Smith charged, wanted the land of the Boers; Rhodes and his company wanted their gold. Had there been no mines in the Transvaal, he suspected that the Boers and the Uitlanders would have been left to settle their political differences by themselves. However tempting the Johannesburg mines, they were not identical with British supremacy in South Africa, much less with Anglo-Saxon civilization. "Who can believe," he asked, "that a nation which has a House of Lords and is holding in subjection three hundred millions of Hindoos has undertaken a crusade for the diffusion of political equality?"[28] Religion, the former great cause of wars, had been replaced by commercial greed, veiling itself under the pretended mission of the race. War had been called the game of kings. It was now the game of capitalists. But its relation to the welfare of the people remained to be seen.

As the South African War proceeded, he was more and more depressed at what he considered the worst stain on England's honour since the execution of Joan of Arc. She could well afford the war's expense, but not its odium. It would be easier, he thought, to kill the two little republics than to lay their ghosts. From a friend of long standing (though the two men never met), John Xavier Merriman, treasurer and later premier of Cape Colony, he received numerous detailed accounts of South African politics. Goldwin Smith never publicly referred to Merriman by name, but often used in his Bystander column in the *Weekly Sun* material on South African affairs gleaned from these personal letters. This first-hand information lent an authoritative air to his analysis of the Boer War, though it made his views on the subject no more palatable to imperially minded Canadians, whose military enthusiasm ran

[28]Letters to General J. H. Wilson, Oct. 10, 1899, Jan. 18, 1900.

high. "To appreciate the full moral beauty of the war fever," he wrote Charles Eliot Norton, "you should see it in a colony."[29]

Merriman's opinion of imperialism was identical with that of Goldwin Smith, and both sympathized with the Boers. Such sympathy aroused sharp criticism in Canada, but in South Africa it placed an English-speaking statesman in a far more difficult position. So few Englishmen shared this attitude that it formed a close bond between the two friends. "Believe me," wrote Merriman, "you can never appreciate the moral support that men like you by your views and writings give to those who are trying to fight against overwhelming odds for the ideals that we believe to be the heritage of Englishmen." Goldwin Smith, for his part, confided that he fought as well as he could in Canada, "though as you may imagine I am not . . . crowned with roses."

Merriman felt that Britain was playing the part of a bully, and longed to see the "rowdy imperialism" of men like Rhodes and Chamberlain and Milner replaced by a return to the saner counsels of the Little Englanders. A wilderness of gold mines, he wrote bitterly, would not repay Britain for the criminal blunder of implanting in the Boers a hatred of England so intense that in days to come it might well lead to another war. To his mind the prevalent concept of imperialism would ruin England and the ideals which had made her great. Whatever the outcome of the war, Britain would gain no glory.[30] Her Liberal imperialists he dismissed with the comment that they had touched pitch and would not escape defilement. Annexation would be a failure, on practical as well as moral grounds. He did not wonder that the Boers found intolerable the arrogance of English officials, backed by the cosmopolitan financier. He invited Goldwin Smith, living in the ancestral home of the Family Compact, to imagine a repetition of similar machinations at the Transvaal. At the end of the war Merriman prophesied that it would leave its trace upon the national character of the English as well as upon the face of an unhappy South Africa. The Boers at least had nothing of which to be ashamed.[31] When the Canadian Parliament passed a resolution regretting the Transvaal's refusal to grant political rights to the Uitlanders, Goldwin Smith was outraged, and sent Laurier one of Merriman's letters, giving the other side of the picture.

[29]Jan. 4, 1904.
[30]Letters from J. X. Merriman to Goldwin Smith, Aug. 9, Oct. 10, Dec. 27, 1899, Jan. 22, Dec. 3, 1900; from Goldwin Smith to Merriman, Dec. 9, 1900, Merriman Papers, South African Library, Cape Town.
[31]Letters to Goldwin Smith from J. X. Merriman, Nov. 27, 1900, July 6, 1902, and June 22, 1903; letter from Goldwin Smith to the *Press* (Philadelphia), April 11, 1902.

Early in 1901 Merriman went to London to urge the imperial Government to offer the Boers better terms than unconditional surrender and the reduction of the two republics to the status of crown colonies. Campbell-Bannerman, then leader of the Liberal Opposition, found him "a most taking and effective envoy." Merriman hoped to obtain a union of the four provinces under a system of responsible government like that of Canada or Australia. Through newspaper reports and letters from Merriman, Goldwin Smith followed these negotiations with intense interest, though he was not sanguine about the outcome. At one juncture he cabled Merriman, "Accept settlement. Independence hopeless." Merriman explained that he was in no sense a plenipotentiary with power to persuade the Boers in the field to adopt a given course. He was grateful, however, for the interest of this adopted Canadian who had never set foot in South Africa. "You will be able to feel," he wrote appreciatively, "that you have preached a rational and manly freedom, that will I hope emerge some day from the depressing flood of shoddy Imperialism which now submerges it."[32]

From the beginning Goldwin Smith took it for granted that defeat was inevitable for the two little republics, confronted by the armed power of the British Empire. Long before the war ended he was sure that the English Liberal party offered the only hope of a moderate and generous policy for the future. Bitterly disillusioned by the role Britain had played, he wrote an American friend: "I am as personally loyal I hope as any Englishman can be to my own country. But I owe no allegiance to the vast predatory Empire of which it is the aim of Jingoism to make England the basis, and which, I am convinced, would be not less baneful in its effects to the British masses than to the rest of mankind."[33]

Few Englishmen criticized Britain's South African policy with the frankness, vigour, and pertinacity of Goldwin Smith. But a minority, although less vocal, shared his views. Notable among these was James Bryce, who in private letters freely expressed opinions which in Parliament he voiced somewhat more moderately. "As to equal rights," he wrote Campbell-Bannerman, "we had no more title to interfere with the franchise in the Transvaal than in New York." Bryce shared Merriman's and Smith's detestation of Chamberlain, whose imperialist policy

[32]Letters from J. X. Merriman to Goldwin Smith, June 17, 1904, March 6 and 24, 1901, from Goldwin Smith to Merriman, March 23, 1901, Merriman Papers. Campbell-Bannerman's comment on Merriman occurs in one of his letters to Bryce, Feb. 9, 1901. A copy is in the Campbell-Bannerman Papers in the British Museum, Add. MS. 41211, V, f. 155.

[33]Letters to Bourke Cockran, Dec. 23, 1899, and May 25, 1900.

they held responsible for the Boer War, and whose preferential tariff schemes they as ardent free-traders loathed. Late in 1899 Bryce said gloomily to Goldwin Smith that he and Campbell-Bannerman were the only Opposition members who were not supporting the Government on the war issue. "It is a dismal close," he wrote, "to the century and the reign; and from what we can learn, no one has been more distressed than the Queen, who had hoped to close her days in peace. To us here it seems to be solely Chamberlain's war . . . but those who profess to know declare that it is at least equally Milner's war." When the general election of 1900 returned the Conservatives to power again, with Chamberlain as the strongest single force in the party, Bryce commented: "We are tempted to regret Disraeli: what more could one say? He was after all not quite so sordid as the present leader of the gentlemen of England."[34] No less than Goldwin Smith he deplored the vainglorious spirit in which the claims and achievements of "Anglo-Saxondom" were then vaunted, as contributing to make the British objects of suspicion and dislike throughout Europe.

At the close of the war Goldwin Smith spoke his mind with customary vigour in a little book called *In the Court of History*, published in 1902, and translated into French by Henri Bourassa. In the introduction the translator coupled the author's name with those of Morley and Bryce as distinguished English opponents of the Boer War, who by their stand had won a place in the esteem of the world, and in particular of the French Canadians. Bourassa believed he expressed the views of his compatriots when he said that if they hated Chamberlain's empire, they admired and loved Gladstone's England. The mutual liking between him and Goldwin Smith dated from the time when Bourassa resigned his seat in the Commons, in protest against Laurier's decision without parliamentary sanction to send a Canadian military force to the Transvaal.

IV

The resurgence of concern for the Empire in the last twenty years of the century was shown not only in the scramble for Africa and the extension of British interests in Egypt and the Sudan, but in more pacific schemes for imperial federation. Canadian support for this project, which was never widespread, was largely a reaction against the move-

---

[34]Letters from James Bryce to Goldwin Smith, Dec. 24, 1899, Nov. 15, March 23, 1900, Jan. 25, 1901; to Campbell-Bannerman, Nov. 1, 1899, Campbell-Bannerman Papers.

ment for commercial union with the United States, whose chief exponent was Goldwin Smith. As far back as 1846, in a letter to Lord John Russell, Joseph Howe had suggested the desirability of colonial representation in the British Parliament. In the early eighties Alexander Galt complained to a Scottish audience that the colonies had no share in the government of the Empire or the shaping of its foreign policy. As a remedy he proposed federation of the Empire, or at least of its self-governing portions. But Sir John A. Macdonald, in a famous speech at Toronto on November 3, 1881, declared that imperial federation was utterly impracticable, and that Canada could never consent to send to Westminster representatives who would there vote away their fellow-countrymen's rights and privileges. "We will govern our own country," Sir John asserted, "we will put on the taxes ourselves. If we choose to misgovern ourselves we will do so, and we do not desire England, Ireland or Scotland to tell us we are fools."[35]

The Imperial Federation League was founded in 1884 in London, where Sir Charles Tupper, then Canadian High Commissioner, addressed its first conference.[36] The next year a Canadian League was established in Montreal, and other branches were set up later at various centres in the Dominion. Among the most enthusiastic Canadian proponents of the cause were George Parkin, Colonel George Denison, and Principal Grant of Queen's University. An independent Canada, they asserted, was out of the question, since the days of small nations were gone forever. They were equally opposed to the idea of either commercial or political union with the United States, which they attacked through the counter-proposal of commercial and political federation of the Empire.

The editor of the *London Advertiser*, John Cameron, criticized imperial federation as "a senseless, snobbish, Jingoish bit of humbug."[37] Its chief Canadian critic, however, was Goldwin Smith, who embarrassed the imperial federationists by asking pertinent questions about their precise proposals. Thus he put his finger on the cloudy vagueness

[35]Sir John's speech was quoted verbatim by Goldwin Smith in a letter on imperial federation published in the *Mail* (Toronto), Feb. 18, 1888. This provoked an indignant reply, signed "Imperial Federationist," dated Feb. 23. Its writer cited remarks made by Sir John in both 1884 and 1888, warmly supporting the cause of imperial federation. Galt's speech was published as *The Relations of the Colonies to the Empire, Present and Future* (London, 1883), 8-21.

[36]By 1900, however, Tupper said he thought that a parliamentary federation of the British Empire was impracticable, and that no intelligent Canadian would be willing to see the control of his country's national interests transferred from Ottawa to Westminster. Speech at Lindsay, May 4, 1900, on "The Past, Present and Future of Canada," reported in the *Globe*, May 5, 1900.

[37]*London Advertiser*, Nov. 28, 1893.

which was a major weakness of the scheme. In this attack he showed for once, at least, genuine understanding of the growing nationalism of most Canadians and of many citizens in other British settlement colonies. He wanted to know what portions of the Empire were to be included, what was to be the link between the dependent and self-governing parts, what representation was to be given the colonies to ensure a real voice in the conduct of imperial affairs, and what relationship was envisaged between the imperial and colonial parliaments. How was the sovereign to act as the head of several legislatures which might easily come into conflict with each other? In numerous English journals he pointed out that no one who lived in the colonies could believe that they would ever consent to give up their power of taxing themselves. A common imperial tariff for widely separated communities, with very different economic circumstances, seemed to him to present almost insuperable problems. If anyone wanted to break up the British Empire, Goldwin Smith suggested that he could not do better than impose upon all its members a uniform policy, especially in commercial matters. From Canada's point of view, this would amount to the surrender of fiscal independence. What, he asked, constituted the fundamental unity of an empire whose heterogeneous parts were scattered over the globe and connected only by the chances of war or maritime adventure? Such an empire was simply a group of historical accidents, without unity of race, language, or circumstances. He could not believe that the colonies would contribute to imperial armaments, pay for imperial wars, or conform to an imperial tariff. If Chamberlain tried to insist that they do so, he might well complete the work of George III. Nor did Goldwin Smith see any prospect that communities where the whole current of events had hitherto set steadily toward national independence would suddenly renounce this aspiration, and submerge their dreams of nationality in a subordinate membership of a distant whole. It was significant that no colony had shown the least willingness to part with any portion of its self-government.[38]

The aims of imperial federationists were as vague as their ideas about organization. What, he demanded, was the object of an association in which the centrifugal forces must be exceptionally strong? Since the whole tendency of the past century had been toward colonial decentralization, some tremendous motive power would be needed to reverse this

[38]*Week*, Aug. 7, 1884; letters to *The Times*, Dec. 31, 1887; to Henri Bourassa, Aug. 29, 1903, Gregory Papers; *Weekly Sun*, Feb. 1, 1889, Sept. 25, 1901, Aug. 19, 1903. The views of Canadian advocates of imperial federation are set forth in George M. Grant, *Imperial Federation* (Winnipeg, 1890), and George T. Denison, *The Struggle for Imperial Unity* (London, 1909).

natural course of events. He appealed to the developing sense of Canadian nationalism, aroused in 1888 by resentment over the recent fisheries dispute with the United States. In every disagreement with the Americans, the Canadians had been made to feel that Great Britain neglected their interests, and that jealousy or hatred excited by her was fully extended to her colonists. Both Canada and Australia had shown more enthusiasm for curtailing the powers of the Judicial Committee of the Privy Council than for strengthening the bonds of empire. He appealed to Canadians to let the misty phantom of imperial federation "cloud our perception of our own destiny no more."

He was convinced that the democracy which then ruled England had no interest in any concerns but its own. If the imperial Parliament legislated for Canada, its enactments would be those of ignorance. Between communities on opposite sides of the Atlantic the identity of interest, on which alone a federation could be founded, did not exist. He called on the imperial federationists to note the change in the political spirit of England. The monarchy, to which the hearts and eyes of loyalty once turned, had become a mere figurehead, and the power of the aristocracy had almost departed. In modern times maintenance of the colonial relation simply meant the subordination of one democracy to another, with no perceptible benefit to either, but with obvious detriment to the subordinate partner. As long as Canada remained a dependency she must lack genuine self-government. Sir Wilfrid Laurier asserted that Canada was not a colony but a nation. Goldwin Smith granted that she had in her the making of no mean nation, but held that no community, however great, could really be a nation while its constitution was imposed upon it from without and it was incapable of conducting its own foreign affairs.

He thought, in short, that imperial federation was largely a chimera of Englishmen, based on essential misunderstanding of the real strength of colonial nationalism. The whole idea he dismissed as "simply one of the changes of hue on the dying dolphin of the old colonial system."[39] He rallied the framers of such vast political schemes, whose eyes were always fixed on the political firmament, with forgetting that the ideas of men in general were turned on the path they trod. Seeley's *Expansion of England*, published in 1883, was widely acclaimed in Great Britain. But in colonies such as Canada, Goldwin Smith pointed out, there were many people who believed less in the expansion of England than in the

[39] Letter to the *Mail*, Feb. 18, 1888; "The Canadian Question," *Independent* (New York), Feb. 23, 1888; *Weekly Sun*, Oct. 9, 1901.

multiplication of Englands. By more than a quarter of a century he anticipated Unwin's argument that the British Empire was not the deliberate expansion of the English state emphasized by Seeley, but the unplanned expansion of a people. The social and labour problems looming on the horizon toward the end of the century would soon, he suggested, give politicians more serious cause for thought than "the airy fabric of imperial federation." Even the people of Great Britain were beginning to be suspicious about the prospect of a world-wide league wherein they had to bear all the military and naval expenses, while the colonies declined in any way to sacrifice their interests to those of the imperial country. Goldwin Smith appealed to the English Conservative to say what he expected to gain from pressing to Great Britain's heart "the socialist and feminist democracies of Australasia," currently engaged in enacting exclusion laws against some three hundred odd millions of the black and brown subjects of the Crown. The chief interest hitherto shown by Australians in British politics was when they abetted the dock strike. "Have you not enough of that element already," he inquired, "without going to the antipodes for further instalments?"[40]

When Winston Churchill spoke on South Africa at Toronto in 1900 he lunched at the Grange, where his host privately considered him "a lively talker but a shallow young man." The posters advertising Churchill's lecture dubbed him "the future premier of Greater Britain." Goldwin Smith admitted that if Greater Britain ever came into being, it was likely enough that Mr. Churchill would be its premier. But despite the hopes of the imperial federationists, he could not see that Australian or South African union would be a step in that direction. Imagination boggled at the thought of a confederation of confederations. A Dutchman in a dozen pairs of breeches would be simplicity in comparison with such an arrangement. In any event, he was suspicious of Dilke's phrase "Greater Britain," which reminded him of the old belief that the earth was the centre of the solar system. "Standing on his historical island, the British expansionist sees all the other communities of the race revolving round him, and fancies that they neither have, nor ever will have, any relations but to him."[41] This centripetal view irked his patience. Surely, he argued, it was conceivable that under independent

[40]"The Political Aspect of Imperial Federation," *Saturday Review*, LXXXIII (Feb. 20, 1897), 187-8.
[41]"The Expansion of England."
Goldwin Smith's opinion of Churchill was given in a private conversation with W. D. Gregory, who on Dec. 31, 1900, recorded the incident in the diary preserved among the Gregory Papers.

auspices these young nations might lead a distinct, perhaps a greater, life of their own, that would reflect enhanced importance and interest on the land from which they sprang. He wished England would have the good sense to confine herself to her own sphere and stop clinging to an expensive and purely nominal dominion, fraught with danger of future dissension.

By the end of the century he was confident that the Boer War would kill imperial federation. He could not believe that Canadians would commit themselves to a system liable to entangle them all over the world in quarrels not their own.[42] On the whole he thought it safe to conclude that the movement was dead. Rising from its grave he discerned two phantoms, joint imperial armaments and fiscal union of the Empire, neither apt to be clothed with real flesh and blood. The colonial conferences, more practical offshoots of the imperial federation movement, also filled him with suspicion, as likely to return the colonies to their former dependent position. In 1895 he argued, as in his *Empire* letters thirty years earlier, that since the colonies would not help to defend the Empire, Great Britain would be left to carry the burden alone, and should therefore consider what advantages the political connection offered to countervail the cost and peril of supporting remote dependencies. He did not see why a man should be dubbed a traitor, or even a Little Englander, for espousing such views. In his opinion the jingoes were angry "because they think that we are trying to make them moral, when the fact is we are only trying to make them safe."[43]

In retrospect the colonial and imperial conferences seem major steps on the road to the modern co-operative Commonwealth. At the end of the nineteenth century, however, in the hey-day of aggressive imperialism, Goldwin Smith thought they required watching, lest they conceal veiled interference with colonial self-government. He described the Conference of 1907 as "a highly speculative palaver," and viewed it with a caution tinged with mistrust.

Half a century ago [he commented], the colonial policy of Great Britain was founded on the assumption, shared by almost all the statesmen of the day, that the colonies were destined to become independent nations bound to their Mother-Country only by the tie of affection, which, however, it was believed would be strong. . . . Now the policy is completely reversed, and the Colonial Minister of a Liberal Government is throwing himself into the movement for the strengthening and perpetuation of the colonial tie. Certain

[42]Letter to Henri Bourassa, Feb. 8, 1900.
[43]"The Colonial Conference," *Contemporary Review*, LXVII (Dec., 1895), 105–16.

it is that if he succeeds another part of the Liberal policy must be renounced. Britain must go on struggling to maintain, while other nations will struggle to prevent her maintaining, her empire over all the seas. There can be no reduction of armaments, while without reduction of armaments there can be no security for peace.[44]

V

One of his counts against imperial federation and even colonial conferences was that such pan-Britannic schemes excluded the larger portion of the English-speaking peoples in what he believed must soon become the greatest of their communities, the United States. He was relieved that the Anglo-phobia so prevalent during the eighteen-sixties and seventies in the United States was by the eighteen-nineties slowly giving way to a realization of the bonds created by a common respect for law and a common attachment to personal liberty and freedom of opinion. As the memory of the old quarrel between England and the United States faded, and both countries saw a threat in the rise of such powers as Germany, Goldwin Smith welcomed an increase in kindly intercourse between them. He had no sympathy, however, with pretensions founded on an alleged superiority of race. To him Rosebery's desire to cast the world in an Anglo-Saxon mould seemed a conspiracy against other nations, which could only provoke merited hostility and lead at last to disaster.

The United States alone, to his mind, deserved the title of the Greater Britain, since, if not within the dominion of the British Crown, it was yet within that of the British race, the British intellect, and the British civilization. While he considered imperial federation impracticable, he was convinced one federation was feasible, and, to those who measured grandeur not by physical force or the expansion of empire, at least as great as that of which the imperialist dreamt: "a moral, diplomatic and commercial union of the whole English-speaking race throughout the world."

Opponents too often dismissed Goldwin Smith's attacks on British imperial policy as those of a purely destructive critic. He believed profoundly that the British Empire of ideals, literature, and political institutions had no peer in history. In his positive contribution to problems of empire he was three-quarters of a century ahead of his times. Fired by his idea of Anglo-Saxonry, a *rapprochement* between the scattered members of a famous race, he envisaged its parts morally united though

[44]*Weekly Sun*, April 17 and 24, 1907.

politically independent, its qualities variously displayed in different parts of the world. This, he held, was no dream, but by a rational policy might be translated into a glorious reality. What he did think chimerical was faith in the political union of all these communities, or even of those still nominally ruled by Britain.[45] After his first visit to the United States in 1864 he tried to inspire his fellow-countrymen with this vision. For the rest of his days he was consumed by a desire to do all he could to further its realization.

His enthusiasm was shared by only a few contemporaries. In 1869 the founders of the Royal Colonial Institute had invited the American Minister to England to join representatives of the various colonies at their inaugural dinner. Immediately after they had drunk the health of the Queen and royal family, the chairman proposed a toast to the United States, concluding with the words: "The descendants of Great Britain's younger sons greet the representative of the eldest born!" The Prime Minister, Gladstone, spoke warmly of the Institute's aim to hand down from one generation to another "the great and noble tradition of the union of the British race.[46] At a time when little love was lost between England and the United States, such a meeting bore significant witness to an underlying if seldom acknowledged community of interest.

Such sentiments, however, were rarely expressed. The profound faith in all the English-speaking peoples affirmed by Goldwin Smith and Dicey and Bryce was shared only by two of their friends, Sir Charles Dilke, and the historian, E. A. Freeman. In the United States, Dilke observed, the polyglot peoples of the world were being fused into an English mould, so that through America England spoke to the world. The development of Elizabethan England Dilke saw "not in the Britain of Victoria, but in half the habitable globe. If two small islands are by courtesy styled 'Great,' America, Australia, India, must form a 'Greater Britain.' "[47]

In his historical study of federalism Freeman dismissed imperial federation as nonsense. To his mind it did not involve true federation, but its opposite, subjection, because the colonies were not in a position to grant powers to a central body, since they themselves possessed only such authority as the mother country had given them. It would be a strange federation of the English-speaking people, he suggested, which excluded the inhabitants of the United States, who had established, if

[45]Letter to the *Daily News*, July 4, 1866; "The Organization of Democracy," *Contemporary Review*, XLVII (March, 1885), 315–33; "A Federation of the English Speaking People," *Sun* (New York), Sept. 2, 1894.
[46]Royal Colonial Institute, *Proceedings*, I–II, 21–8.
[47]Sir Charles Dilke, *Greater Britain* (London, 1868), i.

not a greater Britain, at least a newer England. Freeman hazarded the opinion that a lasting friendly alliance between the scattered English people of the world, including the Americans, was a far higher object than maintenance of "any so-called British Empire." In a letter to Goldwin Smith he wondered whether there might be some kind of mutual citizenship between Great Britain, the United States, and the English-speaking colonies. Of the possibility of any closer union he was doubtful. Smith thought there might at least be ultimate hope of an Anglo-Saxon franchise, a conception which to him seemed no less visionary and at least as grand as imperial federation.[48]

In America, as in England, few men of the time shared such views. One who did was Goldwin Smith's friend, T. F. Bayard, sometime Secretary of State and later American ambassador to England. On the eve of taking up this latter post Bayard declared that what he most hoped to achieve in England was strengthening the common sympathies, affection, and traditions of the two peoples.[49] Among the few Canadians who cherished the same ideal was John Cameron. Unlike Goldwin Smith he believed that Canada's destiny was independent nationhood. Only one prospect appealed to him more: the fusion of Canada, Great Britain, and the United States into "a world wide English-speaking union."[50]

At the end of his days, as at the beginning, Goldwin Smith avowed that his loyalty was to England, not the Empire. Yet he referred to the United Kingdom as the "British Commonwealth" in 1882, two years before Lord Rosebery described the Empire as "a commonwealth of nations." The time, Smith foretold, would soon come when the beat of the British drum would no more go around the world with the rising sun. Yet as it died away there would be heard the voice of civilization, law, and literature speaking in the English tongue in "that grander and better Empire to which all whose language is English must for ever belong."[51] Throughout his eighty years he believed, not in dominion over dependencies, but in a community of independent nations, each contributing from its own resources to the common store of humanity,

---

[48]Letter from E. A. Freeman to Goldwin Smith, Aug. 19, 1888, published in W. R. W. Stephens, *The Life and Letters of E. A. Freeman* (2 vols., London, 1895), 384; E. A. Freeman, "Imperial Federation," *Macmillan's Magazine*, LI (April, 1885), republished in *Greater Greece and Greater Britain* (London, 1886); letter from Goldwin Smith to *The Times*, Dec. 31, 1887.

[49]Letter from T. F. Bayard to Goldwin Smith, April 16, 1893, Autograph Album.

[50]*London Advertiser*, Nov. 28, 1893.

[51]*The Political Relations of Canada to Great Britain and the United States: An Address Delivered to the Nineteenth Century Club, New York, on the 31st of January, 1890* (Toronto, 1890), 7-8.

and each by its example aiding the others. The chief future interest of English history would lie in the fact that Great Britain was the source of political and social institutions transplanted to new lands throughout the world. The power to establish and work such free institutions seemed to him the special gift of the Anglo-Saxon. Although at the close of the nineteenth century the shadows of Britain's day of empire began to lengthen, the friendly co-operation of English-speaking people throughout the world, as Goldwin Smith emphasized, was all but complete. The new concept was an empire not of ascendancy, but of free association. He admitted that he could not help loving all the English-speaking peoples better than some of them loved the others, but prophesied that their misunderstandings and quarrels would one day end.

To advance this goal he had done all he could. Charles Eliot Norton paid tribute to his services to "the Cause to which your life has been given,—the promoting of a good understanding between England and America, and . . . uniting . . . them in bonds of mutual good will."[52] In the faith that such good will would prevail Goldwin Smith died in 1910, still considering himself "a citizen of the Anglo-Saxon race," proud of its traditions and confident in its future.

[52]Letter from Charles Eliot Norton to Goldwin Smith, Oct. 27, 1893.

IX. RELIGION AND ETHICS

LIKE MOST OF HIS FELLOW VICTORIANS Goldwin Smith was deeply interested in religion. He lived through the great age of questioning, when orthodox Christianity was shaken by the higher criticism of the Scriptures, the Darwinian doctrines, and the general development of the natural sciences. In his youth as he once observed, geology nervously strove to accommodate itself to Genesis; soon Genesis strove to accommodate itself to geology.

John Stuart Mill was only one of many contemporary Englishmen who, like the St. Simonians in France, thought of their time as a period of transition, an era of intellectual anarchy in which old institutions and doctrines were discredited before new opinions had been adopted to fill the void. Amid the disintegration of old beliefs men yearned to discover some certainties on which they could take their stand. Goldwin Smith, like Mill, was unconvinced that his contemporaries had a firm grasp of any principle which would render them much less open than their predecessors to sophistry and prejudice. Erroneous convictions were bad, but far worse were no convictions at all. Before he complimented a man or a generation on having got rid of prejudices he wanted to know what had been substituted in their stead. People were too inclined to think the new light which had broken upon them was the only light. Hence they blithely blew out the ancient lamp which, though it did not show them what they now saw, had served to light their immediate path.[1]

If it was an age of uncertainty it was not one of indifference, as Goldwin Smith's writings amply illustrate, but of inquiry and discussion. If men did not reason better than in later days about the questions of life and death, they at least reasoned more, and through examination of established opinions attempted to sift the true from the false. In this process the claims of the new science and the old religion were subjected

[1] J. S. Mill, essays on "The Spirit of the Age," published by the *Examiner* in 1831, when he was twenty-five.

to searching scrutiny. Some smiled at the idea that on the answers to such questioning depended their hopes of eternal salvation, but more were inclined to tremble than to smile. For the most part free-thinking agnostics were as serious in their speculations as those who clung to the doctrines of Christianity. Amid his responsibilities as Prime Minister, Gladstone found time to conduct a public controversy with Huxley on the accuracy of the account of creation in Genesis. Through the pages of the *Nineteenth Century* for 1885-6, the reading public followed the debate with genuine concern.

The Victorian liberal had a real belief, though with Tennyson he might find more faith in honest doubt than in half the creeds. Goldwin Smith's views on religious questions were not simply his own, but were shared by many contemporary liberals. If in retrospect they seem, like some of his political ideas, to lack originality, it is because they reflect the issues which most concerned his age. On religious as on other problems, however, few men were more articulate. To the end of his life he had an impulse to confess the faith—political, religious, or economic—that was in him. The unpopularity of his religious views concerned him little more than that of his political opinions.

I

As a young man of twenty-four he wrote Roundell Palmer (later the first Earl of Selborne) that the problem of church and state was crucial in British politics. He soon became an outspoken foe of the establishment, and in the interests of free-thought rather than nonconformity bent all his energies toward abolishing religious tests in the universities. Yet one of his Oxford students afterwards observed that he was always religious, though unorthodox, and recalled that Goldwin Smith told him he had never doubted the belief in immortality.[2] This doubt, like others, grew upon him. From the position of a relatively orthodox though conspicuously liberal churchman in his youth, he moved in later years to that of a free-thinker. Throughout his life, however, he remained deeply concerned with moral questions and with the ethics as opposed to the doctrinal dogmas of religion. As he grew older he turned increasingly from current political controversies to enduring spiritual problems. Intense as was his interest in politics, like most of his Victorian contemporaries he was even more interested in religious issues. His political opinions and religious views were linked. What he came to consider most important in Christianity was its ethics. His conception of morality

[2]Lionel Tollemache, *Nuts and Chestnuts* (London, 1911), 30.

imbued his treatment of political issues such as slavery and imperialism as well as his concept of history. His high-minded austerity recalled Milton to Lord Selborne, who in 1893 wrote of Goldwin Smith: "In religious views I doubt his being a Churchman; he is certainly not too fond of the clergy or of church establishments, and he was quite out of sympathy with the Oxford Movement, its leaders, and its school. But positively religious (as Milton was, and I should think very much in Milton's way) he is."[3] By the eighteen-nineties Goldwin Smith had left orthodoxy well behind, although his friends were right in thinking him still profoundly religious in temperament.

He followed his early plea for the abolition of tests at Oxford by criticism of the Bampton lectures for 1858 on the limits of religious thought. Their author, J. L. Mansel, then reader in moral and metaphysical philosophy at Magdalen, had argued that an infinite God was incomprehensible to finite man. Men could not know God, only how He willed that they should think of Him. Mansel's attempt to defend conventional orthodoxy by philosophic skepticism provoked protests from clerics like F. D. Maurice and laymen like Goldwin Smith. The latter maintained what Mansel denied, that divine and human morality were the same. He attacked Mansel's empiricism and materialism, declaring that the only cry in which he himself was willing to join was one for freedom of religious thought.[4] Goldwin Smith's complaint that Mansel's lectures left the world without God, truth, or morality was oddly similar to criticisms in after years directed against his own religious position. Mansel comfortably survived the onslaught, for he was subsequently appointed Dean of St. Paul's.

Goldwin Smith's attack on the Bampton lectures was a liberal defence of orthodoxy, and his position in the eighteen-fifties far removed from that which he reached forty years later when most of his religious studies were written. Temperamentally, however, he was never a conformist. During his Regius Professorship he wrote the Bishop of Oxford an open letter (prudently signed with a pseudonym), criticizing that prelate's advice that men should cast doubt from them. "I confess, my Lord," Goldwin Smith declared in tones like those of Mill, "I know but one way in which men can distinguish truth from error, and this is by freely admitting doubt and fairly dealing with it when admitted." Faith which forbade doubt pronounced itself incapable of undergoing the test of

[3] Letter from Lord Selborne to Lord Stanmore, Dec. 30, 1893, published in Roundell Palmer, Earl of Selborne, *Memorials* (2 vols., London, 1898), II, 389. Goldwin Smith's letter to Roundell Palmer, dated Aug. 30, 1847, is published in *Goldwin Smith's Correspondence*, 2-3.

[4] *Rational Religion and the Rationalistic Objections of the Bampton Lectures for 1858* (Oxford, 1861), v, 144.

truth. Inquiry necessarily began in uncertainty, and without free inquiry there could be no assurance of truth, nor anything left but blind submission to the church into which each man happened to be born. The suppression of conscientious doubt, not its fair admission, was really subversive of true faith, for what but reason could be the judge of truth? To forbid any departure from established dogma was a standing invitation to schism. "I do not doubt," he concluded, "that the time is rapidly approaching when all men will see that the protection of particular religious opinions by the State is a thing not to be justified; that the faith needs and can accept no 'defender' but One; and that religion can be 'established' only in the hearts and minds of men."[5] This letter provoked indignant protests from churchmen. He contented himself with the rejoinder that there was no hope of bringing all the Christian world to the precise ecclesiastical position of the last Tudor despot. After all, honest inquiry was but the most fervent prayer for truth.[6] This was plain speaking for 1861.

When a few months later Goldwin Smith resigned from the *Saturday Review*, he wrote its proprietor about the differences of opinion between them. The most important of these was his conviction that state churches presented a fatal barrier to a pure religion and a reconciled Christendom, which were, he thought, the great remedies for the social and political evils of the day. An established church he detested as an institution which simply made the church political without making the state religious. Himself a member of the Church of England, he considered political conservatism her only certain and unchanging doctrine. Precisely because he was her faithful son he was an open and hearty enemy of the establishment. To expect a state church, the negation of religious liberty, to be other than reactionary in politics was to expect a contradiction in nature. A creature of privilege and of patent injustice, subsisting by a stationary creed, it necessarily felt itself threatened by progress. A decade later he was convinced that the state church must disappear, unless mass endowments and legal establishment by themselves were strong enough to hold together people whose beliefs ranged from "Roman Catholicism to extreme Rationalism and beyond."[7]

[5]*The Suppression of Doubt Is Not Faith: A Letter to the Lord Bishop of Oxford by a Layman, April 12, 1861* (Oxford, 1861); letter to the *Daily News*, Dec. 31, 1861. John Stuart Mill's *Essay On Liberty* had been published two years earlier.
[6]*Concerning Doubt: A Reply to "A Clergyman", by a Layman, May 26, 1861* (Oxford, 1861).
[7]Letters to G. W. Curtis, July 3, 1877; to A. J. Beresford Hope, Jan. 22, 1862; to the *Daily News*, Sept. 24, 1866; "The Defeat of the Liberal Party," *Fortnightly Review*, XXII (July, 1877), 1–24; "Whigs and Liberals," *ibid.*, XXIII (March, 1878), 404–16.

II

One of the things which first attracted Goldwin Smith to Cornell was its nonsectarian character. Its emphasis on practical studies and applied science, however, gave him pause. In lectures to the students at Ithaca he suggested that the achievements of science raised questions which must disturb the complacent pursuit of improved railroads and telegraphs. The coming age might be fruitful, not only of marvellous inventions, but of inquiries into the state of man, the government of the universe, the nature of conscience, and the immortality of the soul. To his way of thinking, the data of the physical sciences must be supplemented by those of philosophy and history. He pleaded for recognition of the whole nature of man, both spiritual and material. He saw no natural conflict between religion and science, but looked for their reconciliation, not through curtailment of the conquests of science, but through the conviction that beyond its sphere there remained other phenomena of lasting importance.

In later years Goldwin Smith found himself less and less able to accept theological dogmas. For the ethics of "rational Christianity," however, he never lost his respect. To the Christian code he still adhered for want of a better, since utilitarian morality, which made no appeal to conscience, as far as he could see was no morality at all. In an address at Victoria College he urged his hearers to remember that they were not Methodists or Episcopalians or Presbyterians, but "Christians and nothing else." It was an advanced point of view to propound in 1873 to a Methodist institution. The simple morality of the gospels, he suggested, would carry them through the perplexities of the times. In a period of religious divisions and diverse sects, of doubt and disintegration of faith, ultra-scepticism confronted the ecclesiastical forms of the Middle Ages. For himself, he still held that the great truths of religion had not lost their vitality, and that men would come again to believe in the paramount importance of the spiritual life. The saying that "we are all members one of another" was a Christian doctrine long before it became a tenet of sociology. He believed that the wealth of mankind was morally a common store which the individual was in conscience bound to waste as little, and increase as much, as he could.

Two years after he settled in Canada he wrote a friend at Oxford that his North American experiences had left him "pretty much what I was when you saw me last, advanced in politics, but still in the theological stage of my spiritual evolution." Among the English friends with whom he stayed in 1874 was the Archbishop of Canterbury, with whom, as A. C. Tait, Goldwin Smith had worked on the Oxford University Commission. Their talk ranged widely over the affairs of heaven and earth, and the Archbishop, with an obvious effort to be fair, later wrote, "Though many of your utterances were very different from what I could approve, I know that you speak what you believe, and that in these days is something. I know also that in the conflict which impends between Materialistic Atheism and Christianity you are on our side."[8] In years to come the accuracy of this judgment was amply confirmed.

Fundamental problems of religion increasingly absorbed Goldwin Smith's attention. The evidence of conscience, he granted, was different from that of the senses and of reason. Was it therefore less trustworthy? Conscience was "the great and hitherto unshaken proof at once of the immortality of the soul and of the existence of God."[9] If agnosticism meant suspension of judgment and refusal to accept the unknown as the known, it seemed to him a natural frame of mind for anyone resolved upon loyalty to truth. To such a man existence must appear an overwhelming and unfathomable mystery. Man being what he was, however, would never lay aside his desire to learn the truth about his own origin and destiny; he would never be content simply to enjoy life on earth without thinking of anything beyond. Professed acquiescence in ignorance might sound philosophic, but man remained an inquisitive animal; as often as he raised his eyes to the stars his curiosity would be called into play. Goldwin Smith himself could not accept the doctrines of the Trinity, the incarnation, redemption, and atonement. He never faltered, however, in his belief that although Christianity could no longer be considered a miraculous revelation, it yet remained the most important fact of history.[10]

During the eighteen-eighties and nineties the controversy between theism and agnosticism was fought in North American as well as British journals. The vigour of the debate belied the common assumption that Canadians had no interest in ideas. This wide concern did not surprise Goldwin Smith, for compared with such problems he thought all others trivial and superficial. In the *Bystander*, the *Week*, and the *Weekly Sun* he reviewed recent studies in philosophy and theology, and renewed his

[8]Letter from A. C. Tait, Dec. 31, 1874; letter from Goldwin Smith to Mrs. Hertz, Sept. 30, 1873.
[9]"The Immortality of the Soul," *Canadian Monthly*, IX (May, 1876), 408–16; "Will Morality Survive Religion?" *Forum*, X (April, 1891), 146–56.
[10]"The Prospects of a Moral Interregnum," *Atlantic Monthly*, XLIV (1879), 629–42; "Evolutionary Ethics and Christianity," *Contemporary Review*, XLIV (Dec., 1883), 789–811.

early controversy with the Positivists. To his mind Herbert Spencer abolished morality by attempting to place it on a scientific basis, and by denying the existence of moral laws and conscience. Spencer drew no decisive line between the ethics of the oyster and those of man, and evidently believed that the only difference was that the greatest of mammals was more highly evolved and more perfectly adapted to its surroundings. Goldwin Smith remained unconvinced that the reign of law in nature meant the dethronement of God. Fanatical unbelief he deplored as much as fanatical belief.[11]

To Mrs. Humphry Ward, Matthew Arnold's niece, he wrote in 1888 that *Robert Elsmere* was making a great stir "even in this sequestered nook of the theological world."

> Churches are still being everywhere built, money is freely subscribed, young men are pressing into the clerical profession, and religion shows every sign of vitality. I cannot help suspecting however that a change is not far off. If it comes it will come with a vengeance; for over the intellectual dead level of this democracy opinion courses like the tide running in over a flat. . . . A wonderful period of transition in all things has begun, and I should like very much to see the result. However it is too likely that very rough times may be coming and that one will be just as well out of the way.[12]

III

With advancing years most men grow more conservative, and in many respects Goldwin Smith was no exception. His political liberalism reached its zenith before he left England at the end of the eighteen-sixties. But in religious matters he became increasingly liberal. To the end of his days his attitude was one of honest inquiry and a sober confession of ignorance, never the scepticism of indifference. He grew more impatient, however, of anthropomorphic ideas about religion and naïve acceptance of unquestioned dogmas. Our angels, he observed wearily, are lovely insipidities with impossible wings. Prayer for specific favours struck him as childish. On one occasion when a thunderstorm had disrupted his wife's plans for a garden-party, he wrote a friend, "I tell her next time she must have it announced in church that a lady about to give a garden-party desires the prayers of the congregation for fine weather. This would be at least as rational as praying, which they still do, for

[11]*Bystander*, III (Jan., 1883), 56; I (Feb., 1880), 107–8; II (June, 1881), 366.
[12]Mrs. Humphry Ward, *A Writer's Recollections* (London, 1919), 249.

people going to sea, when a Cunarder is about the only place except the gallows in which it is impossible to get drowned."[13]

His lack of sympathy with dogma made him impatient of interdenominational disputes. Invitations to speak in Unitarian, Baptist, or Friends' churches he gladly accepted, and indeed felt himself closer to the latter two denominations than to any other. It seemed to him that all Christians should be in communion, and that the controversies which divided the Protestant churches belonged to a past age. More than once he suggested that clerical incomes might be increased if churches between whose creeds there was no essential difference would combine, especially in country districts, instead of competing. They could then give a good stipend to one pastor instead of poor ones to three. Since clergymen were still the guides of moral civilization, their temporal position ought to be decent. To the clergy themselves he suggested that if their defence of religion were less dogmatic and more ethical, the effect might be better. He discerned no immediate prospect of formal union between the churches, but hoped that from the tendency to mutual recognition and interchange of pulpits might some day come at least a working union.[14]

The Baptists he particularly respected for their hatred of war and their insistence upon the separation of church and state. An unusual tribute to a man often regarded as an heretical free-thinker was the honorary degree conferred on him by McMaster University, a Baptist institution whose liberality was indicated by its action. Although not a regular member, he often attended a little Baptist church at the doors of the Grange. He had a personal liking for its liberal minister, W. Harris Wallace, and appreciated his willingness to welcome to the congregation one whom the ultra-godly shunned as an atheist. Mr. Wallace, for his part, dismissed the allegation that Goldwin Smith was an agnostic with the comment, "He walked according to the light God had given him, was true to his convictions, and an example to many of us." Their friendship suffered some strain when the minister expressed a desire that Goldwin Smith should write a brief history of the Baptist Church. He got as far as looking up various authorities before confessing that he found the task almost impossible. Nothing further was heard of the project.

At the age of seventy-three he published a little volume of his articles on religious subjects which had originally appeared in American

[13]Letter to Charles Eliot Norton, June 29, 1888.
[14]"The Question of Disestablishment," *Essays on Questions of the Day* (Toronto, 1893), 72.

journals. As the title, *Guesses at the Riddle of Existence* suggested, they put forward possible solutions to some of the great moral and theological issues, not dogmatic statements of personal belief. Profession of an assured faith would have been impossible for Goldwin Smith. If he did not solve the riddle of existence to the satisfaction of others it was because he had arrived at no solution satisfactory to himself. To the end of his days, however, he remained in religion, as in political and social matters, an honest seeker after truth. He could not see why the most momentous of all questions should be the one on which thought was least free.[15] The theory that truth was the privilege of the enlightened few and unquestioning acceptance of traditional dogma the duty of the masses, repelled him. In the preface he expressed the hope that, since he took care not to be irreverent, his heterodoxy would give no offence. He desired to show no lack of tenderness to the creed in which he himself had been reared, which he long held, and only reluctantly resigned.

If agnosticism meant despair of spiritual truth, he professed himself no agnostic. He simply thought that if free inquiry was to lead to rational faith, the way must be cleared by abandoning doctrines of which men were no longer convinced. Although he regretfully decided that there was no conclusive evidence for personal immortality, he refused to believe that all ends here. To him as to others in his day, the thought of death without an after life seemed repugnant to the sense of justice, as that of a world without religion seemed repugnant to the moral sense. It was a common nineteenth-century view that morality could not survive loss of faith in a world to come, where compensation would be found for the hardships and inequities of life on earth.

His friend Judge Longley of Nova Scotia admitted that there was a problem, but argued that under no conditions could happiness in this life be attained save by virtuous living. "With all my heart," he wrote, "I hope there is another existence, but if fully assured there was not, I would still be certain that the only way in which I could secure the largest measure of happiness in this was by the practice of virtue and the exercise of constant self-sacrifice." Like Goldwin Smith he considered religion the greatest topic a man could think or talk about, and it often formed the subject of their letters. Longley had much sympathy with Smith's speculations on religion, though he granted they would please neither the orthodox nor the superstitious. Although the principle of love had made comparatively little headway in the last nineteen hundred years, Longley still looked to it as the only means for the redemption of mankind. Both men were temperamentally religious and

[15]"Liberal Orthodoxy," *Agnostic Annual* (1898), 10–13.

intellectually sceptical. In a letter telling Smith about the christening of his namesake godson, Goldwin Longley, the judge observed cheerfully that the theological regularity of the godfather, about which Goldwin Smith had expressed some doubts, was no more open to question than that of the real father.[16]

Smith's writings on religion endeared him to the godly of Toronto little more than his political ideas to its Empire Loyalists. A bishop's public criticism of his *Guesses at the Riddle of Existence*, however, so largely increased its sale that the booksellers could scarcely supply the demand. The religious intolerance of the New World was well illustrated by orthodox attacks on his infidel writings. More generous Canadian critics sometimes found his speculations on theological problems infinitely depressing. He was encouraged, however, when he received letters from clergymen of various denominations, thanking him for his public expression of doubts which in private pressed heavily upon them. A few reviewers, particularly in England, found Goldwin Smith's honest search for truth a weightier testimonial to religion than most volumes of apologetics.

In his writings on these matters, as in the studies of political and economic problems which appeared during the latter part of his life, he frequently seemed out of date. He was largely concerned to discuss eighteenth-century rationalist objections to theological dogmas and mid-nineteenth-century onslaughts on orthodoxy. Without taking the trouble to read what had been written in the past twenty-five years, he tended to assume that the new "higher criticism" had demolished all claims of the Old Testament to historical accuracy. Hence he sometimes laid himself open to the charge of fighting phantom battles. There was more than this, however, in his speculations on religion.

Challenges presented by modern biblical criticism and by advances in scientific knowledge gave him genuine concern. The uneasiness of intelligent clergymen, struggling to reconcile belief with unbelief, seemed to him illustrated by their growing inclination to substitute philanthropy and social reform for spiritual guidance. On the other hand he supported the churches' new tendency to recognize both worlds, and approved the interest in labour and industrial questions of the Lambeth Conference of 1897. He urged acceptance of the new criticism and of modern scientific ideas in place of uncritical adherence to the older doctrines of divine inspiration. The current assumption that such acceptance meant the end of religious belief, he constantly combated.

For his own part he cheerfully abandoned faith in the story of the

[16]Letters from J. W. Longley, Nov. 7, 1904, May 26, 1903, June 5, 1902, and Jan. 11, 1908.

creation and in the stern God of the Old Testament. He rejected the authenticity of miracles, but never relinquished belief in what to him were the fundamental teachings of the New Testament, the fatherhood of God and the brotherhood of men. This, the real essence of Christianity, he argued, had for eighteen centuries been the soul of moral civilization. No other faith had shown such power for good. Christ never formulated either a creed or an ecclesiastical polity. Formal liturgies and ritual were alike alien to Him. Between ecclesiastical dogma and what he considered the fundamentals of Christianity, Goldwin Smith distinguished sharply, holding that the validity of the latter did not depend on that of the former. If Genesis was rejected and with it the fall of man, he saw no occasion for either the incarnation or the atonement. There still remained, however, the character and teachings of Christ, with their profound effect upon human history and character. If men wished to understand the real meaning of Christianity, they must return in spirit to a hillside in Galilee. There a wandering preacher taught a little group of disciples that the condition of entrance into the kingdom of God was renunciation of the things on which the heart of the world, in the twentieth century as in the first, was most intensely set. A figure less divine, he observed in an address to a Unitarian club, could scarcely have been deified. If people nowadays believed in Christ's divinity, it was because spiritual perfection was divine. Despite all the fanaticism and impostures practised in its name, Christianity had proved by its fruits a solution to the ethical problems of humanity.

Many of these ideas were akin to the religious opinions of Tolstoi. Goldwin Smith agreed that the kingdom of heaven was within. From a brave new world of material progress he expected little, unless men's hearts could be so changed that the brotherhood of men was transmuted from a phrase into a practical creed.

IV

During the last twenty years of his life he frequently wrote letters and short articles on religious topics for the New York *Sun*, where discussions on immortality contrasted oddly with accounts of prize fights and current political controversies. These letters aroused a surprisingly wide interest, and provoked lively correspondence. In them Goldwin Smith described his position as that of many thoughtful men who had renounced dogma but were not prepared without further evidence to embrace materialism. Sharing to the full the doubts and uncertainties of the time, he did not presume to offer any theory of his own. For his part he preferred to rest the claim of Christianity to serious consideration on nothing mystical or supernatural, but on the evidence of the character it had produced and on the relation of that character to the progress of humanity. To him these seemed facts as indubitable as any that could be submitted to scientific investigation.[17]

With the peculiar capacity to antagonize two schools of thought which was an intrinsic part of his independent liberalism, Goldwin Smith challenged the conclusions of fundamentalists and materialists alike. Naturally both attacked him. Many found it easy as well as congenial to dismiss him as a destructive critic, since much of his writing, whether religious or political, was negative rather than positive, as the stand of the liberal often must be. He was not alone in finding criticism of a position easier than proposing alternatives.

The London *Daily Telegraph* gave space in 1905 to a lengthy correspondence on the subject "Do we believe?" In this interchange of opinion some nine thousand persons took part. Interest in the discussion was aroused in the United States as well as in England, with the result that the New York *Sun* invited similar correspondence, to which Goldwin Smith was one of the ablest and most frequent contributors. The next year he collected excerpts from his letters to the *Sun* in a small volume with the characteristic title, *In Quest of Light*. Here again he was a rational pessimist, a critic of established views, and a seeker for truth. He affirmed nothing; he simply stated a case as he saw it, and invited the expression of opinion. He did not tender proofs, but asked for them. As he was then eighty-three, it was not surprising that for the most part he elaborated his earlier ideas. Although men were happily casting off superstition, he thought there was still scope for faith: not the faith which rejected or supplanted reason, but that which was the evidence of things unseen. Seeking the foundation for a reasonable belief, he never wearied of quoting Bishop Butler's remark that "the faculty of reason is the candle of the Lord within us, against vilifying which we must be very cautious." He urged his readers to remember that human knowledge was bounded by the senses and that they might be in a universe quite other than that revealed by sense. The world might be still in its childhood, and the faith which seemed to be collapsing be only that of the child. "Old men," he observed three years before his death, "cannot look for certainty; they can only hope to die in hearty allegiance to truth."[18]

[17]Letters to the *Sun* (New York), March 13 and July 16, 1904, April 28, 1901.
[18]"Evolution, Immortality and the Christian Religion: A Reply," *North American Review*, CLXXXVI (Oct., 1907), 195–9.

Goldwin Smith's last book, *No Refuge But in Truth*, published in 1908, was another collection of letters and articles on religion. In these he discussed such questions as the destiny of man, the scope of evolution, the immortality of the soul, and the imminence of a revolution in ethics. Here he argued that belief in materialistic evolution did not account for man's spiritual nature. Beavers were doubtless wonderfully cooperative, but they had as yet shown no tendency to establish a church. Although evolution was perhaps the most momentous discovery ever made, it was simply a record of observed succession. He wished people would pay more attention to the ascent of man and less to his descent. Despite the great contributions of Darwin, "still we are what we are, not apes but men."[19]

Many of his letters to the *Sun* were reprinted in Canadian papers, where they aroused much comment. From all over Canada and the United States he received replies in support or rebuttal of his position. Complaints by Catholics that he was an intolerant enemy of their faith distressed him, though it may be doubted whether his explanations palliated his offences in their eyes. The Catholic religion, he reiterated, was one thing, and papal theocracy another. Liberal Catholics like Lord Acton were as opposed as himself to the doctrine of papal infallibility. Had not Acton commented on the Council of Rome which evolved this doctrine, "we have to meet an organized conspiracy to establish a power which would be the most formidable enemy of liberty as well as science throughout the world." Notwithstanding his criticism of indulgences and shrines, Goldwin Smith had many Catholic friends, and he particularly appreciated a letter of sympathy on his wife's death from the editor of the *Catholic Register*. "Believe me," he wrote in reply, "I am no enemy of Catholicism. . . . The character of Christ, in my belief, is the creed of Christendom."

To American friends like President Schurman of Cornell and Andrew Carnegie, he sent copies of *No Refuge But in Truth*. He knew Schurman would find the articles heretical, but he hoped not irreverent. Carnegie replied, "Thanks, my dear mentor" (his customary form of address to Goldwin Smith). A sceptic who viewed religious problems with a light-heartedness alien to Smith, Carnegie suggested that "Heaven as described is far from attractive, and the company of the prophets leaves much to be desired. It is said Queen Victoria always drew the line at David, no, to him she would never be introduced." In more serious vein he added that he hoped for eternal life, provided his wife and child and all his friends were to be with him. "The man who says there is none is

[19]*In Quest of Light* (Toronto, 1906), 14.

just as foolhardy as he who says there is. Neither can know—all can hope, and I certainly do." Yet since men had as yet no duties in any other life, he concluded more casually, "Why so inquisitive about another?"[20] Lack of such inquisitiveness Goldwin Smith could not understand.

A journalist's comment on his "profound agnosticism" pained him, and he declared that he would be sorry to think the designation deserved. He craved for light, but thought a careful reader of what he had written would see that he had not renounced religion.[21] The last letter he was able to sign was written to the Bishop of Toronto three days before his death. It thanked him for having called a number of times during Goldwin Smith's illness to see him and pray with him. Among his unpublished manuscripts was an article on "The Religious Outlook" prepared for an address at the Unitarian church in Toronto, but never delivered. In this he asked, "Without God, moral freedom, or hope beyond the grave, what would man and his life be?" Characteristically he concluded that men should accept what was really proven, however unwelcome.

There is abundant evidence that in the truest sense Goldwin Smith was religious, although a reverent and reluctant doubter in a doubting age. In later years when the riddle of existence pressed heavily on his mind, his concern with spiritual questions was paramount. Through his writing on these matters, as on secular problems, ran a note of wistful scepticism. He was caught in the dilemma of the liberal intellectual, so anxious to weigh competing evidence objectively and to be fair to all points of view that he found difficulty in adopting a definite position. He continued to place the liberal's emphasis on the private conscience and the individual judgment. Critics often accused him of opinionated dogmatism, a charge not altogether fair, even when confined to his political views. He believed in democracy, for instance, but saw its faults so clearly that his approval was qualified. Hence his ideas sometimes appeared uncertain or contradictory. Like any sensible person he was less dogmatic in matters of religion than in questions of politics. His deep-rooted liberalism made him hesitate to espouse a position to which he was temperamentally attracted, lest his preferences lead him from the path of reason. He would have liked to accept more Christian teaching had he been able to do so honestly. Some of his ideas developed

---

[20] Letter from Andrew Carnegie to Goldwin Smith, Jan. 12, 1909, Andrew White Papers, Cornell University Archives.

[21] Editorial, *New York Times*, Dec. 27, 1908; letter from Goldwin Smith to the *Sun*, Jan. 17, 1909.

little after he reached middle life, yet in many ways his vision continued to embrace wide horizons. As in politics he looked to a more comprehensive union even than that of the English-speaking peoples, namely the brotherhood of men, so in religion he looked beyond the differences of church and sect to a reunion of Christendom, based upon common agreement on the Christian ideal of character.

Anxious to make his position clear before he died, with one of his last letters to the *Sun* he enclosed a note to the editor, requesting early publication, since he did not wish "to go out of the world as a reputed enemy of religion." On the great religious problems which so deeply interested him he spoke as a learner, not a teacher. A man in extreme old age, he added ruefully, had little time left in which to learn.[22]

[22]*Sun*, April 10, June 11, and Sept. 18, 1910; Sept. 5, 1909.

X. DEMOCRACY IN CANADA

FROM THE OUTSET Canada interested Goldwin Smith more than any other British colony. He had discussed its problems and prospects in his early *Empire* letters, where as a solution for two nations warring in a single state he prescribed a federal union of all British North America into one independent country. What, he demanded, did Canadians hope to gain by remaining a dependency, or fear to lose by becoming a nation? His analysis rankled all the more for its truth, and was not calculated to endear him to most Canadians who had no desire to be independent of Britain. Before his first visit to North America he had declared categorically that the traveller who journeyed from the British colonies to the States passed from a smaller to a greater, from a less prosperous to a more prosperous country, from a province to a nation. Yet he believed in the future of these colonies, which seemed destined to form a united confederation. Rare was the Englishman, in 1862, who was interested enough to have such convictions.

I

Within three years his prediction had passed from abstract theory into practical politics. In March, 1865, when the Canadian legislature was discussing the Quebec Resolutions, Goldwin Smith published an arresting article on the proposed constitution for British North America. The framers of Confederation emphasized their wish to perpetuate the connection with the mother country. He deplored the continuance of a political bond, arguing that a complete break, with a new constitution for an independent new nation, was preferable. The colonists had expressed their desire to form a federal union, with a constitution similar in principle to that of Great Britain. Goldwin Smith thought a unitary government an inappropriate model for a federation, but considered that the Quebec Resolutions really provided, not a federal, but a unitary state, in which the independence of the provinces would be practically extinguished. As instances of the overriding superiority of the central government he cited its unlimited right to tax, to disallow provincial acts, and to appoint lieutenant-governors. Provincial powers seemed to him not much more important than those delegated to local authorities in the United Kingdom. Here lay seeds of possible future discord. The provinces might temporarily be content to subordinate local independence to a mutual desire for combination against the mythical danger of American invasion. Once the danger was clearly over, however, provincial sentiment, fed by divergent interests, might well reappear. Hence he contended that the framers of the constitution should make a clear choice between federal and unitary government. A hybrid compromise, leaving doubtful the object of citizens' ultimate allegiance, was based on the fallacious hope that difficulties would eventually settle themselves.

Divergent interests, especially between French Catholics and English Protestants, he thought inevitable. American experience suggested that the best safeguard against disruption of the new constitution was to be sought in strong local governments, not centralization, in the elasticity rather than the rigidity of the federal framework. Flexibility, though apt not to be appreciated by the framers of constitutions, was to his mind an important advantage. He attacked the proposal that the members of the Senate should be nominated by the executive. Such a plan might be tolerated in a kingdom where the power was exercised in a monarch's name, but scarcely in a democratic community. Fashionable as bicameralism was, in a popular government it represented a futile attempt to make the sovereign people, whose will must inevitably be supreme, impose a check on itself. Canadians, like Americans, he pointed out, were democrats. Their fundamental institutions—the acceptance of political and social equality, the absence of hereditary rank, the common schools and free churches—were all essential products of the New World, not the Old. In conclusion he observed that Europe was covered with the wreck of constitutions patterned on the British, and, even more deplorably, with the wreck of political faith. Workable constitutions must be more than imitations of foreign models; they must reflect the national temperament and political circumstances of the people whom they were designed to serve. Whatever the merits of the English constitution, it could scarcely be regarded as the normal and final state of man.[1]

[1]"The Proposed Constitution for British North America," *Macmillan's Magazine*, XI (March, 1865), 407–12.

The Nova Scotian allegation that their province had been tricked into Confederation was accepted by Goldwin Smith. From the beginning he attacked the failure to submit the terms of the new constitution to the people affected, and declared roundly that Confederation was the offspring, not of statesmanship, but of deadlock. As long as the country was prosperous and all went smoothly, few questions might be raised about the manner in which the union was carried. But when discontent arose, as was inevitable, more would be heard of the failure to submit the constitution to the direct vote of the people.

II

Thus when Goldwin Smith first settled in Toronto he was already known as a student of Canadian politics and a critic of the British North America Act. First-hand contact with democracy in Canada confirmed his original misgivings. Within a year he was declaring that unfortunately the colonies had reproduced British institutions, dry-rot and all. He never accepted the need for regional recognition, and had no sympathy with sectional considerations which influenced the composition of the federal cabinet and led to the Maritime demand for "better terms." If local susceptibilities were allowed to determine the membership of cabinets, he roundly declared, all hopes of Canadian statesmanship would be ended. It was ridiculous to demand ministerial representation not only for various sections of the country, but also for different races and creeds. Such was the triumph of parochial considerations that apparently the only nationality whose claims could be safely neglected was the weak and self-depreciatory Canadian nationality. Was Canada, he demanded impatiently, only a league for peace and security, or was it a nation with a federal structure?[2] A decade later, analysing the new Dominion's problems in an English journal, he remarked bitterly: "From the composition of a cabinet to the composition of a rifle-team, sectionalism is the rule."[3] Intercolonial free trade was the only good result of Confederation, which in his opinion had done nothing to fuse the races and little to unite the provinces.

As an Englishman and historian he found it hard to conceal his amusement at Canadian reverence for the venerable ark of the con-

[2]A Bystander, "The Dominion Parliament," *Canadian Monthly*, I (Feb., 1872), 149; II (July, 1872), 56–67; "Colonel Gray on Confederaton," II (Aug., 1872), 173–83; Rose-Belford's *Canadian Monthly*, II (Jan., 1879), 115.
[3]*The Political Destiny of Canada* (Toronto, 1878), 16–17.

stitution, then some eleven years old. His new compatriots did not welcome Goldwin Smith's comment that the framework of their union was necessarily experimental, and at least in part the product of accidents and compromise. Their reluctance to consider the need for alteration he dismissed as absurd. The constitution, like other mortal works, was imperfect, a nondescript cross between federal and unitary forms. He could think of no more legitimate subject for reconsideration and amendment. It was the role of genuine conservatism, by recognizing and removing defects, to avert violent and sweeping change. He continued to insist that "ruinous cracks" were beginning to appear in the fabric of Confederation, and that its terms should first be revised and then submitted to the people.

He saw no reason to consider the arrangement of 1867 sacrosanct, nor to fear that correction of its proved defects would shake the popular allegiance to established institutions whose value every statesman acknowledged. The imperial Parliament, from which the British North America Act ostensibly emanated, never really considered it seriously, and far from being able to give adequate attention to Canadian affairs was unable to find enough time for its own. Necessary changes in the terms of Confederation were impossible since there was practically no power of revision. Tupper's theory of a compact between the provinces, alterable only with their unanimous consent, would, if accepted, prevent political development, since a reactionary party could always gain control of a single province. One of the first critics of the compact theory, Goldwin Smith argued that it was untenable, because the British North America Act was an imperial statute, interpreted by an imperial court and subject to amendment by the same authority by which it was made, due deference being paid to the expressed wishes of the Canadian people. The "provincial rights" cry made no appeal to him. As firmly as John Stuart Mill he believed in local administration of local affairs combined with as much centralization as possible in all truly national matters.

Twenty years after Confederation he saw few grounds for optimism in the development of faction, increased taxation, debt, demagoguery, and corruption, with their inevitable effect upon political character.[4] He discerned no appreciable development of national feeling—his greatest and most lasting mistake about Canada. While Canadians respected Goldwin Smith's ability and integrity they found it difficult to like a

[4]"The Canadian Constitution," *Contemporary Review*, LII (July, 1887), 1–20; *Bystander*, III (Oct., 1883), 257–61; *Weekly Sun*, Jan. 25, 1899.

mentor who in leading English and American journals portrayed the young country in such unflattering terms. His reputation in Canada would have been even worse had he been identified as the writer of three articles on Canadian politics in the *New York Times* signed "A Canadian." Their title, "Government by Bribery," with the sub-heading "The Dominion of Canada Ruled by Corruption," suggested the contents. The events leading up to Confederation were briefly described. The two political parties, suddenly "finding that they could not overcome each other, the leaders agreed to bury the hatchet, bury their principles, embrace one another, and divide the country between them."[5] This was not the account given in Canadian history books.

Such strictures sound extreme, but at the time had some relevance. During the last three decades of the nineteenth century the Canadian political scene presented grounds for pessimism. The Pacific Scandal of 1873 was only the most famous instance of a corruption widespread in both parties, which, although largely condoned by the electorate, disgusted not only critical journalists like Goldwin Smith, but high-minded statesmen like Edward Blake. Smith liked to recount how he had once asked a British Columbia farmer what his politics were, and received the reply: "Government appropriations." These appropriations admittedly played a part in building up national unity. Goldwin Smith thought the price too high. Unlike most reformers he was by temperament a pessimist. His persistent criticism of abuses sprang from no optimistic faith in the goodness of man. What was wrong with a situation always struck him much more forcibly than what was right. His own austere integrity made him acutely conscious of human frailty. He realized that motives were commonly mixed, but too often assumed that the worse prevailed.

It seemed to him unwise to leave open many questions of prerogative and constitutional convention, in the faith that as need arose they could be settled according to "the well understood principles of the British Constitution." Well understood they might be in England where the practice of centuries had stamped them indelibly upon the minds of public men. There great political families with unbroken traditions had the strongest reasons for respecting a polity which was their own heritage. Canada's case was different. To his mind the Dominion needed a complete written constitution and its own court of final appeal (as opposed to the Judicial Committee of the Privy Council), with powers of interpretation as ample as those of the American Supreme Court. He was torn between amusement and annoyance at E. A. Freeman's

[5] *New York Times*, April 13, 20, and 27, 1890.

enthusiasm for "the singular clearness and accuracy of the British North America Act as compared with the blundering language" of most modern acts of Parliament.[6] He pointed out that many gloomy predictions of Christopher Dunkin, the chief critic of the Quebec Resolutions, had been fulfilled. Certainly the equal provincial representation which the Senate failed to provide was unfortunately recognized in the composition of the federal cabinet, and there was aptness in Dunkin's description of the provinces as a bundle of fishing-rods tied together by the ends.

During the first thirty years after Confederation Canadians were much less concerned than Goldwin Smith about constitutional limitations on their national sovereignty. At the beginning of the twentieth century, however, annoyed at the decision in the Alaska boundary case, they began to demand the right to make their own treaties. This, Goldwin Smith reasonably observed, was to demand independent nationality. Great Britain would not enforce treaties she had not made, nor would foreign governments negotiate with any but a sovereign power.[7] His analysis was shrewd. Most Canadians in fact failed to realize the logical implications of their own demand. Unfortunately, after the demise of the Canada First movement, Goldwin Smith was never willing seriously to envisage the possibility that Canada could remain independent in a continent shared with so powerful a neighbour as the United States. Nevertheless he was convinced that her relationship to the mother country ought to be defined. To his mind no community, however important and full of hope, could be called a nation while its constitution was imposed from without, its legislation remained subject to an external veto, its appellate jurisdiction was vested in an external court, and control over foreign affairs lay with another country.[8] In the nineteenth century Canadians resented such comments, but in the twentieth they themselves became increasingly irked by these limitations on their nationhood.

"To impart anything like liveliness to a discussion of the British North America Act," Goldwin Smith once remarked, required "the touch of Voltaire." This feat he managed to accomplish, but Canadians would have been willing to exchange some of the liveliness of his candid analysis for a more sympathetic understanding of their problems.

---

[6]Letter from E. A. Freeman to Goldwin Smith, April 25, 1888; "Current Events and Opinions," *Week*, May 29, 1884.

[7]Unsigned review of Sir John Bourinot's *Lord Elgin* in the *Nation* (New York), LXXVIII (Jan. 7, 1904).

[8]*Weekly Sun*, Aug. 23, 1899.

III

These general criticisms of the Canadian constitutional framework Goldwin Smith supplemented by specific attacks on particular political institutions, chief among them the party system, the governor-generalship, and the Senate. His outspoken censure of British party politics has already been noted. Even in England, where distinctive principles appeared to divide the parties, he had found in them more to condemn than to admire. In Canada, where there were no such real issues of principle, the situation was far worse. No one could say what the conservatives were to conserve or the reformers reform. In certain so-called Canadian Liberals he discerned a singular resemblance to the most arbitrary British Tories. With Macdonald's enthusiasm for nation-building Goldwin Smith was unsympathetic, partly because he thought the scheme impractical. In any event it was hard to see why a national policy in the political sphere was more Conservative than Liberal. With the abolition of the seigniories and the overthrow of the Family Compact, he saw no basis for conservatism in a country without an established church or governing class, with the possible exception of Orangeism and its strange ally, the Roman Catholic theocracy of Quebec. Compared with the power of material interests, religious influences on politics seemed to him feeble. He prophesied that there would appear no adequate successor to Macdonald, able to hold together the motley group of followers from every camp who had combined under a leader of genius and good fortune.[9] He did not foresee that strong leaders and an appeal to the most diverse interests and sentiments were to become permanent characteristics of successful Canadian parties.

Goldwin Smith insisted that he had as much sympathy for rational conservatism as for liberalism. The only conservatism he thought possible in the New World, however, was that which looked to the mature opinion of the community as the basis of government. As a radical he

---

[9]The task of Sir John's political life, Goldwin Smith wrote in the *Week* for April 10, 1884, "has been to hold together a set of elements, national, religious, sectional and personal, as motley as the component patches of any 'crazy quilt', and actuated, each of them, by paramount regard for its own interest. This task he has so far accomplished by his consummate address, by his assiduous study of the weaker points of character, and where corruption was indispensable, by corruption. It is more than doubtful whether anybody could have done better than he has done. His aims, if they have not been the loftiest, have always been public, and in the midst of daily temptation he has kept his own heart above pelf. Indeed, if he had not, he could scarcely have played so successfully upon the egotism and cupidity of other men."

thought that Liberals formed parties of opinion, whereas Conservatives formed parties of interests. Hence Liberal parties were more subject to splits, since opinion groups tended to divide in proportion to their activity, while interest groups tended to consolidate in proportion to their strength. Claims of Canadian Conservatives that they drew their inspiration from England Goldwin Smith countered by pointing to corruption connected with the tariff, railways, public works, and political patronage. Any British politician who attempted the sort of bribery common in Canada would be forced to leave the country within twenty-four hours. In forthright terms he spoke his mind about the corruption of Canadian politics in general and of the Conservative Government in particular. Ultra-Conservatism he disliked; political corruption was worse. Their combination he found singularly distasteful. In his opinion the Canadian party system had saturated with corruption a people naturally well qualified for free institutions.

By the turn of the century, however, Goldwin Smith was hoping that the Conservatives would win. He described the election campaign of 1900 as a struggle for place between two factions, both Tory and imperialist. "They are abusing each other heartily," he wrote an American friend, "and every word that each of them says is true. . . . The straight Tories do us less harm, and the Pseudo-Liberals occupy the ground on which, if they were out of the way, something really Liberal might be formed. But the whole country is so venal that the chances are always in favour of the Judas who carries the bag."[10] He saw no hope for Liberalism while Laurier and his cabinet were in power. Canadians would be better off with the avowed Tories in office, for at least there would then be a real Opposition.

Neither Conservatives nor Liberals were much amused at such pictures of Canadian politics portrayed in American journals by an Englishman resident in Canada. Few stopped to reflect that he frequently described British politics in terms little more flattering, although there the cause of such strictures was not corruption, but Irish Home Rule or votes for women or old age pensions: all catastrophes whose origin he traced to the iniquitous operations of the party system.

Goldwin Smith was but the first of many who found it hard to discern any clear-cut differences between Canadian Conservatives and Liberals. Sir Charles Tupper's speeches, he blandly observed, might almost as well have been delivered by Sir Wilfried Laurier. It would only be neces-

[10]Letters to Bourke Cockran, Oct. 14, 1900; to W. D. Gregory, Jan. 12, 1900, Gregory Papers, Douglas Library, Queen's; *Bystander*, II (Jan., 1881), 7-9; I (Feb., 1880), 58.

sary to transpose the personal or party recriminations. But from one rising young Liberal he hoped for better things. He had known Mackenzie King as a young man, and noted with interest his translation from the civil service to active politics. King, if anyone, he prophesied in 1908, was likely to succeed in the arduous endeavour to combine patriotism with party. Perhaps he might also succeed in distinguishing Canadian Liberalism from Conservatism. To a letter of congratulation from Goldwin Smith upon his appointment as Minister of Labour, King replied with characteristic elaboration:

In nothing do I regard myself more fortunate . . . than in holding any place in your regard. It will be my earnest endeavour to strive after the realization of those principles of government by which the common good is best fostered, and to administer the affairs of the department over which I have been called to preside without fear or favour, and in so far as I may be equal to the task, in a broad and progressive manner. I shall continue to look in the future as I have in the past to your writings for guidance and assistance.[11]

IV

If there was one political institution which Goldwin Smith disliked more than another, it was the office of governor-general. This chiefly reminded him of the appendix, which served no purpose, but sometimes did serious harm. For British royalty and aristocracy he had little liking, but they were at least indigenous growths springing from ancient historical tradition. The idea of grafting the sins of the Old World on to the New through the gratuitous establishment of a puppet governor-generalship and a make-believe aristocracy outraged all his republican instincts. To his way of thinking the Canadian constitution could well do without a false front of monarchy, in which the king who reigned but did not govern was represented by a governor-general and lieutenant-governors who did likewise. "Religious Canada," he observed dryly, "prays each Sunday that they may govern well, on the understanding that heaven will never be so unconstitutional as to grant her prayer."[12] So far as he could see, these functionaries merely served as a ventriloquial apparatus for the prime minister and provincial premiers, meekly repeating words put into their mouths in the speeches from the throne.

The vice-regal court at Ottawa struck him as a childish parody of British monarchy which wasted money and encouraged the worst type

[11]Letter from W. L. Mackenzie King to Goldwin Smith, June 8, 1908.
[12]*Canada and the Canadian Question* (Toronto, 1891), 147–55.

of social snobbery. Had the governor-general retained any real authority, Goldwin Smith thought something might be said for the institution. He believed that the monarch's representatives ought to have some discretionary power and on occasion refuse dissolutions, but for the most part they lacked the courage to do so. They should consider themselves guardians of the prerogative, and hence responsible for seeing that it was not abused by colonial politicians. They ought to feel responsible for the character, though not the policy, of the servants of the Crown, and for the purity, though not the expediency, of appointments to public office.

This somewhat unusual conception of the governor-general's role under a responsible government Goldwin Smith defended by arguing that the Crown's representative should always remember that he was an English gentleman and in the last resort go home rather than consent to anything dishonourable. He would, for instance, be justified in refusing to appoint a senator whose nomination he suspected had been bought. In practice, however, the governor-general did none of these things. It was difficult to say what purpose he served, save possibly "to throw a slight veil of decorum over such Ministerial acts as need it."[13] As an authoritative interpreter of Canadian sentiment to the imperial government, the governor-general necessarily suffered from certain practical disadvantages which could not easily be overcome. A newcomer to the country, he laboured under the double disability of being a personage to whom it was difficult to speak the truth, and of living in an official capital where, on certain subjects at least, not much truth was spoken. As a channel of English influence on Canadian thought, in Goldwin Smith's opinion, the governor-generalship might profitably be exchanged for the free importation of British books.

He showed little understanding of the difficulties of the early governors-general who performed a dual role as representatives of both the sovereign and the British government. Colonial ministers, as Dufferin aptly observed to Carnarvon, were "a kittle team to drive," especially when there were "two loose horses like Brown and Blake rampaging about on either side of the leaders."[14] Goldwin Smith lacked the imagination to perceive that the governor-general's lot was seldom a happy one. They all came, he protested to Dicey, ignorant of a country in which they could have no permanent interest. At their departure they

[13]*Weekly Sun*, Jan. 27, 1909, Jan. 11, 1905; "The Empire," *Essays on Questions of the Day* (Toronto, 1893), 162.
[14]Letter from Lord Dufferin to Lord Carnarvon, Dec. 21, 1874, C. W. de Kiewiet and F. H. Underhill, *Dufferin-Carnarvon Correspondence, 1874–1878*, (Toronto, 1955), 126.

forgot what they had learned. "When," he demanded, "will this farcical subordination end?"[15] He was a difficult man to please. Outraged by the suspicion that Lord Minto had encouraged Laurier to send Canadian contingents to the Boer War, he complained that governors-general were prone to irresponsible meddling.[16] What he really wanted was for them to intervene only where he thought they should.

When in 1903 an Australian suggested that Sir Wilfrid Laurier should become the next governor-general of Canada, Goldwin Smith protested indignantly. Laurier would doubtless fill with grace any role assigned to him, but to make him or any other Canadian politician governor-general was absurd. How could he be expected or believed to be free from party bias?[17] This argument was to be heard frequently in the half century that elapsed before the appointment of the first Canadian governor-general.

In his opinions on the utility of governors-general, Goldwin Smith for once expressed a widely held, though minority, view. Twenty-five years after his death a constitutional authority observed that the self-governing dominions were convinced that the governor-general served no purpose more distinguished than that of a rubber stamp. To Goldwin Smith's popularizing of this idea in Canada he attributed much of the criticism of Lord Byng's refusal in 1926 to grant the dissolution requested by Mackenzie King.[18]

Goldwin Smith's failure to acknowledge that the Crown was a necessary constitutional entity in responsible cabinet government was based on his preference for a republic and his belief that parties played no vital role. He did not confine his strictures to abstract generalizations about the uselessness of representing the Crown in virtually independent colonies, but frankly criticized the sins of omission and commission of successive governors-general. Lord Dufferin's speeches struck him as "a collection of elegant flummery almost unique in literature," containing scarcely a word of truth from beginning to end. Their dislike was mutual. Dufferin complained privately to Carnarvon that Goldwin Smith did all the mischief he could by advocating independence for Canada, and laying down the law to a group of young men in Toronto whom he tried to inspire with his "eminently wrong headed ideas."[19]

The advent of Lord Lorne "and his princess" Smith anticipated as

[15] Letter to A. V. Dicey, April 30, 1910.
[16] Letter to J. X. Merriman, Oct. 14, 1902.
[17] *Weekly Sun*, Jan. 14, 1903.
[18] A. Berriedale Keith, *The King and the Imperial Crown* (London, 1936), vii.
[19] Letter to Lord Carnarvon, April 25, 1874, *Dufferin-Carnarvon Correspondence, 1874–1878*, 36.

an invitation to the worst excesses of colonial snobbery.[20] After Lord Lorne's term of office was completed he repaid these criticisms by embarking on a journalistic controversy with Goldwin Smith about the political future of Canada.[21] Of Lord Minto Smith was little less critical, although some friendly letters passed between them about General Middleton, whom they both admired and whose defence Goldwin Smith undertook when accusations were made against Middleton's conduct during the Northwest Rebellion. They also held similar views about political corruption in Canada. "Ever since I have been here," Minto wrote Goldwin Smith, "I have used whatever influence I possessed against the abominable political 'pull', which nearly everyone in Canada looks to and which is ruining the individuality of the people."[22]

Lord Lansdowne Goldwin Smith genuinely liked. The two became good friends, and found bonds of union in their common disapproval of imperial federation and Irish Home Rule. Before Lansdowne's arrival in Canada Goldwin Smith wrote a friend that the new Governor-General, by all accounts, was "fit for better things than cultivating Colonial flunkeyism and struggling to avert that which must come and ought to come, and which the true interest of the English people would lead everyone to wish should come—the union of Canada with the continent of which nature has made her a part."[23] Lord Lansdowne often visited the Grange, and before his return to England sent Goldwin Smith an engraving of his great-grandfather, Lord Shelburne, as a reminder of one "who is very grateful to you for your kindness during his stay in Canada."[24] Goldwin Smith was not the man, however, to allow his real personal liking for Lord Lansdowne to modify his low opinion of governors-general and aristocrats in a New World democracy whose chief asset was the absence of marked class distinctions. He was happy to find that some individuals had the force of character to rise above the disabilities inherent in their rank and office. Further than this he was not prepared to go.

[20]Letter to G. W. Curtis, Nov. 11, 1878; *Bystander*, I (March, 1880), 128.

[21]Goldwin Smith's article on "Canada and the United States," *Forum*, VI (Nov., 1888), 241–56, was countered by the Marquis of Lorne on "Obstacles to Annexation," in the same journal for Feb., 1889. Goldwin Smith replied in "The Interference of Aristocracy in the New World," *Independent* (New York), Feb. 28, 1889.

[22]Letters from the Earl of Minto, Aug. 11 and July 8, 1904. Three letters to Lord Minto from Goldwin Smith, dated July 8, 28, and Aug. 13, 1904, supporting General Middleton, are in the Minto Papers, XXX, 4–8, Public Archives of Canada.

[23]Letter to Mrs. Hertz, Oct. 8, 1883, *Goldwin Smith's Correspondence*, 152–3.

[24]Letter from Lord Lansdowne, May 8, 1888, Autograph Album, The Grange, Art Gallery of Toronto.

V

The Canadian Senate, which he described as "the House of the political dead," seemed to him only less indefensible than Britain's hereditary second chamber. Within twenty years after the passage of the British North America Act he observed that the intentions of constitution builders concerning an upper house had never more signally failed of achievement. Under Sir John A. Macdonald the Senate had become a political infirmary and bribery fund, destitute of any moral influence whereby it might render a real service to the nation. Such a bulwark against rash action could be swept away in a moment by gusts of popular passion. A second chamber nominated by the executive was an outrage against the elective principle. Prime ministers as party leaders were bound to do what they had done, bestow seats in the Senate as rewards for party services. If the upper house was composed of old men, it would be impotent, if of rich men, odious, and if of the wisest and best men in politics, then the more powerful lower house would be deprived of its natural leaders. From this quandary he saw no escape, although he thought the election of senators by the provincial legislatures would be an improvement on the existing system. Any idea that a nominated senate would be the serene abode of men of high character, special knowledge, or commercial experience, was belied by the Canadian Senate, which had become merely a home for superannuated party politicians. Its work as a divorce court was as anomalous as that of the Lords as a court of appeal.

Most Canadians at the time agreed that their Senate had proved a disappointment. Their mistake, in Goldwin Smith's eyes, lay in adopting the antiquated figments of the British constitution as well as its living parts, under the delusion that the figments were realities. Furthermore, different social conditions in England and Canada were bound to affect the way in which political institutions worked. Parliamentary democracy was based on responsible government. The Canadian Senate was irresponsible, and few considered it a body to which irresponsible power could safely be entrusted. On the other hand he granted that a second chamber was needed as an organ of legislative revision and second thought. When Laurier proposed the possibility of a joint sitting of the two houses in case of deadlock, Goldwin Smith argued in rebuttal that if the two chambers were to fuse whenever they disagreed, there was no point in having more than one. The Senate's power to veto measures passed by the Commons, however, seemed to him indefensible. A simple reform, he suggested, would be to empower the Commons to pass measures by a two-thirds majority, over the veto of the Senate. This would not provide an ideal constitution, but would give some opportunity for reconsideration, would leave intact the special character of each house, and would avoid a joint sitting. Over and above all these practical considerations, he attacked the Canadian Senate on the same ground that he attacked titles for colonials and the governor-generalship, as attempts to graft the faults of British aristocracy on to the democracy of the New World.[25]

These criticisms of the Senate, like his attacks on the governor-generalship, met with more popular support in Canada than many of his other views. The senators themselves were uneasily aware that sound reasons lay behind the disapproval so often publicly directed against the Canadian second chamber. They were not prepared, however, to grant that this was always justified. When in 1881 the *Bystander* observed that the only sign of life in the Senate during the previous session was its passage of an amendment to the Scott Act, one of its members, Sir Alexander Campbell, was moved to protest. He wrote Goldwin Smith citing a number of important measures which had originated in the upper house, and as an illustration of the calibre of the discussions sent him a copy of the Senate debates. These, he suggested, showed that the second chamber had discussed public affairs with an intelligence and thoroughness which compared favourably with the deliberations of the Canadian Commons or of other British legislative bodies. "My writing," he added, "bears tribute to the weight which I attach to the views which the Bystander offers to the Canadian public."[26] Goldwin Smith replied courteously, but reiterated his opinion that in a democratic country like Canada no political institution without an elective basis could be really strong. One difficulty about giving the Senate such a basis was that then the relative importance of the two houses might perhaps be reversed.

VI

Other Canadian political institutions also drew his fire. He sometimes wondered whether parliamentary government could ever work well in a colony lacking an independent class. That this doubt was inconsistent

[25]*Week*, May 1 and Aug. 7, 1884; *Weekly Sun*, Jan. 11, Feb. 8 and May 30, 1899, May 28, 1902.
[26]Letter from Sir Alexander Campbell to Goldwin Smith, April 14, 1881, Campbell Papers, Public Archives of Ontario. Goldwin Smith's letter of reply, dated April 17, 1881, is also in the Campbell Papers.

with his attacks on the power of the wealthy governing class in Britain apparently did not deter him or perhaps occur to him. He was concerned by the fact that in frontier democracies where everyone's attention was focussed on vote-getting and where minorities were outcasts, political courage was uncommon. Goldwin Smith was far from convinced that without such courage democracy could succeed. Cowardice, next to corruption, seemed to him the besetting political sin of the continent.

Men of independence and courage were rare in any country, particularly in a colony without a leisured class. In his *American Commonwealth* Bryce devoted a chapter to the reasons why great men did not become presidents. In Canada Goldwin Smith thought the situation was more difficult, because there leading men, occupied with their own personal and business concerns, did not even go into Parliament. To make matters worse, the country was over-governed. Four million people had to produce eight prime ministers (one federal and seven provincial), as many legislatures, and some sixty-five ministers of the Crown. England, with ten times the population, was content with one king, one Parliament, and a single cabinet normally smaller than the ministry at Ottawa. Canada also had judges and chief justices "as the stars of heaven in number."[27] He doubted whether any country in the world had as much government as this colony which perhaps required least. The results achieved compared with the energy expended reminded him of drawing a cork with a steam engine.

The low calibre of men in public life led naturally to a low standard of legislative debate and achievement. More than once Goldwin Smith commented that it would be difficult for the tone and manners of the Ontario legislature to sink much lower. Little was accomplished during the session because so much time was wasted in personal altercations. He saw no use in observing all the forms of the British House of Commons if the ordinary rules of parliamentary decorum and even of social decency were to be completely disregarded. He had no sympathy with proposals for attracting abler men to public life by increasing the salaries of parliamentarians, and was outraged, in 1905, at the Canadian innovation of paying a special salary to the leader of the Opposition. Both measures struck him as bribes. The latter he particularly disliked as a legislative recognition of the importance of parties, which he always hoped might be diminished if judiciously ignored. He feared also that by accepting a salary the leader of the Opposition would become a pensioner of the Government, and thus jeopardize his independence.[28]

[27]*Bystander*, I (March, 1880), 127; I (April, 1880), 175.
[28]*Weekly Sun*, Aug. 23 and Sept. 6, 1905; "Current Events," *Canadian Monthly*, III (March, 1873), 230; III (April, 1873), 336; letter to James Bryce, Aug. 7, 1905.

VII

Two major components of Canadian thought Goldwin Smith largely misunderstood. The first was the strength of national sentiment. The second was the French community. In his enthusiasm for union with the United States he ignored not only Canadian nationalism, but French-Canadian opinion on the subject. Both mistakes were serious. In his early *Empire* letters, written before his first visit to Canada, his Anglo-Saxon prejudices were as evident as Lord Durham's twenty-five years before. Here Goldwin Smith had described Quebec as "an antediluvian relic of old French society with its torpor and bigotry, utterly without value for the purposes of modern civilization." This judgment he qualified by explaining that he naturally referred to their institutions, not to the French people, whose qualities might prove invaluable in tempering the character of the English. With or without qualification, the description stung.

Fifteen years later, when he had lived in Canada nearly a decade, but had acquired little real knowledge of Quebec, his early estimate was scarcely modified. "French Canada," he wrote, "is a relic of the historical past preserved by isolation, as Siberian mammoths are preserved in ice. . . . The French Canadians are an unprogressive, religious, submissive, courteous, and, though poor, not unhappy people." Perhaps it was as much due to the climate as to their lack of intelligent industry that they had an indifferent reputation as farmers. He prophesied, however, that "even the 'paleocrystallic' ice which envelops French Canada will melt at last, and when it does French reaction will be at an end."[29] The courtesy of the French was never more signally illustrated than in the tributes of Quebec newspapers at the time of Goldwin Smith's death to a man who never really understood them. He did try, however, to understand. Few Torontonians troubled to subscribe, as he did, to a leading French-Canadian journal, *Le Nationaliste*, and few numbered among their friends such a leader of French opinion as Henri Bourassa.

Yet although Goldwin Smith's prejudice about French Canada can scarcely be denied, he himself always maintained that he felt no racial bias and attacked not Frenchmen or Catholics as such, but ultramontanism, the desire of certain clerical elements to control the politics as well as the religion of their people. Jesuit political influence particularly annoyed him, and he criticized the federal government for not disallowing the Quebec law which compensated the Order for the ancient loss of its estates. The British North America Act, he pointed out, did not

[29]*Political Destiny of Canada*, 10–29.

restrict the federal veto to cases where provincial legislation was unconstitutional. That it should generally be so limited seemed to him proper. Flagrantly unwise or unjust statutes, however, he thought should also be disallowed, and in this category he placed the Jesuit Estates Act, for he considered the Society a "political and social conspiracy."[30]

To the Jesuits in particular Smith traced the marked development of French nationalism. Thirty years' residence in Canada convinced him that Lord Durham erred in expecting the French, as the weaker race, to be absorbed. French nationalism had become not less but more pronounced and aspiring in these three decades. Tension between French and English reached fever pitch in 1885 during the crisis over the rebellion and the subsequent hanging of Louis Riel. The racial and religious animosities of the day made others beside Goldwin Smith wonder whether dreams of a Canadian nationality were vain. To him it seemed that the French did not intend to form one nation with English-speaking Canadians, but to be a people apart, with their own language, state religion, flag, and institutions. The growth of French nationalism prevented the real unification of the Dominion. The French province, sandwiched between English-speaking sections of the country, marred the solidity of British Canada, weakened its sense of community, and interfered with the development of a truly national opinion. Yet he believed that the French and English, despite all difficulties, might work out a modus vivendi, provided ardent imperialists exercised some discretion.[31] In any event, his hopes for Canadian nationalism were dimmer than his hopes for the union of Canada and the United States, which he liked to describe as the reunion of the English-speaking peoples of the continent. Into such a picture it was awkward to fit French Canadians.

Despite his uneasiness about the resurgence of French nationalism, he found the contented, simple, and devout people of Quebec a refreshing exception to their materialistic and commercially minded Anglo-Saxon compatriots. French Canada, he once remarked, was probably the best product of Catholicism. With these views his friend Matthew Arnold agreed. During his North American tour in 1884 Arnold paid a brief visit to Quebec, and wrote Goldwin Smith that it was "the most

[30]The Jesuit Order was suppressed by the Pope in 1773 and not refounded until 1813. Their estates in French Canada were taken over by the British government in 1773. More than a century later the Quebec legislature passed a bill granting compensation for this loss to the refounded Order. A series of editorials on this question, unsigned but written by Goldwin Smith, was published in the *Mail* on Jan. 26, Feb. 5 and 9, March 2, 9, 11, and 13, June 27 and July 6, 1889. One consequence was that the Society of Jesus brought a libel suit against the *Mail*.
[31]*Weekly Sun*, June 30, 1909; letters from Goldwin Smith to the *Mail*, dated Oct. 8, 1888; to Lord Grey (then Governor-General of Canada), Dec. 12, 1906,

interesting place we saw in America. And the French population there seemed amiable and moderate; at Montreal, on the other hand, ultramontanism was in the ascendant, and took much offence at my saying that with high ultramontane pretensions on the one side, and Orangeism on the other, there could be no real fusion of the people."[32]

Through his friendship with Henri Bourassa, whom he considered the best representative of French Canada, Goldwin Smith eventually came to a more sympathetic understanding of Quebec and its people. Correspondence between them was begun in 1900 by Bourassa, who said he was encouraged to write because ever since his stand against the prevailing current of jingoism in Canada during the Boer War, Goldwin Smith had occasionally spoken well of him in the *Weekly Sun*. This approbation, "from such a high and disinterested authority," he wrote, "has been an ample compensation for the attacks, the suspicions and the sneers which I have received from several quarters." Goldwin Smith was in Italy when this letter reached him. On his return to Canada he urged the young French Canadian to visit him at the Grange, where he welcomed him, as Bourassa said, like a son. When Bourassa went to England the following year Goldwin Smith gave him letters of introduction to Morley and Bryce. In the next ten years the two wrote each other often. During their common attack on the Boer War Goldwin Smith frequently suggested to Bourassa questions that he might ask in the Commons and papers he might request to have tabled. The *Weekly Sun* reported Bourassa's speeches fully and did what it could to strengthen his stand.

Despite decided differences of opinion on such questions as the separation of church and state, and denominational schools, a real, if somewhat odd, friendship grew up between the two men. Based on a common enthusiasm for several ideas, their liking for each other was a tribute to the innate liberality of both. In his youth Bourassa prided himself on being a Liberal of the English school, a disciple of Fox and Gladstone and of "all those Little Englanders who have made England and the Empire what they are." After the outbreak of the First World War, however, he became a more uncompromising French nationalist who considered the real enemy of his compatriots not Prussian militarism but Anglo-Saxon materialism.

Bourassa was qualified to appreciate Goldwin Smith's comment that in politics courage always told, and in no country more than in Canada

---

[32]Letter from Matthew Arnold, May 2, 1884, Goldwin Smith Autograph Album; Goldwin Smith, "Canada, the Empire, and Mr. Chamberlain," *Monthly Review*, Oct., 1903, 38–54.

where the political variety was rare. Participation in the South African War was strongly opposed by most French Canadians, between whose position and that of the Boers it needed little imagination to see some parallel. At the turn of the century Goldwin Smith came to view them as the chief bulwark against the military and ultra-patriotic spirit of the times, which threatened to drag Canada into imperialist wars. When Chamberlain proposed a preferential tariff throughout the Empire, Goldwin Smith promptly recognized that the suggestion was unlikely to appeal to French Canadians. Their opposition to military contributions was apparent. "Your people," he wrote Bourassa in September, 1900, "are a power in the dominion. In the Empire they would be a nullity. In the chapter of political accidents they have become for the present the sheet-anchor of Canadian self-government." He urged Bourassa to point out to his compatriots that an imperialist policy led not only to military expenditure, but to some form of conscription, which they would not like. Nothing in Goldwin Smith's life gave him more satisfaction than his solitary stand in English-speaking Canada against the Boer War. To Bourassa he wrote, "You have reason to feel the same pleasure in a higher degree."[33]

Goldwin Smith looked to Bourassa as the natural leader of a new and genuinely Liberal party, since the two old parties in Canada had in his view been rolled into one. He thought in 1902 that there might be a chance for a third party which would represent all the racial elements in the country, and guide policy in the interests of Canada alone. In the spring of that year Laurier went to England to attend the Colonial Conference and confer with Chamberlain on Canadian relations with Great Britain. Goldwin Smith suggested to Bourassa that before Laurier's departure a meeting should be held (probably in Montreal), to protest against any surrender of Canadian self-government, political, military, or commercial, and also against any sacrifice of Canadian policy to interests solely British. Such a meeting, he thought, might be the foundation of a movement, if not of a party, which was purely Canadian. Bourassa hesitated, on the ground that it would be necessary to be sure that such a meeting would be largely attended and would not give rise to counter-demonstrations in the English-speaking provinces. Should the question divide Canadian public opinion on racial lines, the result, he

[33]Letters from Goldwin Smith to Henri Bourassa, March 16, Sept. 7, Oct. 8 and 19, 1900, Nov. 16, 1903, Gregory Papers; letters from Henri Bourassa to Goldwin Smith, Jan. 20, 1900, Sept. 21, 1901; letter from Goldwin Smith to W. D. Gregory, Dec. 18, 1899, Gregory Papers.

pointed out, would be disastrous. He preferred first to sound English-speaking opinion by a meeting in Toronto. This took place the next year, but without significant results.

Despite their interest in creating a third party, both men underestimated the value of parties in representative government. Goldwin Smith agreed strongly with Bourassa that there should be co-operation between those who placed principle before profit and country before party. Bourassa's avowed ambition was to work for a disinterested and truly national government. "My first object," he wrote Goldwin Smith, "is to develop a keener, a broader and a more effective public spirit among my own compatriots. The second is to bring a more sincere and honourable understanding between both races, the basis of which would be a truer, less bombastic and more defined Canadian patriotism. So far," he added, "I have found no difficulty in practising O'Connell's maxim, that is, in taking my theology at Rome and my politics at home."[34]

Independent journalism was another cause both men had at heart. When in 1900 Bourassa established *Le Devoir*, he told Goldwin Smith that it was to be completely free from control by party or business interests. He hoped it would prove strong enough to struggle against corruption, and be less recalcitrant than Olivar Asselin's *Nationaliste*. He himself left federal for provincial politics because he thought French Canadians could not be politically effective without a strong sense of their rights and duties as a constituent part of Canada and the British Empire.

Goldwin Smith greatly regretted Bourassa's departure from the House of Commons, but continued to watch his career with great interest and pleasure. "We who do not desire to be the toys of British Jingoism," he wrote, "have reason to be heartily thankful that Lord Durham's prediction of the absorption of the French element by the British was not fulfilled." In the last year of his life he tried to enlist Bourassa's aid in attacking proposals for Canadian contributions to the British navy. Was Canada, he asked, to have a voice in the declaration of war? Was she to be taken into confidence about the cause of it?[35]

Laurier's charm, good manners, and obvious ability attracted Goldwin Smith, and he had high hopes of the Liberals when in 1896 they

[34]Letters from Henri Bourassa, Feb. 1, 1907, and May 7, 1906, Bourassa Papers, Montreal; letters from Goldwin Smith to Bourassa, March 26 and April 10, 1902, and from Bourassa to Smith, April 3, 1902, Gregory Papers.

[35]Letters to Bourassa, Jan. 16, 1905, and Nov. 13, 1909, Gregory Papers; letters from Henri Bourassa, June 14 and Nov. 19, 1909, Bourassa Papers.

came to power after the long period of Conservative rule. In particular he hailed Laurier's accession as the death knell of the National Policy. Laurier himself he described as "a gallant gentleman of the French school who hit his opponents hard but courteously." By 1897, however, he was concerned by Laurier's conversion to imperial federation and to protection. The Liberals had made much of Conservative corruption under Macdonald, but once in office found it difficult to demonstrate that their own hands were cleaner. Critics complained that Laurier had been ruined by knighthood and association with the great in England. Goldwin Smith's bitterness was the measure of his disillusionment, which was completed by Laurier's willingness to allow recruitment of a Canadian contingent for the South African War. He came to the conclusion that Laurier was an opportunist without fixed political or economic convictions, who had thrown all his former principles to the winds, and, if the Atlantic could be bridged with phrases, would be the man to do it. To speak of him and his party as Liberals was a misapplication of the name. Although he recognized that a French Catholic Prime Minister had to balance on a political tight-rope, Goldwin Smith never fully appreciated the necessity of reconciling French and English interests in order that the two peoples could live together amicably. Hence he underestimated Laurier's services as a conciliator, and considered Bourassa the more genuine representative of French Canada. He also underestimated the extent to which Laurier, like Bourassa in his earlier days, was a Liberal of the English school.

An Englishman and free-thinker could scarcely be expected to understand French Canada. It so happened that Bourassa, more than any other Canadian public man, shared many of Goldwin Smith's most cherished convictions: his hatred of war, imperialism, and parties, and his faith in independent journalism. The fact that few French Canadians were enthusiastic about the union of Canada with the United States, and that this alone made the scheme impractical, Goldwin Smith conveniently chose to ignore.

VIII

Comparative political institutions and problems in the English-speaking democracies always fascinated Goldwin Smith. Long before his first visit to North America in 1864 he had been interested in the similarities and diversities of the British and American political systems. This early concern was quickened by first-hand knowledge of America, and he wrote much on the strength and weakness of parliamentary *versus* presidential government, as exemplified in Great Britain and the United States. He was also interested in comparing Canadian institutions with those of South Africa and Australia.

Although he never visited South Africa, his concern about the Boer War and his friendship with John Merriman gave him an abiding curiosity about that country's political problems. His acquaintance with Merriman began in 1878, when the Colonial Office was undergoing one of its recurrent attacks of enthusiasm for a federal solution to South African problems. In his first letter Merriman apologized for troubling a man he had never met with the concerns of a colony about which, in all probability, Goldwin Smith had scarcely heard. He was writing, he explained, because "we are threatened with an application of the great colonial office nostrum 'Confederation', which like a good many other specifics, is sometimes administered without much reference to the condition of the recipient."[36] Downing Street dangled Canada before the eyes of South Africans as "the modern political elysium." Hence Merriman wanted the opinion of an objective critic with first-hand knowledge of Canadian conditions. In particular he wanted detailed information on how the Canadian constitution worked. Did the powers of the federal government tend to increase? Was friction between the Dominion and the provinces diminishing? Was federalism expensive? Did it encourage log-rolling for public works in certain districts? Merriman was opposed to South African federation, which he thought unsuited for a scanty and scattered population, where the chief issues of party politics were expenditures on public works. He may well have hoped that Goldwin Smith's views would support his own.

Had Canadians known that an outspoken critic of the British North America Act was being consulted by a South African about the success of Confederation, they would have thought it a bad joke. Goldwin Smith, however, was naturally delighted to give an opinion. He replied to Merriman that federalism was too complicated and expensive for a country like Canada, whose population was too small to provide the requisite number of competent public men. Legislation was often entrusted to the unfit. Forced upon the framers of Confederation by the insistence of Quebec, federalism had done nothing to mitigate sectional feeling. Despite the grant of residual powers to the national Parliament,

[36]Letter from J. X. Merriman, Nov. 3, 1878, Merriman Papers, South African Library, Cape Town.

he had so far perceived no tendency towards its aggrandizement at the expense of the provinces. Provincial demands for better terms were likely to continue and to increase friction between different levels of government. Each party accused the other of trying to buy political support through the use of public works as bribes. Goldwin Smith was not prepared to attribute this to federalism, except in so far as the multiplication of legislatures provided a larger field for intrigues of every sort. Before South Africans decided on constitutional change, he suggested that they send to Canada delegates who could examine for themselves the practical working of its federal system.[37]

Such criticism of Canadian political institutions was precisely what Merriman wanted to hear. Goldwin Smith's comments merely confirmed his mistrust of federalism, and provided evidence against what he called the "sub-federation" of dependent colonies where subjects usually assigned to the central government in a federation of independent communities were administered by Downing Street. His fear that bilingualism would prove difficult or impossible, however, Goldwin Smith did not support. He admitted that the bilingual Parliament of Canada made for a certain clumsiness in debate and increased the cost of Hansard, but he thought its obvious advantages outweighed these minor defects. By 1880 Merriman reported with satisfaction that the plan for South African confederation had been quashed. During the debate on the subject in the Cape Assembly he had used extracts from Goldwin Smith's letters, and thought these had carried real weight.[38]

For the next thirty years the two men continued to correspond. During the Boer War Merriman found time almost every fortnight, in the middle of his duties as a cabinet minister, to send long, hand-written reports on the progress of hostilities and the state of public opinion. When union was again being discussed in South Africa from 1907 to 1909, he once more consulted Goldwin Smith, asking advice about shaping the new constitution, and in particular about the difficult problem of the franchise. As a good Liberal Merriman would have liked to see the Cape franchise (which imposed property and educational tests, but made no distinctions as to colour) adopted by the Union. He realized that local colour prejudices would probably make this impractical, but believed denial of all political rights would turn non-white peoples into helots and lead eventually to revolution. Would Goldwin

---

[37]Letter from Goldwin Smith to J. X. Merriman, *Goldwin Smith's Correspondence*, 72–7.

[38]Letters from J. X. Merriman to Goldwin Smith, March 17, 1879, and July 9, 1880; from Goldwin Smith to Merriman, Aug. 25, 1881, Merriman Papers.

Smith, he wondered, know any precedents for the plan (eventually adopted), of keeping the Cape franchise for the Cape, and having a different franchise for the other provinces? Smith apparently did not cite the American example on this point, but suggested that the broad outlines of the Swiss constitution might provide useful hints for South Africa. He particularly liked the Swiss custom of electing the executive from the legislature, because he thought this tended to weaken the power of parties. Merriman sympathized with his distaste for parties, but considered corruption no problem in his country. Nor was he enthusiastic about the Swiss referendum and initiative.

Goldwin Smith looked forward with much interest to the launching of the new constitutional barque in South Africa, and hazarded the suggestion that it might be helpful to give the natives some sort of head man, "of course with very limited powers," to represent them. Before the Union of South Africa came into being, however, Goldwin Smith was dead. He did not live to read Merriman's last letter, which confided his disappointment that the launching of the ship in whose building he had taken such a part had been entrusted not to him, but to Botha.[39]

Plans for federation in Australia also interested Goldwin Smith, although he had there no friend like Merriman to keep him closely informed on political opinion. Some letters, however, passed between him and G. B. Barton, the brother of the Attorney-General of New South Wales, who, as Sir Edmund Barton, became the first Prime Minister of the Commonwealth. In 1891 G. B. Barton sent a copy of the proposed constitution for Australia to both James Bryce and Goldwin Smith, as the two ablest students of comparative government in the English-speaking world. Six years later he sent Goldwin Smith some notes on federation, asking his opinion on whether Australians might wisely model their new constitution on that of the United States. Goldwin Smith replied that he did not see how the British party system could be fitted into the American pattern, where cabinet members had no seats in Congress and no control over legislation. In the very act of centralization, he cautioned, all the centrifugal forces were called into play. Australians should profit from Canadian mistakes, and avoid in particular the problems of bicameralism. Where there were two Houses, each with power, deadlock was probable. If he were an Australian, Goldwin Smith would be inclined to try first a system less difficult than federalism. A simple federal council, he suggested, elected by the state

[39]Letters from J. X. Merriman to Goldwin Smith, Oct. 26, 1907, Aug. 31 and Nov. 15, 1908, June 5, 1910; letters from Goldwin Smith to Merriman, July 24, 1908, Aug. 20, 1909, Merriman Papers.

legislatures, might work well. Such a scheme would be unpretentious and cheap. He feared it would also be deemed timid, and therefore wished the Australians all success with a more imposing project. Barton explained in reply that the Canadian model "never received a moment's serious consideration, either in the Conventions or out of them. It was regarded as a piece of 'old fogeyism' that might be good enough for Canadian folk, but would never suit Australian democrats."[40]

The two federal countries of North America also provided material for interesting comparisons. Goldwin Smith's were usually unfavourable to Canada, although he distrusted the American enthusiasm for lofty abstractions. Rufus Choate's description of the principles in the Declaration of Independence as "glittering generalities" struck him as more sensible than Emerson's "blazing ubiquities." He thought the chief weaknesses in American government were the elective presidency and judgeships and the powerful party machines. To the important differences between the two political systems he did less than justice, since he always hoped to convince Canadians that they had little to lose and much to gain by joining the United States. It was reasonably clear that in such an event the institutions and practices of Canadian cabinet government would have to be abandoned. This prospect caused Goldwin Smith little concern. There was a time when he had thought two political experiments on the North American continent better than one. But eventually he came to believe that actually they were not two distinct types of state, since the Canadian political institutions derived from England were largely dummies. In his opinion the two democracies of the New World were essentially the same.

Although Canadians liked to plume themselves on their superior political virtue, he thought they could easily fit into the American party system. Scarcely a wire or a wire-puller need be disturbed. Political corruption was on a larger scale in the wealthy United States, but was more shameless in Canada. Happily, in neither country were party politics the whole of life. More difficulty would be created by the differences between their banking systems. The franchise and municipal government, with their attendant liabilities, were similar on both sides of the line. The referendum used by some American states might to his mind be adopted by Canadian provinces with advantage, because provincial acts, no matter how unwise, unless *ultra vires* were seldom reserved by lieutenant-governors or disallowed by the federal government.

---

[40]Letters from G. B. Barton to Goldwin Smith, Aug. 18, 1899; to the *Daily Telegraph*, dated March 2, 1892. Goldwin Smith's letter of Nov. 26, 1897, to G. B. Barton is published in his *Correspondence*, 308–9.

Submission of certain measures to the direct verdict of the electorate might be an improvement. His desire to see Canada a united country and not merely "a bundle of provinces" made him warmly approve the federal power of disallowance.

Canadians cherished their system of responsible government, but Goldwin Smith thought they overrated its virtues. He believed that the practical result of making the executive dependent on the support of the legislature was a constant effort by the government to corrupt both Parliament and the constituencies. To his mind party leaders commonly misused the prerogative of dissolution, and were not justified, for party advantage, in keeping the threat of a general election hanging over the country. He could not agree that decisions about the duration of Parliaments should rest with the prime minister, because he objected to the great power which this gave party leaders. A set time for election and dissolution seemed to him preferable, for he considered the right to summon and dissolve Parliaments at will simply a relic of feudal prerogative, which had clearly become obsolete. So long, however, as it continued to exist, Goldwin Smith maintained that the governor-general or lieutenant-governors, as representatives of the Crown, were responsible for its exercise.[41]

His hopes for American democracy, as for Canadian nationalism, ebbed and flowed. More than once he described the United States as the greatest experiment ever made in popular government, on whose success or failure the fate of democracy everywhere, and especially in Canada, depended. At other times he was downcast by the growing influence of wealth, the bane he had early deplored in Great Britain and whose relative absence in the United States he had admired during the eighteen-sixties. When at the turn of the century American imperialist aspirations seemed paramount, Goldwin Smith began to wonder whether the New World was going to adopt all the worst vices of the Old. The English radical who admired the republic of Lincoln argued for years that a little country like Canada should throw in her lot with the most progressive nation in the world. At the beginning of the twentieth century, however, the power of the presidency and Senate made him think the United States in some respects the most conservative of modern democracies. So far from being in the vanguard of democracy, America might almost be called its rearguard.[42] He had often contended that if Canada joined the United States, its people would exercise a

[41]*Weekly Sun*, June 8, 1904; "Anglo-Saxon Union," *North American Review*, CLVII (Aug., 1893), 170–85; letter to the *Speaker*, Jan. 1, 1898.
[42]"Then and Now," *Cornell Era* (Dec., 1908).

beneficial conservative influence on the American tendency to excessive democracy. Americans viewed the revolution as the salient fact in their history, whereas Canadians had some sense of unbroken and ancient traditions. Towards the end of his life, however, he began to think that the United States needed more radicalism, not less, and doubted that Canada could provide it.

More conservative critics greeted this American development with enthusiasm rather than regret. A. V. Dicey traced the change in English public opinion toward the United States, from widespread criticism at the beginning and middle of the century to warm interest and growing approval in the eighteen-eighties. A very slight knowledge of America, he observed, showed that it was not a land where socialism could flourish. Hence modern English radicals were naturally less partial to the United States than earlier reformers like Cobden and Bright. Among thoughtful British Conservatives, however, the American republic now excited profound admiration, as the best example of a conservative democracy. As England was becoming democratic, its people began to wonder whether American institutions might provide a model whereby the forces of political conservatism might be preserved.[43] It was typical of Goldwin Smith that his enthusiasm for America was strongest in the eighteen-sixties when the British governing class loathed everything American, and most qualified at the end of the century when English Conservatives applauded the conservative republic.

His analysis of political institutions in North America was always coloured, like much of his thought and writing, by a vision of healing the schism between the English-speaking peoples of the continent. He took it for granted that the Americans would remain predominantly Anglo-Saxon and Protestant. Since Canadians were obviously reluctant about the prospect of union between the two countries, he devoted his journalistic powers to presenting the politics of the United States in the most favourable light. In addition, his forty years in Canada, compared with two in the republic, naturally made him more familiar with Canadian public affairs, and if familiarity did not breed contempt, it at least bred distaste and pessimism. To him Canadians seemed more concerned with equality than liberty, with conformity than courage, with personal gain than honest independence. Hence as public prosecutor, jury, and judge, he tried Canadian democracy and found it wanting.

[43]A. V. Dicey, "Americomania in English Politics," *Nation* (New York), XLII (Jan. 21, 1886). In the *Contemporary Review*, LXXI (April, 1897), 457–76, Dicey advocated a common citizenship for Englishmen and Americans.

XI. THE DESTINY OF CANADA

A CENTURY AGO Canada's destiny was far from self-evident. Even after the British North American colonies had united, Canadians differed widely among themselves about the future of their country. The framers of Confederation meant to build a new nation, but were not agreed on whether it should remain a British colony or become completely independent. Practical men, pointing to the handful of people strung out across a continent with major geographic obstacles to unity, considered annexation to the United States probable. Few envisaged what actually happened, the growth of an independent nation, little less closely linked to Britain than in colonial days and far more closely linked to the other English-speaking countries of the world. Ultimately, the vision of the Little Englanders has been fulfilled, if not precisely in the way they anticipated, at least in a way they would have approved.

Goldwin Smith was the most lucid and persistent advocate of Canada's union with the United States. Annexation was a term he never used, since it implied forcible absorption by the States against the wishes of Canadians and without the consent of the mother country. For this he had no sympathy. What he had in mind was not the forced subordination of a lesser to a greater power, but a free union between two independent countries, like that between England and Scotland, which produced one united kingdom without submerging the indivduality of the constituent parts. Toward the end of his days he often spoke of how over the years his views on the future of Canada changed. He had left England imbued with the opinion then prevalent among most Liberals and emphatically avowed even by Disraeli, that the colonies were destined to be independent. This was his position when he settled in Canada, but first-hand knowledge of the geographical difficulties, internal cleavages, and commercial interests of the country led him to change his mind. He came to believe in a union on equal terms of the English-speaking peoples in North America, a union in the best interests of Canada, the United States, and Great Britain alike. This account of his views, given in old age, Goldwin Smith undoubtedly thought correct.

Examination of what he said half a century before, however, suggests that his memory played him false, and that from the early eighteen-sixties he considered union between Canada and the United States at least a logical possibility. Numerous Englishmen agreed with him. Nor was this surprising, since two decades before Confederation many Canadians considered such union much more than a possibility.

I

Great Britain's repeal of the Corn Laws in 1846 produced various developments in Canada: a free trade league in Montreal, a movement for a protective tariff, a pressure for reciprocity with the United States, and an agitation for annexation. The latter culminated in manifestoes published in Montreal and Toronto in 1849, which attributed the current depression in Canada to Great Britain's adoption of free trade and the consequent loss of a preferential market in England. These manifestoes, favouring "a friendly and peaceable separation from the British connection, and a union upon equitable terms with the great North American Confederacy of Sovereign States," were signed by over a thousand prominent Canadians, among them Alexander Galt, and John Abbott who later became a Conservative Prime Minister. Partly as a device to quell the movement for annexation on both sides of the border, the Governor-General, Lord Elgin, devoted himself to securing the reciprocity treaty of 1854 with the United States. Not until its abrogation twelve years later did annexation again become a live issue. Rightly or wrongly, Canadians believed the chief reason for abrogation was the American conviction that Canada was so contented with reciprocity that she did not want political union. If reciprocity were ruled out, she would be forced to seek admission to the United States. From abrogation in 1866 until the rejection of reciprocity in 1911, closer trade relations with the States was a major concern of Canadian governments, both Conservative and Liberal.

During most of this period Great Britain was prepared to see Canada take her own way, whether this led toward independence or annexation. On more than one occasion the union of Canada and the United States was advocated by Cobden and Bright, from whom Goldwin Smith may have caught some of his first enthusiasm for the project.[1] In his *Empire* letters, however, Smith urged the desirability, in both Canadian and

---

[1] Cobden's prophecy of the ultimate union of Canada and the United States, at least "for all purposes of free intercommunication," was made in a letter of March 9, 1848, to Senator Charles Sumner, quoted in J. A. Hobson, *Richard*

American interests, of Canada's becoming a separate nation. It would be good for her to learn independence instead of colonial subjection, and good for the United States to learn what nations, like men, could derive from the society of their equals. Once Canada attained independence she would be free, if she so desired, at some later date to join the United States.

When in 1864 he first crossed the Atlantic Goldwin Smith heard talk of annexation in American political circles. On returning to Britain he wrote Seward that Canada seemed likely to fall voluntarily into American hands, perhaps even before they wanted her. "To us," explained the staunch Little Englander, "this and the other distant and helpless dependencies are a mere source of embarrassment and weakness, as the English people are beginning to perceive."[2] Yet he supported the proposed Confederation of British North America, on the ground that otherwise Canada would soon join the United States. Hence he urged the imperial government to co-operate fully with the eminent Canadians who went to London to discuss the project. That all the English-speaking colonies of the continent, both British and American, would ultimately form a federal union seemed to him not only probable but almost certain. He saw no virtue, however, in hurrying the natural course of events, although he found it difficult to stand beside the Mississippi or St. Lawrence without feeling that union was the behest of nature, which would eventually be fulfilled. Thus as early as 1865 Goldwin Smith envisaged union between Canada and the United States as probable. He did not reverse this stand in supporting, as he did, first the cause of Canadian independence and later that of commercial and political union with the States. In after years he spoke of union in almost the same words, and provoked the retort from Canadians that they frequently stood beside the St. Lawrence without experiencing such sentiments.

A letter to the *Daily News* in which he set forth these views aroused much discussion in Canada, where it was reprinted in the Toronto *Leader*, a journal which supported Confederation but strongly opposed annexation. The *Leader* argued that proposing an immediate grant of

---

Cobden (New York, 1919), 339–40. Bright expressed similar views in speeches at Rochdale, on Dec. 4, 1861, and at Birmingham, on Dec. 18, 1862. On the latter occasion he envisaged "one vast confederation stretching from the frozen north in unbroken line to the glowing south, and from the wild billows of the Atlantic westward to the calmer waters of the Pacific main . . . one people, and one language, and one law, and one faith, and, over all that wide continent the home of freedom, and a refuge for the oppressed of every race and every clime."

[2]Letter to W. H. Seward, April 16, 1865, Seward Papers, University of Rochester Library.

independence to the British North American colonies was tantamount to suggesting that England abandon them. It agreed that sooner or later colonies became independent, but saw no reason to hasten a separation from Britain which most Canadians desired to postpone indefinitely.[3]

George Brown, who was in London when the Quebec Resolutions were being considered by the British government, wrote Macdonald of his regret at finding an almost universal desire that the British American colonies should soon shift for themselves. During the debate in the imperial Parliament on the defences of Canada, Lord Palmerston argued that her destiny was in her own hands, and that she was free to choose whether or not the connection with England should be retained. Robert Lowe, for once on John Bright's side, declared that Britain ought to tell Canada that she was free either to set up for herself or join the United States. With equal frankness Cobden announced that he was interested in Confederation as a step toward amicable separation from the mother country. In Canada these remarks provoked the comment that Goldwin Smith's ideas, of which a year earlier he had seemed the solitary advocate, now divided public opinion in England and might tomorrow prevail.[4]

A major reason for Confederation was the widespread conviction among the colonists that they must choose either such a union or absorption by the United States. As Cartier pointed out in the Confederation Debates, the seventh article in the original draft of the American Constitution provided for the admission of the British colonies on terms easier than those required of other new states. Most Canadians accepted D'Arcy McGee's view that it was not their destiny to be "engulphed into a Republican union . . . that we have theatre enough under our feet to act another and a worthier part; we can hardly join the Americans on our own terms, and we never ought to join them on theirs."[5] McGee believed in a Canadian nationality, not a hyphenated French-, British-, or Irish-Canadian hybrid. This nationality Canadians should labour to secure and be prepared to defend. On such a concept Confederation set the seal. Part and parcel of the sentiment for Canadian nationality was fear of American aggression and absorption into the United States. This attitude Goldwin Smith disapproved without fully understanding it,

---

[3]*Leader*, May 11 and April 14, 1865. Goldwin Smith's views on colonial emancipation were attacked in a series of articles in this journal on June 5 and 16, and July 3, 1865. His letter on "The Crisis in Canada" was published in the *Daily News*, April 27, 1865.

[4]*Leader*, April 5, 1865.

[5]Address to the Irish Protestant Benevolent Society, Quebec, May 10, 1862, published in D'Arcy McGee, *Speeches and Addresses* (London, 1865), 34–5.

with unfortunate results for his aspiration to mould the destiny of Canada and to interpret her people to Great Britain and the United States.

In the latter country annexation of some or all of the British North American colonies was freely discussed by the press, public speakers, and Congress from the eighteen-forties until the Treaty of Washington in 1871, and on various occasions thereafter. Goldwin Smith heard such proposals when he first visited the United States in 1864, but returned to England convinced that Americans should not incorporate a disaffected population by attempting to take Canada by force. They need only wait patiently for the natural course of events, which patently tended toward the amicable union of all the English-speaking states of North America. By ties of blood, geography, commercial interests, and political institutions Canadians were already a part of the Anglo-Saxon peoples of the New World. Hence he viewed their ultimate political fusion with the United States as a gradual emancipation which a student of history and politics and a well-wisher of both countries awaited with interest but with no desire to hurry.[6]

Canadian-American relations, already strained, were not improved when in July, 1866, Mr. Banks, the chairman of the Foreign Affairs Committee, introduced in the House of Representatives a bill to annex all British North America. Canadian papers protested that so gross an outrage had seldom been committed by the legislature of a presumably friendly country.[7] The measure passed a second reading, however, before it was quietly pigeonholed. The failure of the United States to discourage a small Fenian raid into Canada caused further irritation between the two peoples. Four years later the Massachusetts legislature passed a resolution favouring annexation. During the negotiations preceding the Treaty of Washington many Americans thought Britain should settle the claims for the depredations of the *Alabama* by ceding British North America to the republic. Senator Sumner was the best known of many advocates of such a scheme, which Gladstone himself at one time seemed to countenance. Thus Canada's fear of the United States had some real basis.

Charles Tupper, who went to London to combat Howe's efforts to secure Nova Scotia's withdrawal from Confederation, wrote Macdonald that he anticipated no difficulty with the Colonial Office. He did fear,

[6]"The Case of the Alabama," *Macmillan's Magazine*, XIII (Dec., 1865), 162-76; *The Civil War in America* (Manchester, 1866).

[7]*Gazette* (Montreal), July 5, 1866. American interest in annexation in the eighteen-sixties and seventies is discussed in detail by L. B. Shippee, *Canadian-American Relations, 1849-74* (New Haven, 1939).

however, an unpleasant parliamentary debate, which might foment the agitation in Nova Scotia and encourage American annexationists. Goldwin Smith's comments in *The Times*, supporting the Nova Scotians and foretelling Canada's eventual union with the United States, added to an already difficult situation.[8]

Among the prominent Englishmen who agreed with Goldwin Smith was Sir Charles Dilke. He returned from a trip around the world convinced that no one gained from Britain's retention of Canada. The fact that the Canadians hated the Americans was to him no reason why Englishmen should spend blood and money to protect them against the consequences of their hate. In all history, he suggested, there was nothing stranger than the narrowness of mind which led Britons to see in America a hostile nation, and in Canada a piece of England.[9]

Residence in Ithaca at a time when American dislike of England and indirectly of Canada was at its height modified Goldwin Smith's views. He continued to believe in Canadian independence (with retention of the British flag and British citizenship), but now admitted that only in Nova Scotia was there any real opinion favourable to annexation. He still thought political union would eventually come, but considered immediate annexation not in the interest of either Canada or the United States. It would involve the Dominion in the consequences of a civil war in which she had not participated, would expose her to the effects of a ruinous tariff, and would open her political offices to the patronage of American party machines. In short, Canada would become an appendage, and might well find herself at war with England. For the time being, at least, he thought she would be better independent. He even admitted that certain Canadian institutions, such as an appointed judiciary, were superior to those of her neighbour. Since politicians were fallible, there was something to be said for two diverse experiments in democracy in the vast North American continent. Canada might one day help to retrieve some of the errors into which the impetuous democracy of the United States, with its conflicting interests and heterogeneous population, was certain to fall. From this point of view her premature absorption would be a misfortune.[10]

---

[8]Letter from Charles Tupper to Sir John A. Macdonald, April 9, 1868, published in Sir Charles Tupper, *Recollections of Sixty Years in Canada* (London, 1914). Goldwin Smith's speech on the subject was reported in *The Times*, April 11, 1868.

[9]Sir Charles Dilke, *Greater Britain* (London, 1868), 65-7.

[10]Letters to the *Daily News*, Oct. 5, 1869; to Charles Eliot Norton, Aug. 30, 1869, published in Massachusetts Historical Society, *Proceedings* (Dec., 1915), 154.

Goldwin Smith made no other such pessimistic assessment of American democracy until the turn of the century, when under President McKinley the United States emerged as an aspirant to imperial power. To Lord Salisbury early in 1870 he expressed fear that "the annexationist passion" in the United States was steadily gaining ground and that Canadians could not long withstand the pressure of the tariff imposed against them by the Americans. In the long run the most they could do would be to exact certain favourable conditions of annexation.[11]

II

When in 1871 Goldwin Smith moved to Canada, its relation to the United States was the major political problem of the day. The previous year the Hon. L. S. Huntingdon had introduced in the Canadian Commons a resolution for a "continental system of commercial intercourse." Sir John Macdonald had unsuccessfully attempted to include trade among the questions settled by the Treaty of Washington. Then as later the chief support for reciprocity came from farmers throughout the country, and from Maritime fishermen who had long desired access to the New England market. Americans interested in commerce, however, tended to support annexation in preference to reciprocity.

Despite the desire of Conservatives and Liberals to increase trade with the States, it became apparent that failing American co-operation Canada must learn as best she could to stand on her own feet. These were the economic circumstances that gave birth to the movement for nationality known as Canada First, which was already under way when Goldwin Smith moved to Toronto, where W. A. Foster's pamphlet, *Canada First*, had just been published. The Governor-General, Lord Dufferin, was thus mistaken in considering Smith the creator of Canada First. Its members did not aspire to found a new political party. They simply appealed to those who put country above party, and looking neither to Britain nor the United States, would help to build an independent Canadian nation. This was precisely the enterprise to appeal to Goldwin Smith, just as Edward Blake, their political hope, was the Canadian statesman most certain to attract him. Since in his *Empire* letters he had already won a reputation as an advocate of Canadian nationality, it was natural that in Toronto he should be promptly drawn into the counsels of the movement. In after years he pointed out that

[11]Letters to the Marquess of Salisbury, Jan. 31 and March 23, 1870, *Goldwin Smith's Correspondence*, 21-2.

when Canada First began, the Northwest had been only recently acquired and British Columbia had not yet come into Confederation. Hence the lack of geographical compactness, which he later came to think so serious an obstacle to independent nationhood for Canada, was then less apparent.

Goldwin Smith too easily assumed and too frequently said that although most British statesmen considered the union of the provinces as the seal of Canadian nationality and the forerunner of independence, the real cause of Confederation was deadlock. Had he troubled to read carefully the debates on the Quebec Resolutions, he would have perceived that a new nation was precisely what the framers of the 1867 agreement hoped to achieve. Clearly, however, Confederation alone did not secure this end. Throughout the nineteenth century, as Goldwin Smith constantly emphasized, Canada remained a dependent colony, self-depreciatory, and internally rent by cleavages between the French and English. In the early eighteen-seventies he opposed union with the United States, and was alarmed at the signs of a "moral annexation," which under pressure of economic distress might lead to "political catastrophe." At that time he believed that Canada, free from revolutionary bias, had her own political mission on the North American continent, and he welcomed anything which helped to foster a united, vigorous, and self-reliant nationality. He hoped the new Dominion might develop not only a better government than that of the United States, but eventually a model for American imitation.[12]

The aim of the Canada First movement was not entirely clear. Some of its members looked for a truly independent nation, while others wished only for responsible government in domestic affairs. All, however, wanted to create a Canadian patriotism, and to raise the country above the position of a dependent colony. All cherished the memory of D'Arcy McGee and hopefully turned their eyes toward the rising star of Edward Blake. Their programme included the maintenance of some connection with Britain, a voice for Canada in treaties affecting her, the encouragement of immigration, and a reorganized Senate. A few members advocated compulsory voting, and representation of minorities in the legislature.[13]

Opponents of the movement for the most part believed with the Governor-General that the prompt result of early independence for

[12]"Current Events," *Canadian Monthly*, III (Feb., 1873), 145–7; III (Jan., 1873), 63; III (April, 1873), 332.

[13]*Canada First: A Memorial of the Late William A. Foster*, with introduction by Goldwin Smith (Toronto, 1890), 3–10. The leading spirits were W. H. Howland, W. A. Foster, James H. Coyne, and the poet, Charles Mair.

Canada would be annexation to the United States. To Lord Carnarvon, the Colonial Secretary, Dufferin privately confided his suspicion of a growing desire among the younger generation to consider independence Canada's manifest destiny. He saw something to be said for this novel idea, provided that for the next two or three decades it remained only a vague aspiration. Heretofore Canadians had conspicuously lacked the self-assertion and self-confidence characteristic of Americans. The Governor-General regarded the rise of national feeling among them as neither antagonistic to British interests nor inimical to the imperial bond. He was astute enough to realize that Canada's deep-rooted devotion to England rested on the consciousness that the maintenance of the connection depended on her own free will. Hence he cautioned against the capricious exercise of imperial authority, lest the cry for independence be raised a generation too soon. In the course of time, he admitted realistically, some change in the relations between Canada and the mother country was inevitable.[14]

As a newcomer Goldwin Smith considered himself disqualified from joining Canada First, but he warmly sympathized with it, gave financial assistance, and spoke and wrote much on its behalf. His services to its organ, the *Nation*, have already been noted. By the end of 1873 a *Grip* cartoon portrayed him as "the political giant-killer, or Canada First." Temperamentally he had much in common with Edward Blake: both were austere, upright, and independent. Both opposed the Canadian Pacific Railway, and shared a common dislike of George Brown and the *Globe*, a sentiment fully reciprocated. Imperial federation, however, Blake supported and Goldwin Smith rejected.

Blake's famous Aurora speech on October 3, 1874, outlined the main principles of the Canadian National Association, founded by the Canada First group. Two days earlier Goldwin Smith had laid the cornerstone of the new National Club. As president he delivered an inaugural address to the committee and stockholders, wherein he expressed the hope that the idea of nationality might bind Canadians together by a tie stronger and more reputable than better terms and sectional cabinets. To love Canada more was not to love the mother country less. By naming their organization the National Club, the members implied that Canada was a nation. They hoped that a faith in nationality would produce Canadian statesmen, lend dignity to public life and the press, and give an impulse to Canadian literature and intellectual interests. The present transition of

[14]Letters from Lord Dufferin to Lord Carnarvon, April 23 and 25, 1874, March 10, 1875. C. W. de Kiewiet and F. H. Underhill (eds.), *Dufferin-Carnarvon Correspondence, 1874–1878* (Toronto, 1955), 28, 35–7, 136–7.

the British colonies from dependence to autonomy in his opinion must end in "a family of self-governed nations."[15]

For such sentiments he was violently attacked by the *Globe* as a traitor who should be ridden out of town on a rail. Liberals and Conservatives alike considered the Canada First movement a potential threat to the older parties. Notwithstanding George Brown's interest in reciprocity, he had personal reasons for disliking both Goldwin Smith and Edward Blake. The former, as an outspoken advocate of an independent press, threatened the *Globe*'s local monopoly of Liberal journalism. The latter, as a brilliant statesman, challenged Brown's influence in the Liberal party. Hence he devoted his energies and the powerful venom of the *Globe* to silencing both.

The situation, as the *Nation* observed, was awkward. There was Mr. Blake with whom the *Globe* "cannot afford to quarrel; Mr. Goldwin Smith, whom it cannot afford to ignore; and there is the 'insipid' journal [the *Nation*] of whose existence it cannot but, however unwillingly, take cognizance. The problem is how to smash the third, discredit the second, and gently lead back the erring first to the paths of rectitude and the green pastures of Gritism. Unfortunately . . . the process requires very careful manipulation." To the *Globe*'s complaints that the Canada First group preached treason against the British Crown, dismemberment of the Empire, and revolution, the *Nation* rejoined that they preached independence from the tyranny not of Downing Street, but of the *Globe*. Of all tyrannies the most degrading was government by anonymous slander.[16] The *Globe*'s attacks continued unabated, and as Goldwin Smith remarked later, he was tested more than most men by bitter vituperation for his belief in Canadian nationality.

Canada First came to an untimely end in 1875 with Blake's return to the political fold as Minister of Justice in Mackenzie's federal cabinet. The *Globe*, Goldwin Smith lamented, had largely succeeded in killing the liberal spirit which had seemed to be awakening among the younger men who now began to stream into the United Empire Club. By the spring of 1876 he agreed with Blake that the outlook for Canadian nationhood was dark. "*My* dream," he wrote sadly, "has fled through the ivory gate. There was a chance of making Canada a nation while, from the Civil War and its effects in the States, the balance of prosperity was on the Canadian side. Now the balance has turned, and no one who looks much below the surface can doubt whither things are tend-

[15]As reported in the *Nation* (Toronto), Oct. 15, 1874.
[16]*Nation*, Oct. 22 and 29, Nov. 19, and Dec. 31, 1874.

ing."[17] Years afterward he wrote Dilke that he had originally believed in an independent Canada, as a separate trial of democracy, until Sir John Macdonald stretched the country out in a broken line from the Atlantic to the Pacific. All unity was then lost.[18]

Goldwin Smith never recovered from his disillusionment at what he considered Blake's defection and the consequent demise of Canada First. His hopes for Canadian nationality vanished, and he reverted to his earlier view that Canada should first become independent of Britain, and then align herself more closely with the United States. This transition in his thought was illustrated in a letter to the Toronto *Telegram*, where he prophesied that the political separation of the New World from the Old would soon be completed. Canada must choose between nationality and union with the United States. For his part, he had supported nationality in the belief that democracy in North America might better be entrusted to two friendly nations than to one. He did not wish, however, to be the dupe of an illusion. The golden opportunity for making Canada a nation had been allowed to pass, the movement for nationality conceived at Confederation had proved abortive, and Canada's destiny was now indubitably linked with that of the United States.[19] Henceforth he tried to win Canadians and Americans to his point of view, and found himself more and more out of sympathy with both Liberals and Conservatives and with the great majority of Canadians who refused to dismiss nationhood as a dream of the past.

III

The Liberal Government in office at Ottawa from 1873 to 1878 had no more success than its Conservative predecessor in securing a new reciprocity treaty. Canadian interest in the matter was stimulated by the acute depression which began in 1873 and lasted for the greater part of the next twenty-three years. During the eighteen-eighties Canada's prospects seemed darker than at any other period in her history. A brief improvement from 1879 to 1883 was naturally though erroneously attributed by the Conservatives to Macdonald's National Policy. While still in opposition Sir John had declared at Napanee in 1877 that he was a free trader if he could get free trade, but that he did not intend to have a jug-handled policy. If they could not have reciprocity of trade,

[17]Letters to Edward Blake, May 7, Feb. 8, and April 10, 1876, Blake Papers.
[18]Letter to Sir Charles Dilke, Nov. 29, 1901, Dilke Papers, British Museum.
[19]*Evening Telegram*, Oct. 10, 1876.

they would have reciprocity of tariffs. He originally defended the National Policy as retaliation, designed to force down the high American tariff. Macdonald's attempt to make the best of two worlds, by asserting that he favoured both reciprocity and protection, was more astute than convincing.[20] He managed, however, to win the support of manufacturers who believed in protection and of farmers who hoped the National Policy might eventually lead to reciprocity.

From the beginning Goldwin Smith doubted that protection in Canada would compel tariff reduction in America. Considering both free trade and protection inexpedient in new countries, he assumed the absolute truth of neither. A low tariff for revenue was necessary for most nations and far more defensible than duties designed to benefit specific industries, which simply levied tribute on the community to advance private interests. He looked to the day when Canada and the United States would see the error of their ways and again become low tariff countries. Hope deferred brought neither disillusionment nor doubt that he was right. At the beginning of the twentieth century he was still prophesying that in North America the winter of protection was breaking up and that the spring of free trade was at hand.

His first major study of his adopted country's position and prospects, *The Political Destiny of Canada*, appeared in 1877 as articles in the *Fortnightly Review*, and in book form the following year. Here he described imperial federation as a mere chimera, Canadian nationality a lost cause, and Canada's ultimate union with the United States a moral certainty. Four main forces were tending to sever the political connection between Canada and Britain: distance, divergent interests, different political character, and the attraction of the great English-speaking people with whom Canadians shared the continent.

These views provoked a public rebuke from Sir Francis Hincks, and a barrage of criticism in the Canadian press. A Toronto journalist justly commented that since no Canadian accepted Goldwin Smith's opinions, the soundness of his conclusions was dubious.[21] The people of Quebec hardly wished to be dismissed cavalierly as "a million of unassimilated Frenchmen" whose opinions carried little weight. Yet, although most French Canadians had no desire to join the United States, some did. In an American journal Louis Fréchette argued, like Goldwin Smith, that the existing situation was untenable, and that there were only three

[20]In the Can. H. of C. *Debates*, 1878, 854, Sir John explained that the National Policy, among other advantages, "moving as it ought to do, in the direction of reciprocity of tariffs with our neighbours so far as the varied interests of Canada may demand, will greatly tend to procure for this country eventually reciprocity of trade."   [21]*Mail*, June 13, 1877.

roads open to Canada: imperial federation, independence, and annexation. French Canadians were not prepared to support imperial federation or perpetual vassalage to Britain. With three thousand indefensible miles of border, independence was impractical. Hence, Fréchette thought that union with the United States was Canada's "manifest destiny," and that it would free the people of Quebec from English-Canadian superiority toward a conquered race.[22]

Goldwin Smith continued to prophesy that Canada and the United States were irresistibly drawn to each other by economic forces. If he lived another decade, he declared in 1880, he would probably die an American citizen, through Canada's incorporation into the United States. Commercial union must be kept before Canadians "without fluttering their political susceptibilities."[23] In the *Bystander* he enumerated the advantages to Canada. Without access to the main markets of the continent, she could never hope to enjoy full economic prosperity. Her climate was too severe, her range of production too limited, her markets too small, and her frontier too long to make commercial isolation feasible.

At the time these views appeared plausible. It required idealism and patriotism in the first three decades after Confederation to believe that four million people could weld together a half continent with such natural barriers as the Laurentian Shield and the Rocky Mountains. Goldwin Smith was right in maintaining that for Canada the price of independent nationhood was a lower standard of living than that in the United States. But he was wrong in thinking that nationalism made less appeal to Canadians than material advantage. His conviction that here economic forces would prevail contrasted oddly with his reiterated criticism of a purely materialist interpretation of history or religion, and with his usual stress on intangible considerations. Yet in part his advocacy of commercial union sprang from idealism. To him the schism between the Anglo-Saxon peoples of the continent which resulted from the American Revolution seemed an unfortunate accident of history. Hence he thought of union between Canada and the United States as a desirable reunion of like-minded peoples, the undoing of an historical wrong. To achieve this end he was ready to sacrifice time, labour, and reputation.

Goldwin Smith was among the first to emphasize the triangular nature

---

[22]Louis Fréchette. "The United States for French Canadians," *Forum*, XVI (Nov., 1893), 336–45. The same issue carried an attack on Goldwin Smith's views by Castell Hopkins.
[23]Letters to G. W. Curtis, May 24, 1880; to Mrs. Hertz, Jan. 22, 1880.

of Canada's relationship to the United States and Great Britain. That Canadians should recognize the inescapable realities of this relationship was his constant theme. He reminded them that in commerce and economics Canada was part of the American continent, although politically she was a dependency of Great Britain. Thus willy-nilly she was affected by the fiscal policy of the United States.[24] Although at the end of the nineteenth century few Canadians thought in these terms, the fact that Canada is North American geographically, though European by tradition and history, has long been accepted as the foundation of twentieth-century Canadian policy, in foreign as in economic affairs. Goldwin Smith's belief in this matter was closely linked to his faith in commercial union, which he considered the logical prelude to political union between Canada and the United States.

At the same time he protested that no one could be more eager than he to strengthen Canadian links with the mother country. More than ever he cherished the moral bond and rejected the political tie as worse than useless. Canada's continued allegiance to Britain, he observed in *The Times*, was entirely voluntary, and she continued to pay it precisely because it was voluntary.[25] As "a loyal and even ardent citizen of the Greater Britain," he wanted to see all children of England, including the United States, linked to her by ties of affection. In her interest as well as in that of the colonies he deprecated the perpetuation of dependency, with its constant liability to disputes, and wished to see it replaced by mutual citizenship. From Britain's point of view, the union of Canada with the United States would mean the substitution of a broad and secure empire of affection for a precarious and almost nominal supremacy.[26] He could never understand the indignation which such sentiments aroused in Canadian loyalists. Already, he pointed out, the Dominion had "extorted legislative independence, administrative independence, fiscal independence, and all but extorted judicial independence; she is now laying claim to diplomatic independence; yet she vows all the time that she is a dependency, destined ever to remain so, and even makes a creditable show of indignation if, when the whole of the substance is gone, anyone speaks with levity of the shadow."[27] This assessment was not palatable to those Canadians who refused to believe that a man of Goldwin Smith's views could really be loyal to Britain. The annexationist programme, according to the *Globe*, was "first, N.P., then distress;

[24]Letter to the *Montreal Witness*, March 25, 1874.
[25]*The Times*, Feb. 14, 1887.
[26]Letters to Professor Tyndall, Oct. 6, 1882; to J. W. Longley, Jan. 15, 1887, *Goldwin Smith's Correspondence*, 137, 195.
[27]*Bystander*, III (July, 1883), 196.

then commercial union, then more distress; then annexation, then the deluge."[28]

IV

Renewed economic depression in 1884 reawakened the interest in trade relations which had slumbered fitfully during four years of comparative prosperity. Canadian nationalists had practical reasons for their disillusionment. Prices for farm produce were low, and the home market was too small to absorb the output of local manufacturers. Manitoba and the Northwest were not being settled as rapidly as had been hoped. During the decade from 1881 to 1891 their population doubled, but this increase was slight compared with that in the neighbouring American states. Men streamed across the border to seek their fortunes, until by 1890 Canadians in the United States would have made up a third of the population of the Dominion. Since the National Policy had not inaugurated an era of prosperity, Canadians began to look for other solutions to their economic problems. Among these commercial union won more support than the counter-proposal for imperial federation. A widespread belief that in negotiations with the United States Britain had commonly sacrificed Canadian interests weakened enthusiasm for the political tie with the mother country. Yet since commercial union was undeniably a possible if not probable precursor of political union, the proposal was strongly opposed by those most devoted to the British connection, as well as by business men who wanted a protective tariff. There was also opposition from Quebec, where most French Canadians dreaded that absorption in the United States would mean losing the safeguards for their language, religion, and culture. With no sympathy for imperial federation, which they feared might drag them into European wars, the French largely rejected the schemes of federationists and commercial unionists alike. A minority of Canadians dimly perceived, though few openly declared, that neither commercial union nor imperial federation was compatible with Canada's aspirations for independent nationhood. By the mid-eighteen-eighties, however, acute economic distress made Conservatives and Liberals alike eager to secure another reciprocity treaty with the United States. It began to look as though Goldwin Smith's hopes might be fulfilled.

Many advocates of both schemes failed to differentiate clearly be-

[28]*Globe*, June 26, 1880. Editorial attacks on commercial union also appeared in the issues of Feb. 16, March 27, June 18, 23, 28, 29, and July 3, 1880.

tween commercial union and unrestricted reciprocity. Americans were inclined to consider the terms synonymous. The distinction hinged on whether the two countries should have joint or separate tariffs. Commericial union implied a joint tariff, and was thus a more comprehensive proposal than reciprocity in certain specified products. In practice commercial union would have meant that Canada adopted the American tariff, including its discrimination against Great Britain. Under unrestricted reciprocity Canada and the United States would erect no tariffs against each other, but each could determine as it saw fit its tariff against other countries. For the most part, however, only purists drew this clear-cut distinction between the terms, and contemporary discussion of the subject was often confused. Goldwin Smith, with customary inconsistency, sometimes distinguished between them and sometimes did not. Usually he maintained that commercial union simply meant reciprocity which was complete instead of incomplete and lasting instead of unstable. He himself preferred to speak of continental free trade.

To T. F. Bayard, the American Secretary of State, he wrote optimistically in 1886 that Canadians were almost ready for commercial union, if the question could be brought before them.[29] As Secretary of State (1885-9) and later United States' Ambassador to Great Britain (1893-7), Bayard was one of the earliest Americans in public life actively to espouse the cause of Anglo-Saxon unity. This enthusiasm, extending beyond support of reciprocity, formed a natural bond between him and Goldwin Smith, who considered Bayard a sound free trader, and one of his best friends at Washington. Both men liked to refer to Canadians and Americans as the two great branches of the English-speaking race.

From 1887 to 1888 trade relations with the United States were the chief political issue in Canada and support for free trade between the two countries more widespread than it ever again became. Under these promising circumstances Goldwin Smith redoubled his efforts to persuade Americans and Canadians that commercial union was to their mutual advantage. He avowed his belief that the two peoples would one day unite, but tried to allay Canadian fears that commercial union led inevitably to political fusion. The propositions, he maintained, were quite distinct. Reciprocity between 1854 and 1866 had not led to annexation; why then should commercial union? If, as was hoped, it increased the country's material prosperity, Canadians might be more content than before with their political position. Despite Goldwin Smith's protests, there was truth in the prevalent view that if one

---

[29]Letter to T. F. Bayard, Jan. 29, 1886, cited in Charles Callan Tansill, *The Foreign Policy of Thomas F. Bayard* (New York, 1940), 530.

scratched a commercial unionist one would find a political annexationist. Yet the majority of the Canadians who advocated free trade with the United States did not want their country to lose its independence.

Among the leading commercial unionists in Canada were Henry W. Darling, former president of the Toronto Board of Trade, and V. E. Fuller of Wentworth, president of the Council of Farmers' Institutes. Most Canadian manufacturers were opposed, but Darling declared that every natural industry in the country would benefit from reciprocity, and the *Acadian Recorder* maintained that every merchant in Halifax was interested in commercial union. In the United States the chief supporters of the movement were Congressmen Benjamin Butterworth and R. R. Hitt, C. A. Dana, proprietor and editor of the New York *Sun*, S. Ritchie, a mining magnate with large interests in Canada, and Erastus Wiman, a former Canadian who had become a New York business man. Twenty-five years earlier Wiman had been a reporter on the *Globe*. He worked up to the position of commercial editor before moving across the border, where he finally became the first president of the New York City Canadian Club. A strong advocate of commercial union, Wiman, like Ritchie, was an equally strong opponent of the forcible annexation of Canada by the United States.[30]

Since 1849 support for closer trade relations with the United States had been traditional in the Maritime provinces, where the ablest advocate of the cause was J. W. Longley, Attorney-General of Nova Scotia. His friendship with Goldwin Smith had begun in the eighteen-seventies when Longley was finishing his law studies at Osgoode Hall. Smith was then active in the Canada First movement, which Longley supported and for which he occasionally wrote in the Toronto *Nation*. Wiman, Longley, and Goldwin Smith were the most effective speakers and writers for commercial union, and the latter two did not conceal their hope that political union would eventually follow. To Longley, for example, commercial union was the most important question confronting both countries, since tariff barriers were absurd between peoples "identical in race, language, laws and institutions."[31] In his view it was the logical step to an ultimate reunion of the English-speaking peoples of North America.

---

[30]Wiman wrote much on commercial union. In 1889 and 1891 the *North Amercian Review* published four of his articles on the subject. In May, 1891, it also published attacks on the proposal by Sir Charles Tupper and the Marquis of Lorne, former Governor-General of Canada.

The *Acadian Recorder*'s views were given on Dec. 1, 1885, in a leading editorial on commercial union.

[31]Letter from J. W. Longley to Erastus Wiman, March 28, 1887, cited in Charles Callan Tansill, *Canadian-American Relations, 1875-1911* (New Haven, 1943), 393. This study gives an able and detailed discussion of the movements for reciprocity and commercial union.

In Toronto a Commercial Union League was formed in 1887, with Goldwin Smith as president and G. Mercer Adam as secretary. Branches arose throughout the country, and in the cause Goldwin Smith addressed numerous meetings from Winnipeg to Washington. The most receptive group in Canada were the farmers, who obviously suffered most from protection. Representatives of the Farmers' Institutes at an annual meeting in Toronto advocated the removal of all trade restrictions between Canada and the United States. Similar resolutions were passed by local institutes in various parts of Ontario. Some slight support came from commercial interests. The Toronto Board of Trade, for example, favoured the largest possible measure of reciprocity compatible with Canada's relationship to Great Britain.

Both Canadian parties had difficulty in deciding what stand to take, and preferred to follow rather than lead public opinion. There were good reasons for their reluctance. The Conservatives depended largely for support on the manufacturers whose industries in many cases had been kept alive by the protective tariff. These were almost certain to be alienated by the adoption of commercial union. On the other hand the party had nothing to gain from premature opposition to a policy which attracted much support from farmers and some prominent Conservatives. Macdonald himself objected to commercial union, but not to closer trade relations. He explained cautiously to the Canadian Commons in June, 1887, that his ministry was doing what it could to foster the friendly attitude of the American government toward the extension of commercial relations with Canada.

Laurier, like Macdonald, was unsure of public opinion and hesitated to commit his party, since the Liberals were not anxious either permanently to estrange the manufacturers or to antagonize French Canada. In a private letter to Sir Richard Cartwright he confessed his fear that the party was doomed to continual defeat unless it came out squarely for commercial union.[32] On the other hand he was unsure whether such a policy was consistent with Canada's duty to the mother country. Great Britain's lack of enthusiasm for the proposal was clearly shown by Joseph Chamberlain's declaration at Belfast that Canada knew perfectly well that commercial union meant political separation from Britain— a comment much criticized by the Canadian press.

Meanwhile Sir Richard Cartwright announced in October, 1887, that he supported commercial union, although he strongly opposed annexation. He spoke for himself alone, without committing his party. The first

---

[32]Letter from Wilfrid Laurier to Sir Richard Cartwright, Aug. 8, 1887, Cartwright Papers, Public Archives of Ontario.

Canadian statesman publicly to espouse this cause, he remained its most enthusiastic advocate in the House of Commons. There was, in fact, much difference of opinion within the Liberal ranks. Alexander Mackenzie, the former Prime Minister, wrote privately to Cartwright that he considered commercial union impracticable. Commercial unionists complained of Sir John's protective tariff, but proposed to bind themselves to the far higher American tariff and to duties against English manufactures. Espousal of commercial union might be good party tactics for the Liberals, but the proposal revolted Mackenzie, who much preferred reciprocity. He resented not being taken into Laurier's confidence, and commented bitterly that the new leader apparently meant to ostracize him.[33]

Goldwin Smith's jubilant announcement that commercial union was sweeping the country was doubtless prejudiced. There was enough enthusiasm for the scheme, however, to persuade the Governor-General, Lord Lansdowne, that he should inform the imperial government about the state of Canadian opinion. At the end of October he sent the Colonial Secretary an able analysis of the situation, expressing views remarkably similar to those of his friend Goldwin Smith. Up to that time, Lansdowne explained, neither party had formally adopted commercial union. For the past six months, however, it had been advocated with much ability and persistence by men who were not professional politicians, chief among them Goldwin Smith. Meetings in support of the project had been attended by large and representative audiences all over Canada. From a strictly economic point of view, Lansdowne thought commercial union would greatly benefit the majority of Canadians. He was equally sure that it would tend to estrange Canada from the mother country and to encourage political union. It would also give much offence to the people of the United Kingdom. Fairly enough, he pointed out that Canada could not then afford, like Britain, to have free trade with all the world. If she were to trade freely with anyone, she stood to gain most from doing so with her immediate neighbour, the country with which she already did most business. "Should Great Britain," he concluded, "herself so deeply committed to a free trade policy, deny to Canada the advantages of free trade with the United States, the refusal could be defended only upon what would be regarded as purely selfish grounds."[34]

Lord Lansdowne was anxious that the British plenipotentiaries meet-

[33]Letter from Alexander Mackenzie to Sir Richard Cartwright, Sept. 27, 1887, ibid.

[34]Letter from Lord Lansdowne to the Rt. Hon. Sir Henry Holland, Secretary of State for the Colonies, Oct. 31, 1887, Macdonald Papers, Commercial Union, 1886–7, vol. 44, Public Archives of Canada.

ing in Washington in November to discuss the fisheries question should have this information. A wider measure of international free trade might, he thought, be proposed as a solution for the current difficulties between Canada and the United States. When the British and Canadian delegates reached Washington Joseph Chamberlain showed this memorandum (which Lansdowne had marked "extremely confidential") to Sir Charles Tupper in his capacity as an imperial representative. Tupper promptly sent a copy to Macdonald, who replied with restraint that since the despatch was confidential, he doubted Tupper's right to show it to him. He had read it with some regret but no surprise, since he knew Lansdowne was "a free trader to the bone." In any event, commercial union was "a dead duck"; Canadians connected it with annexation and repudiated both. He thought the Governor-General now recognized the wisdom of the policy which Macdonald had announced to him in the spring, namely "allowing the cry of Commercial Union to blaze, crackle and go out with a stink, without giving it undue importance." The Government could afford to disregard Lord Lansdowne's private opinions about its policy, since as long as it was supported by the Canadian people he must obey its behests. "I dare say it would astonish us," Macdonald concluded philosophically, "if we saw the confidential despatches of the Governors-General from 1867 until now."[35]

Early in 1888 Laurier made up his mind that the Liberals should take a definite stand. The party caucus decided to support unrestricted reciprocity rather than commercial union, as they wished to avoid any possible political connotations. For the next three years reciprocity remained the most important plank in their platform.

In February and March, Congressmen Butterworth and Hitt introduced in the House of Representatives further resolutions in favour of commercial union with Canada. While the House Committee on Foreign Affairs was discussing this matter, they asked Goldwin Smith to go to Washington to tell them his views, an invitation which he gladly accepted. The Committee subsequently reported favourably on Mr. Hitt's motion, which over a year later passed the House only to be rejected by the Senate.

Meantime at Ottawa on March 14, 1888, Sir Richard Cartwright introduced in the Commons a resolution in favour of reciprocity. After a lengthy debate it was defeated, as was his similar resolution the following year. Goldwin Smith refused to accept this rejection as the decision of the Canadian people. He wrote Bayard that it was simply

---

[35]Letter from Sir John A. Macdonald to Sir Charles Tupper, Jan. 15, 1888, *ibid*.

the view of "a Parliament elected before commercial union had come into the field," and that the next election would be sure to tell a very different tale.[36] Notwithstanding the rashness of this prophecy, it was clear that the Conservative ministry was readier to defeat a Liberal motion for reciprocity than to propose a better alternative.

Goldwin Smith kept bombarding Canadian, American, and British journals with arguments for commercial union. Soon, however, the movement's popularity in Canada waned. During the summer of 1889 the *Mail*, which for the past twelve months had been strongly annexationist, abandoned the cause, and the next year began to attack it. The *Globe* continued to advocate reciprocity but not political union.[37]

Goldwin Smith for his part was untroubled by doubts as to the wisdom of his beliefs, although he admitted that Canadians were slow to recognize their own best interests. He delivered one of his ablest speeches in January, 1890, to the Nineteenth Century Club of New York on the political relations of Canada to Great Britain and the United States. Here he argued that Canada and America were really one people under two governments, with a customs line drawn between them. In a notice of this address the *Spectator* commented acidly that no section of English public opinion would try to prevent Canada joining the United States if it really wished to do so. Its editor did not believe, however, that colonial sentiment was accurately represented by Goldwin Smith, who he understood had established a reputation in Canada for "crankiness" and wrong-headedness.[38]

Dilke's recently published *Problems of Greater Britain* was critically reviewed in the *Bystander* for April, 1890. Dilke had described as unfortunate Goldwin Smith's attacks in English and American journals on Macdonald's National Policy. Canadians, he justly remarked, preferred to settle their affairs among themselves. Goldwin Smith resented the comment. He also thought Dilke overestimated the success of Canadian Confederation, the prosperity of the country, and the achievements of the National Policy. Dilke's disapproval of commercial union, and his statement that there were hardly any annexationists in Canada, Goldwin Smith considered unwise and inaccurate. Dilke's analysis, how-

---

[36]Letter to Bayard, April 11, 1888, Bayard Ms., cited by C. C. Tansill, *Canadian-American Relations, 1875–1911*, pp. 408–9.

[37]Among the newspapers which supported commercial union were the *Globe*, the *Manitoba Free Press*, the Hamilton *Times*, the Ottawa *Free Press* and the Montreal *Herald*. It was opposed by such journals as the Montreal *Gazette*, the Halifax *Morning Herald*, the Hamilton *Spectator*, the *Ottawa Citizen*, the London *Advertiser*, and the Regina *Leader*.

[38]*Spectator*, Feb. 8, 1890.

ever, contained shrewd sense. In his opinion the first result of commercial union would be the destruction of Canada's protected industries. Furthermore he thought free traders illogical to advocate a scheme which would commit the Dominion to the high American tariff. In any event, protection appeared more popular in Canada than free trade. Dilke's own avowed preference for free trade lent weight to his estimate about the strength of Canadian public opinion. His assessment was unquestionably more sane and realistic than Goldwin Smith's. The Liberal party's devotion to free trade never got beyond the stage of abstract theory. Even this was rapidly vanquished by the conclusive argument of electoral defeat.

The McKinley high tariff act of September, 1890, increased American duties on various Canadian goods, and made the prospect of reciprocity appear remote. In public Goldwin Smith confessed little discouragement, but in private he admitted that the new American tariff was "a sad relapse and a great disgrace to democracy, though it is not the only proof that the folly and wastefulness of the people can out-Herod the folly and wastefulness of kings."[39]

On February 3, 1891, the dissolution of Parliament was announced. During the election campaign the Conservatives concentrated on denouncing the Liberals as annexationists and traitors, who if returned to power would allow the country to be swallowed up by the United States. The truth was that Liberals believed in reciprocity and opposed political union, but they were not able to contend against the charge of disloyalty and the personal popularity of Macdonald. The Conservatives fought and won the election (though with a reduced majority) with the slogan, "The old man, the old flag, the old policy." The Liberals fought and lost on a slogan of unrestricted reciprocity, which was as far as Laurier would go, although Cartwright and some others would have preferred to stand for commercial union. The Conservatives' return to power on March 5 was undoubtedly due in large part to the electors' suspicions that beneath the Liberal enthusiasm for unrestricted reciprocity lurked a design for future political union.

During the campaign Goldwin Smith had done what he could to support the Liberals. In lectures on loyalty, aristocracy, and jingoism he had indignantly denied the allegation that commercial unionists were disloyal. To his mind it was disloyal to bribe manufacturers and virtually sell them the policy of the country. It was disloyal to pander to sectional interests or particular constituencies against the broad interests of the community. It was disloyal to sap the independence of the provinces,

[39]Letter to Mrs. Winkworth, Oct. 20, 1890, *Goldwin Smith's Correspondence*, 227-8.

and reduce them to servile pensioners of the federal government. "If it is not disloyalty to a crown on a cushion, it is disloyalty to the commonwealth."

One of his ablest studies, *Canada and the Canadian Question*, was written as a campaign document, but failed of this purpose because it was not off the press until April. Provocative and pessimistic, the book had more than transitory interest. It appeared at a time when optimism about Canada's future was difficult. Economic depression was severe, crops were poor, banks were failing, and emigration to the United States was increasing. If the Americans were not annexing Canada, Goldwin Smith observed, they were annexing the flower of the Canadian population. The only force against commercial union was pro-British sentiment. In favour of union he listed an impressive array of factors: geography, trade, and common ties of blood, language, and democratic institutions. He envisaged a great continent, almost unlimited in productive possibilities, forming the home of a united people, eschewing war, and presenting a fair field "for a new and happier development of humanity."[40]

Everything he wrote attracted wide notice owing to the reputation and ability of the writer and the controversial nature of his subject matter. *Canada and the Canadian Question* received even more than usual. Principal Grant of Queen's agreed with another reviewer that the book was "so brilliant, so inaccurate, so malicious even that it is enough to make one weep."[41] At the same time he thought Canadians must be grateful to the writer for casting in his lot with Canada and doing his best to awaken the people and to purify journalism and political life. His complaint that the author did not understand the deepest feelings of Canadians was certainly fair, although Goldwin Smith bitterly resented the charge. Principal Grant and he admired each other's intellectual capacity and integrity, but their views on the destiny of Canada and on imperial federation were too diverse to make it possible for them to be friends. The Montreal *Gazette* was irritated by Andrew Carnegie's comment in a British journal that "the most eminent man in Canada to day" espoused union between Canada and the United States.[42] George (later Sir George) Parkin, the chief Canadian advocate of imperial

---

[40]*Canada and the Canadian Question* (Toronto, 1891), 233, 278–9.
[41]G. M. Grant, "Canada and the Canadian Question," *Week*, May 1 and 15, 1891. Interesting unsigned reviews of the book appeared in the *Spectator*, April 4, 1891, and the *Saturday Review*, LXXI (April 18, 1891), 474–5. The latter reviewer may have been Frederic Harrison.
[42]*Gazette*, Nov. 7 and 25, 1891. Carnegie's article, "Imperial Federation: An American View," appeared in the *Nineteenth Century*, XXX (Sept., 1891), 490–508.

federation, also attacked Goldwin Smith's pessimistic analysis of the country's prospects, and his reiterated prophecy that her destiny was union with the United States.[43] Other critics were kinder. The *Globe* admitted that many would dissent from the writer's views on political union and on French Canada, but thought the book the best, clearest, and most interesting account available of Canada and Canadian affairs.

Condemnation of Goldwin Smith's opinions about the future of Canada as perversely unrealistic is in retrospect easy. They were certainly not those of most Canadians, and were not commended to them by American comment like that which appeared in the *Detroit Free Press* on July 29, 1895. "In the far distant days," wrote its editor, "when the star spangled banner floats alike over New Mexico and New Foundland [sic], Manitoba and Michigan, and Ohio and Ontario, his name will be cherished as the first Canadian statesman who saw with prophetic eye the dawn of that brilliant future and endeavoured in every . . . conscientious way to promote it." Nevertheless some of the most thoughtful Englishmen of the day agreed with Goldwin Smith, although they did not always say so in public. Bryce, for example, granted that the stream of events was carrying Canada towards annexation, though he was doubtful about the ultimate benefit to the Dominion.[44] In the second edition of his *American Commonwealth*, however, Bryce said he discerned no immediate disposition of Canadians to join the United States. As the American continent already lacked political variety, he thought it best for the time being that both countries should develop independently, since each might have something to teach the other.

V

During 1892 Goldwin Smith spent some weeks in Washington, whence he frequently wrote Laurier about the prospects of commercial union, cheerfully admitting that political union was his private heresy. In these letters he offered unasked advice on policy and tactics as freely as in earlier years he had made suggestions to Macdonald. By summer he admitted that both unrestricted reciprocity and commercial union seemed "pretty dead." On the other hand, Americans were keenly interested in political union, and he thought support for this was unquestionably gaining ground in Canada. All that was needed was a leader and an

[43]George Parkin, *Imperial Federation* (London, 1892), and *The Great Dominion* (London, 1893). From 1895 to 1902, while principal of Upper Canada College, Parkin also acted as special correspondent for *The Times*.
[44]Letter from James Bryce to Goldwin Smith, April 24, 1891.

organ. A note of weariness crept into his later letters. He was tempted to shut his library door on political questions such as commercial union, as he began to feel old and wanted time to complete some literary and historical work. "Besides," he added unexpectedly, "I have said my say, and have no predilection whatever for the part of an agitator out of Parliament."[45] Predilection or not, it was a fair description of his career. His library door remained sufficiently ajar for him to accept the honorary presidency (and become the chief financial supporter) of the Toronto branch of the Continental Union Association, established in 1892 to obtain the imperial government's permission to submit the question of union to the people of Canada, and to provide information on the subject to anyone interested. The organization had its chief strength in New York, where it was called the Continental Union League, and numbered among its members both Theodore Roosevelt and Andrew Carnegie. If he could die in Canada an American citizen, with England's blessing on the arrangement, said Goldwin Smith, the height of his ambition would be fulfilled. Since he was already seventy, he feared this was unlikely to happen.[46]

The first National Liberal Convention at its meeting in Ottawa in June, 1893, adopted as a plank "a fair and liberal reciprocity treaty." Under Cleveland's second administration at Washington the prospects of concluding such an agreement for a time seemed brighter. In an address at Winnipeg Laurier denounced protection as bondage, When, however, he attained office as prime minister in 1896, he made no effort to strike off the shackles. By that time renewed prosperity made Canadians less anxious for reciprocity, and the return of the Republicans under McKinley indicated little American enthusiasm for lower tariffs. Early the next year Laurier proposed reciprocity, but President McKinley was opposed. The Dingley Act of July, 1897, raised American tariff barriers higher than they had ever been before, and for well over a decade put an end to all real prospect of reciprocity. Two months before the bill's final approval Goldwin Smith went to Washington, where he appeared before the Senate tariff committee, in a vain endeavour to secure some modification of the high duties imposed against Canadian products.

From 1898 to 1899 the Joint High Commission considered various questions, including tariffs, at issue between the United States and Canada, but negotiations broke down because of disagreements about

[45]Letters to Wilfrid Laurier, July 10, Feb. 15, and Aug. 2, 1892, Laurier Papers, vol. VI, ff. 2109–10, 2159–60, 2202–5, Public Archives of Canada.
[46]Letter to General J. H. Wilson, Sept. 15, 1893.

the Alaska boundary. The only important fiscal change made by Laurier's Government was introduction of an imperial preference carefully designed not to injure the susceptibilities of protected Canadian manufacturers. The Liberals never forgot that they had lost the election of 1891 on the slogan of unrestricted reciprocity, and did not propose to make the same mistake twice. Although Laurier continued to pay lip service to freer trade, once the Liberals took office it became difficult or impossible to distinguish between their tariff policy and that of the Conservatives. By 1897 faith in a tariff for revenue only, which had been Liberal policy ever since 1846, was permanently abandoned in favour of moderate protection. Goldwin Smith never forgave Laurier for what he considered this shameless betrayal of principle.

His hopes for continental union were dealt an even worse blow when in 1898 the United States developed imperialist aspirations. He did not believe that any wise Canadian would wish to join the American career of barbarian and tropical expansion. He sympathized neither with Cleveland's tacit apology for American policy in the Philippines as "a peaceful acquisition of territory for truly American uses and purposes," nor with the defence of imperialism implicit in Theodore Roosevelt's statement that they had never tried to force an unsuitable form of government on any new territory.

Since under these circumstances he began to doubt the wisdom of union with the United States, the question arose what Canada's destiny should be. Was independence possible after all? When in 1903 Canadians were annoyed at the arbitration award in the Alaska boundary dispute, Laurier urged that Canada should be given power to make her own treaties. To obtain this power, said Goldwin Smith, she must become a nation and hoist her own flag. In a moment of insight he suggested that she might become a nation without parting company with the British monarchy, since the United Kingdom itself illustrated the possibility of two monarchies under the same crown. He criticized the Canadian suspicion that British diplomats were indifferent to their interests and had not tried to preserve them. England could scarcely insist on concessions, when the bare possibility of war with the United States over a Canadian dispute would bring defeat to any British government. As long as Canadians remained dependent they must expect their interests to be subordinate, and on occasion to be sacrificed to imperial interests. He granted that in diplomatic negotiation they sometimes got less than they wanted and perhaps less than they deserved. Nevertheless they should frankly face the practical alternatives. Did they really think Great Britain should go to war and involve Canada in war with the

United States about the Oregon or Maine boundary? If the Americans were intransigent, what means of coercion would Canadians suggest?[47] Since the issues of peace and war were not in their hands, they must not allow their irresponsibility to make their demands unreasonable.

Canadians commonly complained that Goldwin Smith was pro-American and anti-British. When, however, he defended the imperial government with such plain speaking, they were outraged, and thought him ready to support any country except the one he had adopted. Actually, he adopted Canada more wholeheartedly than Canadians ever adopted him. There was truth, unwelcome as it was, in his contention that Canada could not expect to combine the advantages of independence with the protection of the British forces, and that if she wished to enjoy the rights and privileges of a nation she must be prepared also to assume its responsibilities.

No one in either Canada or the United States, he admitted in 1907, any longer talked or thought about political union; it seemed improbable that anyone would do so for some years to come. An octogenarian could have no practical interest in the matter. At the same time he considered that a movement for commercial reciprocity, apart altogether from political relations, was gaining ground. He still believed in an eventual free and honourable union between the two countries.[48] If ever a liberal offer came from the United States, Canada would be pretty sure to embrace it. Her farms, forests, fisheries, and mines all craved for their natural markets. Fortunately he did not live to see Canada reject in 1911 the first and last serious opportunity for reciprocity since 1866. At the time of his death Goldwin Smith was still looking forward to the voluntary reunion of the British race on the North American continent as the ultimate solution of "the Canadian question."[49]

In unpublished draft notes for his reminiscences he frankly declared that he never could see the slightest difference in ideas or sentiments between British Canadians and Americans in the northern states. Between the Englishman and the Canadian, on the other hand, there were marked distinctions which could hardly fail to interfere seriously with their political partnership. The ferment of anti-Americanism kept up by United Empire Loyalists he thought largely an indulgence of personal and family vanity. Fully realizing how unpopular this view would be in Canada, he was never equally outspoken in his published

[47]*Weekly Sun*, Oct. 14 and 28, 1903, March 16, 1904, April 10, 1907.
[48]"Canada, England, and the States," *Contemporary Review*, XCI (March, 1907), 344-54.
[49]Letter to Lord Charles Beresford, Aug. 31, 1909.

opinions. Had Canadians not realized that Goldwin Smith's views on the political destiny of their country were as the voice of one crying in the wilderness, they would have disliked him even more. The real cause of their quarrel was not far to seek. He never understood that Canadians valued their nascent independence as much as Americans or Englishmen valued theirs. George Parkin wrote in 1895 that no political passion in Canada was as strong as opposition to absorption into the United States. This estimate of Canadian opinion was more accurate than Goldwin Smith's. Ever since Confederation on one issue at least French- and English-speaking Canadians have been largely united: their common determination to preserve the identity of Canada as a separate state.

Nevertheless it is specious to conclude that Goldwin Smith was not merely a prophet without honour in his own country, but a false prophet. Was it really unfair to argue that some Canadians had an incurably colonial mentality? Almost two decades after Goldwin Smith's death, Mr. Bennett, then leader of the Conservative Opposition, attacked the establishment of a Canadian embassy at Washington. In his view this implied a doctrine of separation and the end of Canada's connection with Britain. "If we are a sovereign state," he declared, "we cannot belong to the British Empire."[50] Goldwin Smith might be forgiven for believing, half a century earlier, that it would be difficult to combine Canadian autonomy with a political connection to the mother country. He was at least prescient enough to realize that the links of sentiment and common institutions would be stronger than any formal commitments. He was clearly right in considering profoundly significant the bonds which united the English-speaking peoples of the world. Commonplace in the twentieth century, this concept was not widespread in the nineteenth. Goldwin Smith's belief that Canada's eventual destiny was union with the United States was no stronger than his belief in the emancipation of colonies. He wanted to see the dominions become independent of the mother country without diminution in their mutual bonds of affection. Although he grossly underestimated the strength of Canadian nationalism, he was yet well aware that what he did for Canadian letters and in particular for Canadian journalism were steps toward building up a feeling of nationality in the people of a new nation. The Canadians who rejected union with the United States in favour of independent nationhood in a real sense accepted the core of Goldwin Smith's doctrine while they rejected the unpalatable husks.

[50]Can. H. of C. *Debates*, 1927, 2472. Shortly after Mr. Bennett became Prime Minister in 1930 he overcame his repugnance to Canadian representation at Washington sufficiently to appoint his brother-in-law as Minister.

XII. EPILOGUE

BORN FOURTEEN YEARS before Queen Victoria's accession, Goldwin Smith lived for nine years after her death. He came to manhood trailing such multi-coloured clouds of eighteenth-century ideas as the belief of Bolingbroke that party meant faction and of Tom Paine that an active government meant tyranny. He died in 1910, confident that the common heritage of the English-speaking peoples was the central fact of modern politics. To an unusual degree he linked the Old World to the New, and the nineteenth century to the twentieth.

In what sense was he a typical Victorian liberal? He was perhaps most typical in conforming to no type, in making a virtue of intellectual nonconformity and independence. In his moral earnestness and belief in the primary importance of individual character as a guide to history and politics as well as to day by day living, he was certainly Victorian. Lord Acton once remarked that an historian's preferences betray him more than his aversions, since a writer's interpretation of history gives the measure of the man himself. Of no one was this more true than of Goldwin Smith. If he spoke less than Matthew Arnold about high seriousness, he no less profoundly believed in it. Like many English public men of his day, he was always ready to make personal sacrifices for his principles. In his humanitarianism, faith in reason, and conviction that responsibilities complemented privileges, he again represented significant strands in Victorian thought. The apparent Victorian worship of material progress, however, was completely alien to Goldwin Smith. Concerned though he was with economic questions, he never considered them the most permanent or most important problems of mankind.

His belief that colonies were destined to become independent illustrates a characteristic, if unpopular, aspect of nineteenth-century political thought. His strictures on imperialism were based on the tenet of classic liberalism that exercising power over other peoples was immoral and benefited only special interests. Hence he failed to appreciate that British imperialism sprang in part from the seapower inevitably created in the process of commercial and industrial expansion. On occasion, like other men, he tilted against windmills, and in retrospect some of his opinions seem even more quixotic than they did at the time. A true son of Oxford, he was the advocate, not so much of causes already lost, as of those yet to be won. As for loyalties, those which most imperialists thought impossible seemed to him common sense. Time has justified his belief that loyalty to England and to British traditions is compatible with the conviction that empire over unwilling peoples is outmoded.

His political thought had serious defects. Both in Canada and in Ireland he misjudged the forces that made for nationality. The characteristic Manchester illusion that free trade would ensure international peace, Goldwin Smith shared to the full. That free trade might be only a fortuitous episode in British development occurred to him no more than to other liberals of his day. The idealized and somewhat romantic conception of American democracy which he brought with him from Britain coloured his judgments of English and Canadian institutions. Thus, for example, he underestimated the remarkable flexibility and strength of the British cabinet system.

A busy publicist can scarcely be a serious and consistent political philosopher. Goldwin Smith's thought contained contradictory elements which were the inevitable defect of a prolific journalist who never stopped writing, and whose opinions were often based more on moods and emotions than on rational analysis. He neither set out (nor took the time) to present an integrated political creed. In this, of course, he was not peculiar; many leading nineteenth-century English liberals were like him. Seldom, save by a few philosophers like T. H. Green, was the liberal position presented in a form strictly coherent. Some liberals were interested in one objective and some in another. All were enrolled under one banner, but within the larger struggle vigorously engaged in their own minor and separate skirmishes.

Liberalism in its widest sense may be interpreted as the extension of freedom and political equality to all members of the community. In concrete circumstances, however, this may imply different things, and in England certainly did imply different things with different exponents. Goldwin Smith, for instance, fought for Gladstone's Second Reform bill, but considered manhood suffrage for the totally uneducated absurd. And his belief in individual freedom was a far cry from the individualism of extreme laissez-faire, since he was prepared to restrict the less important liberties in order to enlarge the more significant. He had certain rooted prejudices which his thinking never transcended. Perhaps if he had not removed himself from the British political scene and intellectual environment he might have conquered some of these prejudices or thwarted their growth. Life in Toronto neither discouraged his original biases nor widened his intellectual horizon. Like most men, perhaps more than most, he had blind spots. He hailed as an historical landmark the repeal of the Corn Laws, but showed no sympathy for the Chartists. He looked back with pride to his association with Joseph Arch, but had little interest in the Fabian Society. The Fabians themselves, however, showed no more thorough-going revulsion against unproductive wealth and conspicuous waste than Goldwin Smith, himself wealthy, nor any more acute awareness of social obligation.

In an optimistic age which clung to a belief in progress amid the passing of other beliefs, Goldwin Smith was more than half a pessimist. Modern inventions, improved methods of warfare, the enfranchisement of the illiterate, and new relations between capital and labour all provoked his apprehension rather than his acclaim. He was far less confident than many of his contemporaries that such developments illustrated the march of progress. Yet he was rationalist enough to believe that through just laws, good education, and free discussion men could become more virtuous and more happy. His most striking characteristic was a passion for justice. During Goldwin Smith's last illness Dicey wrote to assure him that everyone in Britain believed his life and writings had done much to keep alive the hatred of injustice in England.[1]

An ordered society, which reverenced the best traditions of the past and eschewed the untried panaceas of idealists, was as dear to him as to any conservative. Yet he began as a radical and to his death still considered himself one. Like other radicals of his school he remained an ardent individualist. In an age of compromise he believed strongly that on some subjects conciliation and neutrality were impossible. The competing pressures of interest groups formed appropriate matters for compromise; principles did not.

It is not difficult [wrote his friend Judge Longley] to secure contemporary approval if we will only consent to be neutral, negative and average, and conform invariably to the regnant sentiments of the hour. But to utter fearlessly and manfully one's honest conviction even when counter to popular ideas, and in spite of common views to proclaim new advanced and unpopular ideas requires courage and force of character. This, I think, you have persistently done during a whole life-time and with a very large audience. That you should have preserved the respect and regard of all thinking men, and grown steadily in the appreciation of the intellectual

[1] Letters from A. V. Dicey, April 5 and 19, 1910.

world, ought to be a matter for profound congratulation and a matter of joy and pride in your advancing years. Ultimately the world has never worshipped trimmers and time-servers, and I think you can feel pretty sure of the admiring judgment of posterity—which seems a worthier ambition than contemporaneous applause.[2]

The very strength of Goldwin Smith's opinions in itself made him unpopular. In addition he was by temperament a reformer and critic, never so happy as when exposing an abuse or rousing public opinion about an injustice. Despite his keen and penetrating intellect he was usually a destructive rather than a creative critic. He shut more doors than he opened, and his influence was correspondingly less. His criticisms, like those of most men, were coloured by his prejudices. Yet the biases and inconsistencies which he never attempted to conceal were one facet of his intellectual independence.

His friends took for granted that he would support any cause he thought just, but they never felt sure which side he would espouse. The wide circle of able men who liked and respected Goldwin Smith was a tribute both to him and to them, for with many of them he strongly disagreed on various important issues. A. V. Dicey, for instance, was also a Liberal Unionist, but approved England's part in the Boer War. James Bryce's experience in Ireland converted him to Home Rule. John Morley advocated Home Rule and votes for women; Goldwin Smith no less strongly opposed both. These differences of opinion, however, in no way affected his friendships. By the end of his days he had lived down many of the enmities he had aroused. Even those who disliked his ideas could not help admiring him as a person. None of his friends was more delighted by this fact than Bryce. After a visit to the Grange in 1907 he wrote Goldwin Smith from the British Embassy at Washington that "one of the best parts of it was to see how the Toronto people, many of them differing wholly from your views, honour you and are proud of your presence among them."[3]

Despite the warm friendships which meant much to him, Goldwin Smith was a lonely man. Physically isolated by his self-imposed exile from the English political and literary circles in which he had matured, he was more effectively isolated by his ideas and his passion for expounding them even to the unsympathetic. By temperament a mentor, he was perpetually indignant: with the defects of democracy, with political corruption, with jingoism. He hated cruelty and he hated shams. His

[2]Letter of Aug. 19, 1908, on the occasion of Goldwin Smith's eighty-fifth birthday.
[3]April 13, 1907.

influence as a journalist was great, but he would have persuaded more had he inveighed less. His masterly invective irritated or silenced opponents oftener than it convinced them. The respect accorded his later years was a tribute in part to his ability, in part to his age, and in part to the fact that constant reiteration caused his more unpopular views to be dismissed as those of a crank.

In a sense he fell a victim to his gift for expression. Too often he thought he solved a complicated problem by summarizing it in an epigram. His judgment about British politics may have been partially warped by a voluntary exile, but it was even more unreliable about affairs in Canada, where he lived almost forty years. More than once Bryce tried in vain to get from him a real conception of Canadian politics. Some three decades before his death his friends noticed in him a failure to grasp current facts and a tendency to think sweeping phrases explained all phenomena. The oracular habit grew upon him, and little fresh light seemed to dawn. "Everything was judged by the old doctrines," Bryce commented in a letter to Dicey, "and condemned in the old phrases. Often, no doubt, he was quite right, but even when he was condemning—as when he condemned Gladstone for one set of acts and Chamberlain for another—he showed little insight into the causes that were at work."[4] With a temperament at once sensitive and aggressive he combined a preconceived devotion to unshakeable convictions. Intellectual rigidity was the defect of his virtues. If he had been less sure he was right, he would have crusaded less keenly against what he believed to be wrong.

The fairest contemporary assessments of his strength and weakness were made by two close friends, Dicey and Bryce.

It seems to me [wrote Dicey after reading Goldwin Smith's *United Kingdom*] as if the old story of the fairies was truer in his case than in that of any other man I have ever known. Every gift was showered upon him except two, which some offended fairy seems to have denied, and these are sound judgment and a real sense of justice. I take him to be a man who is never consciously, either in deed or word unfair; but I can hardly read a page of his reflections on history in which I don't feel an element of unconscious unfairness.... Goldwin Smith ... seems to me by nature made for a public spirited statesman in an aristocratic republic. He is by nature as little of a monarchist as of a democrat and is neither a Liberal nor a Conservative in the modern sense of those terms, whatever that sense may be.[5]

[4]Letter from James Bryce to A. V. Dicey, Nov. 14, 1913, Bryce Papers, Bodleian Library.
[5]Letter to James Bryce, quoted in Robert S. Rait, *Memorials of Albert Venn Dicey* (London, 1925), 180–4.

At the same time Dicey thought Goldwin Smith had some of the rarest gifts a man could possess, and had used them for noble ends. Few people cared enough about wrongs which affected neither themselves nor their class to spend a lifetime combating them. Sympathy for all sorts and conditions of underdogs was Goldwin Smith's abiding passion. Dicey placed him among the greatest of the pamphleteers, and thought that if their long line was finished it could not end more appropriately.

Almost everyone who knew him felt that he accomplished less than his unusual powers had seemed to promise. Had his career in England not been cut short by his father's death and his marriage to a Canadian his life might have been very different. Many men with less reason to complain about the unfairness of fate are embittered. Goldwin Smith did not become either indifferent or cynical. If he disappointed friends it was because, in an age of great men, their expectations for him were high.

Yet in the distinguished ranks of British political journalism he occupies an honourable place. A journalist's influence is always intangible and hence difficult to assess, but unquestionably his achievements were significant. The pamphleteer's appeal is to his own time, and on his own generation Goldwin Smith left his mark. First and foremost he aimed at clear thought and expression, believing that a good style interposed nothing between the idea and the mind to which it was presented, that the form should not distract the reader's attention from the matter. He not only reflected the early ideas of Victorian liberalism, but helped to mould them. Few bystanders kept in closer touch with the great movements of their day, political, religious, and social. It often seemed a case of Goldwin Smith against the world, for he had no desire to be a popular leader. He knew the price of popularity, and had no wish to pay it. To party advancement and public office he preferred the position of independent critic. If his followers were few, his readers were many. In England he helped to free the universities from religious tests, to popularize the study of history, and to support the Jamaica Committee. In the United States his services to the North during the Civil War and to education at Cornell won him a deserved reputation as perhaps the warmest English admirer of the American republic. In Canada, if on politics his effect was slight, on the press and on letters it was supreme, and his death closed a journalistic epoch. On numerous social problems his views were half a century in advance of his times.

His influence—and want of it—was illustrated by the saying that there were three parties in Canada: the Liberals, the Conservatives, and Goldwin Smith. In many ways he fulfilled the functions of a third party, although he would not have liked the comparison. During a period of Canadian development when there were only two parties, with few significant differences between them, his ideas pervaded both, goaded the sluggish, and roused the complacent. In his self-appointed role as keeper of the nation's conscience he never flagged. E. A. Freeman called him a "prophet of righteousness." Like the *Manchester Guardian* to which he was a frequent contributor, Goldwin Smith managed to make righteousness readable. If he sometimes mistook his own conception of morality for a universal categorical imperative, he might be forgiven by a country more prone to self-approval than to self-examination. He saw too many sides of a question to give unmixed satisfaction to any one, but by cutting at the roots of colonial provincialism he liberalized Canadian thought. Although Canadians almost always refused to follow his advice, they came in the end to respect him as a cross between a censor and an oracle.

During his lifetime, as Judge Longley observed, what Goldwin Smith wrote was "read and quoted throughout all the English-speaking world, and at his death he received the universal homage of the intellectual world."[6] His study was his arsenal, and the periodicals of England, Canada, and the United States his field of battle. This had its unfortunate side. He was too much a man of letters to move freely among ordinary people. His own philosophic belief in eternal principles and in the rationality of man made him singularly ignorant about human nature. Yet if he often misunderstood others, it was his own lot to be misunderstood. He was accused of being a snob, a hypocrite, and a traitor. The Grange, remarked a Toronto journalist, was a dispensary for grievances, and few who devote their life to the cure of abuses are loved. On one occasion shortly before his death he spoke of the advances made during his life in the sense of social responsibility, public and private charity, and facilities for education and recreation. "This world of ours," said Goldwin Smith, "is still a good deal out of joint, though not quite so much as it was eighty years ago." According to his lights, he did all that one man could to set things right. That more often than not his lights differed from those of others, is perhaps irrelevant.

Nothing ever estranged him from Britain. In a real sense he was both an English and a Canadian patriot. Bred in England, domiciled in Canada, and a frequent visitor to the United States, he had friends in all three countries. "Goldwin Smith, controversialist," begins the article in the *Dictionary of National Biography*. The description is apt, but even apter might have been "Goldwin Smith, Anglo-Saxon," for it was as a

[6]J. W. Longley, "Mr. Goldwin Smith," *Canadian Courier*, July 9, 1910.

member of the English-speaking peoples that he preferred to think of himself. His energies and ability were primarily devoted to furthering friendship and understanding among them. He was more responsible than any other man for initiating the idea of English-speaking union.

When critics charged that he was a false prophet, who invariably espoused the losing side, Goldwin Smith calmly countered that he was content to await the verdict of history. He pointed out that he had supported repeal of the Corn Laws, an extended suffrage, and university reform. He had advocated colonial independence, disestablishment of the Irish Church, and legalization of trade unions. He had defended the North in the American Civil War, and attacked the part played by England in both the Crimean and Boer Wars. Admittedly, his views on the destiny of Canada had not been vindicated, but the story was not yet ended. Somewhat surprisingly he added that he was always for Canadian nationality, and the trend was in that direction.[7]

A letter to a friend, written a few years before his death, illustrated characteristic aspects of his liberal thought. He granted the justice of a comment recently made about him by the Canadian correspondent of *The Times*, that an old man was apt to cleave to old ideas. "My old ideas," Goldwin Smith observed, "are that morality is the foundation of the State, that a free commonwealth is better than an empire, that unnecessary war is crime and folly, and that a great industrial nation, dependent for its supplies of food and raw material on importation from abroad, is especially interested in the maintenance of peace. A tidal wave of the opposite sentiments just now prevails. But I am old enough to have stood more than once on the dry shore where a tidal wave has been."[8]

[7] Interview with Goldwin Smith, *World* (Toronto), Nov. 14, 1903.
[8] Letter to John Ogilvy, vice-president of the Dundee Liberal Association, published in the *Manchester Guardian*, March 31, 1902.

INDEX

ABBOTT, SIR JOHN, 254
Acadian Recorder, 269
Acton, Lord, 18, 113, 140, 143, 223
Adam, G. Mercer, 72, 270
Agassiz, Louis, 40
Alabama, 30, 38, 45–6, 49–50, 257
Albany, Duchess of, 88–9
Albany, Prince Leopold, Duke of, 19, 63, 88–9
Albert, Prince Consort, 150
Anarchism, 170–1
Anglo-Saxonry, 38, 207–10, 287–8
Anthony, Susan B., 48
Arch, Joseph, 175, 283
Aristocracy, 54, 153–9
Arnold, Matthew, 25, 56n., 153, 186n., 281; opinion of Goldwin Smith, 25n.; on Canada and the United States, 63–4, 242–3; on the American press, 91
Ashburton, Lady, 10
Asquith, H. H. (Earl of Oxford and Asquith), 173
Asselin, Olivar, 245
Atkinson, J. E., 14
Australia, 204–5; conciliation and arbitration in, 175; federation, 249–50

BACON, SIR FRANCIS, 139
Bagehot, Walter, 13, 38, 137, 144, 152, 193
Bailie, John, 103
Bakunin, Count Michael, 163, 171
Banks, N. P., 257
Barton, Sir Edmund, 249
Barton, G. B., 249–50
Bayard, T. F., 209, 269, 272–3
Bennett, R. B., 280

Bentham, Jeremy, 7, 135
Bismarck, Otto, 189
Blake, Edward, 59–60, 147, 230; connection with the *Nation* and the *Liberal*, 75–80, 97; Canada First, 259–63
Blanc, Louis, 10
Bloomfield, Bishop, 6
Boer Wars, 93, 94n., 124–5, 141n., 195, 198–201, 206, 236, 243–4, 246–8
Boston, 32–4
Boulton, D'Arcy, 62
Boulton, William Henry, 36, 60
Bourassa, Henri, 124, 200, 241, 243–6
Bourinot, Sir John, 88
Bowell, Sir Mackenzie, 114
Bradford, 89
Bright, Jacob, 55
Bright, John, 13, 19, 38, 129, 177, 185, 195, 197; on English universities, 8–9, 20; connection with Jamaica Committee, 23–4; supported the North in American Civil War, 28–9, 33, 37; on public education, 57; friendship with Goldwin Smith, 82, 133; Manchester Liberal, 117, 136; on the franchise, 139, 148; on colonial emancipation, 187, 191, 256; on the United States, 252; on union of Canada and the United States, 254, 255n.
Brodrick, G. C., 6, 55
Brown, George, 37, 114, 256; attacks on Goldwin Smith, 59–60, 72–3, 75–6, 261–2; Goldwin Smith on, 80, 86
Brown University, 33, 40

Browning, Robert, 89, 111
Bryant, William Cullen, 37
Bryce, James (Lord), 9, 50, 82, 93, 145, 158, 168, 208, 243; friendship with Goldwin Smith, 9n., 22, 284-5; visit to United States, 47; on the *Bystander*, 88; on parties, 140, 142, 173-4; on votes for women, 149-50; on the United States, 196-7; on the Boer War, 200-1; on Disraeli, 201; *American Commonwealth*, 240, 276
Buller, Charles, 187
Burke, Edmund, 35, 112, 141, 150
Burns, John, 175
Bury, Viscount, 193
Butler, B. J., 37, 45
Butler, Joseph (Bishop of Bristol), 222
Butterworth, Benjamin, 269, 272
Bystander, 72, 87-90, 94, 96-7, 109, 123, 216, 239, 265

CABINET SYSTEM, 143
Cairnes, J. E., 37n., 182n.
Cambridge, 9
Cameron, John, 78, 89n., 202, 209
Campbell, Sir Alexander, 239
Campbell, Wilfrid, 90
Campbell-Bannerman, Sir Henry, 157, 173, 200-1
Canada, 84; Goldwin Smith's visit in 1864, 36-7; his early views on, 186-92; his ideas on Confederation, 190, 226-9, 247; democracy in, 228-40, 250-2; Goldwin Smith on the political destiny of, 47, 96-7, 113, 192, 230, 242, 250-80
Canada First, 60, 76, 79, 122, 231, 259-63
Canada Temperance Act, 181
Canadian Authors' Society, 98
Canadian Monthly, 71-3, 75, 77, 97, 123
Canadian Pacific Railway, 93
Canadian Press Association, 80, 88, 114
Canning, Lord, 7
Cardwell, Edward (Lord), 92
Carlyle, Thomas, 10, 16, 23
Carman, Bliss, 90
Carnarvon, Lord, 235, 261

Carnegie, Andrew, 101, 196, 223-4, 275, 277
Cartwright, Sir Richard, 270-2
Catholicism, 223, 242
Catholic Register, 223
Cavour, Count Camillo, 147
Chamberlain, Joseph, 141, 244, 270, 272; Goldwin Smith on, 91, 141n., 198-201, 203; republican views, 150, 152
Channing, Sir Francis (Lord), 159, 180
Chatham, Lord, 35
Chelsea, 24, 89, 135
Chicago, 63-4
Choate, Rufus, 250
Churchill, Lord Randolph, 55
Churchill, Sir Winston, 159, 205
Clarendon, Lord, 39
Clark, W. R., 120
Cleveland, 24, 46
Cobden Club, 136
Cobden, Richard, 8, 16, 164, 177, 197; on *The Times*, 13; friendship with Goldwin Smith, 19-21, 32-3, 37-8, 133; support of North in American Civil War, 29-31, 37; attitude toward United States, 48, 252; Manchester Liberal, 117, 136-7; on imperialism, 184-5, 187, 191; views on union of Canada and the United States, 254, 256
Cody, H. J., 121
Coleridge, John Duke (1st Baron), 88
Coleridge, Sir John Taylor, 5
Collins, Sir Robert, 88
Colquhoun, A. H. U., 121
Colonial conferences, 206-7
Commonwealth, 206, 209
Communism, 163, 165
Colonial emancipation, 16, 19, 30, 133, 183-8
Conservative party (England), 11, 136; (Canada), 73-4, 107, 270, 274
Conservatism, 135-6, 192, 232-3
Contemporary Review, 72
Continental Union Association, 115, 122, 277
Cook, John Douglas, 12-13
Cornell, Ezra, 41-3, 48-9, 51
Cornell University, 22, 40-52, 68, 70, 117, 215
Coyne, James H., 260n.

Crime, 100, 103n., 163
Cromwell, Oliver, 20
Crowe, Eyre, 13
Curtis, George W., 34, 37n., 43, 87

Daily News, 13, 16, 23n., 46, 255; Goldwin Smith's *Empire* letters to, 14, 19, 126, 183, 186; Goldwin Smith's letters on American Civil War to, 29-31, 36
Daily Telegraph, 222
Dana, C. A., 269
Darling, H. W., 269
Darwin, Charles, 193, 223
Darwinism, 194, 211
Democracy, 29, 51, 148, 168-9, 176, 182; Goldwin Smith on dangers of, 137-9, 224; parties in, 140-3; and imperialism, 195; in Canada, 228-40, 250-2
Denison, George Taylor, 74, 114, 119-20, 202, 203n.
Dent, John, 79
Derby, Lord, 15, 24, 28, 146
De Tocqueville, Alexis, 36, 100
Detroit Free Press, 276
Devoir, Le, 245
Dicey, A. V., 145, 159, 168, 235; on Goldwin Smith, 16, 22, 283-6; on the United States, 47-8, 208, 252; on life at the Grange, 64-5
Dickens, Charles, 13
Dilke, C. W., 13
Dilke, Sir Charles, 13; republican sympathies, 150-1; *Greater Britain*, 205, 208, 258; *Problems of Greater Britain*, 273-4
Dilke, Lady, 3
Disraeli, Benjamin (Earl of Beaconsfield), 3, 74, 146, 201; feud with Goldwin Smith, 11, 82, 184; Second Reform Act, 133-5, 147; *Lothair*, 184; imperial policy, 187, 192, 198, 253
Dixon, Benjamin Homer, 61
Dixon, Thomas, 61
Doukhobors, 107
Dublin, 92
Dufferin, Lord, 75, 235, 261
Dukinfield, Lady, 6
Dukinfield, Sir Henry, 6
Dundas True Banner, 115
Dunkin, Christopher, 190-1, 231
Durham, Lord, 187, 241f.

Edinburgh Review, 12-13
Education, 44; 1858 Royal Commission on Popular, 6, 56, 178; Goldwin Smith's views on, 44-5, 133, 167-8, 175; co-education, 48-9; in Canada, 55-9, 117-18, 121-2
Edward VII, 18-19, 39, 130, 153, 158
Elcho, Lord, 145
Elgin, Lord, 254
Emerson, Ralph Waldo, 33, 250
Empire (Toronto), 96, 98, 106, 108, 115, 116n.
Engels, Friedrich, 92
England, 134, 196; political institutions of, 138, 144, 150-60, 172; public affairs in, 173
Essays on Reform, 145
Eton, 4-5
Evening Telegram (Toronto), 78-9, 263
Eyre, Governor, 22-4

FABIAN SOCIETY, 283
Factory legislation, 177
Falconbridge, Justice, 119
Falconer, Sir Robert, 122
Family Compact, 62, 117, 199, 232
Fawcett, Henry, 152
Financial Post, 128
Flavelle, Sir Joseph, 121
Forster, W. E., 152
Fortnightly Review, 13, 72, 82, 141, 264
Foster, Mr. and Mrs. Colley, 54
Foster, W. A., 259, 260n.; *Canada First*, 259
Fourier, Charles, 164
Fox, Charles James, 243
Franchise, extension of, 16, 145-50, 154, 160; First Reform Act, 3, 134, 154; Second Reform Act, 133, 144-8, 160, 282; Third Reform Act, 133, 147, 149; votes for women, 64, 148-50, 179, 233; university representation, 146
Fraser, James, 34n.
Fréchette, Louis, 264-5
Freeman, E. A., 13, 95n., 287; on the English-speaking peoples, 208-9; on the British North America Act, 230-1
Free trade, 133, 136-7, 187, 254, 282
French Canada, 178, 241-6
Froude, J. A., 186n.

Fuller, V. E., 269
Function of the state, 162–8, 174, 177, 180, 182

GALT, ALEXANDER, 202, 254
Garibaldi, Giuseppe, 183–4
Garrison, Wendell, 95
Gazette (Montreal), 192, 275
George III, 27, 153, 203
George, Henry, 165
Gibraltar, 183–4
Gibson, Sir John, 130
Gladstone, W. E., 24, 134, 201, 208, 243, 257; connection with university reform, 7–8, 10; relations with Goldwin Smith, 11–12, 21, 89, 93, 173; views on American Civil War, 28; advocacy of Home Rule, 91–3; Third Reform Act, 133; on liberalism, 135; on parties, 140; on *Genesis*, 212
Globe, 37; attacks on Goldwin Smith, 59–60, 73, 76–7, 261–2; influence on Liberal party, 72, 75, 84; changed attitude toward Goldwin Smith, 95, 116, 126; support for unrestricted reciprocity, 114, 273; on *Canada and the Canadian Question*, 276
Globe (Boston), 80
Godkin, E. L., 95–6, 124
Governors-general, 234–7
Grant, George M., 118, 119n., 202, 203n., 275
Grantham, 89
Granville, Lord, 39
Greeley, Horace, 37, 48
Green, T. H., 13, 149, 282
Gregory, Walter Dymond, 122–3
Grey, 3rd Earl, 15
Grey, 4th Earl, 130
Griffin, Martin, 66

HAGUE TRIBUNAL, 194
Hamilton, 36, 80
Hamilton, Alexander, 28
Harcourt, Sir William Vernon, 13, 134
Harper's Magazine, 34, 87
Harrison, Frederic, 17, 25–6, 121, 129, 150
Haultain, Arnold, 65, 124n.
Hawthorne, Nathaniel, 50
Herald (Hamilton), 115
Hincks, Sir Francis, 264

Hirst, F. W., 82n.
Hitt, R. R., 269, 272
Hobhouse, L. T., 162, 165, 167
Hope, A. J. Beresford, 12, 14–15, 214
Hopkins, Castell, 115–16, 121, 265n.
House of Commons, 138–9, 154–7; payment of members, 142, 144, 179
Houston, William, 79
Howe, Joseph, 148, 190–1, 202, 257
Howell, George, 150–1
Howland, W. H., 260n.
Hughes, Thomas, 23, 29, 47
Huntingdon, L. S., 259
Huxley, T. H., 9–10, 23, 186n., 212

IMMIGRATION, 106–8
Imperial federation, 201–7
Imperial Federation League, 115, 202, 237
Imperialism, 183–210; Goldwin Smith on Rosebery's views, 179; American imperialism, 195
India, 183–6
Inglis, Sir Robert, 7
Ionian Islands, 21, 152, 183–4
Ireland, 38, 184–6; Irish Home Rule, 64, 79, 91–3, 95, 150, 156, 160, 172, 186, 233, 236
Ithaca, 40–2, 44–5, 47–9, 51, 215
Ithaca Journal, 43

JAMAICA COMMITTEE, 22–4, 29
James, Henry, 95
Jefferson, Thomas, 28
Jesuit Estates Act, 96, 241–2
Johnson, Pauline, 90
Journalism, 6, 285; in London, 10–16, 60; in Canada, 68–81, 94–9, 122–9
Jowett, Benjamin, 7n., 9, 89, 186n.

KING, JOHN, 99n., 102, 126
King, W. L. Mackenzie, 102, 175, 234, 236
Kingsley, Charles, 23, 170
Kropotkin, Prince Peter, 63, 107, 171, 194

LABOUR MOVEMENT, 168–76
Labour party, 173–4
Lake, W. C., 7n.
Lampman, Archibald, 90
Lansdowne, Lord, 63, 237, 271–2

INDEX 293

Lassalle, Ferdinand, 163
Laurier, Sir Wilfrid, 67, 98, 130, 204, 233, 238, 244, 278; stand on Boer War, 199, 201, 236; Goldwin Smith's views on, 245; on commercial union, 270–2, 276
Leader (Toronto), 255–6
Leeds, 82
Lewes, 89
Lewis, Sir George Cornewall, 12, 187
Liberal (Toronto), 76, 77n., 78–80
Liberal Party (England), 8, 34, 134, 136, 173–4, 206–7; (Canada), 72, 84–5, 107, 270, 274, 277–8
Liberalism, 35, 133–6, 149, 160–3, 166, 170–1, 177, 180, 224, 282; liberal democracy, 137–44; laissez-faire, 167–8, 177; liberal socialism, 172–3; in Canada, 233
Libraries, 100
Lieber, Francis, 37
Lincoln, Abraham, 28, 34, 37–9, 152–3, 181, 251
Lindsey, Charles, 59n., 80
Lingen, Lord, 91
Lisgar, 93–4
Little Englanders, 117, 183, 188, 190ff., 243, 253
Lloyd George, David, 134; budget, 134, 158–9
London, 6, 10
London Advertiser, 78
Longfellow, Henry Wadsworth, 33
Longley, J. W., 219–20, 269, 282, 287
Lorne, Lord, 236–7, 269n.
Loudon, James, 120
Lowe, Robert, 82, 147, 256
Lowell, James Russell, 32, 140
Loyola, Ignatius, 163

MACAULAY, T. B. (Lord), 153, 185
McCarthy, Justin, 14, 93
Macdonald, D. Bruce, 121
Macdonald, J. A., 126
Macdonald, Sir John A., 73, 96, 190, 202, 246, 256–7, 274, 276; relations with Goldwin Smith, 83–6; Goldwin Smith's estimate of, 86, 232n., 238; National Policy, 107, 160, 232, 263–4, 271; views on relations with the United States, 259, 270, 272
Macdonald, Lady, 85
Macdonnell, James, 13n.

Macdougall, William, 70
McGee, D'Arcy, 60, 70, 256, 260
Mackenzie, Alexander, 72, 76n., 262, 271; Goldwin Smith's views on, 75, 83–4
McKinley, William, 195–6, 259, 274 277
McMaster University, 218
Magdalen College, 4–5, 213
Mail (Toronto), 73–4, 77, 96, 119, 273
Mail and Empire, 96, 119
Maine, Sir Henry, 12, 140, 148; *Popular Government*, 148
Mair, Charles, 90, 260n.
Manchester, 55, 89
Manchester Guardian, 91, 95, 157, 287
Manchester School, 187–8, 190–1; Goldwin Smith's connection with, 11, 25, 129, 133, 160; ideas on the function of the state, 136, 178; view of the aristocracy, 154, 159
Manchester Union and Emancipation Society, 30
Manitoba, 93
Mansel, J. L., 213
Martineau, Harriet, 14
Marx, Karl, 92, 163, 165
Marylebone, 24
Maurice, F. D., 170, 213
Mavor, James, 107, 119n.
Mazzini, Giuseppe, 10, 188
Mercury (Leeds), 91
Meredith, Sir William, 121
Merriman, John Xavier, 198–200, 247–9
Mill, John Stuart, vi, 11, 129, 133, 175, 211, 213, 214n.; connection with Goldwin Smith, 16; chairman of Jamaica Committee, 22–4; attitude toward American Civil War, 29; *Representative Government*, 38n., 140; liberal views, 134–5, 137, 143, 146, 154, 162, 188–9, 229; on votes for women, 148; *Spirit of the Age*, 211n.
Mills, David, 78
Milner, Lord, 121, 128, 201
Milton, John, 181, 213
Minto, Lord, 236–7
Molesworth, Sir J., 187
Monarchy, 134, 138, 144, 152–3

Montreal, 36, 98, 242, 244, 254
More, Sir Thomas, 164, 166
Morley, John, 13, 82, 140, 243, 284; on Goldwin Smith, 3, 22, 55; visit to the Grange, 63-4; opponent of Boer War, 201
Morning Chronicle, 11-12, 184
Morning Post, 91
Morris, William, 111
Mortimer, 4
Mowat, Oliver, 75, 85
Mozley, J. B., 10
Müller, Max, 16, 25
Mundella, A. J., 146
Municipal government, 99-100, 142

Nation (New York), 32, 95, 109
Nation (Toronto), 60, 74-7, 79, 97, 261-2, 269
National Policy, 83-4, 107, 160, 263-4, 266-7, 273
Nationaliste, Le, 241, 245
Negroes, 24, 29
New York, 37, 99
New York Times, 37, 95, 121
New Zealand, 186; conciliation and arbitration in, 175
Newcastle, 152
Newcastle Programme, 172
News (Toronto), 122
Nicoll, W. Robertson, 126, 128
Nihilism, 171
Nineteenth Century, 212
North American Review, 32
Northwest, 93-4, 97, 107, 260
Norton, Charles Eliot, 25, 40, 48, 54, 61, 199; friendship with Goldwin Smith, 32-4, 43
Nottingham, 89
Nova Scotia, 190, 258

OBERLIN COLLEGE, 48
O'Brien, Colonel and Mrs. William, 46, 47n.
O'Connell, Daniel, 245
Old age pensions, 64, 178-80, 233
Ontario, 74, 93, 117, 175; journalism in, 71, 88, 97-8, 123-4; provincial politics, 85; universities in, 117; Lord's Day Alliance, 180
Ontario Agricultural College, 124
Orange Order, 92-3, 96, 117
Oriel College, 22
Orillia, 100

Ostrogorski, M., vi, 109
Ottawa, 67-8, 83-5, 98, 117, 235
Owen, Robert, 164, 166
Oxford Movement, 5, 213
Oxford University, 11, 89, 111, 117; Goldwin Smith at Magdalen, 4-5; university reform, 6-10, 15, 21, 89; Goldwin Smith Regius Professor of Modern History, 16-19, 27, 32, 108, 112; contrasted with Cornell, 41-2, 46, 51

PAINE, THOMAS, 136, 281
Pall Mall Gazette, 75, 150, 193
Palmerston, Lord, 21, 28, 34n., 198, 256
Parke, Sir James, 5
Parkin, Sir George, 202, 275-6, 280
Parks, 100-1
Party system, 138, 140-3
Patrons of Industry, 89n., 122-3
Patteson, T. C., 72, 119
Pattison, Mark, 7n., 12
Peel, Sir Robert, 11, 20, 136, 147
Pell, J. E., 103
Philippines, 196, 278
Pigou, Francis, 4
Pitt, William, 20, 137, 147
Potter, Thomas Bayley, 30
Prohibition, 100, 182
Providence (Rhode Island), 33, 40
Public assistance, 103-6
Public ownership, 166, 170
Pym, John, 23

Quarterly Review, 13, 16
Quebec, 96, 232, 247, 265, 267; Goldwin Smith on, 241, 243
Queen's University, 118-19

RADICALISM, 158, 160-1
Raymond, H. J., 37
Reading, 4, 6
Recorder (Brockville), 77
Reform League, 135, 145
Religion, 211-24; Established Church, 214; Baptists, 218; Unitarians, 218, 221, 224; agnosticism, 219, 224
Republicanism, 150-2, 161
Rhodes, Cecil, 198-9
Riel, Louis, 96, 242
Ritchie, S., 269
Roberts, Sir Charles G. D., 90
Roberts, Lord, 185

Robertson, John Ross, 79
Robespierre, M., 163
Rogers, Thorold, 19–20, 38n.
Rolleston, George, 86
Roosevelt, Theodore, 37, 196, 277–8
Rosebery, Lord, 207, 209; definition of liberalism, 135; on parties, 143; on the Lloyd George budget, 158–9; Goldwin Smith's views of, 172, 179; on socialism, 174
Royal Colonial Institute, 193, 208
Royal Society of Canada, 98
Ruskin, John, 23
Russell, Lord John, 3, 7, 34n., 39, 202
Russia, 171–2
Ryerson, Egerton, 58–9, 191

ST. GEORGE'S SOCIETY, 102, 115–17
Saint-Simon, Henri, Comte de, 164
Saint-Simonians, 211
Salisbury, 3rd Marquess of (Lord Robert Cecil), 12, 74, 259
Saturday Night, 96
Saturday Review, 10, 29–30, 110, 134; Goldwin Smith on staff of, 12–16, 126, 214
Schnadhorst, Francis, 141
Schurman, Jacob, 51, 185, 223
Scotsman, 91
Scott, C. P., 95
Scott, Sir Walter, 111
Second chambers, 156; American Senate, 143–4; House of Lords, 146, 153–60; 178, 198; Canadian Senate, 156, 227, 238–9
Seeley, Sir John, 204–5; *Expansion of England*, 204–5
Selborne, Roundell Palmer, Earl of, 173, 212–13
Seward, William H., 34, 37, 39
Sheffield, 55, 146
Shelburne, Lord, 237
Smith, Adam, 136–7; *Wealth of Nations*, 187
Smith, Elizabeth Breton, 4
Smith, Goldwin (1823–1910), early years, 3–5; active in university reform, 5–10; tutor at University College, Oxford, 6; secretary, Commissions on Oxford University, 6; member, Royal Commission on Popular Education, 6; journalism in London, 10–16; Regius Professor of Modern History at Oxford, 14, 17–18; as an historian, 16–19, 112–13; *Lectures on the Study of History* (1859), 16; *Lectures on Modern History* (1861), 16; *Irish History and Irish Character* (1861), 92; *Rational Religion and the Rationalistic Objections of the Bampton Lectures for 1858* (1861), 3n., 213; advocate of colonial emancipation, 16, 19, 30, 133, 138; interest in American Civil War, 16, 20, 28–39; *Empire* (1863), 19, 126, 183–8, 226, 241, 254, 259; views on imperialism, 19, 183–210; *Does the Bible Sanction American Slavery?* (1863), 31; *A Letter to a Whig Member of the Southern Independence Association* (1864), 31, 34; visit to United States (1864), 22, 32–8; visit to Canada (1864), 36–7; views on religion, 17, 21, 32, 211–24; *A Plea for the Abolition of Tests in the University of Oxford* (1864), 9; friendship with Cobden and Bright, 19–21; *The Civil War in America* (1866); interest in extension of the franchise, 19, 144–50; views on liberal democracy, 133–42, 166–8, 170–3; resignation of Oxford chair, 22; father's death, 22; work for Jamaica Committee, 22–4; *Three English Statesmen* (1867), 18, 23; *The Reorganization of the University of Oxford* (1868); at Cornell (1868–71), 41–52; republican ideas, 150–2; settled in Toronto (1871), 53; visited England (1872 and 1873–4), 54–5; member, Council of Public Instruction, 57–8; marriage and life at the Grange, 60–8; visited England (1876–8), 81–2; views on socialism, 164–78; journalism in Canada, 68–81, 94–9, 122–9; *Political Destiny of Canada* (1878), 264; relation to Sir John A. Macdonald, 83–6; started *Bystander* (1880), 87–91; *Cowper* (1880), 109–11; visited England (1881–2), 88–9; *Lectures and Essays* (1881); revived *Bystander*

(1883), 89–90; founded *Week* (1883), 90–1; visited England (1886), 89, 91; views on Ireland, 91–3; interest in Northwest, 93–4; letters in Canada, 94–9; active in movement for commercial union (1887–8), 268–73; *A Trip to England* (1888), 109; revived *Bystander* again (1889), 96–7; social welfare activities, 99–108; literary criticism, 109–11; *Jane Austen* (1890), 110; *Bay Leaves* (1890), 112; *Loyalty, Aristocracy and Jingoism* (1891), 114, 274; views on aristocracy, 153–9; *Canada and the Canadian Question* (1891), 85, 275–6; *The Moral Crusader, William Lloyd Garrison* (1892), 110; *Specimens of Greek Tragedy* (1893), 112; *Essays on Questions of the Day* (1893), 166n., 218n.; *The United States* (1893), 112–13; views on Canadian democracy, 228–40, 250–2; views on the political destiny of Canada, 226, 242, 250–80; controversies with Colonel Denison and the St. George's Society, 114–17; visited England (1893–4), 117; views on education, 117–19; *Oxford and her Colleges* (1894); controversy concerning honorary degree at University of Toronto, 119–20; connection with *Weekly Sun*, 122–8; *Guesses at the Riddle of Existence* (1897), 218–20; *The United Kingdom* (1899), 113, 154, 285; *Shakespeare: The Man* (1899), 110; opposition to Boer War, 198–201; *In the Court of History* (1902), 201; *Commonwealth or Empire* (1902), 95; *The Founder of Christendom* (1903); *Lines of Religious Inquiry* (1904), 110; *My Memory of Gladstone* (1904), 110; *Irish History and the Irish Question* (1905); member, Commission on University of Toronto, 121; member, University Board of Governors, 121–2; *In Quest of Light* (1906), 222; *Labour and Capital* (1907); *No Refuge But in Truth* (1908), 223; death, 130

Smith, Harriet Elizabeth Mann Dixon, 36, 60–2, 64–6, 89, 115, 117, 128–30
Smith, Katharine Dukinfield, 4
Smith, Richard Pritchard, 4, 22, 34n.
Smith, W. L., 122
Socialism, 164–74, 182; Christian socialism, 170
Social reform, 99–108
South Africa, political institutions, 247–9; Boer Wars, 93, 94n., 124–5, 141n., 195, 198–201, 206, 236, 243–4, 246–8; constitution, 205
Spanish-American War, 125, 197
Spectator, 75, 128, 178, 188, 273
Spencer, Herbert, 23, 129, 166–8, 193, 217; *Man versus the State*, 166–8
Standard (London), 91
Stanley, A. P., 7, 25, 39
Stanley, Lord, 148
Stephen, James Fitzjames, 12
Stephen, Leslie, 29, 145
Strachey, St. Loe, 18, 178
Stubbs, William, 22
Sumner, Charles, 33, 45–6, 50, 257
Sun (New York), 128, 221–4
Syracuse, 42

TAIT, A. C., 216
Taylor, Bayard, 43
Tennyson, Alfred (Lord), 10, 110–11, 212
Thackeray, W. M., 10
Thoreau, H. D., 33
Tilley, S. L., 190
Times, The, 68, 94n., 150, 152, 258; Goldwin Smith's letters to it on university reform, 7; influence of, 13, 91; attacks on Goldwin Smith, 14, 116, 183–4, 192; attacks on the North during the American Civil War, 29, 31, 35
Tolstoi, Count Leo, 171, 197, 221
Toronto, 3, 36–7, 46–50, 53–4, 93, 96–7, 245; in the seventies, 66–7; social welfare in, 99–108, 254, 259; as centre of United Empire Loyalism, 116–17; University of Toronto, 36, 46, 56, 64, 100, 118–22
Trade Disputes Act, 176
Trades and Labor Congress, 176
Trade unions, 55, 120–1, 160, 174–6

Trevelyan, G. M., 197
Tribune (New York), 37, 42
Tribune (Winnipeg), 94, 119n.
Trinity College, 118
Trollope, Anthony, 13
Tupper, Sir Charles, 202, 233, 257, 269n., 272
Turgot, A. R. J., 147
Tyndall, John, 10, 186n.

UNIONIST PARTY, 91–3
United Empire Loyalists, 62, 116–17
United States, 27–8, 53, 207, 286; Civil War, 16, 28–39, 112, 114, 197, 286; Goldwin Smith's views on relations with England, 27–8, 34–5, 38–9; political institutions of, 36, 117, 139, 143–4, 246–7, 250–2; American imperialism, 195–7, 259, 278
University College, 6, 38, 89
Unwin, George, 205

VICTORIA, QUEEN, 15, 39, 134, 150, 152, 201, 208, 223
Victoria College, 118, 215

WAKEFIELD, GIBBON, 187
Walker, Byron E. (Sir Edmund), 121, 129
Wallace, W. Harris, 218
Walpole, Sir Robert, 86
War, 125, 197
Ward, Mrs. Humphrey, 184n., 217; *Robert Elsmere*, 217
Week, 119; Goldwin Smith's connection with, 72, 90–1, 96, 98, 99n., 123–4, 216
Weekly Sun (*Farmers' Sun*), 86, 95, 122–8, 198, 216, 243
Wellington, Duke of, 3
Westminster Review, 13, 110
White, Andrew D., 22, 40–4, 46–52, 55, 56n.
Whitney, James, 122
Williams, Sir Edward Vaughan, 5
Willison, Sir John, 79, 95, 125
Wilson, Sir Daniel, 58
Wilson, Woodrow, 112
Wiman, Erastus, 269
Winnipeg, 93–4
World (Toronto), 119

ZOLA, EMILE, 181

www.ingramcontent.com/pod-product-compliance
Lightning Source LLC
Chambersburg PA
CBHW071150070526
44584CB00019B/2730